Empires of the Imagination

Empires of the Imagination

A Critical Survey of Fantasy Cinema from Georges Méliès to The Lord of the Rings

ALEC WORLEY
Foreword by Brian Sibley

McFarland & Company, Inc., Publishers
Jefferson, North Carolina, and London

*A film is a ribbon of dreams. The camera is much more than
a recording apparatus; it is a medium via which messages
reach us from another world that is not ours
and that brings us to the heart of a great secret.
Here magic begins.* — Orson Welles

LIBRARY OF CONGRESS CATALOGUING-IN-PUBLICATION DATA

Worley, Alec, 1974–
Empires of the imagination : a critical survey of fantasy cinema from
Georges Méliès to The Lord of the Rings / Alec Worley ; foreword by Brian Sibley.
p.   cm.
Includes bibliographical references and index.

ISBN 0-7864-2324-2 (illustrated case binding : 50# alkaline paper) ∞

1. Fantasy films — History and criticism.   I. Title
PN1995.9.F36W67   2005   791.43'615 — dc22   2005017001

British Library cataloguing data are available

On the Cover : A scene from *The Golden Voyage of Sinbad* (1974)

Manufactured in the United States of America

*McFarland & Company, Inc., Publishers
Box 611, Jefferson, North Carolina 28640
www.mcfarlandpub.com*

For my grandparents,
Percival and Lillian Sprague,
and in memory of Muriel Alice Cattermole

Contents

Acknowledgments   viii

Foreword by Brian Sibley   1

Preface   3

1. Locating Fantasy   7

2. The Birth of Fantasy Cinema   17

3. Fairy Tales   25

4. Earthbound Fantasy   83

5. Heroic Fantasy   162

6. Epic Fantasy   232

Bibliography   273

Index   275

Acknowledgments

First of all I must thank *Shivers* editor David Miller, who came up with the idea for this book and was generous enough to let me run with it, and also helped me out with the photographs. Thanks also to Steve Jones, who recommended McFarland and offered vital professional advice, to Brian Sibley and Vivien Green for providing the foreword and for their patience, to Adrian Bales, without whose gloriously extensive video library Chapter Five would have been much shorter, to Marie O'Regan, for allowing me to pester her with stupid questions, to Jeff Gardiner, for the same, and to the unfailingly polite and efficient staff at the BFI library.

For their constant support and for letting me borrow/steal videos, books and cutlery, I must also thank Dave "Diesel" Bezzina; Saxon and Georgina Bullock; Gary Couzens and Pam Creais; Bob "the Barbarian" Covington, for knowing more about men in loincloths than is surely healthy and Richard "Two-Gun" Toogood for knowing even more; the Dastardly Darbyshires, Iain and Louise; a special thank you to those who inspired my forthcoming musical *West End Knights*, starring Dame Judi Dench as Sir Steve Larcombe, Dame Edith Evans as Sir John Sharp and Martita Hunt in a big hat as Sir Robert Waghorn (music by Stephen Sondheim and script by Tom Stoppard); Mum, Derek and Christopher; Nana; Chris and Cathy Ruane (the most generous in-laws ever); my sister-in-law, Tracey "Red Sonja" Ruane; Keith "But is it fantasy?" Shadbolt, who thankfully never found "the Blackadder Sausage"; Vicky Moore (soon to be Shadbolt); Andrew "Thrud" Xinaris, as well and Nic and Izabel; Stuart "Little" Young; and anyone else who had to listen to me rant about fantasy for the last three years.

Thanks also to David Bassom; Tony Benham; the BBC's *The Late Review* and *The Big Read*; Chris Colclough, David J. Howe; Maria Kyriakides; Mano Lanza; Michael Moorcock; latecomers Daniel and David Rajah; John Travis; David Valchera; the British Fantasy Society; and His Holiness the Pope, the King of Norway and our other honoured guests, for all those little cogs that kept the whole thing rolling.

Most of all I owe more thanks and love than I could ever write to my wife Lisa, who endured *everything* and more, and without whom there is no way this book would ever have been, except by magic.

Foreword

by Brian Sibley

When Hollywood finally, almost belatedly, acknowledged the triumphant success of *The Lord of the Rings* trilogy by giving *The Return of the King* the Academy Award for Best Picture (along with almost every other available Oscar), it was seen as an astonishing breakthrough: the very first "fantasy film" to be so honored. Think of some of the best-loved films of all time — *King Kong, Snow White and the Seven Dwarfs, The Wizard of Oz, Star Wars* and *E.T.: The Extra-Terrestrial* — they don't have a "Best Picture" Oscar among them.

After reading Alec Worley's meticulously researched and reasoned appraisal of over 100 years of fantasy pictures, from the magical conjurations of Georges Méliès to Peter Jackson's tours of Middle-earth, you may wonder why such a rich vein of creative filmmaking, one that has yielded so much gold (and no little dross), should have been so shamefully neglected, not just at movie prize-givings, but also in the area of critical analysis and appreciation.

One reason, perhaps, is that fantasy movies are a reminder that all film is "fantasy" and, even more than that, an *illusion*: a trick of the eye, called "persistence of vision," that is a shameless cheat and deception, regardless of whether those so-called "moving pictures" are depicting the real or the fantastic.

Mary Poppins may have been pipped to the post for the Best Picture Oscar by *My Fair Lady*, but is the tale of Eliza (itself inspired by the myth of Pygmalion and Galatea) any less a fantasy than that of the magical nanny? Is the studio recreation of London's Covent Garden any more realistic than that of the imaginary Cherry Tree Lane? Of course not; it merely disguises its fantastical features beneath a mask of verisimilitude.

Alec Worley has rummaged through the film vaults, pulling forth legions of wonders: wizards and witches, fiends and faeries, mermaids and monsters, heroes, angels and ghosts — even God, Satan and Santa Claus. He whisks us back to Camelot and old Baghdad, leads the way to Shangri-La and Neverland and holds the carriage door as we board the Hogwart's Express. Along the way, he explains, examines, compares and contrasts with great perception and admirable, if sometimes painful, frankness.

1

For we love or loathe our fantasy movies: *It's a Wonderful Life* and *Willy Wonka and the Chocolate Factory* are hardy perennials, screenings of which we await or avoid with either unalloyed delight or utter disgust.

But even as you cheer the author's exoneration of Disney's much-vilified *Alice in Wonderland* or boo his snappish dismissal of *Chitty Chitty Bang Bang*, the realization dawns that some other readers will be experiencing entirely opposite emotions!

It is a reminder that aficionados of the fantasy film genre are passionate folk. More so, I surmise, than fans of the Western, the musical or the murder mystery. And why? Because more than any other type of film, the fantasy — in all the many and varied manifestations catalogued in these pages — is the most primal.

This is the closest movie storytelling ever comes to its older ancestors: the sumptuous picture-book visions of faerydom; the mythic tales of idealized heroism and ruthless brutality; the sinister absurdities of masques, mummers' plays and marionette shows; and, even earlier, the shifting shadows dancing on the cave walls around the fireside teller of tales.

Fantasy films are their often beautiful, sometimes deformed but always intriguing offspring. They beg affection and understanding. This book offers both — and a reward to every cineaste who shares the author's fascination with films of the fantastique.

Brian Sibley has written and broadcast extensively on the subject of film and is a specialist on animated, fantasy and musical films as well as on many of the writers whose work has been brought to the screen, including J.R.R. Tolkien, Lewis Carroll, Charles Dickens, Roald Dahl, J.M. Barrie, P.L. Travers, C.S. Lewis and others.

Preface

The absence of any comprehensive critical survey of fantasy cinema was one of the most intimidating things about putting this book together. With the exception of Peter Nicholls' *Fantastic Cinema*, John Clute and John Grant's *Encyclopaedia of Fantasy* and David Pringle's *The Definitive Illustrated Guide to Fantasy* (three pathfinders to whom this survey owes much), most detailed studies either qualify fantasy as the illegitimate offspring of science fiction or horror (its cousins in the triumvirate of the *fantastique*), or else witter on with the indiscriminate ardor of a fanboy.

As far as I can tell (with apologies to any notable books out there I may have missed), serious criticism of fantasy cinema is astonishingly lacking, leaving a wealth of movies out there awaiting analytical plunder. Isolated favorites like *The Wizard of Oz* and *It's a Wonderful Life* already get plenty of press, but what about forgotten movies like *The 5,000 Fingers of Dr. T*, *Labyrinth* and *Conan the Barbarian* (not the camp sequel it always gets mistaken for)? And what about all those fantasy pictures hiding in the arthouse closet? (Think of me as the Peter Tatchell of fantasy cinema.)

Unlike horror and sci-fi, fantasy has no unifying definition to call its own, and here the problem resides, since what qualifies as fantasy depends entirely upon the perceptions of the individual. While we can generally agree on what constitutes the horrific or the futuristic, our regard for the spiritual concepts made flesh by fantasy are as varied as the movies themselves. To the fundamentalist Christian, Jean-Jacques Annaud's authentic caveman caper *Quest for Fire* is pure Darwinian fairy tale; to the atheist, Mel Gibson's *The Passion of the Christ* is a bloodthirsty epic fantasy as fanciful as *Excalibur*. For the purposes of this survey I remain strictly agnostic, but out of respect for the faiths of others I have avoided direct religious adaptations such as *The Ten Commandments*, whose inclusion would have been tantamount to blasphemy. For similar reasons I have sailed close to the shore when it comes to animation, whose perceptions of reality exceed fantasy's own in terms of complexity.

One of the things that spurred the writing of this book was the cultural debate concerning fantasy ignited by the success of Peter Jackson's *The Lord of the Rings*, based on fantasy's reluctant ur-text by J.R.R. Tolkien. The arguments, largely negative, illustrated just how maddeningly ignorant even the most literate of pundits are when it comes to fantasy, and just how ghettoized the genre itself really is. Germaine Greer ranted for the umpteenth time about the idiocy of Tolkien and his acolytes, while Philip Pullman's admirers, desperate to keep the author's *His Dark Materials* off the fantasy roll call, treated us to some wonderful euphemisms (my favorite has to be "metaphysical fabulism"). Although I raged at the time, in hindsight I sympathize. The industry Tolkien has become is commonly regarded as the acme of what the fantasy genre has to offer, which, of course, is simply not the case.

In the meantime, poor old J.R.R. has shouldered the blame and suffered renewed invective in the last three years (all of which turned embarrassingly petulant in 2003, during the BBC's televised literary survey *The Big Read*). Detractors see Tolkienesque fantasy as spitting in the eye of reason. Several articles have vilified *Lord of the Rings* (both book and films) as symptomatic of the spread of religious fundamentalism. But all too often this argument ignores the rational political minds herding such national hysteria. Modern wars are just as much failures of reason as imagination, and strangely enough the same can be said of bad fantasy.

If this survey could banish any single misconception about the fantasy genre (and there are dozens to choose from), it would be the idea that fantasy amounts to nothing but meaningless escapism. This lie oozes so much honey that the genre itself is often smitten. So let's clear this one up right away. Fantasy is inextricably defined by reality; how else can one define what doesn't exist except by what does? Unlike horror (fantasy's evil twin), whose murk gives us even more reason to be afraid of life's dark corners, fantasy spotlights our fears so we can better wrestle them into submission. Muhammad Ali claimed to have beaten his opponents before even entering the ring, having mentally rehearsed the bout beforehand in the same way Judy Garland's Dorothy (now there's a comparison) defeats Miss Gulch in Oz so profoundly we don't even need to see the real-life rematch when she wakes up back in Kansas.

Although fantasy often engenders a sense of departure from earthbound reality, it remains stubbornly anchored by a processing of life's challenges, redefining the world in a fresh and foreign language. "Escape," however, is only half the story. If the fantasy experience is to have any relevance, the fantasist must complete the circle by returning home, with renewed understanding of how to live in accord with the irresistible flow of life. In Peter Weir's *The Last Wave*, Richard Chamberlain's haunted lawyer is told "a dream is a shadow of something real," an idea that became a guiding principle in this book.

Fantasy, like Story, like language itself, has the quality of sand; fluid in its entirety, concrete in its constituents. Just as it is impossible to erect sandcastles dry, I make no claim to having formalized the genre, only identified its narrative strategies and their recurring components. As a fiction writer I am fascinated by the way in which Story subsists, and understand that it cannot be summoned by rote. This book is not an Ordnance Survey map of fantasy cinema but more a sort of "spotter's guide," enabling the critical filmgoer to recognize fantasy's component forms as the genre goes about its business.

Fantasy is already a considerable cultural force, in both film and literature. In pop culture its name is "Tolkien"; in highbrow culture it hides incognito. Now is the time, however, for the genre to raise its wings and tear off its disguise. This is a genre fuming with potential. Yet if it is to avoid either mainstream consignment to habitual Hobbit-dom or the shame of highbrow euphemism, it must form ranks now. George Bailey and Dorothy must draw swords. "Magic realist" draft dodgers must be dragged back in line. Frodo and Arthur must escape the borders of Middle-earth and Logres. May this book steer them into the startled enemy ranks and demolish their misconceptions for good. The fantasy genre is vast and it will have your attention.

Alec Worley
Fall 2005

1

Locating Fantasy

Here Be Dragons

Defining fantasy is difficult. Before we can reach any concrete definition, we must clear away a tangle of misconceptions, connotations and jargon, which the term "fantasy" has accumulated over the years. The *Oxford English Dictionary* defines it as "a day-dream arising from conscious or unconscious wishes or attitudes—the process or the faculty of forming mental representations of things not actually present." Fantasizing actively engages the conscious imagination, unlike passive dreaming, although Freud points out similarities between the two in *The Interpretation of Dreams*. "Like dreams, [fantasies] are wish-fulfilments; like dreams, they are based to a great extent on impressions of infantile experiences; like dreams, they benefit by a certain degree of relaxation of censorship. If we examine their structure, we shall perceive the way in which the wishful purpose that is at work in their production has mixed up the material of which they are built, has rearranged it and has formed it into a new whole." Today the concept of fantasy takes Freud's psychosexual cue, soliciting from the back pages of the tabloids next to a row of Xs and a phone number.

When not lurking behind beaded curtains, fantasy goes abroad as a mode of pop-fiction, and it's here where the real identity crisis begins. An encyclopaedia's worth of equivalent labels and haughty euphemisms presently smother fantasy fiction, most of the reading public having no idea how far reaching a genre it really is. As far as many publishers, readers and (sad to say) many writers are concerned, "fantasy" comprises J.R.R. Tolkien's *The Lord of the Rings*, Robert E. Howard's Conan tales, and anyone who sells books by ripping them off. Valuable fantasy writers like Lord Dunsany, Mervyn Peake, Ursula Le Guin, Jonathan Carroll, M. John Harrison, Ray Bradbury, Neil Gaiman, Michael Moorcock, Roger Zelazny, Phillip Pullman, Jane Yolan and China Miéville (to name a handful) must compete for shelf space with seemingly endless volumes of generic tosh, which try to distance themselves from their own banality by claiming they belong to phantom genres like "High Fantasy," "Urban Fantasy," "Dark Fantasy" and so on. Those celebrated outside the genre ghetto are rarely identified as writing fantasy. When referring to certain books by literary VIPs like Gabriel García Márquez, Isabel Allende, Angela Carter and

Salman Rushdie, critics would rather we use the now-euphemistic term "Magic Realism."

In the movies, fantasy has a fractionally more coherent sense of identity, of which magazines that specialize in the media of the fantastic have the clearest grasp. Judging by the films that fall within their remit, these magazines uniformly identify the genre as part of a triumvirate that includes science fiction and supernatural horror. But still fantasy feels poorly defined as a film genre, and often acts as a dumping ground for movies that fail the more recognizable dress code of sci-fi and horror.

The few accounts of serious film criticism that discuss the fantasy genre almost invariably treat it like a whimsical offshoot of its genre cousins, or else seem unable to define it at all. Stuart M. Kaminsky, in his otherwise comprehensive study *American Film Genres*, acknowledges the presence of fantasy, but defines it as, "usually presented as a personal, dreamlike, childhood exploration of our less-than conscious thoughts." This uncertain definition may account for dream-fables like *The Wizard of Oz*, *The 5,000 Fingers of Dr. T* and *The Company of Wolves*, but fails to account for movies like *The Thief of Baghdad*, *The Golden Voyage of Sinbad* and *The Dark Crystal*.

This lack of definition has never been satisfactorily addressed, and Steve Neale's *Genre and Hollywood* suggests a likely reason why. "The predominance of ideologies of realism in our culture tends to mean that, unless marked as high art, many avowedly non-realist genres are viewed as frivolously escapist, as 'mere fantasy,' and thus as suitable only for children, or for 'mindless,' 'irresponsible' adults."

Attempts to define the fantasy genre have been invariably restricted to literature. Bulgarian-born critic Tzvetan Todorov was among the first to point the way towards a formal clarification in his *The Fantastic: A Structural Approach to a Literary Genre*. Here he proposes a definition of "the fantastic": "In a world which is indeed our world, the one we know, a world without devils, sylphides, or vampires, there occurs an event which cannot be explained by the laws of this same familiar world. The person who experiences the event must opt for one of two possible solutions: either he is the victim of an illusion of the senses, of a product of the imagination—and the laws of the world then remain what they are; or else the event has indeed taken place, it is an integral part of reality—but then this reality is controlled by laws unknown to us... The fantastic occupies the duration of this uncertainty." Todorov's favorite example of the sustained fantastic is Henry James's ghost story *The Turn of the Screw* (1898), in which the book's viewpoint character (and hence the reader) is unsure whether the depicted apparitions are real or imagined.

The second half of Henri-Georges Clouzot's *Les Diaboliques* (*The Fiends*) (1954) demonstrates on film what Todorov is getting at. This icy thriller pictures the murder of a despotic headmaster (Paul Meurisse) by the two women in his thrall, his wife (Vera Clouzot) and his mistress (Simone Signoret). Having succeeded in drugging his whiskey and drowning him in a hotel bathtub, they plant his body in the brackish waters of the school's outdoor swimming pool, hoping that when the corpse is discovered his death will look like an accident. But, when the pool is drained, the women are horrified to learn that the body has disappeared. Then the dead man's face shows up in the background of a school photograph, glaring balefully at the camera from a nearby window. Such photographic evidence opposes the theory that the women are hallucinating. The headmaster still lives, but the question remains: Did he survive the murder attempt, or has he clambered out of his watery grave like some vengeful phantom from an EC horror comic?

Though vastly and necessarily simplified here, Todorov's definition of the fantastic is nonetheless limited. The perceptual ambiguities of the fantastic are rarely sustained throughout an entire story, and surely describe a narrative technique, not a genre proper. However, Todorov's idea highlights the issue central to any debate on defining fantasy: perception.

Most fantasy films occupy a domain some distance away from the ambiguous turf of Todorov's fantastic. As the critic explains, "If [the reader] decides that the laws of reality remain intact and permit an explanation of the phenomena described, we say that the work belongs to another genre: the uncanny. If, on the contrary, he decides that new laws of nature must be entertained to account for the phenomena, we enter the realm of the marvellous." The moment a text steps off the ambiguity tightrope is the moment it leaves the fantastic and falls into a neighboring genre, either the "uncanny" or the "marvellous." *Les Diaboliques* makes an unequivocal left turn down the road of the former in which "events are related which may be readily accounted for by the laws of reason." Towards the end of the film, in a hair-raising scene, the timid wife enters a bathroom and sees her dead husband rising, white-eyed and fully clothed, from a brimming bathtub. The poor woman's heart seizes with fright, after which the "dead" man pops white contact lenses out of his eyes and embraces his mistress. His "murder" was all an elaborate sham to dispose of the wife so that he could sell his dilapidated school and elope with his floozy.

In addition to such *Hound of the Baskervilles*–type revelations, Todorov's uncanny applies to texts in which the fantasy phenomena are revealed to have taken place entirely within a character's mind, maybe as a dream or as part of a psychotic episode. Filmic examples of these so-called "perceptual fantasies," like *The Enchanted Cottage* (1945) and Roman Polanski's *Repulsion* (1965), do not fall within the remit of this survey. But the point must be stretched. The dream-worlds of *The Wizard of Oz* and *Alice in Wonderland* may end with "And then I woke up," but it would be absurd to ignore such vital films on the grounds of pedantry. Quasi-fantasy films like Baz Luhrmann's *Moulin Rouge* and Jean-Pierre Jeunet's *Amélie* (both 2001), heading a strain of uncanny movies that have blossomed in recent years, are also (regretfully) excluded. These films envision ingeniously skewed alternatives of our own world, but feature no actual fantasy characters or devices. These are basically perceptual fantasies that take place not within the minds of their characters, but the fertile minds of their directors.

If the headmaster of *Les Diaboliques* had been revealed as a bona fide zombie, maybe collapsing into a soggy heap before the astonished eyes of the police, the film would have toppled into Todorov's realm of "the marvellous." Here extraordinary events are explained as unexplainable, "the class of narratives that are presented as fantastic and that end with an acceptance of the supernatural."

Here the fantasy prospector hits paydirt. Although Todorov describes various degrees of the marvellous, there exists between them an element that unifies all fantasy, an ingredient nailed by Peter Nicholls in his survey *Fantastic Cinema*: "The essence is that a fantasy film must contain a miracle — at the film's heart, there is some sort of magic."

Magic. This is a key word in the definition of fantasy. A fantasy film may take place in a magical world like Oz, Wonderland or Middle-earth. It may involve magical characters, like a flying nanny, or a boy with scissors for hands. It may concern a miracle that takes place in our own world, like the granted wish that turns a New Jersey kid into a grown man.

Magic fuels fantasy, manifesting as miracles, mysterious forces or inexplicable events, none of which can be ascribed to the laws of rationality, nature or science. Magic in fantasy films is ultimately unexplainable. This vital clause, however, must be coupled to a second crucial factor.

Any attempt to differentiate fantasy from reality begins with the question, "Can I believe my eyes?" In the case of fiction and cinema, we must determine who is telling the story. Is it a character within the narrative or the author-director, and can they be trusted to tell the truth? If the answer is no, if it was all a dream, or a delusion, or Mr. Franklin the caretaker dressed up as a ghost in order to scare those pesky kids away from the hidden treasure, then the text is not fantasy; it is what Todorov described as the uncanny, that is, the supernatural explained.

If we define fantasy cinema in terms of Todorov's marvellous (the supernatural left unexplained), then we can unequivocally trust the storyteller (or at least *a* storyteller), and what they describe can be safely construed as an objective fictional reality, no matter how bizarre that reality may be. For the duration of any given fantasy film, magic must be accepted as real. In other words, the audience must temporarily believe, or at least accept, that princes *can* turn into doves, wizards *can* command magic, and fairies *do* exist. Within the bounds of the fantasy genre, magic, though unbelievable, is as unquestionably real a force as gravity.

All films require suspension of disbelief to a degree, but fantasy films require the greatest of all, since their currency is the unbelievable. In the rapport that exists between viewer and film, the viewer may be required to consider the existence of fairies or even the existence of an entire world peopled by ogres and dragons. The greater the imaginative distance, the harder some audiences find it to make the jump. As Steve Neale notes, adult viewers of fantasy, "have often to disown their enjoyment by maintaining that such genres— and such pleasures— are not really for them, but for children, teenagers, others less 'responsible' than they are themselves." Many film critics reserve a warmer regard for more obvious allegorical fantasies, like *The Seventh Seal,* or else children's fluff, like the *Harry Potter* movies, since these make the least pretense at presenting an objective reality. Dramatically earnest or adult-orientated adventure fantasies, like *Conan the Barbarian,* demand a much greater leap of fancy that only certain audiences are prepared to take.

Weird Science and Grim Reaping

Fantasy's sister-genres, science fiction and supernatural horror, also accept the impossible as possible; their very appeal lies in envisioning for us what we can never see in reality. Although there is plenty of overlap between the three genres, fantasy is unique like its brethren.

Sci-fi films distinctively employ some kind of science to rationalize their miraculous events, even though cloned dinosaurs, assembly-line cyborgs or interplanetary travel may be worlds away from what is presently possible. Therefore, rationality is the key difference between sci-fi and fantasy. If a fantasy film ever elucidates its magic through scientific reasoning, it ceases to be fantasy. For example, the first *Highlander* movie is pure fantasy; the origins of its wandering immortals and the nature of the Grail-like prize they fight for remains scientifically vague. In the words of its hero, "Hey, it's a kind of magic." But *Highlander*'s first sequel, *Highlander II: The Quickening* (1990), qualifies itself as sci-fi with the revelation that its immortal heroes are actually aliens, whose physical makeup surpasses our own and somehow accounts for their extraordinary powers. Of course this is not really a science at all, but feasibility doesn't matter. Any film that offers a scientific explanation for its miraculous events, however whacked out that scientific explanation may be, must still come under the generic umbrella of sci-fi.

Imagine that every sci-fi film can be placed somewhere along a straight line with plausible science at one end and implausible science at the other. At the plausible end of the scale one might place technologically credible sci-fi, like Kubrick's *2001: A Space Odyssey* (1968) or maybe Peter Hyams' *Outland* (1981), films whose science (arguably) bears the greatest degree of technological credibility. At the other end, the absurdist end, we enter the eccentric realm of science fantasy, films whose science is so incredible it could never possibly be achievable. Here goes *Ghostbusters* (1984), *Bill and Ted's Excellent Adventure* (1988) and *Mars Attacks!* (1996), many comic-book superhero movies like *Batman* (1989), *X-Men* (2000) and *Spider-Man* (2002), and the improbable prehistories that make up *King Kong* (1933), *One Million Years* B.C. (1966) and *The Land That Time Forgot* (1974). The excuses these films come up with may be as gonzo as the notion in *Superman II* (1980) that the hero's powers derive from his proximity to Earth's sun (yeah, right), but such justifications must still be accepted as rational in order to absorb the film.

It may be pertinent at this point to locate George Lucas' influential space opera *Star Wars* (1977). When measured by the above criteria, the film proves something of an anomaly. Its mystical concept of the Force, coupled with an underlying moral about rejecting technology and embracing the spirit, certainly lends *Star Wars* a close kinship to fantasy films like *Excalibur* and *The Lord of the Rings*. But the film's hi-tech milieu locates it most comfortably within the bounds of science fantasy. But *The Phantom Menace* (1999), the first film of Lucas' reclaimant prequel trilogy, actually contradicts the spiritualist message of the original films by explaining the mystical Force as a science (special molecules in the Jedi's bloodstream, you see), a move that decisively cuts the entire series off from fantasy.

Horror films fit a similar hypothetical scale to the one just applied to sci-fi. Rational horror films, dealing in mundane terrors like madness and serial killers, lurk at one end, while supernatural horror, dealing in devils and multi-headed monsters, sits at the other. It is the latter end that falls under the remit of the fantastical, and which bears close similarities to fantasy. The most obvious difference between the two genres is that horror intends to frighten its audience, whereas fantasy generally does not. (Compare the spooks of *The Evil Dead* to those of *Blithe Spirit*.) But their narrative approach differs also. Horror aims to generate an atmosphere of dread, decay and death, its greatest films (among them Roman Polanski's *Rosemary's Baby*, George A. Romero's *Night of the Living Dead* [both 1968] and Wes Craven's *A Nightmare on Elm Street* [1985]) leave us with a sense that all is not well with the world; those that do not — in which everything turns out fine in the end — ultimately fail.

Conversely, fantasy films attempt some form of healing, whether the psychic wound of a hero or an entire land crippled by dark sorcery. Tim Burton's *Sleepy Hollow* (1999), though creepy, follows the cyclic pattern of fantasy, as its querulous hero (Johnny Depp) confronts his fears in the process of healing the wounded land of Sleepy Hollow, and returns home a changed man.

An effective horror film like *The Blair Witch Project* (1998) charts a narrative descent, as its characters mentally unravel and the film concludes in despair. Admittedly, *The Blair Witch Project* is an extreme example, since most horror films save their heroes at the last minute, but still those surviving characters have been made aware of a horrifying world that exists beyond their own, which they can now never comfortably ignore. Thus their psychic wounds fester. The horror film's ultimate concern, then, is death — whether it comes dressed as a werewolf, a vampire or a chainsaw-lugging lunatic — while fantasy clings to life, even when its films conclude in death. Consider James Earl Jones disappearing into the Iowa corn at the end of *Field of Dreams* (1989), surrendering to the afterlife not with trepidation but with an elated chuckle. We accept his departure from the land of the living because the film suggests we have nothing to fear from whatever may await us on the other side.

Fairies, and Angels, and Wizards, Oh My!

So the fantasy genre is a branch of fantastical cinema that never rationalizes the impossible and generally seeks to reconcile us with a more positive state of being. This constitution, however, leaves us with a hodgepodge of movies, from gentle fairy tale adaptations like *Sleeping Beauty*, enigmatic arthouse fare like *Last Year at Marienbad*, swashbucklers like *The Sword and the Sorcerer* and epics like *Die Nibelungen*. It's clear from this that fantasy films cannot be examined in any depth as a gestalt genre and must somehow be broken down. Fantasy deals in magic, in the unexplainable, but we must go deeper than this and identify a less nebulous element that typifies all fantasy films.

In *The Encyclopaedia of Fantasy*, John Clute and Gary Westfahl describe the relationship between fantasy and story. "Fantasy texts ... can be characterised as always moving towards the unveiling of an irreducible substratum of Story, an essence sometimes obscure but ultimately omnipresent; the key events of a fantasy text are bound to each other, to the narrative world, and ideally to the tale's theme in a way that permits endless retellings, endless permutations of the narrative's unbound motifs, and a sense of ending." If we agree and say that all fantasy films tell a story, then we can identify them by types of story and the manner of their telling.

Louis Gianetti's *Understanding Movies* categorizes films on a scale that reaches between two modes of filmmaking: avant-garde expressionism and documentary realism. Generally speaking, expressionism covers visually flamboyant films that obviously convey the presence of the storyteller/director, while realism refers to those films that record their material with the minimum of manipulation or optical trickery. Popular fiction films, which tend to avoid both extremes, fall directly in between. If we take Gianetti's scale, redefine expressionism and realism to infer a particular *type* of fantasy story, we find that fantasy cinema arranges itself into a general order, with expressionistic types of story at one end and realistic types at the other. They can now be labelled as five separate subgenres of story, five loose sets of narrative scheme, which deal in the same motifs.

Beginning in the center of this new scale, we find films that can be regarded as "earthbound" fantasy, films directly connected to the world as we know it, peopled with realistic, rational and identifiable characters. Into this world, however, some kind of magic either intrudes or is intruded upon. In *Darby O'Gill and the Little People*, magic intrudes when leprechauns start pestering Sean Connery. In *Lost Horizon*, the magical outpost of Shangri-La is intruded upon by Ronald Colman. In earthbound fantasy, magical forces collide with the mundane world. This class of fantasy film can be further identified by its dominant themes, their various insistence on the existence of angels (*Wings of Desire, Dogma*), lost worlds (*She, Lost Horizon*) or individuals with extraordinary powers (*Harry Potter, Bruce Almighty*).

In earthbound fantasy, realistic elements and fantasy elements are easily divisible, but as we move away from this subgenre, towards either realism or expressionism, the line between the two is blurred or even obliterated. Contact with the real world (as depicted in fiction film at least) diminishes since the majority of these other films take place in a universe located far from our own. In his essay *On Fairy Stories*, J.R.R. Tolkien refers to this wholly invented place as the "secondary world," as opposed to our own or "primary" world. The structure of these secondary worlds and the style of their description rely upon either the logic of realism or the chaos of expressionism. The closer a film falls towards realism, the more its fantasy elements will be depicted realistically; the closer a film falls towards expressionism, the more its realistic elements will be distorted fantastically.

The most extreme incarnation of expressionist fantasy is surrealism. Surrealist films feature among the very first examples of fantasy cinema. Luis Buñuel *Un Chien andalou (An Andalusian Dog)* (1929) and *L'Âge d'or (The Golden Age)* (1930) envisage a dream-like playground of ideas and images where reality has no command. This is fantasy at its most chaotic and unadulterated. But surrealism, like animation, is chiefly a mode rather than a subject in itself and must therefore be put to work on a given theme, as in Buñuel's *Le Fantôme de la liberté* (*The Phantom of Liberty*) (1974), which mocks the social niceties of the middle-classes, or Derek Jarman's *Jubilee* (1978), which derides the British monarchy. This book does not include a chapter on these already exhaustively documented films, but does discuss those that take fantasy as their subject.

Falling between surrealism and earthbound fantasy are fairy tales, a term loosely employed here to include any kind of fable, folktale or fantasy allegory. The stories told in fairy tale fantasy are often symbolic or allegorical, their characters usually representative or else necessarily strange in order to correspond to their weird surroundings. Fairy tales may employ all manner of weird phenomena without having to explain themselves, like the psychedelic phenomena that befall Alice during her trip through Wonderland, or the worlds of the Disney fable, where everyone thinks it perfectly normal for chipmunks to burst into song. Fairy tale fantasy may take place in a world that resembles our own, but whose settings are usually twisted or exaggerated to symbolize some aspect of the story.

The further fantasy moves from the earthbound towards realism, the more magic becomes regimented by the rational laws of psychics, social interaction and even politics. The term "realistic fantasy" may sound like an oxymoron, but these films must actually convince their audiences of the objective reality of the fantasies they depict. Between earthbound fantasy and the farthest extreme of realism lies heroic fantasy. These are invariably action movies of some description and feature the exploits of larger-than-life superheroes like Hercules, Sinbad or Conan. The stories these heroes inhabit must be realistically detailed to a degree for the audiences to invest in the adventure. If a heroic fantasy operates by the same cartoon physics that dictate the fairy tale (with wolves swallowing grandmothers, small girls drowning in their own tears, etc.), the exploits of the hero would become meaningless.

At the farthest outpost of fantasy realism resides epic fantasy. Unlike the heroic fantasy picture, epic fantasy films usually concern a vulnerable hero rather than a nigh-indestructible one, while the setting — essentially a backdrop in heroic fantasy — becomes a focal point of the story. Peter Jackson's *The Lord of the Rings* (2001–03) provides the model for this type of fantasy, its secondary world wholly imagined, yet rigorously detailed in terms of history and politics, so much so that it suggests a world that lives and breathes beyond the borders of its story.

Expressionism ————————————————————————————— Realism

Surrealism	Fairy Tale	Earthbound Fantasy	Heroic Fantasy	Epic Fantasy
(L'Âge d'or)	(Edward Scissorhands)	(It's a Wonderful Life)	(Conan the Barbarian)	(Lord of the Rings)

Mythopoetic License

Science fiction films extrapolate the possibilities open to science, while horror films allow their audience to safely confront their most sordid fears. If fantasy films are to be considered an equal, then what is their function? At their most basic, fantasy films offer their audience the superficial thrill of seeing life as it is not. The superheroes of heroic fantasy allow us to see ourselves as gender ideals. The landscapes of the fairy tale and the epic fantasy give us glimpses of scenic worlds we would otherwise never see. The angels and miracles of earthbound fantasy offer the chance to believe without faith. By bending the laws of reality, these films give us a contrasting view of life, so that we might better evaluate the reality we live.

We know what is real, ergo, we know what is unreal; reality defines fantasy and vice versa. As Tolkien points out in *On Fairy Stories*, "Fantasy is founded upon the hard recognition that things are so in the world as it appears under the sun; on a recognition of fact, but not a slavery to it. So upon logic was founded the nonsense that displays itself in the tales and rhymes of Lewis Carroll. If men really could not distinguish between frogs and men, fairy-stories about frog-kings would not have arisen."

An urge to defy the rules of logic demonstrated itself early in the history of fantasy cinema. Back in the 1920s, when staunch Soviet film theorist V.I. Pudovkin proposed the revolutionary idea of "constructive editing," that shots can be arranged to elicit meaning and tell a story, the mischievous Surrealists responded with films that defied every narrative law. But the psychological function of fantasy runs deeper than the simple urge to jump ship and frolic in the waters of the imagination.

"I have no small opinion of fantasy," writes Jung in *The Practice of Psychotherapy*. "When all is said and done, we can never rise above fantasy. It is true that there are unprofitable, futile, morbid, and unsatisfying fantasies whose sterile nature is immediately recognised by every person endowed with common sense; but the faulty performance proves nothing against the normal performance. All the works of man have their origin in creative imagination. What right, then, have we to disparage fantasy? In the normal course of things, fantasy does not easily go astray; it is too deep for that, and too closely bound up with the taproot of human and animal instinct. It has a surprising way of always coming out right in the end. The creative activity of imagination frees man from his bondage to the 'nothing but' and raises him to the status of one who plays. As Schiller says, 'man is completely human only when he is at play.'"

Jung named our creative capacity to fantasize the "Mythopoeic Imagination." This faculty, which shapes our daydreams and fantasies, as well as our cultural myths, manifests through a store of unconscious images, which the psychologist termed the "archetypes," universal ideas expressed with a primal image, symbol or situation. These mythological motifs recur again and again in folk stories worldwide, changing form with every telling, but never losing their elemental significance. Familiar examples include the figure of the hero, the hero-swallowing dragon, the duplicitous trickster and the wise old mentor who guides the hero on his journey. In Arthurian legend, this last archetype clearly discloses itself as Merlin the magician, whose whiskery cinematic descendents include Obi-Wan Kenobi of *Star Wars*, Dumbledore of the *Harry Potter* films and Gandalf of *The Lord of the Rings*.

Jung became especially fascinated with the archetype of the "Nekyia," also known as "the night-sea journey." In various mythologies, the hero embarks on a voyage, during which he is consumed Jonah-like or else challenged by some monstrous force, like the six-headed sea-monster Scylla, who helped herself to Odysseus' crew in *The Odyssey*. For Jung, the Nekyia "expresses the psychological mechanism of introversion of the conscious mind into the deeper layers of the unconscious psyche."

James Stewart undertakes just such a journey in Frank Capra's earthbound fantasy *It's a Wonderful Life* (1946). Transfixed by the prospect of death as he prepares to drop himself from a bridge, he is engulfed by the monster of uncertainty, as Clarence the angel posits him in an alternate world in which he was never born. Jimmy finally resurfaces, reborn into a new, and wonderful, life.

Fantasy films thrive on archetypes like these, making them more open to psychological analysis than perhaps any other genre. Earthbound fantasies like *It's a Wonderful Life* clothe their archetypes in modernity, while the various motifs of "secondary world" fantasies (fairy tale, heroic and epic fantasy) spring unalloyed from their mythopoeic source, their trolls, wizards and questings having changed little since the days of folk tales and heroic legends.

But the spiritual truths of the archetypes have been suppressed ever since Darwin suggested we are not the children of God. Jung likened the predicament of modern humankind to Goethe's Faust, who gained every insight into the material world, but lost touch with his immortal soul.

In a secular age, cinema serves an almost mystical purpose, a medium dictated by precise scientific principles, yet capable of connecting us to the airy realm of the imagination. Critics like Stuart M. Kaminsky and James F. Iaccino have fruitfully reconciled film and myth by applying Jungian theory to film critique, and yet the fantasy genre, the richest of all mythopoeic sources, remains largely dismissed. Critics do so at their loss, as Jung illustrates in his *Alchemical Studies* by a comparison of eastern and western attitudes to fantasy: "Yoga teaching rejects all fantasy products and we (the west) do the same, but the East does so for entirely different reasons. In the East there is an abundance of conceptions and teachings that give full expression to the creative fantasy; in fact, protection is needed against an excess of it. We, on the other hand, regard fantasy as worthless subjective daydreaming. Naturally the figures of the unconscious do not appear in the form of abstractions stripped of all imaginative trappings; on the contrary, they are embedded in a web of fantasies of extraordinary variety and bewildering profusion. The East can reject their fantasies because it has long since extracted their essence and condensed it in profound teachings. But we have never even experienced these fantasies, much less extracted their quintessence. We still have a large stretch of experience to catch up with, and only when we have found the sense in apparent nonsense can we separate the valuable from the worthless."

2

The Birth of
Fantasy Cinema

Once Upon a Time in Paris

Three days after Christmas 1895, lights dwindle amid Oriental moldings in the Indian Salon basement of Paris' Grand Café. Surrounded by empty seats, 33 doubtful spectators are about to witness the public debut of moving pictures—and to believe in magic. Auguste and Louis Lumière ignite their rattling *Cinématographe*, throwing a beam of light across the smoky room. A glowing image appears on one wall. The old magic lantern trick, no doubt. But just as customers think the one franc they'd paid for their seat might have been better spent, the image—incredibly—begins to move. During the screening of *Cordeliers' Square in Lyon*, patrons gasp as the film's bustling pedestrians turn to regard their audience. Others shriek and impulsively duck as a locomotive hurtles towards them during *Arrival of a Train at Ciotat Station*.

Zeuxis, the ancient Greek artist, reputedly painted grapes so realistic that passing birds tried to eat them; the Lumière brothers achieved a similarly convincing *trompe l'oeil*. They freed the recorded image from a stasis that had endured since the days of the daguerreotype. Now any scene an operator cared to point his camera at could be recorded in its active entirety, not just a frozen slice of time. The arrival of the Cinematograph fired the imaginations of the Parisian press. "What deeply poignant emotions we shall experience on seeing before us those we have loved speaking and moving," wrote *Le Courier de Paris*. "Departed parents or loved ones, suddenly brought back to life, reappearing with their familiar gestures, their soft voices, all those memories that, alas, without this new invention fade further and further into the misty corners of our minds. Why, if this continues we could almost overcome memory loss, almost put an end to separations, almost abolish death itself." Even the scientific community seemed swayed, conceding in *La Science française*, "[T]he show borders on the most unbelievably wonderful sorcery that has ever been dreamed of."

But such bedazzlement faded with familiarity. The Lumières' rivals quickly cottoned on to the financial possibilities of the Cinematograph and began patenting cameras and projectors of their own. Moving pictures became a familiar diversion in the dime stores of America, the music halls of England and the boulevard cafes of Europe. By now only the most hopelessly naïve rube would believe that these flickering images had the power to leap off the screen, as jokingly proposed in the British film *The Countryman and the Cinematograph* (1901). Urbane audiences would never be convinced that a train could fly out of a cinema screen, any more than they believed a magician's stage act was anything but smoke and mirrors. And yet the illusions proffered by both enchanted their respective audiences.

The Merry Frolics of Méliès

Fittingly, the father of fantasy cinema was a Frenchman renowned for his expertise as an illusionist. Georges Méliès, third son of a wealthy industrialist, sold his share of the family boot business at the age of 26 and bought Paris' famed Théâtre Robert-Houdin, where he rose to fame as France's premier stage magician. One of those present at the Cinematograph's public debut, Méliès became intrigued by the device, imagining the creative avenues it could open up as part of his stage act. He immediately offered to buy the Lumière projector, but the brothers refused, eager to get rich off their contraption before its novelty value wore off.

The following year, an undaunted Méliès contacted English technician Robert W. Paul, who produced and sold counterfeit projectors based on the American Kinetoscope, invented by Thomas Edison, who forgot to secure a transatlantic patent. Méliès bought one of Paul's projectors and screened a number of imported Edison films at the Robert-Houdin. Later, using Paul's camera as a prototype, Méliès developed several different cameras of his own, eventually producing one-scene, one-shot, one-minute movies in his backyard, using a canvas enclosure as a rudimentary studio.

Unsatisfied with merely recording stage acts, Méliès determined to adapt them for film, replacing mirrors, pulleys and vampire traps with lens, crank and shutter. His first important discovery in this direction was apparently accidental. The story, as Méliès himself set it down in 1907 (appearing in translation in David Robinson's *Georges Méliès: Father of Film Fantasy*), is questionable, but credible. "The camera I was using in the beginning (a rudimentary affair in which the film would tear or would often refuse to move) produced an unexpected effect one day when I was photographing very prosaically the Place de l'Opéra. It took a minute to release the film and get the camera going again. During this minute the people, buses, vehicles had of course moved. Projecting the film, having joined the break, I suddenly saw a Madeleine-Bastille omnibus changed into a hearse and men into women. The trick of substitution, called the trick of stop-action, was discovered, and two days later I made the first metamorphoses of men into women and the first sudden disappearances which, at first, had a big success."

Escamotage d'une dame chez Robert-Houdin (*The Vanishing Lady*) (1896) was one of Méliès' first optically manipulated films. Méliès himself, in his magician's tuxedo, throws a striped blanket over his seated assistant, and with an appropriate flourish whisks away the mantle to reveal a blackened skeleton. To achieve this effect, Méliès simply stopped his camera at the vital moment and substituted the lady for the skeleton before restarting the film. Although Méliès certainly discovered this early special effect for himself, his was not the first film to employ it. Edison beat him to it with an earlier Kinetoscope film, *The Execution of Mary, Queen of Scots* (1895), which switched an actress for a beheadable dummy. Both films employed the "stop-action" effect invisibly, but whereas Edison's film did so to sustain an illusion of reality, Méliès' did so to achieve the reality of an illusion. Instead of recreating a realistic event, the Frenchman had depicted the blatantly unreal, an event that could never otherwise have taken place in the world we, the audience, inhabit.

Transformation is the essence of magic, be it transforming one thing into another or producing something out of nothing. Thus fantasy cinema was born the moment Georges Méliès turned his assistant into bones. The genre has abounded in such alchemical conversions ever since, as pumpkins metamorphose into coaches, toads into princes, and wayward heroes into kings, who in turn restore crippled lands into flourishing kingdoms.

In the final months of 1896, Méliès produced the first true fantasy film. Whereas *The Vanishing Lady* was essentially an adjunct to its director's stage act, its central miracle rationalized by Méliès' presence as the presiding magician, *Le Manoir du Diable* (*The Infernal Palace*), based on a stage act Méliès presented in 1890, featured a series of impossible events that occurred of their own accord within a self-contained world. *The Infernal Palace* is a lost film, but the following synopsis from the 1901 *Warwick Film Catalogue* survives:

> The picture shows a room in a mediaeval castle; carved stone pillars, low doors and vaulted ceiling. A huge bat flies in and circles around. It is suddenly transformed into Mephistopheles. He walks around, makes a magic pass, and a large cauldron appears and out of it, in a great cloud of smoke, there emerges a beautiful lady. At another magic pass, a little old man comes out of the floor carrying a big book. Then the cauldron disappears. And so it goes on. Cavaliers, ghosts, a skeleton and witches appear and disappear at a sign from the Evil One. Finally one of the cavaliers produces a cross, and Mephistopheles throws up his hands and disappears in a cloud of smoke.

Méliès' fantastical output now branched into two distinct categories: so-called "trick films," like *The Vanishing Lady*, and genuine fantasy films like *The Infernal Palace*. In his trick films, Méliès appeared on-screen as himself, wearing his prescribed stage attire and performing deceptions in much the same way as he would at the Robert-Houdin, albeit through a medium that allowed him greater deceptive scope. In this fashion, he cloned himself enough times to occupy an orchestra in *L'Homme orchestre* (*The One-Man Band*) (1900), inflated his own head to explosive proportions in *L'Homme à la tête de caoutchouc* (*The Man with the Rubber Head*) (1902), and replicated his cranium several times to serve as notes on a huge conductor's sheet in *Le Mélomane* (*The Melomaniac*) (1903).

Méliès' fantasy films contain no such mediator to allow the audience to dismiss the phenomena as a clever trick. Here the miraculous is not the formal product of a conjurer, but operates of its own accord, as part of the fabric of the story and the world in which it takes place. Nothing short of "magic" explains why willful furniture torments a weary traveller in *L'Auberge ensorcelée* (*The Bewitched Inn*) (1897), or how a impish moon can visit a medieval astronomer in *La Lune à un metre* (*The Astronomer's Dream, or the Man in the Moon*) (1898), or makes sense of the subterranean phantoms who menace the heroine of *La Caverne maudite* (1898) [*The Cave of the Demons*]. By the turn of the century, Méliès had demonstrated that cinema was not limited to non-fiction, to the "travelogues," "scenics," "topicals" and other "actualities" exemplified by the Lumières. The camera could indeed lie, and Méliès' did so shamelessly.

For the camera to keep up with his inexhaustible imagination, Méliès developed a repertoire of optical tricks, including double exposure, dissolves, masking, miniatures and fast and slow motion, all of which remain fundamental to special effects techniques today. Of his embryonic methods, Méliès wrote in *Cinematographic Sights* in 1907, "With all these processes mixed one with another and used with competence, I do not hesitate to say that in cinematography it is today possible to realise the most impossible and the most improbable things." As Méliès continued to develop and refine his stock of tricks, he found that fairy tales, with their brisk narrative form and abundant transformations, provided excellent material for his films. In 1897 he produced the world's first filmed fairy tale, the now-lost *La Cigale et la Fourmi* (*The Grasshopper and the Ant*), adapted from *Aesop's Fables*.

Méliès transposed from the page to the screen a fascination with the fairy tale that had existed among his countrymen since the 17th century, when storytelling was a fashionable pastime among socialites. Influenced by earlier Italian tales, these popular stories developed into a literary vogue. Collections appeared, among them *Les Contes des fées* (1697) by Marie-Catherine d'Aulnoy (from which the English phrase "fairy tale" is derived) and the earthy folkloric yarns of Charles Perrault, one of the few men writing in a form dominated by women. His 1697 collection *Histoires ou contes du temps passé* (*Stories or Tales from Past Times*), includes some of the best-known Western fairy tales, whose forms and characters have persisted in literature and film to the present day.

Méliès set three of Perrault's tales to film — *Cendrillon* (*Cinderella*) (1899), *Le Petit Chaperon rouge* (*Little Red Riding Hood*) (1901) and *Barbe-Bleue* (*Blue Beard*) (1901) — and embellished each story with imaginative touches of his own. In *Cinderella*, Méliès stars as a bearded Father Time, pinned to the center of an enormous clock as it strikes midnight. He also appears as the capering Devil in *Blue Beard*, springing from the pages of an open Bible to incite the tyrant's latest wife to marital treason.

Away with the Féeries

As his fantasy films swelled with ambition, Méliès employed a distinctive aesthetic inspired by a form of popular French theatre, which had enchanted the director in his youth. Known as the *féeries*, these colorful vaudeville shows, a combination of pantomime, opera and melodrama, emerged in the wake of the French Revolution, when theatre opened its doors to the great and newly emancipated unwashed. Often filching the plots of romantic 18th century fantasy novels, the French *féeries* featured a repertoire of stock characters similar to the Italian *commedia dell'arte*, incorporating archetypes like the virtuous lovers, the bungling sidekick, the grotesque rival and his assorted demonic minions.

Since revolutionaries like D.W. Griffith, Pudovkin and Lev Kuleshov had yet to establish cinema's common tongue, Méliès instinctively employed the theatrical tropes of the *féerie* in bringing his fantasies to the screen. The director pointed his stationary camera squarely at the stage where the action takes place, suggesting the viewer occupies the front stalls of a theater, while the frame of the picture approximated the proscenium arch. He filmed his actors exclusively in full shot, with no close-ups or cutaways, and moved from scene to scene with a dissolve in lieu of a falling curtain. Canvas backdrops painted to a vanishing point created a sense of depth, an illusion enhanced by the ranks of flat scenery that shuffled into view from the wings or descended from the flies above the stage. Stop motion substitutions and varieties of double exposure created most of the necessary visual effects. Viewed today, these films feel unearthly, as actors scurry around ingeniously designed dioramas like Lilliputians in a toy theater.

Méliès applied this expressionistic style, a unique combination of theatrical and cinematic techniques, to practically every form of fantasy narrative. He freely adapted ballet (1900's *Copélia ou la poupée animée* [*Coppelia, the Animated Doll*]), opera (1905's *La Légende de Rip van Winkle* [*Rip's Dream*], from the comic opera of 1884), folklore (1900's *Le Rêve de Noël* [*The Christmas Dream*]; 1908's *La Cuisine de l'ogre* [*In the Bogie Man's Cave*]), fiction (1899's *La Colonne du feu* [*Haggard's "She": The Pillar of Fire*]; 1902's *Le Voyage de Gulliver* [*Gulliver's Travels*]), classical myth (1903's *Le Tonnerre de Jupiter* [*Jupiter's Thunderbolts, or the Home of the Muses*]; 1905's *Ulysse et le géant Polyphème* [*The Mysterious Island*]), Arabian fantasy (1905's *Le Palais des mille et une nuits* [*The Palace of the Arabian Nights*]) and science-fiction (1902's *Le Voyage dans la lune* [*A Trip to the Moon*]). This last film, a dotty fusion of Jules Verne and H.G. Wells, remains Méliès' most celebrated film. The image of its grimacing piecrust moon with a bullet-shaped rocket lodged in its eye has become an emblem of bygone cinema.

One of the most grandiose of Méliès' post–*Trip to the Moon* fantasies is *Le Royaume des fées* (*Fairyland, or The Kingdom of the Fairies*), a 1903 film based on the ballet *Biche où bois* (*The Forest Hind*). In this opulent romantic adventure, the Prince of Bel Azor embarks on a chivalrous rescue mission when a malicious hook-nosed crone kidnaps his betrothed, the Princess Azurine, and imprisons her in a remote island fortress. When the Prince sails in pursuit, the crone summons a tempest that sinks his vessel. (Méliès employed a detailed miniature to describe this, and somehow shot the following underwater scenes through a fish-tank, so live minnows could flit across the foreground.) A compassionate mermaid revives the drowned Prince and his crew, who ride a cutout parade of lobsters and swordfish to the court of King Neptune. They hitch a ride inside the belly of a cheerful-looking whale, who disgorges the Prince on shore. With the aid of an angelic fairy, he wrests Azurine from a gang of torch-twirling imps before stuffing the crone into a barrel and shoving her off a cliff.

Although *Fairyland* boasts nothing to rival the enduring magic of *A Trip to the Moon*, the film provides a sumptuous example of Méliès' cornucopian style. The director crams his frame to excess, barely containing his sensual décor with its shell-like curves, sprouting fauna and swollen gargoyles. The copiousness of detail suggests a world fit to explode, like the inflated noggin of *The Man with the Rubber Head*.

Although Méliès dabbled in practically every strain of fantasy, from the fireside fable to the operatic epic, he reserved a particular fascination for the tale of Faust. The impish Méliès invariably cast himself as Mephistopheles. As His Infernal Majesty, the director turned himself into a monkey, a pig and a donkey in *Le Cabinet de Mephistophélès* (*The Laboratory of Mephistopheles*) (1897), gave romantic advice in *Faust et Marguérite* (*Faust and Marguerite*) (1897), frightened nuns in *Le Diable au couvent* (*The Devil in a Convent*) (1899), thwarted a thief in *Les Trésors de Satan* (*The Devil's Money-bags*) (1901), learned to dance in *Le Cake-walk infernal* (*The Infernal Cakewalk*) (1903) and did time in *Satan en prison* (*Satan in Prison*) (1907). In all his incarnations, Méliès' Devil delights in dumbfounding mortals as much as Méliès' the filmmaker did his audience.

Easily the most impressive of Méliès' diabolic outings is the lavishly frenetic *Les 400 Farces du diable* (*The Merry Frolics of Satan*) (1906), based on an 1839 *féerie*, *The Devil's Pills*. William Crackford, an excitable engineer in a Sherlock Holmes cloak and deerstalker, buys a basketful of eggs from an alchemist, actually the Devil (Méliès) in disguise. When hurled to the floor, the eggs explode in a burst of smoke and grant their owner's wish. Crackford demonstrates this in front of his wife in a dizzyingly inventive scene. He produces several chests, lifting one out of the other, and out of which burst a troupe of somersaulting footmen, who proceed to fold up the room's furniture like over-starched laundry. The chests form a train, which Crackford rides into the Alps, where Satan's devils await. Crackford tries to escape in a carriage, but the Devil turns it into an astral chariot, drawn by a skeletal horse, and blasts him into orbit.

As the carriage shoots across the night sky, Méliès revels in his own firecracker imagination, letting rip with absurdities that would later endear him to the Surrealists. The coach driver lights his pipe with a star. Crackford hooks a crescent moon with his umbrella and munches on it like a slice of watermelon. Smiling chorus girls recline on shooting stars and beckon as they glide past. Goblin-faced constellations scowl at the vehicle's passage, and a crotchety old geezer clambers out of a trapdoor in Saturn and shakes his fist. But the fun comes to an end when Satan drags Crackford down to Hell, where imps inside a treadmill turn his newly captured soul on a spit.

The Magician of Montreuil Takes a Bow

As cinema matured, pundits began to dismiss Méliès as a vestige of the new medium's infancy. In 1910, after his studio went bankrupt, he was forced to hand over the reins to a successful competitor, Pathé Frères. Under the auspices of producer Charles Pathé and rival fantasist Ferdinand Zecca, Méliès produced a final clutch of *féerie*-inspired fantasies—*Les Hallucinations du Baron de Münchausen* (*Baron Münchausen's Dream*) (1911), *Cendrillon ou la pantoufle mystérieuse* (*Cinderella, or the Glass Slipper*) (1912) and *Le Chevalier des neiges* (*Knight of the Snows*) (1912). They all flopped.

Modern cinemagoers favored realism. As film production in Europe faltered at the approach of World War I, America stepped in to take up the slack, flexing the muscle of its newly established base of production, a cluster of California-based studios collectively known as Hollywood. Méliès' fantasies looked increasingly naïve alongside evermore accomplished American productions, including Bison Pictures' authentic Westerns, Keystone's urban slapstick and Famous Players' reverent stage adaptations. Popular performers like Florence Lawrence, Maurice Costello and Mary Pickford outshone Méliès' antiquated magic. Hollywood trailblazer D. W. Griffith utilized Méliès' optical effects to advance sophisticated narratives, standardizing effects like the fade-in and fade-out as part of cinema's accepted grammar, while Méliès still relied on them for their own sake.

When considered alongside the rest of fantasy cinema, Méliès' films seem to occupy a bubble, sealing them off from the rest of the genre. Despite their various sources, Méliès' fantasies are unified by their peculiar theatricality; the director tarred sci-fi with the same freewheeling absurdist brush as fairy tale, and their differentiating themes fell by the wayside. Story meant little to Méliès; narrative was merely the glue holding together a parade of tricks. French film historian Georges Sadoul quotes the filmmaker. "In this type of film (fantasy films, flights of imagination, artistic, diabolical, fantastical or magical films), the most important thing lies in the ingeniousness and unexpectedness of the tricks, in the picturesque nature of the décors, in the artistic lay out of the characters and also in the main 'hook' and the grand finale. Contrary to what is usually done, my procedure for constructing this sort of film consisted in coming up with the details before the whole; the whole being nothing other than the 'scenario'" (as translated in *The Journal of Popular Film and Television*, 1987, in an article by André Gaudreault.)

While Méliès' fantasy films stagnated, others moved the genre forward. Across Europe and in the U.S., Méliès' imitators and admirers produced fantasy films of their own, developing techniques the Frenchman had pioneered in realizing the fantastic on screen and adapting a range of untapped literary sources, like the *Alice* books, L. Frank Baum's *Oz* series and ancient Norse saga. Few of these could match Méliès' originality of vision, but ironically it was their very banality that enabled fantasy to survive. Free at last of Méliès' constrictive and outmoded aesthetic treatment, story began to dictate style, freeing fantasy cinema to diversify and develop forms of its own.

By the time of his death, the 76-year-old Georges Méliès had amassed a filmography totalling over 500 short films, covering a range of subjects: scenic views, comedies, religious and historical re-enactments, erotica, sci-fi, trick films and fantasy. Sadly, few survived the war. Méliès destroyed many himself, angrily burning them in his yard after the demise of his career. Reserves were either confiscated by the Nazis or melted down to make boot heels for the army. Less than 40 percent of his entire output still exists, leaving his oeuvre impossible to categorize accurately. A few tantalizing titles remain to hint at the full extent of his fantasy output.

Méliès vanished until the late 1920s, when film journalists found him working a cramped toy stall in the corner of the Gare Montparnasse. He received the devotions of several young filmmakers, including future fantasist René Clair, who paid homage to Méliès in his charming tribute to the silent era *Silence est d'or* (*Silence Is Golden*) (1947). Two years after a famous gala celebration of his work in 1929, Méliès was officially honored for his contribution to cinema when Louis Lumière awarded him the Legion of Honor and hailed him as the "creator of cinematographic spectacles." In 1937, German surrealist filmmaker and Méliès devotee Hans Richter proposed a new version of the *Baron Munchausen* story, to be co-directed by his idol, but the project was scrapped after the Frenchman died of cancer the following year.

Although their densely inventive textures echo throughout the work of modern fantasists like Terry Gilliam, Jean-Pierre Jeunet, Jan Švankmajer and Tsui Hark, Méliès' films are too idiosyncratic to have been widely influential beyond his decline. But the "Magician of Montreuil" remains a landmark figure in fantasy film, if not for comprehending the potential of cinema to realize events beyond the actual, then for his consummate sense of wonder, which has remained an indelible part of the genre ever since.

3

Fairy Tales

Seeing Is Believing

Fairy tales are not so much about fairies as the perilous realm they inhabit. Faerie, as it is known, is a world located some distance from our own, although humans often stumble upon its shores. Curious explorers have been known to traverse portals as unexpected as rabbit holes and wardrobes, or have tumbled through their own dreams, or perhaps followed a star until morning. "The realm of fairy-story is wide and deep and high and filled with many things," writes Tolkien, "all manner of beasts and birds are found there; shoreless seas and stars uncounted; beauty that is an enchantment, and an ever-present peril; both joy and sorrow as sharp as swords. In that realm a man may, perhaps, count himself fortunate to have wandered, but its very richness and strangeness tie the tongue of a traveller who would report them." This world may resemble our own, but the illusion is never entire. Like the shape-shifters of legend, some immutable detail will betray its true nature. Perhaps its geography appears inconsistent, and gothic towers loom incongruously over pastel suburbs, or the behavior of its inhabitants seems weirdly irrational, and grown men squabble like infants over tickets to a chocolate factory.

Georges Méliès was the first to document Faerie on behalf of cinema, but the realm was ancient when the fairy tales he adapted were young. What we commonly regard as fairy tales today derive from an elder storytelling tradition, known among scholars as the wonder tale, the socializing folk stories exchanged among communities solely by word of mouth. A fairy tale is a wonder tale set in writing. Lucius Apuleius' Beauty and the Beast prototype *Cupid and Psyche* (a poetic episode from *The Golden Ass* [second century]) is regarded as the world's first fairy tale, but the form developed in earnest during the medieval period, influenced by Boccaccio's *The Decameron* (1348–53) and Chaucer's *The Canterbury Tales* (1386–1400). The genre was formalized in sixteenth and seventeenth century Italy, by Giovan Francesco Straparola's *Le piacevoli notti* (*The Pleasant Nights*) (1550–53) and Giambattista Basile's *Lo cunto de li cunti* (*The Story of Stories*) (1634–36), and popularized in the 1690s by the French noblesse, with whose renditions Méliès was so familiar.

In the introduction to her study *From the Beast to the Blonde*, critic Marina Warner accurately describes fairy tale as "a language of the imagination, with a vocabulary of images and a syntax of plots." This can of course be said of fantasy itself, whose archetypal wizards and ogres we recognize behind various guises in fantasy films across the spectrum. But we are most familiar and perhaps most at ease with these emblems as they appear in fairy tale, as mysterious and as divorced from our world as they were in the tales we heard as children. And yet it is here that fantasy is at its most radical. Echoing the oral hyperbole of the wonder tale, stories set in Faerie do not obey the dictates of time or physics as must its opponent epic fantasy. In short, fairy tale is the most unrealistic form of fantasy. Here an inventor can convert a cookie-cutting machine into a Pinocchio without the story having to explain the science of how he did so, nor will any other character question the impossibility of his accomplishment. But for the necessary strictures of narrative, the stuff of fairy tale is as protean as that of surrealism.

Unlike epic fantasy, fairy tales' transformations do not affect the land so much as those within it. Spontaneous mutations occur every day in Faerie; babies become swine, puppets become boys and maidens become monsters. Prof. Jack Zipes explains the appeal in his introduction to *The Oxford Companion to Fairy Tales:* "The tales seek to awaken our regard for the marvellous *changing* condition of life and to evoke in a religious sense profound feelings of awe and respect for life as a miraculous process which can be altered and changed to compensate for the lack of power, wealth, and pleasure that most people experience."

Since magical transmutations characterize fantasy film, it's unsurprising that the genre's development parallels that of the special effects industry. Since Méliès' day, fantasy cinema has commonly been employed as a vehicle for technical advances in that field, its progress dictated less by cultural climate and more by the innovations of FX gurus like Ray Harryhausen and Rick Baker. Indeed, few filmmakers realize that the creation of fantasy and an excessive effects budget are actually divisible.

In the early days, Méliès' founding box of camera tricks proved simple enough for his less imaginative rivals to emulate. Receiving plainer treatments than they would have under the Frenchman, who lent his adapted tales an idiosyncratic glamour in keeping with their storybook origins, the old school of fairy tale authors were the first to be adapted to film. G.A. Smith's *Cinderella and the Fairy Godmother* (1898) was the first film to bear that fairy tale's title, although it lacked any narrative beyond the conjuration of a ballroom gown. Méliès' version a year later was the first to properly adapt the Charles Perrault version. Cornish wonder tales provided the basis for Edwin S. Porter's *Jack and the Beanstalk* (1902), while two Brothers Grimm stories received their first screen treatments in Sigmund Lubin's *Le Petit Poucet* (*Little Tom Thumb*) (1903) and the Edison-produced *Hansel and Gretal* (1909). E.T.A. Hoffmann's tale *Coppelia* received only a cursory treatment in Méliès' *Coppelia the Animated Doll*, but Lewin Fitzhamon let the story breathe in *The Dollmaker's Daughter* (1906). Percy Stow filmed Robert Browning's 1842 poem as *The Pied Piper* (1907) and was the first to adapt the tale of Beauty and the Beast (from an unknown source author) in 1905, while Lucien Nonguet's *La Belle et la bête* (*Beauty and the Beast*) (1908) was based on the version by Madame Jeanne-Marie Leprince de Beaumont.

By the time Méliès had begun his steep decline in 1910, the literary fairy tale had already undergone a revolution. In the introduction to his groundbreaking *The Wonderful Wizard of Oz* (1900), L. Frank Baum wrote, "[T]he old-time fairy tale, having served for generations, may now be classed as 'historical' in the children's library; for the time has come for a series of newer 'wonder tales' in which the stereotyped genie, dwarf and fairy are eliminated, together with all the horrible and blood-curdling incident devised by their authors to point a fearsome moral to each tale." True to his manifesto, Baum produced an exuberant fairy tale for the New World transposed from the tales of the Old.

Unlike his literary forebears, Baum lived long enough to see his tales adapted to film. He scripted a successful stage musical based on *Wizard* in 1902 and toured in 1908 with a sideshow, including several short films (now lost) based on his books. But he myopically hoped to capitalize on the already diminished vogue for fairy tale films. In 1910, the Chicago-based Selig Polyscope Company produced for him a silent single-reeler, Otis Turner's *The Wonderful Wizard of Oz*, starring a young Bebe Daniels as Dorothy. Turner borrows a number of tricks from Méliès' outmoded repertoire, as the Wicked Witch's minions appear and vanish via stop-action and their boss meets her corrosive end with an appropriate dissolve. Predictably the film flopped, as did its three follow-ups of the same year, *Dorothy and the Scarecrow in Oz*, *The Land of Oz* and *John Dough and the Cherub*. Baum filed for bankruptcy in 1911.

Undeterred, he founded the Oz Film Manufacturing Company in 1914, determined to film his entire literary oeuvre. Before the company went bust a year later, it managed to produce *The Patchwork Girl of Oz*, based on the 1913 novel, *The Magic Cloak of Oz*, based on *Queen Zixi of Ix* (1905), and *His Majesty, the Scarecrow of Oz*, based on *The New Wizard of Oz* (1903). Baum reportedly directed the last two himself, having fired the original director J. Farrell MacDonald. *Patchwork Girl* bombed so badly, distributors didn't touch its follow-ups for years. Given the popularity of the books and Baum's unstoppable hucksterism, the commercial failure of these films is puzzling. Perhaps, as Mark Evan Swartz suggests in *Oz Before the Rainbow*, the films targeted the all-child audience that did not yet exist.

Literary fairy tales were written primarily for adults until the late eighteenth century, when the Enlightenment provoked debates over the moral value of fantastic literature and its possibly detrimental effect on the minds of its readers. Fairy tales now diverged roughly along two paths: didactic "bourgeois" children's literature, and philosophical adult tracts epitomized by the work of German romantics like Ludwig Tieck, Novalis and Goethe. The Brothers Grimm were unique in that their tales addressed both audiences at once.

A similar schism affected American fairy tale films after the failure of Baum's Oz pictures. With multi-reel films the norm by 1910, adult audiences considered one-reel fairy tales passé. The few films that retained the joyful triviality of the trick era were low-budget fare catering exclusively for children, like Chester and Sidney Franklin's *Jack and the Beanstalk* and *The Babes in the Wood*, both released by Fox in 1917 and cast almost entirely with children. If they wanted to reel in the grown-ups as well as their kids, movies now had to work greater spectacle and prominent stars into their fairy tale plots and expand them to feature length. Dominating the genre well into the '20s, Paramount revived flagging interest in fairy tale by headlining Mary Pickford and Marguerite Clark respectively in two prestige productions, James Kirkwood's *Cinderella* (1914), based on the Perrault, and J. Searle Dawley's *Snow White* (1916), a mighty six-reeler based on the Grimms.

The year 1918 saw Paramount launch another high-profile fairy tale, Maurice Tourneur's *The Bluebird*, based on Maurice Maeterlinck's respectable children's play *L'Oiseau bleu* (1909), while Otis Thayer's *Little Red Riding Hood* and Madeline Brandis' *The Star Prince* borrowed Fox's gimmick of an all-child cast. Concerning a boy who falls from the stars and whose haughty nature is changed by the love of an earthly princess, *The Star Prince* is most significant as possibly the first fairy tale written (by Brandis) directly for the screen. Hollywood's search for untapped literary fairy tales had finally uncovered those of Hans Christian Andersen. J. Searle Dawley's *The Seven Swans* (1917) was the first to adapt his work, followed a year later by John G. Adolfi's *Queen of the Sea*, a riff on Andersen's *The Little Sea-Maid*, itself influenced by Friedrich de La Motte Fouqué's *Undine*, filmed in 1916 by Henry Otto.

After Baum's death in 1919, his son sold the film rights to *The Wonderful Wizard of Oz* to Chadwick Pictures, who produced a loose adaptation in 1924. It was directed by popular slapstick comedian Larry Semon and starred a young Oliver Hardy as the Tin Woodsman. A modest success on release, the film had been delayed to avoid competing with yet another Paramount fairy tale, Herbert Brenon's *Peter Pan* (1924), faithfully based on J.M. Barrie's 1904 play, a text which proved as significant to the development of the literary fairy tale as Baum's Oz books. Like Baum, Barrie also lived to enjoy his cinematic offspring and realized the potential for expanding the material through special effects. In a series of notes to the film's producers, Barrie wrote that the play's famous flying sequences "should show at once that the film can do things for *Peter Pan* which the ordinary stage cannot do. It should strike a note of wonder in the first [scene] and whet the appetite for marvels." Barrie also wrote the source play for Paramount's *A Kiss for Cinderella* (1925), again directed by Brenon and starring Betty Bronson, fresh from her career-launching screen turn as Pan.

Aside from numerous versions of Cinderella, another perennial favorite of silent fairy tale film were the *Arabian Nights*. Originally a collection of Arabic fairy tales, *Alf laila wa laila* (*The Thousand and One Nights*) underwent an assortment of Middle Eastern translations before a Frenchman, Antoine Galland, wrote the first European version in the early eighteenth century. The stories became fashionable among the Victorians thanks to Richard Burton's unexpurgated ten-volume English edition. The Arabian Nights are framed by the story of a murderously bigamous Sultan, whose latest wife ingeniously stalls her own execution by reciting a labyrinth of tales, from which cinema managed to extract a few. Ferdinand Zecca for once out-innovated his rival Méliès by producing the first *Arabian Nights* adaptation, *Ali Baba et les quarante voleurs* (*Ali Baba and the Forty Thieves*) (1902), which he followed up with *Aladdin et la lampe merveilleuse* (*Aladdin and the Marvelous Lamp*) (1906). Following Charles L. Gaskill's *A Princess of Baghdad* (1913), Fox cornered the market in Arabian *fantastique* with Herbert Brenon's *A Daughter of the Gods* (1916) and the Franklin brothers' *Aladdin and the Wonderful Lamp* (1917) and *Ali Baba and the Forty Thieves* (1918), both with all-child casts.

The exotic milieu of the *Arabian Nights* provided a sound vehicle for the swash-buckling of Douglas Fairbanks. Fairbanks wrote (under the pseudonym of Elton Thomas) and produced his own fantasy film, *The Thief of Baghdad* (1924), directed

Rising along a gusty floor: The romantic thief, Ahmed (Douglas Fairbanks), gives the Princess (Julanne Johnson) the ride of her life in Raoul Walsh's silent *The Thief of Baghdad* (Fairbanks/United Artists, 1924).

by Raoul Walsh. Surpassing Paramount's big-budget fairy tales, *Thief of Baghdad* became the crowning American fantasy of the silent era, boasting (in addition to the magnetism of its star) an entirely foreign fantasy world and a bestiary of storybook monsters. Yet the film's agenda differed little from the naïve sensationalism of Méliès. Clearly intending to engage the viewer no further than their eyeballs, Fairbanks laid on over six acres of set for celebrated production designer William Cameron Menzies to garnish with towering Art Deco. He also employed thousands of extras to mill about as urchins, fakirs and merchants.

With a joyful grin and effortless grace, Fairbanks bounces around this Arabian Faerie as Achmed the thief. Scorning the words of the holy man who writes his wisdom in the stars ("Happiness must be earned"), the scoundrel disguises himself as a prince in order to win a princess (Julanne Johnston) away from a caricature Mongol prince (Sojin Kamiyama). The film abruptly changes tack halfway through, from patented Fairbanks swashbuckler to a fantasy parade float that steamrollers the star with special effects. Set the challenge of bringing the Princess the rarest treasure in the world, Fairbanks tussles first with a dragon, then with a bat the size of a hang glider. He also revives a spindly tree-man with a magic talisman, beats up a giant spider on the floor of the Midnight Sea (where he grudgingly resists the charms of the local nereids), recovers the cloak of invisibility from the Citadel of the Moon, rides home astride a winged horse and conjures an army from a magic chest, before stringing up the Mongol villains by their pigtails.

The success of *Thief of Baghdad* proved double-edged. It established fairy tale fantasy as a viable commercial genre, but only in the form of movies as overwhelmingly extravagant and prohibitively expensive as this. Any emotional or intellectual engagement in a penetrating secondary world was not yet an option. Fantasy had to be seen, not imagined, in order to be believed, and the costs involved in doing so, particularly after the Wall Street Crash, meant that fairy tale films went untouched by Hollywood for almost a decade thereafter.

In a Wonderland They Lay

Released three years after *The Interpretation of Dreams*, Percy Stow's *Alice in Wonderland* (1903) had to tread carefully. If it let slip that fairy tales comprised the same psychoactive stuff that interested the shrinks, the moral authorities hovering over the nickelodeons would have swooped. Based on *Alice's Adventures in Wonderland* (1865) by troubled Oxford don Charles Lutwidge Dodgson (Lewis Carroll was his pseudonym), Stow's film was the first fairy tale to present Faerie as a place one had to get to rather than a place you already were. Like Baum and Barrie after him, Carroll (who died five years too early to see his beloved Alice on film) had successfully modernized the European fairy tale with the tantalizing proposal of a fantastic world existing separately and parallel to the reader's own.

At the time, Méliès was only just ushering cinema away from its roots in documentary realism, and the lunatics of Faerie were not yet allowed free passage into the world of the sane. Early films had to quarantine munchkins and jabberwocks, setting their stories entirely within an archaic storybook milieu that bore no relation to the world of the viewer, often announcing this divorce with a promulgatory "Once Upon a Time." Other films had to clearly demarcate the line between the irrational world of Faerie and the rational world of the audience. Stow's film sticks close to Carroll, and has nothing untoward happen to Alice (May Clark) until she clambers down the film's cavernous rabbit hole.

Like other trick films of its time, *Alice* compares badly to the frantic confectionary of Méliès. Stow's teenage heroine toddles through a humdrum Wonderland where forced perspective tricks effect potion-induced changes in size, and enlarged animals like a monstrous puppy and a very grumpy-looking Cheshire Cat, at which Alice waves her kerchief in frantic greeting. When a procession of sandwich-board playing cards threatens to chop off her head, the film quickly reels Alice back to the safety of the real world. The it-was-all-a-dream revelation acts as a cut-off point for the imagination of the audience, for fear that the unreal events in which they have so far invested will overwhelm them.

In America, however, producers saw *Alice* as just the upstanding English classic needed to silence the film industry's moral critics. Aside from staying on to describe the trial of the tart-stealing Knave of Hearts, Edwin S. Porter's lavish *Alice's Adventures in Wonderland* (1910) follows precisely the same narrative arc as Stow, while W.W. Young's *Alice in Wonderland* (1915) boasts the first screen appearance of Carroll's hookah-puffing Caterpillar, the Mock Turtle and the Gryphon, as well as staging the Lobster quadrille. Young's was also the first film to adapt elements of Carroll's ominous sequel *Through the Looking-Glass, and What Alice Found There* (1871), notably the pugnacious twins Tweedledum and Tweedledee. As in Young's film, "Bud" Pollard's *Alice in Wonderland* (1931) negates the need for a rabbit hole by making it clear from the outset that Alice is asleep and dreaming. We see the girl leave her sleeping form and join the waist coated rabbit, who escorts her to the Wonderland of the first book, this time with the addition of sound and a title song by Irving Berlin.

In 1932, armed with an Alice of his own, Walt Disney prepared to make his momentous invasion of Faerie. Disney had moved to Hollywood in 1923, with the fabled sum of $40 to his name, and had conquered the field of animation by the end of the decade with his *Silly Symphony* cartoons. Disney would soon become the single most influential figure in the development of American fairy tale film. Conceived in collaboration with Mary Pickford (then hoping to resuscitate her fading post-silent career), Disney planned a feature-length revival of the unofficial *Alice in Cartoonland* shorts he made in the '20s. But Disney's live-action–animation project, along with another Alice proposed by Columbia (based on Eva LeGallienne's 1932 stage play), were scrapped after Paramount snagged the film rights and produced Norman Z. McLeod's *Alice in Wonderland* (1933), the studio's abortive return to big-budget fairy tales, and the first feature length adaptation of Carroll's books.

With the defining opulence of Fairbanks' *Thief of Baghdad* still strong in the public mind, Paramount knew it had to ensure its Wonderland would be a place worth visiting. Hoping some of *Thief*'s magic would rub off, the studio hired

Smoking in Wonderland can cause peculiar side effects, as the Caterpillar (Ned Sparks) demonstrates in Norman Z. McLeod's *Alice in Wonderland* (Paramount, 1933).

Fairbanks' production designer William Cameron Menzies, although not to create sets but to co-write the script alongside Joseph L. Mankiewicz. The same Carrollesque logic applied to the studio's decision to hide most of its highly publicized cast behind pasteboard masks, as Percy Stow had done back in 1903. The scheme did not go down well with audiences, who had paid to see and not just hear Cary Grant as the Mock Turtle, W.C. Fields as Humpty Dumpty and Gary Cooper as the White Knight. Suggesting an Arabian Nights–style tangle of realities by having Alice tumble through the looking-glass *and* the rabbit hole, the film performed a lavish belly-flop. Besides George O'Ferrall's negligible *Alice in Wonderland* (1935), Carroll's inquisitive heroine would not make another live-action trip to Wonderland until the early '50s.

Starring Charlotte Henry (Paramount's Alice), alongside Laurel and Hardy (as the Carroll-inspired "Stannie-Dum and Ollie-Dee"), Gus Meins and Charles Rogers' *Babes in Toyland* (1934) anchors itself in reality in a different manner to the previous *Alice* pictures. Based on the 1903 operetta by Victor Herbert and Glen McDonough, this cutesy musical pantomime, one of Laurel and Hardy's early features, opens with Mother Goose emerging from the pages of her own book, tunefully introducing us to the world within. As formal as Méliès in his conjurer's tuxedo bowing to the audience before a trick, the image of the unfolding storybook and the chaperone figure of the on-screen storyteller became a popular introductory device in fairy tale film. These gestures affirm the superiority of the audience, reminding and assuring them that the film world and all its attendant marvels are only make-believe, and will make no attempt to arrest the viewer with credibility.

The book of *Babes in Toyland* spreads its pages, disclosing a Faerie village where the streets are paved with lettered building blocks and lit by giant birthday candles. Huge gingerbread cottages reduce their adult tenants to the size of children in a nursery. Although it features the Three Little Pigs and gives Red Riding Hood a walk-on part, the film concerns itself chiefly with the characters of nursery rhyme. Happily engaged to Felix Knight's Tom-Tom (the piper's son), Charlotte Henry's Bo Peep is menaced by Henry Brandon's jealous Silas Barnaby. Looking as though he has just scuttled out of the darkest corner of Dr. Caligari's cabinet, the villain threatens to evict Bo's old mother from her cozy shoe, along with lodgers Stan and Ollie. After the boys dupe him into handing over the deeds, the vengeful Barnaby attacks Toyland with a mob of grass-skirted bogeymen. The stop-motion techniques that animated the star of *King Kong* a year before motivate a rallying legion of life-size wooden soldiers.

Perhaps more influential than it is generally given credit for, *Babes* foreshadows some important fairy tale films to come. There is something of Judy Garland's Dorothy in Henry's ankle-socked Bo Peep, and the film presages Disney's animated septet as several inquisitive dwarfs gather to watch Bo fall asleep in their glittering caves. But the most portentous image has to be that of a decidedly Mickey-esque mouse (played by a clearly anguished monkey in dungarees, white gloves and black tiddlywink ears) commandeering a toy airship and gleefully carpet-bombing fairyland.

By the time Warner Brothers had released their own star-studded Faerie frolic in 1935 (Max Reinhardt and William Dieterle's *A Midsummer Night's Dream*), Disney's seminal animated fairy tale *Snow White and the Seven Dwarfs* was scheduled for production. Dubbed "Disney's folly" by doubtful critics as the production sprawled over-budget, the finished film triumphed on release in early 1938. The Disney studio went on to dominate American fairy tale film production for the best part of the twentieth century, its influence so extensive that significant fairy tale films by other Hollywood studios did not emerge until the mid–80s. But before Disney's conquest of Faerie was complete, MGM offered a parting shot whose cultural impact would rival anything from the Disney stable.

Victor Fleming's groundbreaking musical *The Wizard of Oz* (1939) famously flopped on release, a month before Britain and France declared war on Germany. It made a paltry $2 million next to *Snow White*'s then-whopping $8 million, but recouped its losses and garnered a monumental following through annual airings on TV. The homeward journey of Judy Garland's plaintive Dorothy down the Yellow Brick Road to the Emerald City, her persecution by the Wicked Witch of the West (played with bristly malevolence by Margaret Hamilton), and the vaudeville antics of Ray Bolger's brainless Scarecrow, Jack Haley's heartless Tin Woodsman and Bert Lahr's cowardly Lion have become as much a part of popular culture as oft-misquoted lines like, "Toto, I have a feeling that we're not in Kansas any more."

Oh my! The Tin Man (Jack Haley), Dorothy (Judy Garland) and the Scarecrow (Ray Bolger) aghast in Victor Fleming's spectacular musical *The Wizard of Oz* (MGM, 1939), first proposed by the studio in 1933 as a Laurel and Hardy vehicle.

The first talkie fairy tale by a major studio not based on a European or British source, *The Wizard of Oz* wisely tightens Baum's enervated narrative. For the author, fantasy had to be a benign affair, "in which the wonderment and joy are retained and the heart-aches and nightmares are left out." Consequently his books, though deliriously inventive, are often a struggle to read for their very lack of exciting conflict. In a fortunate irony, the film's Wicked Witch keeps Dorothy in a state of peril more in keeping with the very tales of Grimm and Andersen that Baum declared passé.

However, the most significant difference between book and film is the location of Oz itself. The Oz of the book is a genuine secondary world, whereas the film has Dorothy awaken like Alice the moment Faerie threatens to consume her. She finds herself back in the humble monochrome surroundings of her Kansas farmstead, realizing without regret that her Technicolor Oz was as imaginary as Wonderland. Presumably MGM believed Baum's concrete parallel world needed an imaginative commitment audiences would not make. But *Wizard* cannily avoids the trap of writing off Dorothy's sojourn as a worthless hallucination. Bolger, Haley and Lahr's slapstick farmhands, Hamilton's dog-hating Miss Gulch and Frank Morgan's compassionate Prof. Marvel have their equivalents in Oz, presenting Dorothy with a pliable analogy of her life in Kansas. This allows her to negotiate her problems from a symbolic perspective and return empowered to deal with them in the real world.

The connection between these two realms is made clear only after Dorothy has lost touch with rationality, knocked unconscious and carried away by the cyclone, a tubular conduit to another world similar to those traversed by Alice and the body-swapping tourists of *Being John Malkovich*. Offering a sustained view of the gulf between worlds, Dorothy's farmhouse swirls precariously intact inside the twister as the reality of earthbound Kansas liquefies into the surrealism of fairy tale. An old woman knits in her rocking chair as she churns past the window, pausing to offer a friendly wave, before a pair of fishermen cheerfully tip their hats as they ply their oars against the wind. Before landing in the fictional reality of Oz, Dorothy's priggish nemesis Miss Gulch appears, fiercely pedalling her bicycle in midair, and making the transition of worlds complete by dissolving (unforgettably) into her shrieking broomstick-straddling alter ego.

While echoing the theatricality of Méliès with its optical effects, beautiful matte backdrops and spectacular sets, *Wizard*'s influence on future fantasy films is considerable, if not entirely positive. Ever since the Wicked Witch shrieked, "Seize them, you fools," and the Wizard's ersatz green head boomed "Silence," so have countless parrot-like fantasy villains. Also, the simpering camp of the film's candy-colored absurdism has been allowed to bleed into too many tales of sword and sorcery. But the film's sturdy quest plot has been beneficial. With much citing of phallic broomsticks and menses-red slippers (they're a less Technicolor-friendly shade of silver in the book), critics often regard the film as a "rites of passage" tale, even though Dorothy only inadvertently effects the film's two plot points (crushing the Wicked Witch of the East beneath her falling house, and fatally dowsing the Wicked Witch of the West while trying to put out a fire).

More significant is Dorothy's epiphany, "There's no place like home." Taken literally, this becomes a regressive and insular reaffirmation of the pioneer values of land, home and family, although a metaphorical reading reveals a profound spiritual truth. Dorothy realizes the answers to her real-world problems aren't to be found in a distant land somewhere over the rainbow or at the other end of the rabbit hole. "If I ever go looking for my heart's desire again, I won't look any further than my own backyard." Yet, paradoxically, flights of fantasy serve to define reality, and arduous revelatory quests are often necessary before one can realize what was always a present fact.

Walt Disney and the Pursuit of Sweetness and Fright

After the excessive shindigging of the Jazz Age, a period of repentant conservatism followed, as '30s America struggled to drag itself out of the Depression. Pleased to avoid any attention from its own self-censorship body the Hays office, Hollywood regarded fairy tales as a safely inoffensive source of material, but only after having sweetened their often salty original flavor. Today children are less likely to encounter Perrault, the Grimms and Andersen through their original literature than through the animated movies of the Disney studios and their merchandising circus. Since the '30s, these films have canonized fairy tales, and dictated with which partialities they should be told. True to the forward thinking of L. Frank Baum, Disney feeds creaky European tales into a monstrously efficient storytelling machine, producing versions that are bright, positive and thoroughly American. Stripping the old tales' often violent and erotic embellishments, the process installs a thrusting narrative engine and a neatly bisected moral compass. Evil is aged, ugly and cynical; good is youthful, pretty, innocent and destined to conquer evil through idealism.

Hollywood literalism also governs Disney. The magic you see is the magic you get, as the studio's cutting-edge animation techniques leave little room for the imagination. Generally there's no question of the technical virtuosity of a Disney fairy tale, or the entertainment value of their telling, and yet their content is often regressive. As well as the significance of the storyteller's choice of tale, one must bear in mind the principles of the teller himself. As Marina Warner reminds us, "Just as history belongs to the victors and words change their meanings with a change of power, stories depend on the tellers and those to whom they are told who might later tell them again. 'Never trust the artist. Trust the tale,' D.H. Lawrence's famous dictum, fails to notice how intertwined the teller and the tale always are."

Like Baum and Tolkien, studio founder Walt Disney tends to polarize opinion. Following *Fantasia* and *Bambi*, the critics who had hailed *Snow White* a triumph accused Walt of vulgarizing high culture and peddling pap suitable only for infants and the infantile. Walt also got a lot of specious press during the animators' strikes that threatened to cripple the studio in the early '40s. Since then, critics have detected suspect ideologies in the most seemingly innocent of his films, and biographers often cannot resist proposing the irony of "Uncle Walt" hiding devilish secrets. Walt and the studio that became his legacy can be more constructively criticized for homogenizing fairy tale, cutting back its complex forests of the mind to make room for the sort of vacant plastic palaces so deservedly mocked in *Shrek*.

Here rests the bulk of the argument against Disney's animated fairy tales. But it's important to remember that fairy tales are not static things, preserved in literary varnish and shelved for posterity. They thrive by fresh interpretation. The traditional opposition to the Disney fairy tale is really aimed at their conclusiveness in the public mind, that they have become *the* version of a given tale and not simply *a* version.

British critic David Thomson expresses something of this outrage when he describes Disney's *Snow White and the Seven Dwarfs* (1937) as, "a travesty of the original story." In actual fact, the film stays true in essence (if not incident) to the Grimms' *Schneewitchen* (adapted from *Kinder und Hausmärchen* [*Children's and Household Tales*] [1812–15]). As in *Babes in Toyland*, and most Disney fairy tales that followed, an introductory storybook unfolds and ushers us through a prologue, before the jealous queen decides to eradicate the surpassing beauty of her stepdaughter Snow White. Fleeing into the woods after her assassin cannot bring himself to cut out her heart, the girl stumbles upon the picturesque squalor of the dwarfs' cottage. (For all the daily cartloads of jewels these guys heave out of their mine, one would have thought they could afford a maid.) The delightful comic troupe of Doc, Sleepy, Happy, Sneezy, Bashful and Dopey find themselves smitten by their guest, but Grumpy mutters darkly, "All females are poison, they're full of wicked wiles," foreshadowing the Biblical treatment awaiting many future Disney heroines.

Although one of the most influential fantasy films of all time, not to mention a triumph of human craftsmanship, Disney's *Snow White* remains a fairly rudimentary tale. It never penetrates its own presentation of male/female domestic roles, as the manly dwarfs set off to sweat down their mine to the tune of "Hi Ho," while Snow White celebrates the feminine delights of housework with a blissful "Whistle While You Work." The film's not interested in stuff like the Queen's motivating female vanity, driven to murderous extremes by the validating male gaze of her mirror (all this the film leaves to the critics). It would rather garland the plot with comic capering and sweet songs. And why not? All the better to showcase its exquisite animation, for which over 600 artists produced some two million drawings, only an eighth of which made it into the finished film. The movie is also rigorously desexualized. Snow White is chastely corseted and her legs veiled by a voluminous dress. The seven adoring males she lodges with are as asexual as the cute woodland creatures that pitch in with the housework. Freudian critic Bruno Bettelheim affirmed the sexlessness of the fairy tale dwarf, observing there are no female members of the species, but this claim has since been refuted by Gimli, the dwarf warrior of *The Lord of the Rings*.

Snow White is often naïve to the point of parody, but few remember the film for its heroine waltzing through a glade with a train of bluebirds, or warbling "Some Day My Prince Will Come" to an audience of enraptured bunny rabbits. Less forgettable is the equal delight in which the film takes its own grotesquery: the queen magically shrivelling herself into a bubble–eyed crone, the poison slime that congeals in the shape of a skull on Snow White's fatal apple, and the witch taunting a parched skeleton before booting it to pieces. (British censors classified the film as too horrific for youngsters, along with *The Wizard of Oz* two years later.) The shadow of German Expressionism looms long over these scenes, as it does in Snow White's flight through the forest of clawing trees, and the withered Queen's *Caligari*-like mountainside tumble, after which her pet vultures descend in a quietly horrific closing touch. The name of Disney has since become a byword for both simple-minded sweetness and movie-induced childhood trauma.

Snow White's success firmly thrust the Disney flag into Faerie soil. MGM's *Wizard of Oz* and 20th Century–Fox's imitative *The Blue Bird* (1940) both faltered at the box office in the wake of *Snow White*, and Hollywood quickly surrendered fairy tale to Disney. Animation was clearly unsurpassable when it came to depicting such fantasies, a presumption confirmed by Disney's second animated feature, and perhaps his masterpiece, *Pinocchio* (1940).

Far richer in theme than *Snow White* and even more sumptuously animated, *Pinocchio* stays broadly faithful to Carlo Collodi's picaresque fable *Le avventure di*

Pinocchio (1881–83). Set in a gorgeously realized Faerie world (more Austro-Hungarian than Italian; all alpine backdrops, cobbled streets and lederhosen), the film offers the same moral parable as its source book, with the innocent wooden hero struggling through earthly temptation to prove himself worthy of a higher state of being. In the only major amendment to the book, the movie Pinocchio receives his reward only after his death, a Christian revision of the book's folkloric moral, in which Pinocchio has to prove himself a hardworking member of society.

Jiminy Cricket (a dapper little hobo lent the chipper tones of popular entertainer Cliff Edwards) heaves open another preparatory storybook and relates how he was there when Geppeto the toymaker wished upon a star that his latest puppet become a real boy. The angelic Blue Fairy grants Geppeto's wish, but his new son (voiced with immaculate naivety by Dickie Jones) must remain made of wood until he proves himself brave, truthful and generous. She also dubs Jiminy the conscience of Pinocchio in a detour from the original story, where the petulant puppet flattens his mentor with a mallet early on and the insect reappears to offer advice as a disgruntled ghost. His moral slate a blank, the credulous Pinocchio falls easy prey to a foxy conman and an unflatteringly sleazy Italian marionettist, before the boy's moral education takes a turn for the infernal during a trip to Pleasure Island.

This scary sequence presents a sort of Coney Island funfair catering exclusively for aspiring young hoods, where brawling, smoking and wanton vandalism are the attractions. (Disney's overbearing reverence of females is evident in an absence of little girls among these hellions.) While the boys are distracted, the sinister Cockney coachman orders his demons to close the gates, as the boys' wayward behavior transforms them into repentant donkeys. In a shrewdly frightening scene, Pinocchio stares aghast as his panicking chum dwindles into a terrified mule. In an ominous final touch, we never again see the boys who have already been shipped off to labor in the salt mines. Even *Shrek*, for all its anti–Disney swagger, cannot bring itself to end without assuring the audience that its dismembered Gingerbread man was not left to his fate in the torture chamber, and made sure to reattach his missing leg with icing before the end credits.

Pinocchio's Old Testament aspirations become obvious by the end as the hero survives a Jungian *nekyia* by rescuing Geppeto from the belly of a gargantuan whale. Modern critics tend to view religious allegories with distaste or suspicion, but behind *Pinocchio*'s subliminal warnings against the wages of sin and its pedagogic lie that noble deeds will never go unrewarded, shines a sincere conviction that good does exist in the world. Possibly more than any other Disney fairy tale, *Pinocchio* expresses a true sense of wonder, of surrendering to something not apparent, an act of faith aligning fantasy with the divine.

Disney fairy tales rarely address mundane social issues, but *Dumbo* (1941) is an exception. Here the studio cracks a satirical joke at the expense of its then-striking employees, as a bunch of money-grubbing circus clowns conspire to hit the ringmaster for a raise. With Disney brought to the brink of collapse by the double box office crash of *Pinocchio* and *Fantasia* (1940), and a number of animators' strikes, the film can be read as a petition of the studio's plight, using animals to allegorize a human story.

Based on *Dumbo, the Flying Elephant* (a 1939 children's book by Helen Aberson and Harold Pearl), the film sees the tarpaulin-eared baby as an embodiment of the creative ambition of Timothy Q. Mouse (Walt's stand-in), who comforts Dumbo when his mother is wrongly sectioned. Timothy's clumsy bundle of dreams causes catastrophe at first, bringing down the Big Top and uniting the rest of the herd against him. But together they achieve unprecedented success and spawn a commercial empire with the help of a bucket of hallucinogenic champagne and a strutting chorus of ragtime crows. The story is as much a plea for tolerance along the lines of Andersen's *The Ugly Duckling*, as the outcast Dumbo is reintegrated into society by a group of black characters one presumes similarly ostracized. Either way, the film reverses traditional human/animal roles, with the circus animals providing the laughs and drama, while the humans (often faceless or described in silhouette) occupy the periphery.

Before CGI and animatronics allowed live-action animal actors to wag their chops on command, animation was the only way to mount anthropomorphic fables. Thus Disney inherited the mantle of Aesop, coding the timeless dramas of the human world through animals that behave like Man. Essentially a beguiling study in mood, color and movement, *Bambi* (1942) excises human characters altogether, although civilization remains a malignant, unseen presence. Mankind itself is the serpent in the film's Eden, a paradise notably devoid of Adam and Eve figures like Snow White and her Prince Charming.

A considerable softening of Felix Salten's 1922 German serial, *Bambi* underlines the circle of life, a theme Disney re-employed in *The Lion King*. The film's first Spring heralds the birth of the eponymous fawn in a forest populated by over-adorable woodland creatures, like Thumper the gap-toothed bunny and Flower the coy skunk. But cutesy frolics are again balanced by the presence of death, accepted here as a natural step on the road to maturity. The shooting of Bambi's mother is another of Disney's exquisitely manipulative scenes of childhood anguish, and one that requires a heart of flint to sit through unmoved. (The scene also drew criticism from deer-hunting fathers of the film's traumatized child audience.)

The political paranoia reigning in postwar Hollywood would have made an interesting *Animal Farm*–style fable itself, but with the HUAC hearings destroying careers by 1947, no one dared. Although Dr. King's civil rights movement remained another thorny issue during the Cold War, Disney made the questionable decision to adapt the animal fables of the plantation slaves in *Song of the South* (1946). During the film's production, the National Association for the Advancement of Colored People repeatedly voiced concern over the possibility of racial stereotyping. Hollywood did its best to placate them by awarding an honorary Oscar to the film's African-American star, James Baskett. (However, the star was politely disallowed from attending the film's premiere in Atlanta.)

The sort of film which apologists describe as "of its time," *Song of the South* is not explicitly racist, but certainly as sticky as Brer Rabbit's adhesive encounter with the tar baby. Most embarrassing is the film's fondness for the Southern slave age, in which grinning black servants adoringly attend benevolent plantation owners. Here freckle-faced little Johnny (Bobby Driscoll) befriends Baskett's chortling old storyteller Uncle Remus, who regales him with tales of how the cunning scamp Brer Rabbit outwitted ravenous enemies Brer Fox and Brer Bear. ("Brer" is slave dialect for "brother.") The film presents these stories as three brief animated segments, through which the live-action Remus strolls, convincingly passing the time of day with friendly animated animals and yodelling the undeniably uplifting *Zip-A-Dee-Doo-Dah* (which also won an Oscar). But the film's focus is less on the tales themselves and more on the healing power of their telling; a point most thuddingly put in the syrupy scene where Remus nurses a sickly Johnny back to health by reciting stories.

As evinced by the mocking fairy tales of the Mesdames and Mademoiselles of the seventeenth century courts, storytelling has served as a subtle form of empowerment to minorities. Journalist Joel Chandler Harris, author of *Song*'s source book, *Uncle Remus, His Songs and His Sayings, The Folk-lore of the Old Plantation* (1880), revealed the satirical commentaries of the slaves by recording their wonder tales, reciting them in their own communal patois through the representative figure of Remus. This was done through a white author, but one who wrote without condescension by suppressing his own authorial persona in favor of another. Harris also made sure to establish Remus as an ex-slave, whereas his status remains ambiguous though suspiciously subservient in Disney's film. The overriding voice here belongs not to Remus, but to Disney, whose sentimentality dominates the film and whose depictions of Brer Rabbit & Co. as scrawny, excitable black stereotypes feel somehow inexcusable. A bad film however you read it, *Song of the South* nonetheless illustrates how certain tales have difficulty purging the taint of a particular telling. Just as a whiff of fascism will always linger around the story of Siegfried, the fact that Brer Rabbit was a fairy tale hero born of slavery is an issue facing any future teller of his tales.

The Cinderella story is one of the most potent and enduring fairy tales, but also one of the most reactionary. Cinderella's social transformation from drudge to princess is not achieved through active independence, but through her attracting a validatory husband, prompting feminist fairy tale authors like Angela Carter, Jane Yolen and Tanith Lee to redress the balance by empowering the heroine. Charles Perrault's seventeenth century version of the tale has become the basis of much escapist fantasy for women, and the story's rags-to-riches arc is bald enough to work without the crutch of magic animals or fairy godmothers. Non-fantasy Cinderellas include Audrey Hepburn in *My Fair Lady* (1964), Julia Roberts in *Pretty Woman* (1990) and Renée Zellweger in *Bridget Jones's Diary* (2001). Although their fairy tale passivity is usually augmented by a greater degree of personal freedom, such women almost always achieve deliverance solely through an authoritative male. Disney's *Cinderella* (1949) is just as reactionary in its sexual politics.

Disney's fairy tale *oeuvre* can be broadly divided into two sets of archetypal stories: the male rites of passage (*Pinocchio, Dumbo, Bambi, The Lion King*) and the domestication of the female (*Snow White, Cinderella, Sleeping Beauty*). Cinderella herself, like her animated peers, is portrayed with the reverence of a Renaissance Madonna, attended in her joys and sorrows by those enraptured bluebirds, who emerge from the scenery as she leads into pitch-perfect song and pines for a masculine savior. By comparison, the unsightly nemeses of wistful ninnies like Cinderella are usually far more appealing. *Cinderella* benefits from one of Disney's most fearsome matriarchal villains, a wicked stepmother who exudes more menace in a sneer than the pyrotechnics of *Sleeping Beauty*'s Maleficent or *The Little Mermaid*'s Ursula combined. Patiently weathering the calculated cruelty of her stepmother and ugly sisters, Cinderella's constancy is rewarded with a fairy godmother, and in an enchanting scene she conjures a delicate pumpkin-coach out of a swirl of fairy-dust.

But behind its sumptuous animation, *Cinderella* offers feeble consolation, that dreams will come true if you keep believing. While even the most florid of good fantasies will reinforce an emotional reality, *Cinderella* believes daydreaming is the key to a woman's goals. Domestic duties may be dull, says the film, but at least a girl can look forward to a handsome prince, who'll whisk her away to higher social climes where someone else can do the dishes, while she concentrates on squeezing out kids.

Before their revitalization in the late '80s, Disney's fairy tale films rarely committed themselves to earthbound politics, yet the symbolic language of their telling inescapably pins even the most frivolous yarn to a clear critical reading. Defying the notion that it avoids anything of practical human value, fantasy actually has to work hard to detach itself from interpretation. Few achieve the intangible dream-logic of a Carroll or a Mervyn Peake, although Disney took a stab in 1951 with their interesting adaptation of the *Alice* books. Otherwise, Disney's Americanized fairy tales were primarily concerned with entertainment, harnessing fairy tale as a vehicle in which to explore the visual possibilities of animation. Meanwhile, filmmakers in wartime Britain and Europe took greater charge of their material, expressing their own stories through tales of old.

Diamonds from Tears

Disney's animated propaganda short *Education for Death* (1943), based on the polemic by Gregor Ziemer, puts Hermann Göring in Valkyrie drag as Princess Germania, a chubby sleeping beauty awaiting the reviving kiss of Prince Hitler. This is a rare instance of Disney expressing satire through fairy tale, although the studio regarded the genre as an inappropriate means to tackle the more serious aspects of its anti–Nazi campaign. Once Princess Göring has been awakened, the film sheds its fairy tale cloak and segues into a blood-and-thunder expressionist montage, as the Third Reich brainwashes a compassionate German youth and sends him to his death along with hundreds like him.

American fairy tale films would not fully realize the significance of their genre until the 1990s; before then, only their technical excellence separated them from the naïveté of Méliès. Most ultimately regard their genre as trivial escapism of no relevance to the real world. Fairy tale had its uses as a vehicle for bravura special effects, but remained disposable fare fit only for the diversion of children and the amusement of adults. The best fairy tale films of studio-era Hollywood (*Pinocchio* and *The*

Wizard of Oz) succeed in spite of themselves, their enduring potency almost an accident, hardly the result of any conscious effort on behalf of the filmmakers. Their resonance relies for the most part on the effectiveness of the original text and a clever
rearrangement of their motifs, which themselves have been harnessed and arranged
into a patented Hollywood formula, espoused today by the gospels of screenwriting
gurus.

Fairy tale was as new to America as cinema itself. In Germany, however, the genre
had been ingrained in the nation's literature since the late eighteenth century, when
the Romantics adopted the form to extrapolate the spiritual concerns of Neoclassicism. Works like E.T.A. Hoffmann's four-volume *Fantasiestücke* (*Fantasy-Pieces*)
(1814–15) and Ludwig Tieck's *Phantasus* (1812–16) helped canonize fairy tale, as did
the Grimms' quixotic project to make a definitive record of the pre-medieval German wonder tale. The German stage preserved the spirit of Romanticism with various productions of Goethe's *Faust*, Hoffmann's 1816 mermaid opera *Undine*,
Offenbach's operettas and Tchaikovsky's fairy tale ballets. When prestigious German
stage talents like Max Reinhardt began to work in film in 1913, fantasy made the
crossover too.

Having previously dismissed the cinema as lowbrow trash, Germany committed itself to the medium more than a decade later than France, Britain and the U.S.,
but the refined sources of their *Märchenfilme* contrast notably with those of their contemporaries. Curt A. Stark's *Der Schatten des Meeres* (*The Sea's Shadow*) (1912) adapts
the Swedish folktale of an unhappy fishwife lured into the sea by the spectre of Death.
Stellen Rye's *Der Student von Prag* (*The Student of Prague*) (1913) is inspired by tales
of the doppelganger. In what became a common image in early German cinema, the
runaway id appears in Hoffmann's *Das Abenteuer der Sylvester Nacht*, Adelbert von
Chamisso's *Peter Schlemihls wundersame Geschichte* (*Peter Schlemihl's Amazing Story*),
and Poe's *William Wilson*. In Rye's film, the Devil bestows riches upon an impoverished undergraduate in exchange for his mirror image, which steps from its frame and
returns to kill the youth in a duel. Heinrich Galeen directed the definitive version of
this Faustian tale in 1926; Arthur Robison directed a sound version ten years later.

Austrian author Gustav Meyrink popularized Hebrew folktale in his 1913-14
serial *Der Golem* (collected in 1915), in which a hulking clay statue is brought to life
by a Rabbi in order to protect the persecuted Jews of a Prague ghetto. Heinrich
Galeen's *Der Golem* (1914) updates the story as an earthbound artifact movie, in
which the immobile creature is unearthed from the ruins of a synagogue and brought
to life by an antiquarian. Preceding *King Kong*'s first night in the big city, the Golem
goes on a lovelorn rampage and is climatically destroyed in a fall. Richard Oswald's
Hoffmanns Erzählungen (1915) comprises several of the author's tales, as well as
finding room for another adaptation of Chamisso. About the only conventional fairy
tale film Germany produced before the '20s was Educational Pictures' *Schneewitchen*
(*Snow White*) (1916), an obscure adaptation of the Grimms' tale starring Ruth Richey
as the murderous Queen.

Once Germany had signed the 1918 armistice, their films began to be seen abroad.
Hollywood's Douglas Fairbanks borrowed ideas for his *Thief of Baghdad* from Fritz
Lang's *Der müde Tod* (*The Weary Death*) (1921) and *Die Nibelungen* (1924), two

fantasy films born of German Expressionism, itself a significant movement of the *fantastique*. German Expressionism arrived in 1920 with the macabre melodramatics of Robert Wiene's *Das Kabinett des Dr. Caligari*. In an attempt to alienate themselves from the ubiquitous narrative realism of Hollywood (which had seized control of the global film market during World War I) German filmmakers harked back to the theatricality of Méliès, depicting morbid hermetic worlds as wilfully artificial as their painted backdrops and jagged, claustrophobic sets.

German Expressionism lends itself well to fairy tale in striving to create a protean world that mirrors the distorted psychologies of its characters. The movement's retreat from realism uncovered several seminal works of the *fantastique*, most notably F.W. Murnau's unofficial *Dracula* adaptation *Nosferatu* (1922) and Lang's monumental *Metropolis* (1926), cornerstones of horror and sci-fi. But in its presentation of the human psyche as a sort of reality-warping magic itself, German Expressionism is perhaps at its most penetrating in tales of fantasy. Its doomed Faustian heroes are usually as incapable of controlling the unfathomable forces of magic in which they dabble, as they are of containing their own psychoses, which irradiate their surroundings like a Munchian scream.

Lang's *Nibelungen*, a doom-haunted forerunner to *Lord of the Rings*, and Murnau's 1926 *Faust* are Expressionist fantasies that bear less of a relation to fairy tale than does Paul Wegener's 1920 *Der Golem*. Returning to the source tale which the actor-director first heard while filming *The Student of Prague*, this definitive version has the lumbering clay sentinel fall into the hands of its master's reckless apprentice, who orders the automaton to abduct a local girl on his behalf. Like newborn monster Boris Karloff in James Whale's *Frankenstein* a decade later, the Golem rebels against its Promethean master and embarks on an aggravated rampage. But the Golem comes to a less tragic though no less symbolic end, as a little Aryan girl offers him an apple and plucks the enervating Star of David from his chest.

Der müde Tod subtitles itself "A German Folksong" and presents a storm-lashed coaching-inn where Death abducts a young woman's bridegroom. The Reaper recites three morbid tales before she joins her betrothed by taking her own life. Hans Werckmeister's *Algol* (1920) presents Cinderella in negative, as a grasping industrialist receives supernatural aid from an evil star, and uses it to create a malignant empire. Rochus Gliese's apparently minor film *Der verlone Schatten* (*The Lost Shadow*) (1921) and Ludwig Berger's obscure *Der verlorene Schuh* (*Cinderella*) (1923) are further adaptations of Chamisso and the Grimms, while Paul Leni's portmanteau melodrama *Der Wachsfigurenkabinett* (*Waxworks*) (1924) features a nightmarish *Arabian Nights* episode with Emil Jannings as the cut-throat caliph Haroun-al-Raschid.

Less miserable and more conventional in their approach to fairy tale are the delicate shadow puppet films of German animator Lotte Reiniger. First commissioned by Paul Wegener to create silhouette captions and animated wooden rats for his *Der Rottenfänger von Hameln* (*The Pied Piper of Hamlyn*) (1918), Reiniger went on to produce over 50 short films, many of them straightforward adaptations of familiar tales. Most celebrated is her feature-length *Arabian Nights* fantasy *Die Abenteuer des prinzen achmed* (*The Adventures of Prince Achmed*) (1926), cinema's first animated feature film (a credit often erroneously given to Disney's *Snow White*, although that was the first animated feature in Technicolor).

Expressionism reflected the public mood after Britain and France effectively demolished the German economy with the "war guilt" clause in the Treaty of Versailles, making the empowerment fantasies proposed by National Socialism seem ever more appealing throughout the '20s. When Hitler's Nazi party came to power in 1933, they gradually absorbed the German film industry, governing it with strict censorship until it became fully nationalized. To receive funding, film projects now had to be run by Minister of Propaganda Josef Goebbels.

Those filmmakers not already lured to Hollywood fled abroad, taking their stories with them. Lotte Reiniger and her husband left Germany in 1935, leaving many of her film prints in Berlin; Allied bombing destroyed them ten years later. She became a British citizen in 1950 and made fairy tale shorts for the BBC. Her former tutor Max Reinhardt, who fostered the majority of talent during the *goldenes Alter* of early German cinema, departed for Hollywood, where he co-directed 1935's *A Midsummer Night's Dream* with fellow émigré William Dieterle. The film prompted German authorities to notify Warner Brothers that their film would not be screened in Hitler's Germany, where Reinhardt was now considered an undesirable.

Reinhardt's frequent collaborator Ludwig Berger co-directed (with Michael Powell and Tim Whelan) an ambitious Arabian fantasy for producer Alexander Korda (yet another émigré) in Britain, until German bombing forced the production to retreat to Hollywood. An astute sound and color revision of Fairbanks' non-copyright source, Korda's *The Thief of Baghdad* (1940) is too patchy to repeat the unwavering visual impact of its predecessor (despite the involvement of that film's production designer, William Cameron Menzies), but succeeds in being the better remembered of the two. The film splits Fairbanks's starring role between John Justin's tediously virtuous lead and his sprightly shoplifting sidekick, irresistibly played by Sabu, who not only snags the reference of the film's title, but steals the show from his companion's tepid romance with dull princess June Duprez. A German star exiled to Britain with his Jewish wife, Conrad Veidt plays Jafar, the glowering Grand Vizier, while Rex Ingram in a bright red nappy booms as the film's towering genie, whom Sabu tricks into granting three wishes by way of that old ruse, "How did someone so big fit into a bottle so small?" Miles Malleson, the soon-to-be-usurped Caliph, also wrote the script, which translates the relentlessly eventful tales of the *Arabian Nights* far more evenly than the overcrowded Fairbanks film.

Although the film's soaring escapism falters towards the end (as the revived leader of a forgotten race turned to stone pauses to offer a trite commentary on the horrors of war), its best scenes lend a transcendent sense of wonder unusual in Hollywood fairy tales of the time. Along with Disney's *Pinocchio*, this is probably the first Hollywood fairy tale to engage the viewer's imagination through suggestion, implying that the narrative borders of Faerie reach beyond what is presented on screen. In the film's crowning scene, the genie transports Sabu inside a mountaintop temple, where he scales a sprawling spider's web littered with tangled skeletons. After fending off a twitching giant spider, he navigates the treacherous contours of a massive hundred-armed idol, dodging hails of goblin arrows to retrieve an all-seeing

Hands to execute: Villainous vizier Jafar (Conrad Veidt) commands the sultry six-armed automaton (Mary Morris) that will assassinate the Caliph in Powell and Pressburger's colorful *The Thief of Baghdad* (United Artists, 1940). Note the resemblance to the sword-slinging statue of Kali in Harryhausen and Schneer's *The Golden Voyage of Sinbad* (1973).

crystal eye. The viewer subconsciously questions the scene. Who built this place? How long has it been there? Who is the idol meant to be and who are the little green guys dancing around him? The film never answers these questions, but presents the scene with such conviction that we know they could be. The magical props of other scenes are more ornamental and gimmicky. A clockwork horse, a memory-erasing rose, a flying carpet and an enchanted crossbow are presented as casually as if they'd dropped off an assembly line and retailed at the fantasy realm K-Mart where *Dungeons & Dragons*–style fantasy has regrettably been shopping for years.

Having neither the talent to compete with Disney, nor the imagination to emulate the Oscar-winning success of Korda's *Thief*, Hollywood fell back on parody. Howard Hawks' romantic comedy *Ball of Fire* (1941) sets the story of Snow White in the concrete forest of New York with Gary Cooper as one of seven crusty scholars and Barbara Stanwyck as their sultry lodger on the run from the Mob. *A Thousand and One Nights* (1945) typifies the kind of lazy anachronistic comedy to which Hollywood movies resort when they don't want to commit to an antique fantasy. The movie opens with a familiar page-turning introduction, which recites the tale of Scheherazade ("If the old gal were still telling them, the latest would go something like this..."). Phil Silvers, replete with trademark glasses, takes the Sabu role and complains about being born 2,000 years before his time, while Evelyn Keyes plays Babs, an obedient genie.

Also impressed by Korda's *Thief of Baghdad*, Goebbels determined that the fatherland must surpass it with a fantasy of its own. Josef von Baky's *Münchhausen* (1943) was produced to celebrate the twenty-fifth anniversary of Germany's grand Ufa studios, now the backbone of the Nazi-controlled film industry. The irony of the Minister of Propaganda commissioning a film about the master of lies apparently went over the head of Goebbels (who granted the film an unlimited budget), although he should certainly be commended for appointing the first fairy tale film for grown-ups.

Oppositionist author Erich Kästner (forbidden from publishing in Germany and credited here under the pseudonym of Berthold Bürger) toes the party line for the most part as Hans Albers' Baron recites his adventures to an unwitting guest. In an anchoring deadpan fashion, he recalls how he rode a cannonball into a hostile Turkish fort; how he bet the Sultan of Constantinople he could retrieve a bottle of Viennese tokay within the hour; how he out-fornicated Casanova, and how he visited the Moon, where peoples' heads live separate from their bodies and babies grow on trees. Critics detect something of Hitler in Cagliostro, the Baron's power-hungry ally, although Münchhausen himself is too ambivalent a figure to be read as an open dissident.

Modelled on a retired army captain (much to his dismay), who famously entertained his dinner guests with wildly embroidered accounts of his travels, Baron Münchhausen appeared as the narrator of several texts printed in the late eighteenth century. On film, his presence calls into question the identity of the fairy tale storyteller. In *Snow White* and *Wizard of Oz*, the narrators (that is, the filmmakers) are largely unseen, perhaps briefly personified by an unfolding storybook, or an escort like Mother Goose or Jiminy Cricket. In Baky's film, the Baron himself narrates most of the story in the first person, leaving us to assume the world he inhabits is our "real" world and his adventures mere fancy. Films like *Song of the South* and Dallas Bower and Lou Bunin's 1951 *Alice* posit the same set-up, but cannot resist finally obliterating the boundary between the teller and the tale. Here the previously immaterial inhabitants of Faerie pop up in the real world the moment the storyteller's back is turned, and the credits roll before the integrity of all that's gone before can be brought into question.

Teasing its audience from the outset, *Münchhausen* plays this treacherous narrative game more ingeniously, opening on what we are led to believe is an eighteenth century ballroom until a guest snaps on a porch-light and leaves in her car. The film gives several more conspiratorial winks when we believe ourselves anchored in reality by the presence of the Baron, leaving us unsure where the boundaries of his recital lie, or even whether he's the one telling this tale.

The Surrealists shared Münchhausen's disregard for reason, which had failed to avert the catastrophe of World War I. Nourished by the abstract experiments of the Dadaists, the films of the Surrealists shared the mutable logic of fairy tale, as well as its interest in probing the unconscious. Significantly, it was a German Expressionist fairy tale, *Der müde Tod*, that inspired Buñuel's surrealist masterpieces *Un Chien andalou* and *L'Âge d'or*. The protean influence of surrealism touched a number of early French comedies, including Jean Vigo's boisterous *Zero de conduite* (*Zero for Conduct*) (1933). But magic solidified during the Vichy years into more orderly, fatalistic fantasies. In Marcel L'Herbier's *La Nuit fantastique* (*The Fantastic Night*) (1942) Fernand Gravey is escorted through his own dream by an angel, before she materializes in the real world and spirits him away. Marcel Carné's quietly mutinous *Les Visiteurs du soir* (*Visitors of the Evening*) (1942) has the Devil failing to conquer the romantic French hearts of those he has turned to stone for their insolence, while Jean Delannoy commits a contemporary Tristan and Isolde to their doom in *L'Eternal retour* (*The Eternal Return*) (1943).

Artless things: Publicity still of Jean Marais as the byronic beast of Jean Cocteau's *La Belle et la bête* (Discina, 1946), one of the most powerful fairy tales in fantasy cinema.

Delannoy's screenwriter Jean Cocteau went on to contribute two of the richest, most lyrical films in fantasy cinema, *La Belle et la bête* (*Beauty and the Beast*) (1946) and *Orphée* (1950). The former, like Korda's *Thief*, would years later be acquired as a touchstone by Disney, who "homaged" both films for an audience mostly unfamiliar with them. In directly adapting Mme. Leprince de Beaumont's didactic children's tale for a sophisticated adult audience, Cocteau senses the necessity for a caveat and opens the film with a written plea for faith in the power of fairy tale. This is a petition to abide by what might be called "Tinkerbell's Law," which states that fantasy stories will only come alive and work when one commits belief. French audiences living in the aftermath of a world war found the idea offensively escapist, but the film is loaded with pertinent parallels. Belle's dysfunctional family reflects a country struggling for reconciliation, just as her handsome but callous suitor Avenant reflects the frightful but tender Beast. (Both are played by Jean Marais.) In a film rife with reflections, only Josette Day's Belle is an absolute, as remote and idealized as a Muse prompting her disciples to their Byronic gestures.

Cocteau's film makes only two major amendments to de Beaumont's tale. It adds the character of Avenant (whom Disney also adopted for their 1991 film), and a Bluebeard-like twist in which the Beast tests Belle's love by telling her of a treasure-crammed pavilion, which can only be opened safely after his death. Cocteau also vividly sensualizes the story. The very masonry of the Beast's tumbledown chateau is as supple as flesh, with disembodied arms holding candelabra, and watchful caryatids exhaling smoke beside the fireplace. Once Belle has saved her father's life by agreeing to live with the Beast, a strange sort of marriage ensues. She swoons at the first sight of him, his leonine head framed ridiculously by a cavalier's ruff, but finds herself treated with reverence and affection, becoming intrigued, even attracted. She voyeuristically spies on him in all his monstrous glory, and in a sly erotic scene he laps water from her cupped hands. Later she berates him like a wayward husband when he stumbles home one night, steaming with the blood of his latest kill and pleading helplessly for her to forgive his instinctive savagery.

La Belle et la bête wields its genre with an artistic certainty unrealized by few Hollywood fairy tales of its time. What *The Wizard of Oz* achieves with Technicolor pageantry, Cocteau evokes with the simplest and most obvious of conjuring tricks. Like Belle's tears freezing into diamonds on her cheek, these effects lend a tangible realism to the magic. The film has since influenced a host of pretentious fantasy films, although regrettably few follow Cocteau's cue by molding their magic from the stuff of reality.

Senseless Dreaming

Postwar British cinema had no time for fantasy. Realism was its spokesman, documenting the devastation Britain had suffered during the war, as well as expressing the bitterness the conflict had left behind. In a period characterized by dignified literary adaptations like David Lean's *Great Expectations* (1946) and staunch realist dramas like Carol Reed's *Odd Man Out* (1947), the unbridled fantasizing of Michael Powell and Emeric Pressburger's *A Matter of Life and Death* and *The Red Shoes* was considered outrageously inappropriate. Despite producing some of the most unusual British films of the time, the creative team of Powell and Pressburger were relegated to the margins by British critics, who dismissed their films as superficial escapist tosh. Having made his fullest commitment to fantasy (sans Pressburger) by co-directing Korda's *Thief of Baghdad*, Powell progressively withdrew from pervasive secondary worlds, as if striving to corral his own terribly un–British imagination, which like the wilful slippers of *Red Shoes* was driving him into obscurity.

Unlike the sprawling Arabian Faerie of *Thief*, the *Red Shoes* (1948) contains its eponymous fairy tale within a perceptual bubble. This irresistible backstage melodrama opens on the image of a candle burning into a puddle of wax atop a leather-bound copy of Andersen's fairy tales. Unlike the familiar prologue storybooks of Disney, which open their pages to swallow the audience into their world, the fairy tale volume of *Red Shoes* remains tellingly closed. Existing only as a point of reference within the film, Andersen's tale of the waif whose enchanted shoes dance their wearer to her death comments with detached irony on the self-destructive actions of three artists. Moira Shearer plays the doomed ballerina, wrenched to her death not by magic shoes but by a tug-of-love between Marius Goring's adoring young composer and Anton Walbrook's Mephistophelean impresario. Representing not an actuality but the ecstatic perceptions of Shearer's heroine, the film's celebrated fantasy sequence sees the proscenium arch of the theater dissolve into the very Faerie it represents.

Based on Offenbach's unfinished opera, Powell and Pressburger's *The Tales of Hoffmann* (1951) offers a triptych of such perceptual fairy tales, framed by the drunken recollections of the author (Robert Rounseville). His quixotic search frustrated throughout each story by a satanic Robert Helpmann, Hoffmann envisions himself pursuing a trio of unattainable females: a lifeless clockwork doll given the illusion of life when her unwitting suitor dons a pair of enchanted spectacles, a witchy Italian courtesan who drags Hoffmann's soul from a mirror like the devilish patron of *The Student of Prague*, and a girl for whom singing rather than dancing brings about her doom.

The closing shot of Dallas Bower and Lou Bunin's *Alice in Wonderland* (1951) tries to play the perceptual fantasy game both ways, as an apparently fictional White Rabbit emerges from a hole in the Oxford riverbank to speciously confirm the truth of the teller's tale. In a common ploy established by *Wizard of Oz* and adapted by several films since, this *Alice* further mingles reality and imagination by constructing its fantasy world from elements of the real. Like actors assuming roles in a play, characters and even landmarks from the story's primary world become characters in the secondary. Ernest Milton's Oxford don becomes the pernickety White Rabbit, and Great Tom, the college bell, appears on the collar of a monstrous puppy. Pamela Brown's comically haughty Queen Victoria is transformed into the bellowing Queen of Hearts, a satirical touch that offended distributors in Britain, where the film went unreleased until 1986.

Bunin's film opens with an extended live-action prologue set in Victorian Oxford, where the storytelling of Stephen Murray's stammering maths professor segues into a pastel-colored Cubist Wonderland. Here Carol Marsh's Alice endures benign encounters with inexpressive stop-motion Wonderlanders. With tedious songs trilled along the way (the chant of the Fish Footman and the Mock Turtle's lament are particularly awful), this *Alice* clings to Carroll's text, but retains none of its flavor. Its skewed checkerboard Wonderland is unusual, but its earthbound sequences rather more interesting, even making a daring reference to Charles Dodgson's real-life relationship with Alice Liddell, the infant muse with whom he became infatuated. Here Dodgson coyly presents Alice with a stolen cherry tart, a subversive gesture given further edge by the miscasting of 21-year-old Marsh, already well known for her sexy turn in *Brighton Rock* (1947).

Refusing to abandon themselves entirely to gauche fantasy, *Red Shoes*, *Hoffmann* and *Alice* maintain a respectable distance from their own fairy tales. Striking a balance between the highbrow and the childish, these films treat their audience like privileged theatergoers, elevating them to the perch of omniscience and allowing a vicarious detachment from the film's enraptured storytellers. It's significant then that so many British fantasy films align themselves with the theater, as do Powell and Pressburger, and the familiar stage troupers seen getting into the pantomime spirit in the *Harry Potter* movies. Perhaps much of the continuing hostility felt among British critics in the '50s towards Disney was down to the studio's refusal to concede this perceptual superiority. Before their '90s revival, when they made sure to crack suggestive jokes over the heads of the children, Disney fairy tales stubbornly dictated events from the storyteller's chair, forcing their adult audience to sit with the children as it were and be addressed as one of them.

Considering the low regard in which they held native fantasist Michael Powell, British critics seemed unusually protective of their native fairy tales when Disney made their reviled versions of *Alice* and *Peter Pan*. Disney's belated *Alice in Wonderland* (1951) suffered poor box office, hateful reviews (mostly from the British press) and a particularly awkward production history. The studio's story department had difficulty coercing Carroll's enigmatic text to conform to the Disney formula, and Walt binned a prospective script by Aldous Huxley, reportedly saying he "could only understand every third word." The studio later took out an unsuccessful court injunction against Bunin's *Alice*, which stole its rival's thunder by opening two days previously.

Walt himself believed his finished film lacked "heart" (originally Carroll's affable White Knight was to lend Alice emotional support), but it's precisely this sense of Carrollean callousness that the film narrowly succeeds in capturing. It opens not on a storybook (correctly affirming that we are not yet in the realm of Faerie), but on an English riverbank, where Alice (voiced with cut-glass vowels by Kathryn Beaumont) becomes bored with her sister's history lesson and fancies the delights of Wonderland. Aside from a church steeple peering over the trees, we see nothing of Alice's world, nor does Carroll himself appear as he does in Bunin's and later films to precipitate the descent into Faerie. Alice imagines her adventure for herself, as she hurries after the White Rabbit and into an angular Wonderland that arranges episodes from both books into a *Silly Symphony* parade of English eccentrics. A garden of contemptuous flowers eject Alice from their flowerbed for being "a weed." A disinterested caterpillar puffs away at his hookah, exhaling dialogue in trails of lilac smoke. The Mad Hatter and March Hare heedlessly conduct an orchestra of piping teapots while munching on the crockery.

Throwing this unreceptive world into sharp relief is the striking humanity of Alice herself. Forcefully well-mannered and struggling to maintain her Victorian dignity in the face of mishap, Alice is a Disney heroine vividly alive in comparison to the mannequins of *Snow White* and *Cinderella*. Like Garland's Dorothy, marooned in Oz as the Wizard's balloon floats back to Kansas without her, Disney's Alice is saved from disaster by waking from her sleep, as Wonderland spirals into kaleidoscopic nightmare and the Queen of Hearts' enraged courtiers strive to cut off Alice's head.

Disney understandably erased the murky undertones of Carroll and Barrie, whose complex anxieties about sex, maturity and loss had to be reassessed for a generation of baby boomers growing up with *Howdy Doody* and *Flash Gordon*. But in the case of *Peter Pan* (1953), the studio threw out the drama along with the Oedipal subtext. The mortal feud between the Lost Boys, the pirates and the Neverland Indians (which has corpses piling up in the play) is here reduced to a meaningless game whereby prisoners are set free moments after capture. Peter himself fades into the background, when not skating through the air or merrily humiliating his buffoonish nemesis Captain Hook. *Peter Pan* is that rare Disney film that really is as mindlessly benign as the critics say. Its only hint of meanness derives from the female characters, all of whom are catty, simpering nitwits—from Peter's preening mermaid groupies to the famously curvaceous Tinkerbell.

The studio apparently shared Peter's adolescent response to feminism ("Girl's talk too much"), as the heroine of *Sleeping Beauty* (1959) also has little to say for herself. After an introductory storybook opens on a strikingly designed Ruritania, the film summarizes the romantic view of women established during Walt's lifetime, and which the studio spent most of the '90s apologizing for. Offended at being left off the guest list for the infant Princess Aurora's christening, the grandly devilish sorceress Maleficent curses the child to die after pricking her finger on the needle of a spinning wheel. But the child is saved by one of three color-coded fairies, who amend the curse from one of death to one of everlasting sleep, which can only be broken by the kiss of true love. Based on Perrault's version of the tale, with a score inspired by Tchaikovsky's ballet, the film tends towards the soporific itself, ironically only waking up once most of its characters have fallen asleep. In an effectively spooky sequence, Maleficent lures the teenage Aurora to her fateful slumber, before her dashing beau battles through an army of goblins, hacks through a cage of snagging thorns, and slays Maleficent, who impressively transforms into a writhing black and purple dragon.

Although having taken on a coat of Disney whitewash, the source story emerges with a symbolist reading far from banal. The studio's insistence on the conservative triumph of true love over carnal lust is never more explicit than in *Sleeping Beauty*. The goatish Maleficent, as the older woman whose transgressions prohibit her from ever getting invited to respectable social gatherings, declares with qualified cynicism that the virginal Aurora will find herself ruptured by the first "prick" she finds. The old-maidish fairies acknowledge this inevitability, but strive to ensure it will be in the name of true love. A symbolic red cloak signifies Aurora's sexual ripening, as the king acts out the preventative measure dreamed of by many a protective father and throws every potential pricker in his kingdom on a bonfire.

Unlike Pinocchio, Aurora is a tethered puppet, her life manipulated by those who know better, and with whose plans she happily falls into line. The inevitable supremacy of spiritual love and the overriding importance of procuring a husband drive the story to its conclusion. However, Aurora's prince finds himself sidetracked from the path of virtue when he falls into the clutches of Maleficent, who gloats kinkily over her manacled captive.

An expensive flop on release, *Sleeping Beauty* was one of Disney's last animated features before the studio began investing in more reliable live-action features, allowing other Hollywood fairy tales to regain lost ground. During the '50s, however, most studios felt any fairy tale spectacular would pale in comparison to the limitless displays of Disney's animation. Instead they tried to dignify the genre, as the British had done. Charles Vidor's breezy non-fantasy musical *Hans Christian Andersen* (1952) announces itself as "a fairy tale about this great spinner of fairy tales." A subdued Danny Kaye plays Andersen, a fanciful cobbler who seeks his fortune in Copenhagen, where he becomes infatuated by Jeanmaire's egocentric ballerina. His yearning expresses itself in a few *Red Shoes*–derivative daydreams, before he returns home a happy bachelor.

Charles Walters's de-fantasized *The Glass Slipper* (1954) also takes up ballet as a passport to respectability. Infinitely more colorful than doughy Drew Barrymore in the comparably deconstructive *Ever After*, Leslie Caron's Cinderella is a temperamental Gallic ragamuffin. Her unlikely romantic mentor is Estelle Winwood's eccentric old bird, who became a reclusive kleptomaniac after she "took to reading books." The film departs from Perrault in making Prince Charming (Michael Wilding) aware of Cinderella's true identity prior to the ball. Thereafter he composes wan love songs over his harpsichord, while she engages in more *Red Shoes*–inspired reverie. Although her ball-gown is stolen rather than conjured, and a pedantic coachman rather than an unstable pumpkin-coach imposes her midnight curfew, the film retains some sense of the fantastic by the end, as Winwood's fairy godmother ambiguously dissolves, "back where she came from."

Despite its failure, Roy Rowland's *The 5,000 Fingers of Dr. T* (1953) is the most notable American fairy tale of the '50s, outside Disney. Historically important as the first live-action fairy tale feature based on an original screenplay, the film was authored by beloved American fantasist Dr. Seuss (a.k.a. Theodore Geisel), whose gleefully imaginative prose and verse tales follow the absurdist tradition of Carroll and Baum. *Dr. T* has young Bart (Tommy Rettig) dream of an otherworldly palace, ruled by his egotistical piano teacher Dr. Terwilliker (Hans Conried), who plans to dupe 500 boys into attending his draconian "Happy Fingers" institute. Padded with awkward songs, the film fails to draw a line between its real and imagined worlds (both are absurd as each other), but sporadically captures Seuss' warped sensibilities better than anything in *The Grinch* (2000) or *The Cat in the Hat* (2003).

With its bowed towers, ladders to nowhere and disembodied gloves signposting unhelpful directions at every corner, the production design of Dr. T's Faerie domain is a triumph, sharing a similar visual sensibility to Disney's *Alice*, all crooked angles and pastel grotesquery. Although crackpot technology takes precedence over outright magic, this world governs itself by a surrealist logic that manifests in inspired touches, like the roller-skating twins who share the same beard and the unfortunate percussionist sealed inside his own endlessly pounded drum. Unfortunately, *Dr. T* was consigned to obscurity after its producer, Stanley Kramer, fell out with Columbia president Harry Cohn. Seuss regretted his involvement, critics dismissed the film and it bombed on release. Other Hollywood fairy tales continued to fight a losing battle against Disney's autocracy well into the '60s.

On the other side of the Iron Curtain, in the cultural vacuum of postwar Russia, fairy tale fought another war against realism and dictatorship. "Senseless dreaming" was how Tsar Nicholas II once described the proposed reforms of the zemstvo socialists, which eventually led to the downfall of the entire Romanov dynasty. Little wonder that the succeeding Soviets regarded the collusive form of fairy tale with suspicion. Having brought about the Revolution through conspiratorial actions of their own, the Soviets strove to prevent the same thing from happening to them, and established a severe vetting system that enforced "socialist realism" as the official agenda of the arts.

The state distrusted the inherently strong social conscience of Russian fairy tales, but authorized those written or filmed specifically for children, provided they display an acceptable degree of patriotic chauvinism. The prolific Aleksandr Rou

Reluctant musician Bart (Tommy Rettig) checks to see if the coast is clear while imprisoned in the "Happy Fingers" institute of crazed piano teacher Dr. Terwilliker in Roy Rowland's notable '50s fairy tale *The 5,000 Fingers of Dr. T.* (Kramer/Columbia, 1953), scripted by Theodore Geisel (aka Dr. Seuss) who loathed the film.

obediently contributed unassuming fairy tale films like *Vasilisa prekrasnaya (Beautiful Vasilisa)* (1939), *Koniok Gorbunok (The Little Humpback Horse)* (1942), and *Kashchey Bessmertny (The End of Koshchei the Deathless)* (1943). To the intelligentsia, forbidden from expressing their views elsewhere, fairy tale films offered an artistic channel free from governmental constraints. Fairy tale films began encoding political critique with a so-called "Aesopian language," as did Nadezhda Kosheverova and Mikhail Shapiro's satirical *Cinderella* (1947), written by outlawed playwright Yevgeni Schwartz.

Polish animator Wladyslaw Starewicz produced several stop-motion animal fables in Russia, among them *The Cameraman's Revenge* and *The Grasshopper and the Ant* (both 1912). After the Revolution, he emigrated to France and made his most celebrated film *Le Roman de Renard* (*The Tale of the Fox*) (1928), while a Ukrainian special effects expert-turned-director, Aleksandr Ptushko, contributed some of the most popular fantasy films of the staunchly realist Soviet era. A figure comparable to George Pal and Ray Harryhausen, although virtually unknown outside his native Russia, Ptushko won the title of Honored Artist of the Republic for his work on *Novyi Gulliver* (*The New Gulliver*) (1935). Concerning a Young Pioneer who falls asleep to a reading of Swift, the film obediently depicts a Lilliput populated by diminutive stop-motion Revolutionaries, who are aided by their colossal guest in overthrowing a half-witted king. Ptushko produced two significant fairy tale films early in his career, *Solotoi kluchik* (*The Golden Key*) (1938), based on Alexei Tolstoy's unofficial version of Collodi's *Pinocchio*, and *Kamenni Tsvetok* (*The Stone Flower*) (1946), based on Pavel Bazhov's *The Malachite Casket*, in which a stonemason's apprentice searching for the legendary blossom is captured by its custodian, the Mistress of the Copper Mountains. Both films won favor for their technical virtuosity and rigid Stalinist ideals.

Cultural attitudes softened in Russia following Stalin's death in 1953, while the strikes and riots that beset East Germany made the Soviet "buffer state" mindful of the content of its own fairy tales. Between the early '50s and mid–'90s, nationalized production company DEFA produced over 200 colorful studio-bound fairy tale features for children, scoring their first commercial success with Wolfgang Staudte's Arabian fable *Die Geschicte vom kleinen Muck* (*Little Mook*) (1953). But the sense of fun that DEFA brought to fairy tale attracted criticism from the Communists, who regarded the films as too similar to the garish capitalist produce of Disney, and determined that East German films should serve a pedagogic socialist function.

The alarming giddiness of Francesco Stefani's *Das singende klingende Bäumchen* (*The Singing Ringing Tree*) (1957) was reprimanded in particular, prompting a debate as to how fairy tales might be constructively turned to propagandist ends. An adroit fusion of several Grimm tales, the film has a conceited prince seek to win the hand of the spoiled Princess Thousandbeauty, who demands he retrieve the titular tree. Once he does so, the sapling refuses to chime, magically consigning the prince to life as a glum but talkative bear. In this form, he carries the Princess away to a Faerie cavern, where her continued heartlessness turns her into a mildew-haired hag. Eventually she wins back her looks by learning compassion and rescues her bewitched suitor from a puckish dwarf (whose snickering mug terrified a generation of British kids when the BBC screened the film in the '60s). It's difficult to detect any precise driving moral at work beyond "a good deed is stronger than any evil spell," a sentiment of persistence apparently shared by DEFA, whose fairy tale production line successfully weathered the constraints of Communism.

Nearer to Life

The fairy tale storyteller is a small god in his or her creation of a secondary world and the government of its invented people. Sometimes this figure is personified by a folkloric chaperone like Mother Goose or Jiminy Cricket, envoys of Faerie who usher us along its treacherous paths. Some storytellers are dreamers like Alice or Dorothy, unconsciously conjuring worlds and navigating a course through them by the compass of instinct. The storytellers behind the bubble-worlds of *The Red Shoes* and *The Tales of Hoffmann* are not idle dreamers but ego-driven fantasists, consciously describing the stuff of Faerie like artists at their easels.

In Ingmar Bergman's *Det Sjunde Inseglet* (*The Seventh Seal*) (1956) and *Jungfrukällan* (*The Virgin Spring*) (1959), the role of the guiding chaperone is invisibly adopted by the director himself, his presence evinced by the lack of any on-screen narrator and in the expressionism of his subjective worlds. In *Seventh Seal*, Max von Sydow's dispassionate knight and Bengt Ekerot's implacable Death are chosen figures as symbolic as a Snow White or a Prince Charming. Bergman's allegorical story of the knight's struggle to find God before plunging into the next world is as edifying as any fable, and its dolorous medieval setting as representative as anything in *Pinocchio*. Based on medieval ballad, *Virgin Spring* is no less obstinate in its storytelling. A Red Riding Hood–like farm girl is raped by wolfish goatherds, whose crimes will eventually verify the compassion of the God absent from *Seventh Seal*.

In *Smultronstället* (*Wild Strawberries*) (1957) and *Vargtimmen* (*Hour of the Wolf*) (1967), Bergman passes the mantle of storyteller onto his characters. Victor Sjöström's elderly professor and Max von Sydow's reclusive painter create self-absorbed fantasies as artistically tragic as those of *Red Shoes* and *Hoffmann*. We do not see the daydreaming narrator of Bergman's autobiographical *Fanny and Alexander* (1982), although his nostalgic presence is implicit in the film's masterful direction. Likening the untrustworthy act of recall to that of fantasizing, the storyteller's tale reconciles the real and the imagined, visualizing his childhood as a production of *Hamlet*, replete with doleful phantoms.

The perceptual borders established by the storyteller must be clearly defined and rigorously maintained, or else a fairy tale risks confusing the audience and breaking the spell. The chaperones of Baky and Gilliam's *Munchausen* films confidently reshuffle these boundaries without losing sight of who is telling the story, while *Dr. T* breaches the perceptions of its young dreamer-narrator whenever its adult characters break into expressive song. The storyteller's grip on the world he has invented must be even tighter when telling more than one tale at a time.

Based on an eccentric novel by Count Jan Potocki, Wojciech Has' Polish fantasy *Rekopis znaleziony w Saragossie* (*The Saragossa Manuscript*) (1964) is a dizzyingly elaborate black comedy that proceeds from the reading of an ancient book unearthed by two soldiers. Tales give rise to tales within, as the book's characters recite stories, whose characters recite stories, and so on, achieving the narrative spiral of the *Arabian Nights*. The film eventually returns its focus to the book's primary tale, that of Van Worden, an army officer (and ancestor of one of the men reading the manuscript) delayed on his journey to Madrid by several inexplicably hostile parties and by friends too preoccupied to help. Whereas Potocki's novel settles on a rationalist, all-in-their-minds conclusion, Has' film becomes lost in its own narrative maze and has to deliver a messily ambiguous pay-off.

Van Worden's scholarly ally, Don Velasquez, appreciates the film's nexus of tales when he suggests that the human mind can never fully comprehend the infinite, only define its components through story. ("I am getting near poetry, which seems to be nearer to life than we suspect.") Pier Paolo Pasolini's *Il fiore delle mille e una notte* (*Arabian Nights*) expresses a similar sentiment in its opening quote, "Truth lies not in one dream, but in many." In his so-called "Trilogy of Life"—comprising *The Decameron* (1970), *I raconti di Canterbury* (*The Canterbury Tales*) (1971) and *Arabian Nights* (1974)—Pasolini celebrates the bacchanalian abandon of the great medieval story-cycles, rejecting cold philosophy and returning to the warm simplicity of emotion.

Set in authentically grubby historical worlds (which found their way into fantasy through an admiring Terry Gilliam), the trilogy's "message" is one of surrender to the simple pleasure of telling stories, an exhilaration that remains inaccessible to the viewer who persists in the search for meaning. Italian fantasy films are generally characterized by this romantic return to an apparently simpler, more sensual age, typified by pre–Biblical heroic fantasies like *Hercules*. Italy had dabbled in fairy tale before Pasolini, but Paolo William Tamburella's bizarre Snow White sequel *I sette nani all riscossa* (*The Seven Dwarfs to the Rescue*) (1952) and Arthur Lubin's tedious desert romance *Il Ladro di Bagdad* (*The Thief of Baghdad*) (1960) only extenuate their enclosed sources into sprawling costume epics. Similarly in Hollywood, fairy tale was not to be intellectualized but written in the brightest colors and decorated with the prettiest effects.

Imaginative independent producers like George Pal were granted a place at the table after the Supreme Court forced the majors to relinquish their monopoly over exhibition in 1948, effectively bringing the golden age of the Hollywood studios to an end. No longer relying on a B-status piggyback from a prestige feature, smaller films attracted attention through technical innovations like Pal's Oscar-winning "Puppetoons" (animated shorts that utilized thousands of different wooden puppets, one for each frame of film). Seeking to finance a vehicle for his special effects, Pal went to the U.K. and made *tom thumb* (1958), for which he won another Oscar. Based on the Grimms' tale, this popular children's musical has a miniature tom thumb (a spirited Russ Tamblyn) stroll out of the woods and announce to a childless couple that he is their new son. Although bedecked with colorful oversized sets and friendly Puppetoon playthings, the film is weak. A pair of rascals (a caddish Terry-Thomas and a dimwit Peter Sellers) dupe the Pinocchio-like tom into a life of crime, while twee songs bolster his insipid misadventures, as well as a soppy romantic subplot concerning the town minstrel (Alan Young) and the Queen of the Forest (June Thorburn).

Pal returned to this benign Bavarian backwater in *The Wonderful World of the Brothers Grimm* (1962), awkwardly shot in triple-framed "Cinerama." Laurence

Harvey's daydreaming Wilhelm and Karl Boehm's pragmatic Jacob narrate a portmanteau of anodyne stories, the third of which, *The Singing Bone*, is the best. Here Buddy Hackett slays a cute stop-motion dragon and is murdered by Terry-Thomas' cowardly knight, whose crime comes to light after his victim's bones are carved into a flute. This tale omits the original bitter ending by restoring Hackett to life. An ailing Wilhelm is similarly restored on his deathbed when visited by the various characters of his tales. Death, whose presence defines the value of life in all stories, is notably absent from Pal's fantasies, as in the majority of over-cheerful family fairy tales that followed.

Like Méliès, Pal quickly exhausted his box of tricks, and his trademark Puppetoons were surpassed by the more economical, single-model animation of Ray Harryhausen. Harryhausen's own breakthrough film, *The 7th Voyage of Sinbad*, was released the same year as *tom thumb* and inspired a cheeky fairy tale rip-off by independent producer Edward Small. Having acquired *Sinbad*'s director (Nathan Juran), its star (Kerwin Mathews), its villain (Torin Thatcher) and Harryhausen's rival animator (Jim Danforth), *Jack the Giant Killer* (1961) has Mathews' humble farm boy rescue Judi Meredith's princess from Pendragon, the Prince of Witches (Thatcher, looking like a cross between Henry VIII and Ming the Merciless). In contrast to the Pal films, this retains much of the brutality of its sources (an assemblage of eighteenth century English folk tales, in which a resourceful Cornish farmer messily vanquishes a number of dimwit giants). Otherwise the film is an odd mix of the hackneyed and the inspired. Although most of Danforth's creations are clearly dupes of Harryhausen designs, a squad of clumping warriors appear out of a handful of gargoyle's teeth in a scene predating the famous skeleton battle of *Jason and the Argonauts*. The wall-mounted limbs of *Belle et la bête* exchange torches for swords, and Pendragon gives the princess a slinky demonic makeover, in a scene echoed years later in *Legend*.

Presented as gimmicks in the same vein as 3D and CinemaScope, Harryhausen's "Dynamation," along with Pal's Puppetoons, helped lure audiences away from their brand new TVs. Although television had contributed to a general decline in box office, it had also been regenerating interest in live-action fairy tales since 1956, when CBS commenced its annual broadcasts of *The Wizard of Oz*. America's gradual rediscovery of the film, next to the success of *tom thumb*, encouraged a hankering for fairy tales in the form of the effects-laden musicals they'd been before Disney forced them into hibernation.

Ironically, it was Disney who answered the call. Sensing the nation's growing appetite for escapist musicals to take their minds off the headlines, they produced their first live-action fairy tale, *Babes in Toyland* (1961). This cloying revision of the Laurel and Hardy film is a cynical reminiscence of *Wizard* to boot, with Oz's Scarecrow Ray Bolger as a flailing Silas Barnaby. Now that the Disney fairy tale had moved away from its secure post in animation, the rest of Hollywood could finally contest its dominance, although the success of the studio's next film would dictate the course of the genre for a few years yet.

Mary Poppins (1964) is a definitive triumph of naïveté over reality. Scattering a queue of prospective matrons with a gust of wind in a moment of quiet surrealism,

Julie Andrews' Edwardian *uber*-nanny presents herself for employment in the regimental Banks household. She promises her patently adorable wards that she will stay until the wind changes—that is, until their pompous father (a wonderfully starched David Tomlinson) can rediscover his sense of joy and nourish their imaginations for himself. Having brought their cluttered nursery to order with a snap of her fingers, Mary chaperones the children on a stroll through a cartoon pastorale with Dick Van Dyke's vowel-chewing Cockney scamp (he's much better as the doddery chairman of Tomlinson's bank), takes tea on the ceiling with her eccentric uncle, and frolics on the rooftops with high-kicking chimney sweeps.

This giddy escapism appalls Tomlinson, although ironically his household was strange long before Poppins showed up. His wife (Glynis Johns) is a committed suffragette when not called upon to dote over her husband, while their servants resignedly cave the china whenever their sea-captain neighbor sounds the hour with a raucous cannonade. Following his ritual humiliation at the hands of his employers, Tomlinson finally sees through his own self-importance and achieves a simple-minded liberation through imagination. Children's author P.L. Travers was annoyed at the studio taking the pepper out of her character, but Disney's Mary is delightful nonetheless. Julie Andrews never lets her Alice-like poise slip, whether sliding demurely up the banisters or floating through the sky, umbrella aloft, heels together and toes akimbo.

The musical and the fairy tale had long been a happy marriage, recognized when *Wizard of Oz* and *Pinocchio* won Best Song Oscars back in the '40s, and cemented when *Poppins* scooped Oscars for both Best Visual Effects and Best Song, an achievement repeated by Richard Fleischer's imitative *Doctor Dolittle* (1967). Based on the first two books in Hugh Lofting's *Dolittle* sequence (1920–52), the film bombed famously. Another composedly eccentric English magician, Rex Harrison's frustrated doctor finds he cannot communicate with his patients and retreats into learning the language of animals. Although he only gets paid in whatever his new patients can afford (he never wants for milk, acorns and—one presumes—fleas), Dolittle happily straightens mouse-tails and prescribes spectacles to myopic horses. Leslie Bricusse's clotted script and inane songs (apart from "Talk to the Animals," which won the Oscar) slow what should have been as exuberant a musical as *Poppins* to an interminable crawl.

Dolittle's shamanistic powers are a gift from the animal kingdom, which itself turns out to be a repository of fairy tale magic. Dolittle's earthbound home of Puddlesby-on-the-Marsh ignores the world of magic ensconcing it, and the doctor must make a plea for tolerance when Peter Bull's blustering magistrate accuses him of insanity. Consequently, the film's first half jars with its second, in which Dolittle escapes mundane civilization and the film slips comfortably into unadulterated fairy tale. Shipwrecked on a floating island inhabited by cultivated savages, the doctor convinces an obliging whale to shove the island back into the mainland, and everyone rides home inside the wobbly shell of a giant snail.

A less sustained musical portrait of Edwardian eccentricity than *Poppins* or *Dolittle* is Ken Hughes's insufferable *Chitty Chitty Bang Bang* (1968). Having spent most of the film's opening hour cobbling together the eponymous car out of a wrecked

Grand Prix winner, failed inventor Caractacus Potts (Dick Van Dyke) amuses his nauseating children with a merrily xenophobic fairy tale. Potts' Heath Robinson workshop, his loopy imperialist father (Lionel Jeffries) and their storybook windmill home indicate we're already in the realm of Faerie. Then the film redundantly segues into "fantasy" with a wavy dissolve, as Chitty sprouts wings and takes off for the Grimmsian land of Vulgaria. Here the film brightens: Once the town's children are rescued from Robert Helpmann's scuttling Child-catcher, the story returns to the "real" world, where the film can't resist tossing its cap by having the car take to the air for a credits-sequence encore.

Co-written by Roald Dahl and based on the stories of Ian Fleming, *Chitty*'s script is as uncertain as *Dolittle*'s as to where its story takes place. It also suffers from the censorious notion that the apparent sensitivities of children must be protected, and their whimsies indulged at all costs. The good guys worship children; the bad guys loathe them. The kids themselves are not so much characters as magical artifacts. Acting rather like the sacred fertility stones of *Indiana Jones and the Temple of Doom*, the children bring light and happiness into the world of reverent adults. The film's protective mojo over pre-teens even affects Chitty. In the opening sequence, the car that Chitty will become crashes and burns for threatening to hit an idiot child who wandered onto the racetrack.

Like their American counterparts, British fairy tales of the '60s prefer to stick to proven and respectable texts, of which the *Alice* books proved popular among both mainstream and exploitation producers. Set in and around a rambling mansion, Jonathan Miller's Cocteau-esque BBC play *Alice in Wonderland* (1966) envisions Carroll's book as a skewed take on '60s Britain. The Wonderlanders, among them Peter Cook's jaunty Hatter and Michael Redgrave's studious Caterpillar (replete with smoking jacket), are entirely human, but act rather like escaped mental patients. This lends a note of alarm without resorting to traditional pantomime excess. Anne-Marie Mallick's tetchy heroine seems in less command of her faculties than most Alices, ambling through the parade with the glaze of a dedicated pothead. The film makes a reference to contemporary drug culture more obviously in a scene where the giggling courtiers of Alison Leggatt's Queen of Hearts attempt a game of flamingo croquet while stumbling about the grounds to the fevered tune of Ravi Shankar's sitar.

William Sterling's apathetic musical *Alice's Adventures in Wonderland* (1972) is more conventionally benign. Her adventures bookended by the picnic recitation of Michael Jayston's implausibly raffish Carroll, Fiona Fullerton's Alice is assured that Flora Robson's "Off with their heads" mantra is only bluster. Again Carroll's unique nihilism is blunted lest it upset the very audience it's intended for, and only the scenes with Peter Bull's monstrous Duchess and Robert Helpmann's babbling Hatter retain anything of their original brittleness.

American counter-culture in the '60s and '70s sympathized with Carroll's heroine, concluding that her author must be partial to mind-bending substances himself. Alice's status as a fellow outsider adrift in a world gripped by unreasoning dementia was famously underlined by Jefferson Airplane as well as embattled U.S. Marines in Vietnam, who adopted *White Rabbit* as an escapist anthem. In a

Of wonders wild and new: Anne-Marie Mallick stars as the rather wolfish dream child of
Jonathan Miller's superb television adaptation *Alice in Wonderland* (BBC, 1966).

simultaneous rebuttal of traditional fairy tale values, and those of the corporations that had appropriated them, Disney's *Alice* became a cult hit in 1974 on its double-bill re-release with the equally freakadelic *Fantasia*. Reprimanding the psychedelia that brought Carroll to the attention of the flower generation, John Donne's hilariously serious anti-hippie docu-drama *Alice in Acidland* (1969) places college student Alice Trenton under the spell of her lesbian French teacher, a predatory White Rabbit–figure who ushers her into the ruinous Wonderland of pot, LSD and group sex. Laura Johnson's *Alice* (1969) relocates the story to Speed City, New York, while Bud Townsend's porno-parody *Alice in Wonderland* (1976) sends up the sugar-sweet pageantry of Disney and rudely denounces Carroll as a dirty old man.

While the author's much-debated preoccupations are put to misogynistic use in Jonas Middleton's pretentious skin-flick *Through the Looking Glass* (1976), several more playful pornos delighted in defiling the fairy tale sweetness cultivated by Disney. Among these were Corey Allen's 1971 *The Erotic Adventures of Pinocchio* ("It's not only his nose that grows") and Rolf Thiele and Helen Gray's 1970 *Grimm's Fairy Tales for Adults*, possibly the only film to feature the original toe-chopping ending of *Cinderella*.

It was during the Watergate era that movies revealed the long-suppressed and long-suspected truth that the fairy tales mother gave you were not innocent at all. While the explicit sexual shenanigans of Pasolini's Trilogy of Life scandalized Italy, Jacques Demy chose to adapt a long-forgotten tale by Perrault in *Peau d'âne* (*The Magic Donkey*) (1970). This tells the story of a princess (Catherine Deneuve) who repulses the incestuous advances of her father (Jean Marais) with the help of a donkey that can defecate a fortune in jewels.

While Demy was less adventurous in his choice of source-tale for *The Pied Pier* (1971), censors considered Walerian Borowczyk's pornographic *La bête* (*The Beast*) (1975) too rude for British screens. Less interested in revising fairy tale than in watching its actors get it on, this playful Gallic fable presents explicitly what *The Company of Wolves* only implies. About to be married off to the crackpot heir of an aristocratic French family, a pretty American girl arrives at their secluded chateau and hears the ancestral legend of a sex-crazed beast-man who stalks the surrounding woodland. Fascinated by the story, the girl has a prolonged orgasmic dream in which an insatiable ursine monster, sporting an obscenely large and continually spouting pecker, chases a woman through the woods Benny Hill–fashion, before lustily deflowering her. But the beast meets its match in beauty as she turns on her pursuer and literally shags him to death.

Although its pretensions are only teasing (Voltaire's opening quote, "Disturbing dreams are but a passing folly"), *The Beast* attempts to reconcile fairy tale with the modern world, affirming its relevance by reinstating contemporary modes of sex and violence, which were part of the Grimms and Andersen long before Disney told audiences they were not.

Mel Stuart's musical *Willy Wonka and the Chocolate Factory* (1971) performs a similar feat for a child audience. Like Hans Christian Andersen before him, screenwriter Roald Dahl (working from his own 1964 book) places fairy tale magic not in the safe and distant past, but in the modern world of the audience. Penniless Charlie

Bucket (Peter Ostrum) wins one of five golden tickets issued by reclusive candy tycoon Willy Wonka, who will give five lucky children a tour of his mysterious factory and a lifetime supply of chocolate. Dahl understands that since Wonka's Wonderland is openly situated in the real world, that world must be equally unreal in order to accommodate it. Charlie resides in Faerie long before he steps through the gates of Wonka's factory, as his adult peers surrealistically submit to Wonkamania (a shrink berates his patient for dismissing a vision telling how to get a ticket, and the wife of a man ransomed for a case of Wonka Bars asks for time to think the offer over).

Dahl also understands that the knockabout brutality of fairy tale is precisely what appeals to children. Wonka's confectionary Eden has its own way of expelling unwelcome snakes, and four grotesque children meet equally grotesque ends in a fashion pleasingly hostile to the child-adoring creed of *Chitty Chitty Bang Bang*. But the film relents when Wonka reassures the surviving Charlie that they have come to no harm, which comes as something of a concession after the consistent sinister streak the film has displayed so far. An ominous tinker warns Charlie of the monstrous things lurking within Wonka's lair, and an extraordinary psychedelic boat trip inside throws up visions of creepy crawlies and a beheaded chicken. Most frightening of all is the dead-pan dementia of Wonka himself (a superb comic centerpiece by Gene Wilder). This enigmatic harlequin is as indifferent to the perils facing his guests as the inhabitants of Wonderland are about the fate of Alice.

Mad for it: Gene Wilder in one of his quieter moments in this publicity still from Mel Stuart's beguiling musical *Willy Wonka and the Chocolate Factory* (Paramount, 1971).

Unfortunately, *Wonka* failed on release (recouping its audience through television like *The Wizard of Oz*). But as Freudian therapist Bruno Bettelheim asserts in his 1976 bestseller *The Uses of Enchantment*, fairy tales were no longer dismissible; "more can be learned from them about the inner problems of human beings, and of the right solutions to their predicaments in any society, than from any other type of story within a child's comprehension." But child-friendly films like George Cukor's *The Blue Bird* (1976) and Bryan Forbes' *The Slipper and the Rose* (1976) were attempting to return to an age of fairy tale innocence that — as far as the '70s were concerned — was dead and rotten. The Sleeping Beauty of James B. Harris's *Some Call It Loving* (1973) is exploited in a carnival sideshow, while the white-bread utopia of Oz is reduced to a decaying urban wasteland in Sidney Lumet's 1978 Broadway adaptation of

The Wiz. The anxious eyes of Diana Ross' Dorothy caution our immersion in the world of Faerie she has been transported to, while the heroine of Jerzy Gruza and Jacek Bronski's bizarre Polish rock musical *Alice* (1981) can only enter Wonderland by committing suicide.

But Faerie was saved from lasting neglect by the decorative special effects that scored so highly at the box office in the form of *Star Wars* and *Close Encounters of the Third Kind*, movies that turned the tide of paranoia and amorality in '70s cinema. The special effects tidal wave broke in the early '80s, manifesting gingerly at first in a couple of nostalgic makeovers for the Arabias of old, Clive Donner's dismal *The Thief of Baghdad* (1978) and Kevin Connor's tacky but enjoyable *Arabian Adventure* (1979). This brought about an unprecedented boom in fantasy film production, from which fairy tale received the most profound benefit.

Walking Dreams

Hollywood in the 1980s lived its own fairy tale. Emulating the effects-heavy spectaculars of Lucas and Spielberg, the bulk of American movies spent the decade singing their nation's praises, while the rest of the world slid into recession. This lavishly self-absorbed spirit manifested in an early deluge of *olde worlde* fantasy films, conversely only rendered filmable by advances in technology. While the newfound genres "heroic fantasy" and "epic fantasy" celebrated the decade's show-off spirit with *Clash of the Titans, Dragonslayer, Excalibur, Conan the Barbarian, Sword and the Sorcerer, Beastmaster, The Dark Crystal* and *Krull*, fairy tale's creaky sensibilities left the genre on the bench for the first part of the decade.

An independent British film spearheaded fairy tale's return, and allowed the genre its first taste of highbrow validity within the U.K. Written by provocative feminist author Angela Carter, from her own revision of Perrault, Neil Jordan's febrile *The Company of Wolves* (1984) is a Tardis of fairy tale in the mold of *The Saragossa Manuscript* and Pasolini's *Arabian Nights*— but its narrative contortionism surpasses both. In the waking world, Rosaleen (played with assurance by 13-year-old non-professional Sarah Patterson) sits in her attic bedroom and dreams of herself as a virginal Red Riding Hood, her Grimmsian village encircled by a wolf-haunted forest (a tangled witch-wood created by Anton Furst entirely within the confines of Shepperton Studios). "Seeing is believing" is the film's rationalizing refrain, as inexplicable dream imagery punctuates its brittle reality. Birds' eggs crack open to reveal weeping stone newborns. A girl's tears turn a white rose blood red. A yellow-eyed Regency dandy (Micha Bergese) half-disgorges a lupine snout (an image that can stand next to anything in Cocteau or Gilliam), while Granny's inedible remains sizzle in the grate. Then the "real" world disintegrates, as the wolves of Rosaleen's dream escape into the waking world and do away with the dreamer, until her parting voiceover (ironically reciting Perrault's priggish moral epilogue) suggests that nothing in the film can be relied upon as reality.

The sexual awakening of the pubescent heroine forms the path through this narrative forest. Rosaleen is clearly another Dorothy (whose ruby slippers match Rosaleen's signature shawl). Both fairy tale heroines resolve an earthbound "rites of passage" through fantasy, but while Dorothy has her companions, Rosaleen walks alone, as fearless, imaginative and wise as the adventurers of Oz combined. Her path is fringed by another forest, this one a mesh of cautionary tales warning of the predations of men. According to Granny (a redoubtable Angela Lansbury), men consort with the Devil (an urbane Terence Stamp) and tear off outer layers to reveal all manner of throbbing red snouts. Yet here women have an equal share of elemental power, as a discarded peasant girl sardonically turns her aristocratic lover's wedding party into a pack of slobbering wolves. Beauty is as carnal as the beast, says the film, rescinding Red Riding Hood's punishment under Perrault by defiantly condoning the prurience he seeks to contain. Embracing her id, Rosaleen becomes a wolf herself, echoing her mother's assertion that "if there's a beast in men, it meets its match in women."

A fascinating film and one of the most remarkable fantasies Britain has ever produced, *Company of Wolves* remains a cult curio. Yet it quietly influenced several high-profile fairy tales throughout the '80s, as well as inspiring a number of independent titles. Márta Mészaros's Canadian-Hungarian *Piroska e farkas* (*Bye Bye Red Riding Hood*) (1988) proposes another feminist revision of Perrault, whose heroine also finds the beastliness of men as magnetic as it is threatening. Will Gould's *The Wolves of Kromer* (1998) less successfully adopts lycanthropy as a fairy tale metaphor for homosexual stigma, as intolerant peasants hound a pair of gay "wolves" out of their village.

Two disappointingly anemic splatter films, impressed by Jordan and Carter's yoking of fairy tale and horror, attempted to restore the gory details of the Grimms. Jeffrey Delman's idiotic anthology *Freaky Fairy Tales* (1986) features another lycanthropic lothario, whose transformation-suppressing pills are mistakenly collected by a cheerleading Red Riding Hood. Michael Cohn's made-for-cable *Snow White: A Tale of Terror* (1996) throws away every opportunity for scares, in favor of Sigourney Weaver's soap-operatics as the evil queen. These films justifiably view the old tales as staid and over-sweetened but, in purporting to tell the "truth" behind the Disney image, they forget just how horrific Disney often is. The studio's counterbalancing sense of horror actually overwhelmed their next attempt to stimulate nostalgia for the pre–*Snow White* fairy tale.

Return to Oz (1985) is uniquely displaced in that it's a sequel to a film never made. Its story infers a previous adaptation of the first *Oz* book more faithful than the MGM film. Disney not only leapfrogs this beloved movie (discontinuing its theatrical songs), but also forgoes the bonhomie that Baum proclaimed as the ethos of his fiction. Such revisionist daring went unrewarded at the box office, and it's easy to see why. Although commendably thrilling, the film is horribly cold-blooded and presents a depressingly bleak view of the imaginative spirit.

Opening like some grand gothic horror, the film appalled both parents and purists by taking ten-year-old Fairuza Balk's haunted Dorothy to a rain-swept sanatorium for electro-shock therapy. These early scenes are pretty sadistic, as Nicol Williamson's avuncular quack and Jean Marsh's austere governess unconvincingly

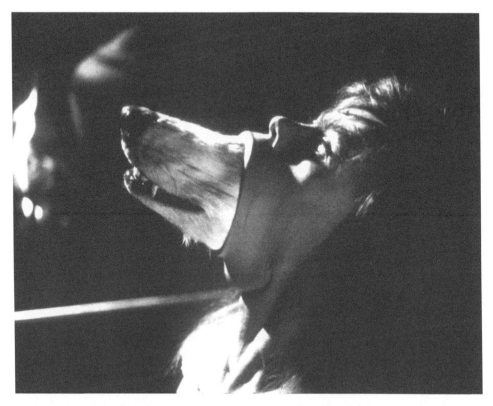

Something he ate? Micha Bergese shows his true colors as the wolfish huntsman in Neil Jordan's exquisite reworking of *Little Red Riding Hood*, *The Company of Wolves* (ITC/Palace, 1984).

assure Dorothy that the screams she hears are not those of accidentally lobotomized patients. As Dorothy is saved by a power cut and escapes (via unconsciousness) into Oz, the film abruptly segues into a world-saving quest plot borrowed from its epic fantasy contemporaries. The Yellow Brick Road has been reduced to rubble and the Emerald City is now in the hands of the spiteful Princess Mombi, who lines her boudoir with living heads.

Dorothy thankfully finds friends in this nightmare world — a dour clockwork soldier, an anxious pumpkin-headed scarecrow and a talkative stuffed moose head. Together they confront the mountainous Nome King, whose elemental minions ingeniously form faces out of stone. The film retains Baum's affection for living objects, but as such (and as the critical cliché went for such genre films of the time), the film is more interested in special effects than in people. What little human warmth Balk's timid Dorothy can summon, the movie regards with suspicion. In a pessimistic twist on the dream/reality dichotomy of the MGM film, *Return to Oz* questions the very mind that would contemplate its own outlandish vision. Dorothy's fantasies have no place in the industrial age, which will extinguish her dreams with the progressive force of electricity.

Like its predecessor, Disney's film posits Oz and Kansas as parallel worlds balanced by similarities (Williamson and Marsh play dual villainous roles, while Dorothy — like the lonely storytellers of *Time Bandits* and *The Usual Suspects* — describes

a matrix of fantasy inspired by the clutter of the everyday). Yet *Return to Oz*'s rationalist conclusion cannot eclipse the possibility that Dorothy may indeed be as insane
as her relatives fear. Like the heroine of *Labyrinth*, Dorothy sees a farewell vision of
her otherworldly friends in her bedroom mirror. But here the reflection ominously
puts a silencing finger to its lips, suggesting Dorothy had better keep her delusions
to herself if she wants to stay out of the rubber room.

By the early '80s, Disney was assuring audiences that it had grown out of the
traditional fairy tale with which it had made its name. While moving into adult production with Touchstone and later Miramax, Disney made failed stabs at flavor-of-
the-month genres with conscientiously "dark" family movies like *The Black Hole*,
Tron, Dragonslayer and *The Black Cauldron*. There remained few old school fairy
tales to tell, and American audiences had little patience with artsy-fartsy attempts to
re-evaluate them. *Company of Wolves* was taken off American screens after a week;
it even caused an opening night riot in one Times Square theater, where poor advertising led audiences to expect a gore-splattered werewolf picture. America needed
fairy tales that retold the ancient stories with a colorful modern sensibility, just as
Baum had done 80 years before, and yet again Disney granted the public's wish.

The studio launched the career of Tim Burton, who would help revolutionize
fairy tale in the '90s and become American cinema's equivalent of Baum or Dr. Seuss.
Burton joined Disney in 1979, toiling unhappily as an animator for several years. His
eclectic imagination cultivated by a love of cheesy sci-fi, gothic horror and morbid
fairy tales, he never conformed to the homogeneity of Disney. But his inventiveness
impressed several of his peers and they funded his first two short films, *Vincent*
(1982), an animated rhyme about a boy who yearns to live in the Gothic world of a
Roger Corman movie, and *Frankenweenie* (1984), in which a little boy happily rean-
imates his dead dog. Their acclaim led to Burton's first feature upon leaving the studio, *Pee-wee's Big Adventure* (1985), a surprise hit that post-modernized fairy tale for
American audiences.

This strangely likable road movie develops the character of Pee-wee Herman (the
slapstick persona of oddball comedian Paul Reubens) into something approaching
the resonance of Peter Pan. Resembling an escaped ventriloquist's dummy, Pee-wee
is a Mad Hatter rather than an Alice. His Wonderland is a toy-box America
overflowing with kitsch relics, through which he rummages in search of a stolen
bicycle. While the fairy tales of Disney are vulgarized amid the pop-cultural clutter,
their innocence is appraisingly reflected by Pee-wee's own. His naïveté overpowers
just about everyone he meets: a manic convict on the run for snipping the "Do Not
Remove" label off his mattress, a ghostly trucker who recalls the expression on her
mortal remains with a crazy cartoon shriek, and a sympathetic waitress with whom
Pee-wee watches the sunrise from inside the jaws of a model dinosaur.

Perhaps a mischievous nod to that urban myth concerning the deceased Uncle
Walt, Pee-wee is an adult frozen in stasis. Reflecting fairy tale's own impasse between
the traditional and the revisionist (which it strove to resolve throughout the '80s),
Pee-wee's eternal pre-pubescence is a state of arrested development also embodied
by the wizened goblin-children of *Labyrinth*, and the eternal infant sought after in
Dreamchild. Burton's film, however, takes this emotional standoff lightly, cracking

several perverse jokes regarding Pee-wee's asexuality. "So is my horn ready yet?" Pee-wee innocently asks his adoring (but unsatisfied) girlfriend as she fixes his bike, voicing the question posed by all such tales of boys who cannot grow up.

Burton repeats this question in *Edward Scissorhands* and again answers "no," leaving Randal Kleiser's subversive sequel *Big Top Pee-wee* (1986) to imagine the sexual anarchy that might ensue should such immortal children ever realize and consummate their adult desires. After a hurricane dumps an entire circus in his back yard, Pee-wee makes it with Valeria Golino's sexy trapeze artist. On the morning after, he realizes he may have broken sacred law, as the fruit of his hot-dog tree shrinks to the size of cocktail wieners. The film ends on a celebratory parade of forbidden romantic couplings. Kris Kristofferson's ringmaster houses a Lilliputian wife in his pocket. Pee-wee's spurned girlfriend (Penelope Ann Miller) finds love in the arms of a troupe of acrobats. Pee-wee's talking pig falls in love with a hippo, and a hermaphrodite marries him/herself.

By the mid–'80s, traditional fairy tales struggled to define their position in modern American cinema, the new effects technology at the genre's disposal proving to work both ways. *Company of Wolves* and the *Pee-wee* films used special effects to elaborate previously inexpressible metaphors, while *Return to Oz* used them to ride the genre like a parade float. A consummate stylist like Ridley Scott was the worst person to resolve this dilemma, and his pompously titled *Legend* (1985) the worst vehicle in which to attempt it.

A pre–*Top Gun* Tom Cruise plays forest boy Jack, and Mia Sara his opalescent lover, Princess Lili, who innocently breaks celestial law by laying hand on a unicorn. This allows Tim Curry's leonine Darkness to steal the creature's horn, plunging the world into *Fimbulwinter*. This mega-budget plane crash of a movie boldly boils secondary world fantasy down to its bare essentials, trying to describe an iconic struggle between good and evil. But the film doesn't know the difference between world-embracing myth and communal fairy tale, ending up with a weird hybrid of the two, a sort of epic fantasy in miniature. The grand plot assures us there's a world threatened by the destruction of these unicorns, yet civilization consists of a single woodland cottage. The sum total of the forces of darkness is a trio of slapstick goblins, while a pair of gambolling unicorns are the sole repository of the world's virtue. Only non-human characters like Anabelle Lanyon's stubborn fairy, David Bennet's gravel-voiced sprite and Curry's blood-red, elephant-horned devil inhabit this simplified world with any credibility.

The film gels just once, in a ravishing scene derived from Cocteau. Ornaments decorating a Gormenghastian fireplace observe a hypnotized Lili waltzing with a faceless lady in black, before Darkness glides magnificently out of a mirror. Otherwise the film sticks to the kind of earnest adventuring and comedy routines laid down by the likes of *Krull*, with dialogue ranging from Curry's cod–*Richard III* soliloquizing, to the annoying contemporary slang of a band of cowardly gnomes.

The film's failure is not entirely its own fault. Noting America's commercial rejection of *Company of Wolves*, Scott reportedly deleted much of *Legend*'s original subtext. But preview audiences were still stumped, forcing Scott to remove two more reels. For years the film existed as two slightly different versions in America and Britain, until Scott prepared a definitive cut for DVD.

While every version of *Legend* fails to reveal an original imagination at work, Jim Henson's Muppet-infested *Labyrinth* (1986) gives fairy tale a rich and more assured post-modernism. Fanciful teenager Sarah (Jennifer Connelly) petulantly recites a spell from her favorite play (entitled *The Labyrinth*) that will have her annoying baby brother spirited away by David Bowie's dashing Goblin King. Bowie unexpectedly obliges, but sportingly gives the remorseful girl 13 hours in which to navigate the protean maze surrounding his castle, after which the child will become one of his cackling goblin subjects. An imaginative triumph, the Labyrinth itself is crammed with scenic sleights-of-hand and visual impossibilities, like the gravity-defying tangle of staircases from which Sarah finally rescues her brother. Conceived by British illustrator Brian Froud, the abundant hobgoblins all have a nice sense of life beyond their function and are as casually contrary to the application of logic as their neighbors in Wonderland. Like Dorothy, Sarah makes supportive friends during her travels, among them a spineless dwarf, a shaggy troll somewhere between a bison and an orang-utan, and a quixotic fox mounted on his Sancho Panza sheep-dog.

Terry Jones' shrewd script weaves familiar strands of Carroll and Baum (whose works— along with the Grimms, Andersen and Sendak — are stacked on Sarah's bookshelves) around a reworking of the tale of Sir Gawain. Like the errant knight who resists temptation in the face of mature responsibility, Sarah must resist the childish temptation to wallow in her own fantasies at the cost of those around her. Like Snow White, she is poisoned by a gift of tainted fruit, causing her to forget her earthbound responsibilities and literally get carried away in a bubble of her own fantasy. She comes to her senses during a romantic daydream, waltzing with the Goblin King at a delirious Regency masque. But a goblin bag-lady offers her further escapist temptations and ushers her back to the security of her toy-littered bedroom. ("Better to stay in here, there's nothing you want out there.") But to opt not to put aside childish things, to remain cloistered in fantasy, at the cost of losing her brother to the world, would mean becoming as much a monstrous child as one of Bowie's goblins. When the King finally offers to cosset her every whim, Sarah again refuses, although wisely concedes she may need the therapy of the Labyrinth in the future. Her triumph is in taming her own imagination, not extinguishing it like the protagonist of *Flight of Dragons*, who denies fantasy at the cost of ever returning to it.

Although occasionally let down by trifles (its superfluous songs recall *The Muppet Show*), *Labyrinth* presents as astute a revision as *Company of Wolves*, whose autumnal hall-of-mirrors ambiance it imitates. The film also subverts expectation far more subtly than a braggart like *Shrek*. The first sight to greet Sarah on entry to her yearned-for fairyland is the Labyrinth's gardener pissing in the lily pond and squirting sweet little fairies with bug spray. We know all bets are off when Sarah tends one of these stricken creatures and it bites her finger. ("What did you expect fairies to do?") By updating the escapist fancies of the old with the rationalist cynicism of the new, the film achieves a synthesis that brought fairy tale into the '90s.

Richard Donner's dry fairy tale romance *Ladyhawke* (1985) similarly attempts to modernize by doing away with the vulgar special effects with which its genre had become so identified. Hoping that its audience will take the story more seriously

No fairies at the bottom of the garden in Jim Henson's marvellously unsentimental *Labyrinth* (Henson/Lucasfilm/TriStar, 1986); groundskeeper Hoggle (pictured, and brought to life by Shari Weiser and Brian Henson) has swatted them all!

without decoration, *Ladyhawke*, like *Ever After*, eschews the traditional Faerie setting for a realistic historical milieu, in this case a Ruritania even more woefully ersatz than the one in *First Knight* (1994). Clearly emulating the shape-shifting mysticism of *Company of Wolves*, Rutger Hauer's frowning soldier and Michelle Pfeiffer's whey-faced noblewoman play star-crossed lovers, cursed by a jealous bishop to occupy separate bodies; Hauer spends his nights as a wolf, while Pfeiffer spends her days as a hawk. It's a poetic idea, but one isolated by the banality of the world surrounding it, and undercut by the anachronistic presence of Matthew Broderick's wisecracking pickpocket.

Rob Reiner's amiable *The Princess Bride* (1987) is equally conscious of the poor company it thinks it's keeping, but a much more successful marriage of fairy tale and effects-free realism. Like *Labyrinth*, it proposes that since life is no fairy tale, fairy tale should do the decent thing by resembling life. However, this commendably pragmatic sentiment deserves a more committed vehicle than this. William Goldman's cynical 1973 novel, on which the film is based, sets itself out as an authentic classical text, whose ramblings have been bluntly abridged. The film's script (faithfully adapted by Goldman) plays a similar narrative game as Grandpa (Peter Falk) reads *The Princess Bride* to his bedridden grandson (Fred Savage), whose impatient interjections replace the book's authorial asides.

Set in the medieval realm of Florin, the story tells of farm girl Buttercup (Robin Wright), whose lover Westley (played with droll dash by Cary Elwes) returns from the sea voyage on which he's believed to have died, to find her engaged to Chris Sarandon's war-mongering Prince Humperdinck. Sardonically recalling the companions of Dorothy are Buttercup's three kidnappers, Wallace Shawn's irate genius, Andre the Giant's lovable strongman and Mandy Patinkin's genial Spanish swordsman, all of whom Westley fights in exquisitely polite duels of brains, brawn and dexterity. Christopher Guest plays the film's Wicked Witch, a six-fingered sadist whose life's work is a torture machine that drains the years of its victims' lives.

Goldman's script brings the pedagogy of fairy tale to task. "Life is pain," sneers Westley. "Anyone who says different is selling something." It also plays further amusing games with our expectations. The film's best joke has Patinkin squaring up to his father's murderer, who poses *en garde* and then runs away. Goldman is clearly laughing along with the material, but the movie resists him by ridiculing its conventions, emphasizing the book's easier jokes with mocking cameos, like Mel Smith's albino torturer, Billy Crystal's kvetching alchemist and Peter Cook's speech-impaired Bishop. The novel ends on a bitterly ambiguous note that questions the conventional "happily ever after," while the film ironically falls prey to its own quip about selling lies, tying up every loose end with a ride into the sunset and the healing kiss of True Love.

Like *Big*, *Princess Bride* opens with a shot of a computer game, lamenting another form of soulless technology enticing children away from the printed word. By the late '80s, fairy tales strove to salvage some measure of this fading humanity from the genre's attendant cavalcade of special effects. Gavin Millar's *Dreamchild* (1985) explores the human pain behind the fantasy. Coral Browne's embittered widow travels to Depression-era New York, where she's haunted by memories of Ian Holm's melancholy Lewis Carroll, whom she inspired as a child. Their monstrousness the measure of Alice's humanity, the Wonderlanders also menace the old woman in the form of hallucinations, spitefully inquiring when she's going to let go and die.

As well as contrasting the human with the inhuman, fairy tale also merges the sentient with the inanimate. A woman's head shatters like porcelain in *Company of Wolves*, while Princess Mombi removes hers like an oversized hat in *Return to Oz*. In *Labyrinth*, doorknockers grumpily refuse to do their duty and an avalanche of rocks is summoned to rescue the cornered heroes. This integration of humanity and the special effects that *Ladyhawke* and *Princess Bride* reject reach an apotheosis in the surrealist masterpiece *Něco z Alenky* (*Alice*) (1988), the first feature film by premier Czech animator Jan Švankmajer.

Here Alice follows a bug-eyed stuffed rabbit into a junkyard Wonderland, whose inhabitants are composed of inanimate clutter brought to frantic life. The Caterpillar becomes a sock with clacking dentures, the Hatter is a clumping marionette, the March Hare a moth-eaten rag doll that skates around in an oily wheelchair, and the Queen of Hearts a vicious playing card, who carries out beheadings with a pair of rusty scissors. Such contradictory fusions abound throughout the film. Tasty bread rolls sprout inedible nails, and creatures are restored to vitality by eating sawdust. Unlike *Song of the South* or *Chitty Chitty Bang Bang*, which reposition their narrative worlds at the last minute, *Alice* (like *Company of Wolves*) doesn't verify the existence of any anchoring primary world. Alice "awakes" to find herself in her room, where the rabbit's exhibit case has been vacated. Delusion and reality fuse, leaving the viewer to decide whether Alice is awake or dreaming.

Terry Gilliam's *The Adventures of Baron Munchausen* (1988) had the last word on whether the '80s fairy tale was still dreaming of the past or waking to the possibilities of the future. A nightmare to produce thanks to the very bureaucracy it lambastes, this enforcedly uneven film was a colossal failure on release, and another excuse for lavish fantasies like it to go unfilmed. Set in "The Age of Reason," in a European city bombarded by Turkish guns, a theater company diverts the besieged citizens with a production of *The Adventures of Baron Munchausen*, until the real Baron (John Neville) turns up, insisting the players have got it all wrong. Recognizing the incredulous actors as his old friends, the Baron claims only he can end the war raging outside since it was he who started it. He recounts his part in the conflict, but no one believes him, not least ruthless bureaucrat Horatio Jackson (Jonathan Pryce), who stands for all the heartless logic in the world. The film asks which reality is true: Jackson's world of realism or the Baron's world of chaos? Although grotesque, the film's primary world is seemingly that of mundane reason, until the absurdities creep in. The Baron builds a hot-air balloon out of ladies' knickers, and floats to the Moon, where he and Robin Williams' lunar king each claim the other is their invention.

The film resolves its grab bag of events with an audacious ending, as the Baron is murdered and lowered into his tomb, only for the film to pull back to a previously unrealized plain of story, where the Baron is still recounting his adventures. ("And that was just one of the many occasions in which I met my death.") Upon opening the city gates, the Turks have been vanquished. What we believed was the world of Jackson the accountant was really the puppet-world of the storytelling

Baron all along. We never see the "real" world or even know if it exists. Josef von Baky's *Munchausen* ends with the revelation (long since dwindled into cliché) that the narrator was a player in his own story. In this case, the division between reality and imagination is clear: It doesn't exist. In Gilliam's film, as in the adjustable worlds of *Company of Wolves*, *Return to Oz*, *Labyrinth* and *Alice*, the real world may well be Faerie in disguise, or vice versa. Fantasy's elusiveness as a genre stems from this uncertainty; magic itself depends upon a perception of it. Rosaleen wisely acknowledges this in *Company of Wolves*: "They say seeing is believing, but I'd never swear to it."

When Worlds Collide

Even when Disney took time out to expand its theme park and media empires, theirs remained the voice of the fairy tale establishment, defining the revisionist agendas of movies like *The Princess Bride*. The studio (or rather the company — Disney changed their title in 1986 to placate shareholders) had not animated a traditional tale since the '50s, but carefully whetted public appetite for more in the late '80s by releasing its self-canonized "classics" on video. According to plan, when their gorgeously animated *The Little Mermaid* was released in theaters in 1989, it was welcomed as a triumphant homecoming for fairy tale.

A sweetening of Andersen's tragedy, *Mermaid* picks up where Disney left off, presenting a bubbly revision of 1959's *Sleeping Beauty*. The kiss of True Love is again the ticket to maturity, although the film's headstrong mer-teen, Ariel (voiced by Jodi Benson), is more commendably proactive in winning it than her predecessor. Having fallen in love with a human prince, she strikes a Faustian deal with oily sea witch Ursula (Pat Carroll). She exchanges her sonorous voice for land legs, but must receive the fateful kiss before the sun sets on the third day of her human life, or else she will shrivel into one of the cowering sea slugs in Ursula's garden. Aided by her on-shore guardian, Sebastian (a melodic Jamaican crab voiced by Samuel E. Wright), Ariel's modern seduction techniques prompt a sliver of old-fashioned disapproval from Ursula ("Little tramp!"). Unfortunately, the film doesn't make good on its feminist promise and lets Prince Eric heroically correct Ariel's mistakes, spearing a Kraken-sized Ursula (in the same fashion that did for the shark in *Jaws: The Revenge*), and leaving Ariel only marginally more empowered than wallflowers like Snow White.

Little Mermaid's technical brilliance, aided by Ashman and Menken's vibrant calypso, reaffirmed the superiority of the Disney fairy tale, whose past crimes were also obliquely confessed in the even more successful *Beauty and the Beast* (1991). This undeniably handsome film also waves the flag for feminism, but the achingly romantic love affair between its bookish heroine, Belle (voiced by Paige O'Hara), and the majestic Beast (Robby Benson) hits the same reactionary note as *Mermaid*. En route to winning the man whom the film assures us she really wants (despite her yearning for adventure and rejecting the subservience offered by Gaston, her narcissistic suitor), Belle spares herself the domestic drudgery of a Cinderella, but still ends up waltzing amid newly earned finery, secured in the arms of a Prince Charming. The film doesn't liberate women as much as it tames men, who are otherwise too ignorant or scary for Belle to approach. The Prince Charmings of old are mockingly typified by Gaston (Richard White), whose virility and enviable physique are found wanting in comparison to the mournful savagery of the Beast. A battle for supremacy takes place between archetypes old and new, culminating in a tooth-and-nail brawl along the gothic battlements of the Beast's castle.

Although critics like Marina Warner were quick to expose its failings, *Beauty and the Beast* was a breakthrough fairy tale, confirming the genre was no longer the preserve of children. The movie's hip sophistication attracted an adult audience who no longer needed to drag the kids along as an excuse to see an animated film, the first nominated for a Best Picture Oscar.

As if recognizing the institution its fairy tales had become, Disney dismantled them even further in *Aladdin* (1992), one of the most commercially successful animated features of all time. Narrated by a verbose Arabian merchant, who relates Aladdin's tale directly to the audience (in the voice of Robin Williams), this essentially straightforward *Arabian Nights* tale (pinching as much from Korda as *Beast* does from Cocteau) hits its dizzying stride when the hero retrieves his magic lamp. Exploding from his prison like a box of fireworks and faced with granting the customary three wishes ("And ix-nay on the wishing for more wishes"), Robin Williams' motor-mouthed Genie yanks the audience out of the world that *Mermaid* and *Beast* take so seriously, exposing its artifice with a staggering (and mostly improvised) vocal torrent of pop-culture references. In a final Brechtian flourish he draws attention to the very mechanics of the film itself, lifting the animation cel of the film's closing frame to throw us a parting quip.

Arab-Americans argued that *Aladdin* (produced during the Gulf War) presented a racist depiction of the Middle East, while critics, already leery of Disney's agenda, scoffed when the company audaciously compared *Bambi* to *Hamlet* in *The Lion King* (1994). James Earl Jones voices the leonine monarch of the African savannah. He is murdered by his fascist brother (Jeremy Irons doing his best George Sanders impression), who coerces young heir Simba into exile. The cub grows to maturity under the irresponsible guidance of his Rosencrantz and Guildenstern (a Yiddish meerkat and a flatulent warthog). When he learns his home has become a blighted wasteland under his uncle's rule, Simba realizes he must take responsibility for his people.

From an original script assembled by a 17-man committee, *Lion King* is technically as polished as its three predecessors, yet its schema is ultimately tarnished. Although the movie makes a clear division between a responsible leader and a self-serving autocrat, it indirectly endorses the very fascism it tries to reject. The species-specific form of the animal fable works against *Lion King*'s monarchical storyline, suggesting that some animals are indeed more equal than others. The film casts its rank and file villains as hyenas, whom a duplicitous statesman allows to cross the border into Simba's utopia; they reduce it to a famished husk. The film veers dangerously close to outright racism here by casting the distinctly ethnic voices of

Whoopi Goldberg and Cheech Marin as lead baddies. Also, the sole factor determining Simba's right to rule is that he belongs to a genetically superior species.

While Disney rehabilitated the Faerie worlds of old, Tim Burton yoked them to the modern world in *Edward Scissorhands* (1990), based on an original story by Burton and regular collaborator Caroline Thompson. The film ingeniously brings the unearthly quality of a Hoffmann fairy tale to the equally romanticized landscape of '50s America, whose Rockwellian suburbanites in turn become the abandoned children, evil queens and villainous noblemen of fairy tale. Bookended by cozy scenes of an old woman relating Edward's tale to her granddaughter, Dianne Wiest's terminally optimistic Avon Lady ventures into the gothic mansion that overlooks her pastel-colored neighborhood. Here she finds an artificial boy named Edward (an almost mute but extraordinarily expressive Johnny Depp). Having cobbled him together from a cookie-cutting machine, Edward's elderly inventor (a poignant cameo by Vincent Price, in his last film role) died before completing his Baumian creation, leaving Edward with twitching shears at the end of each arm.

"I think you should come home with me," Wiest tells him, with the conclusive authority of Mom Eternal. Edward leaves his sinister burrow for the equally grotesque surroundings of suburbia. Here he proves adept at sculpting shrubbery, grooming poodles and fashioning outrageous hairdos for the ladies, while falling dreamily in love with Wiest's teenage daughter (Winona Ryder). But the tide of friendliness turns, and Edward is chased back to his castle by a suburbanite throng, wittily recalling the torch-and-pitchfork mobs that chased the monster back to his castle in a dozen *Frankenstein* pictures.

But for all its enchantments as a modern fairy tale, *Edward Scissorhands* is profoundly neurotic. An androgynous Kewpie doll in an impenetrable fetish-wear outfit, holding the world at bay with his castrating shears, Edward is a vivid symbol of sexual fear. As he comes to terms with the outside world, he emerges into adolescence, undergoing its attendant temper tantrums and the agonizing pangs of first love. When adulthood looms, however, Edward takes fright and, instead of fighting for a place among humanity, he retreats into the cradle of his own imagination. After a tragic parting, the story pulls back to reveal Edward's teenage love, now an old woman, as the film's melancholy chaperone. She also has fallen victim to the regressive influence of Edward, whose gothic nursery still looms outside her window.

Such arrested development became a feature of Burton's fairy tales. The encroachment of sexual maturity threatens the pristine innocence of both Edward and Pee-wee Herman, while the skeletal hero of the innocently macabre *Tim Burton's The Nightmare Before Christmas* (1993) is another misunderstood artist. Painstakingly animated in spidery stop-motion, the film is based on a Seussian poem Burton scribbled down while working for Disney (thus the company claimed the work as its legal property). Bored with the monotony of Halloween, well-meaning spook Jack Skellington (Chris Sarandon) highjacks Christmas, cheerfully distributing gift-wrapped horrors across another suburbia, until the army shoot him down in his Santa suit. Having failed this creative "rites of passage," Jack, like Edward, dusts himself down and falls back on what he does best. Burton's own gothic confectionary, popularized by *Beetlejuice*, *Batman Returns* and *Edward*, had by now become

With these hands: The mercurial Johnny Depp (left) as the star of Tim Burton's *Edward Scissorhands* (20th Century–Fox, 1990), a living mannequin cobbled together from a cookie-cutting machine, here admires his new human extremities. Sadly his inventor (Vincent Price, right) does not live long enough to stitch them on.

enough of a trademark and a box office draw to warrant an authorial prefix on a film written by Caroline Thompson and directed by Henry Selick.

Barry Levinson's disastrous science-fantasy *Toys* (1992) was the first of several failed attempts to simulate Burton's amalgamation of the fairy tale and the everyday. Clearly attempting some kind of parable, the film sees the magic kingdom of Zevo Toys threatened with corruption by a sinister military man (Michael Gambon), and saved by his innocently childish nephew (Robin Williams) and his batty android sister (Joan Cusack). Unlike Burton, Levinson has no clear grasp of where to set his story. His film presents a land of endless emerald pastures, residential pop-up books and candy-colored, bubble-blowing pachyderms. (Ferdinando Scarfiotti's production design — René Magritte by way of Willy Wonka — is the film's only virtue.) Yet this otherworldly facade is undermined whenever Williams is allowed to crack a joke about Jane Fonda, Norman Schwarzkopf or Mother Teresa, occupants of a real world that exists ... where?

Similarly the TV movie *Snow White* (2001), directed by Burton's writing partner Caroline Thompson, frolics in an improbable world of rainbow-colored gnomes, while trying to make sense of the exaggerated behavior of Kristen Kruek's Snow White and Miranda Richardson's evil queen. In the same way that Jim Carrey's expressionist clowning seems merely idiotic in the otherwise rational world of the first *Ace Ventura* movie, so the whimsy of *Toys* and *Snow White* appears farcical when perpetrated by rational characters.

Burton's modern fairy tales maintained a complimentary balance between behavior and setting, which confounded their imitators for most of the '90s. Terry Jones' not-entirely-disastrous *The Wind in the Willows* (1996) and Peter Lord and Nick Park's stop-motion *Chicken Run* (2000) were among the few to get it right. Based on the sedate 1908 animal fable by Kenneth Grahame, *Willows* is set in a jolly expressionist shire overlooked by Michael Palin's talkative Sun and located by signposts accurately pointing "somewhere else" and "not here." Unlike those of Thompson's *Snow White*, Jones' characters do not react rationally to their bizarre surroundings. As in Grahame's book, the film's animal characters interact unobtrusively with the human world of law courts and motorcars. Costumes and makeup cleverly suggest the various species, recalling the human Wonderlanders of Jonathan Miller's *Alice*. Human rabbits canoodle in the hedgerows with their sweethearts, ears and tails poking out of their Oxford tweeds. Foxes stride around the fields in lordly hunting gear, and drunken weasels demolish Toad Hall like Bolshevik revolutionaries.

Another animal fable, *Chicken Run* is a P.O.W. drama relocated to a gloomy Yorkshire farm. Setting itself in the real world, the movie knows that anything untoward must be regarded with astonishment by the film's rational characters. The watchful human farmer sees the hens limbering up for an escape attempt and thinks he's going nuts. The film's deftest touch has Fowler, the patriotic cockerel, spend most of the film surrealistically reminiscing about his salad days in the R.A.F., then appropriately reveal at a crucial moment that he was a mascot, not a pilot. "I'm a *chicken*," he says with exasperation. "The Royal Air Force doesn't let chickens behind the controls of a complex aircraft."

The earthbound setting of *Chicken Run* is superficially fantasized through its animation. (This admission may qualify *all* animated films as fantasy, but the various perceptions presented by the medium are too complex to address here.) Similarly, Philip Ridley's intriguing *The Passion of Darkly Noon* (1995) is a non-fantasy melodrama but for the mythic texture of its telling. A child-like lummox named Darkly Noon (a superb Brendan Fraser) staggers out of an endless forest, the only survivor of a Waco-like massacre. A blithe forest girl (Ashley Judd) and her mute lover (Viggo Mortensen) take him in. Darkly's puritanical upbringing collides with his seething desire for Judd, placing him in the moral bind of a psychopath. Is she some demonic succubus who deserves punishment, as Grace Zabriskie's wild-eyed hermit believes she is? Or is she some pre–Fall dryad whose innocent indulgence in the pleasures of the flesh predates his faith and warrants the same reverence? But the film tends to defuse such poetic ambiguities by grounding them in reality. A giant silver boot floats with mischievously obscure significance downriver, but its spell is broken by a throwaway revelation that it belongs to a travelling circus.

Matthew Bright's grotesque black comedy *Freeway* (1996) similarly interprets the everyday as a fairy tale. Reese Witherspoon's white-trash Red Riding Hood gives her social worker the slip and drives across the West Coast to live with her trailer-park Grandma, while Kiefer Sutherland's wolfish serial killer lays in wait. Some zealous performances save the movie, but otherwise its chosen fairy tale mismatches writer-director Bright's impassioned commentary on the treatment of juvenile delinquents, and quickly feels like an afterthought.

Another awkward but interesting attempt to frame social polemic with fairy tale, John Duigan's *Lawn Dogs* (1997) creates yet another misalignment. The escapist whimsy of ten-year-old Devon (Mischa Barton) and the realist outrage of her parents' trailer trash gardener (Sam Rockwell) would have contrasted better on neutral ground. The film instead takes Devon's side by setting itself in the suburban Faerie of a Tim Burton movie. *Lawn Dogs'* ending is as heavy-handed as its outbursts of Marxist indignation, but rather more appropriate. Devon helps her friend escape suburban hell with the gift of a magic cloth. Dropped from his speeding truck, this causes a river to rise and block his pursuers, while a discarded comb prompts an entire pine forest to erupt out of the tarmac and cover his back.

If these films view the modern world through the prism of fairy tale, movies like *Princess Bride* and Andy Tennant's *Ever After* (1998) view fairy tale through the prism of the modern world, scratching away the glamor to expose the realist truth. In Tennant's apparently pragmatic Cinderella tale, Jeanne Moreau's Grand Dame receives the Brothers Grimm, intending to set the record straight. "The truth of the romance had been reduced to a simple fairy tale," she concludes. This not only dismisses the power of fairy tale, but offers a "truth" every bit as placatory as, say, *Pretty Woman*. Drew Barrymore plays Danielle, Moreau's great-great-grandmother, who unhorses Dougray Scott's runaway Prince, while laboring for her stepmother (an affectedly haughty Angelica Huston) and her two pretty stepsisters. Regarding magic as some kind of narrative cure-all, the film dismisses the schematic fairy godmother. Danielle is left to win the Prince's heart by herself, although Leonardo da Vinci, the father of reason, gives her the required pre-ball makeover. When Danielle is rejected by the Prince after he discovers her identity, the movie takes a bold detour, but commits itself no further. The Prince undergoes an inexplicable change of heart and Danielle escapes her new master by threatening him with a sword. *Ever After* makes as much noise about feminism as Disney's *Beauty and the Beast*, but remains nothing so revisionist as *Pretty in Pink* in Renaissance drag.

Based on Roald Dahl's 1988 book, Danny DeVito's *Matilda* (1996), an outstanding black comedy for kids, presents one of the most confident feminist rewritings of Cinderella. Set in another Burtonsville suburb, the film posits the heroine's traditionally absent family as the very prison from which she must escape. Mara Wilson's self-sufficient young Matilda is incarcerated in a gloriously vulgar small-town bungalow by her selfish parents. Unscrupulous car salesman DeVito and Bingo junkie Rhea Perlman insist their six-year-old prodigy tear up that copy of Melville and sink into blue-collar stupefaction with them in front of the TV. Matilda bails herself out of this domestic hell by becoming her own fairy godmother, cultivating a miraculous I.Q. at the local library and surreptitiously punishing her bullying squirt of a father.

Vexed by their daughter's freakish precocity, her parents send her to school, where the story forms an interesting power struggle between the classical feminine triumvirate of maiden (Matilda), mother (Embeth Davidtz's supportive teacher) and hag (their thunderous antagonist Miss Trunchbull). An inspired performance by Pam Ferris, Miss Trunchbull is one of the most fearsome ogres in fairy tale film. This hulking, child-hating principal launches disobedient children through open

windows and swings over-winsome little girls around by their pigtails. The hyper-
bolic violence of fairy tale has never been put to more hilarious use, and finally puts
paid to the child worshipping ethos of *Chitty Chitty Bang Bang* (although, like *Willy
Wonka,* the movie carefully assures us that Trunchbull's disciplinary methods are non-
fatal).

The contradictory outlooks of the fairy tale past and the down-to-earth future,
which so many films fail to harmonize, also inheres in the opposing sensibilities of
British and American fairy tales. American tales are typified by the pioneer futur-
ism of Baum, Disney, Seuss and Burton, while the British often lament the green and
pleasant land of yesteryear, the golden afternoons of Carroll, the childhood rambles
of A.A. Milne and the idyllic Hobbiton of Tolkien. Hollywood usually overrides these
serene tastes whenever adapting British fantasy, while British films inject an unchar-
acteristically frantic pace into homegrown tales for the benefit of the American market.

This is precisely the strategy that Terry Jones adopts for his slapstick *Wind in
the Willows,* whose Mr. Toad (a splendidly hyperactive Jones) ironically stands for
just the sort of all–American thrill-seeking frowned upon by the English bourgeoisie.
The Anglo-American production *Chicken Run* mines these transatlantic tensions for
laughs, contrasting the American optimism of Mel Gibson's Rocky the rooster with
the British scepticism of Julia Sawalha's Ginger the hen. True to its '40s ambiance,
Rocky struts through the henhouse like an off-duty G.I. while Fowler sums up the
doubtful "bloody Yanks" attitude of an older generation.

But it was American modernity that dominated fairy tale film in the '90s. While
Hollywood emphasized the pro–American sentiments of Roald Dahl's 1961 book in
Henry Selick's efficient *James and the Giant Peach* (1996), the motifs of the traditional European fairy tale were left for mean-spirited independents to savage. The
benign sweetness of George Pal turns to festering rot in the bolexbrothers' (sic) *The
Secret Adventures of Tom Thumb* (1993). Here a helpless Tom (resembling a Puppetoon of *Eraserhead*'s deformed fetus) cringes among all manner of agonized genetic
mutations. Matthew Bright's sleaze-athon sequel *Freeway II: Confessions of a Trick-
baby* (1999) gleefully ticks the boxes on its depravity checklist, as it turns Hansel and
Gretal into a bulimic delinquent (Natasha Lyonne) and a rapidly unravelling psychopath (Maria Celedonio). The tale's cannibal witch, meanwhile, becomes a child-
abusing nun (played with degenerate relish by Vincent Gallo).

While maturing under the guidance of Disney and Burton, fairy tale lost touch
with the children who had formed its audience in the days of *Mary Poppins.* The
shamelessly pretentious *Institute Benjamenta, or This Dream People Call Human Life*
(1995), by animators the Brothers Quay, and Guy Maddin's equally intolerable *The
Twilight of the Ice Nymphs* (1997) are cheerless arthouse guff that haughtily avoid any
sense of the childlike. By contrast, *Toys* and Steve Barron's live-action *The Adventures of Pinocchio* (1996) are children's movies unsure of whom they're talking to.
While Barron's *Pinocchio* collapses Collodi's narrative by extracting its supposedly
outdated didacticism, *Toys* (like *Santa Claus: The Movie*) labors under the delusion
that kids would rather play with wooden penguins than bust caps in each other's asses
in a video game.

Sensing the newfound maturity of child audiences, Rob Reiner's uneven modern fable *North* (1994) switches child/adult roles in the same way as *Matilda*. Elijah Wood's 11-year-old prodigy responsibly follows a court order to find the perfect family and is appalled by the childish-ness of the world's adults. Jean-Pierre Jeunet and Marc Caro's near-masterpiece *La Cité des enfant perdus* (*The City of Lost Children*) (1995) explores this idea further. Densely (if imprecisely) plotted, this sci-fi fable is one of the most astonishing feats of sustained imagination in fantasy cinema, echoing *Star Wars* with its carnival of seamless technical effects masking a profound faith in the unknown.

In a dank seaport, a dimwitted circus strongman named One (Ron Perlman) forms an alliance with nine-year-old Miette (Judith Mittet), the leader of a gang of child pickpockets. Hunting for One's missing infant brother, they learn that a cult of cyborgs is abducting children all over the city at the behest of their anguished benefactor, a lonely genius named Krank (Daniel Emilfork). Reversing the abandoned child premise of movies like *Time Bandits*, the hulking but childlike One is left to fend for himself by Miette's streetwise gang, while Miette herself is a cynical Alice, wise to the ways of Wonderland. This allows for a relationship even stranger than the ambiguous love affair between Jean Reno and Natalie Portman in Luc Besson's *Leon* (*The Professional*) (1994). Miette hopefully inquires whether her naïve companion will ever take a wife, while her stripes and skirts are queasily echoed by the sexy outfit of a wanton saloon girl, who comforts One when he believes Miette dead.

Like *The Secret Adventures of Tom Thumb*, *City of Lost Children* takes fairy tale beyond the present-day Faeries of Burton and into a dystopic sci-fi future, a world of soulless technology in which dreamers are as lonely as Jonathan Pryce's persecuted clerk in *Brazil* (1985). On a forlorn oil rig guarded by a maze of sea mines, Krank uses infernal machines to vicariously inhabit children's dreams, since he's incapable of having his own (perhaps the film's own smug joke at the expense of the audience). Like the genetic mutations that surround him (a miniature den mother, six narcoleptic clones and a migraine-addled brain in a fish tank), the tragic Krank is as flawed a product of science as Burton's Edward. Cloned by an amnesiac inventor, the film's parched villain has a superior sense of reason, but one that fails to keep him warm at night. Modernity and its commodities are here even more sterile and superficial than those in *Edward*, *Darkly Noon* and *Lawn Dogs*. These films liken the modern world to a post-bargain Faust, a perfect but sterile shell to which the mystical imperfection of humanity must be restored.

The same can be said for the dazzling computer-generated effects showcased by *City of Lost Children*, and which became an integral part of fantasy films as they moved into the twenty-first century. Such technology can turn fantasy into as much of a utilitarian prison as science, like the patently artificial CG backdrops that contain the human inhabitants of Neverland in P.J. Hogan's lavishly gloomy *Peter Pan* (2003). The first live-action feature film adaptation since the silent era, the film stays true to Barrie's tragic coda. Jason Isaacs' vicious Captain Hook eventually resigns himself to the crocodile's jaws and Jeremy Sumpter's Peter opts for his cloisters in Neverland over a life with Wendy. Hogan's film understands that no fantasy can offer complete escape from the real world.

Fairy tale worlds composed partially or entirely from CGI not only allow film-makers to manipulate their subjects in a way they couldn't possibly do in front of the camera, they also emulate the hyperbole of the printed fairy tale. Contradictions abound in fairy tale literature, from the enchanted boots of Perrault's *Le Petit Poucet* (*tom thumb*), which allow their wearer to cover seven leagues in a single step, or the treasure-guarding dog of Andersen's *The Tinderbox*, a regular-sized canine with "eyes as big as mill-wheels." Such images do not translate easily to the literal medium of film, although CGI can describe something of their elasticity. Unlike a flat 2D cartoon, CGI affects a realistic texture often indistinguishable from photographed reality, allowing the physical world the mutability of a cartoon.

Live-action films based on popular animation were the first to develop this caricature aesthetic. But while Robert Altman's *Popeye* (1980) is muted enough to look passable, John Goodman's inflexible human frame appears inconsistent amid the plasticity of his Hanna-Barbera surroundings in Brian Levant's *The Flintstones* (1994). Ron Howard's *The Grinch* (2000) and Bo Welch's *The Cat in the Hat* (2003), both based on rhymes by Dr. Seuss, are more confident live-action cartoons. Both employ Burton-like toytowns (Welch was Burton's production designer on *Edward Scissorhands*), while digital effects augment the synchronized gooning of their heavily prostheticized performers (Jim Carrey and Mike Myers, suitably mercurial comedians both), freeing them to perform gravity- and physiology-defying feats almost on a par with the polymorphous genie of Disney's *Aladdin*.

Tormented scientist Krank (Daniel Emilfork) awakes from uneasy dreams in Jean-Pierre Jeunet and Marc Caro's brilliantly bizarre *La Cité des enfants perdus* [*The City of Lost Children*] Lumière/Studio Canal +/France 3, 1995).

Set in a symmetrical primary-colored world, Rob Minkoff's *Stuart Little* films (1999 and 2002) use CGI to much subtler effect, cleverly mirroring the fairy tale incongruities of the 1945 E.B. White book. Their quaint home sandwiched between towering apartment blocks, Geena Davis and Hugh Laurie (deliberately looking as though they've been traced onto an animation cell) are the Littles, the perfect middle-class couple who adopt an affable mouse named Stuart (an entirely CG–rendered "synthespian," keenly voiced by Michael J. Fox). The humans in Stuart's life treat him as off-handedly as the humans of *Wind in the Willows* treat their animal compatriots, while the manager of Stuart's orphanage overturns the chickens-can't-fly-airplanes logic of *Chicken Run* by apologizing for being unable to trace Stuart's real parents. ("Mice aren't very good with paperwork.")

As CGI continued to elasticize the filmable world, the animal fable came into its own. Reversing Hitchcock's crack about actors and cattle, movies could now treat cattle like actors. Synchronizing human voices and animal actors with computer-assisted chin-wagging, the piglet-hero of Chris Noonan's captivating *Babe* (1995), based on Dick King-Smith's 1983 *The Sheep-Pig*, overcomes the dubious species hierarchy proposed by *The Lion King*. George Miller's chaotic sequel *Babe: Pig in the City* (1998) uses CGI to extrapolate the farmyard world of the first film into, "a place just a little to the left of the twentieth century."

Pixar's *Toy Story* was the first feature described entirely in CGI, but the thunder of its follow-up, *A Bug's Life*, was stolen by *Antz* (1998), another CG–animal fable from rival studio DreamWorks SKG. Set in an ant colony beneath Central Park (a horizon of clipped grass wittily resembling the opening shot of *Manhattan*), Woody Allen's anxious worker ant inadvertently instigates a revolution when he falls in love with the discontented Princess Bala (Sharon Stone). The film is a candidly Aesopian treatise on the value of free will, while Pixar's *A Bug's Life* (1998) and *Finding Nemo* (2003) are crowd-pleasing comedies first and animal fables second. A comic take on *The Seven Samurai* and a pleasing undersea road movie respectively, these films sweeten their bluntly delivered moral pills with (very funny) jokes about slapstick circus bugs and stir-crazy goldfish.

Just as these films wittily humanize the animal kingdom, their artificial rendering embraces the real rather than the alien. In the same way that 2D animation freed Disney's artists to realize fairy tale more fully than they could by photographing reality, features rendered entirely in pixels allow the same degree of command, but over worlds almost as photo-real as our own. Unlike Disney (their distributor), Pixar did not adapt the stock eighteenth century tales, but emulated those who first committed them to print. *Toy Story*, *Bug's Life*, *Monsters, Inc.* and *Finding Nemo* all joyously confirm the imaginative notions of children. Toys really do goof around when no one's looking. There really is a monster in your closet, and being a bug or a fish really is no different to being human.

Like *Antz*, DreamWorks' *Shrek* (2001), based on William Steig's satirical 1990 fairy tale, challenges the packageable neatness of the Pixar films. Fluently rendered in storybook-bright CGI, the film makes it clear from the start what it thinks of the classic Disney fairy tale. A prologue storybook falls open in vintage fashion, then the film's eponymous hero, a trumpet-eared, snot-green ogre (voiced with a Scottish brogue by Mike Myers), wipes its butt with its pages. The film continues to cater to children's love of gross humor, so long denied them under Disney, while giving the company itself a churlish satirical kicking. The film's villain is a diminutive megalomaniac (rumored to be modelled on a certain Disney bigwig) and his empire a muzak-filled, but customer-free theme park. Shrek constantly has to restrain his jabber-mouthed sidekick, Donkey (Eddie Murphy), from bursting into hackneyed song, and Cameron Diaz's Princess Fiona charms the birds down from the trees like Snow White. But a sustained high note accidentally detonates one inquisitive sparrow.

Shrek is more about its mocking swagger than its review of fairy tale stereotypes. At its core is a contrary take on Disney's *Beauty and the Beast*, celebrating the monstrousness of the ogre that Disney domesticates. We learn Princess Fiona has been cursed since childhood to turn into an ogre every night until released by True Love's kiss. While echoing Disney's caveat about judging by appearances, *Shrek* mocks that film's transformative climax, as the ogress Fiona dramatically levitates in a swath of light, only to remain an ogre. Her Prince Charming remains revolting and ill-tempered to the end, while she finds beauty in her own beastliness and learns to live "ugly ever after." The film exposes the truth, veiled by Disney (who cut straight to the credits), that the Beast is a good deal more interesting that the vacuously handsome prince he becomes.

Although *Shrek* and its sequel *Shrek 2* (2004) provided the autopsy for fairy tale film as we knew it under Disney, the predominant storyteller of screen fairy tales is likely to retain an American accent. As Hollywood culture became world culture in the '90s, the Faerie of old was absorbed and reinvented by the new. Hollywood technology transformed the medium of live-action cinema into a Faerie of its own, the integration of free-floating CG camerawork changing the very grammar of cinema.

George Lucas (who owned Pixar back when it was called Lucasfilm Computer Development Division) has prophesied that film will become less and less reliant on photography, with computers allowing filmmakers greater creative freedom than filmable reality can afford. Such a move would bring the filmed fairy tale closer to the written, with filmmakers using technology to coerce the real world into serving the symbolic needs of fairy tale as freely as any author. But Lucas himself demonstrates the limitations of his vision with his own unlovable *Star Wars* prequels, whose few human actors are as isolated by technology as the citizens of *The City of Lost Children*. Such untethered retreats into digital escapism equal the retreat from humanity that is the tragedy of *Edward Scissorhands*. As in the '80s, fairy tale film now has the opportunity to launch new and even more penetrating explorations of Faerie, but must resist the temptation to abandon itself entirely to its pleasures. At present, the only certainty is that, happily or not, fairy tale film will live digitally ever after.

4

Earthbound Fantasy

This Magic Earth

Earthbound fantasy is just that, bound to the world of traffic jams, news reports and daily grind that we all inhabit (at least as it's presented by classical narrative cinema). Here, the primordial irrationality of Faerie has been tamed by the advance of civilization, which has become the unfeeling mechanistic prison from which Alice and Dorothy escape. While Wonderland, Cimmeria, Middle-earth and Oz still exist just outside its borders, the human world of the earthbound fantasy film has largely purged itself of the unexplainable, although pockets of enchantment survive in its unfamiliar corners.

Easily the most numerous of fantasy films, since their mundane settings are the easiest to produce, earthbound fantasy stands dead center on the Gianetti scale, sandwiched between the absurdist realism of fairy tale and the realistic absurdity of heroic fantasy. Exemplified by the slick, easily digestible movies of Capra and Spielberg, classical narrative cinema (to which earthbound fantasy belongs) doesn't need to lay down rules for its fictional reality to obey. We don't need to be told how this world works because we've lived there our whole lives. In effect, half the work of an earthbound fantasy film is already done, until it alters what we regard as acceptable reality, and rules must be carefully put in place in order to account for them.

While its neighboring subgenres present invented worlds governed to a greater or lesser degree by the laws of our own reality, earthbound fantasy stands where magic and logic intersect. Invariably presented as a collision of ancient versus modern, the manifestations of magic found inhabiting earthbound fantasy most often stem from a clearly identifiable source. The rampant wildlife that overruns a small town in *Jumanji* has escaped a magical board game. The ghosts of *The Sixth Sense* appear because a frightened little boy has the power to see them. The body swaps of the *Freaky Friday* movies result from idle wishes. These activating devices are the switches that allow a magical current to flow into the mundane world, ushering the motifs of fantasy into existence in a similar fashion to the fairy tale storyteller. Activators allow earthbound fantasy to differentiate magic and reality with relative ease, unlike fairy tale, whose magic irradiates the entire world and needs no excuse for it to burst into being.

Earthbound fantasy usually sees the world through the eyes of an everyday Joe, some dependable James Stewart type as sensible as you or I. If these guys looked out their window one day and saw a Balrog setting fire to the tool shed (a not uncommon occurrence in earthbound fantasy), they'd react much the same as we would, by (a) running away very quickly, while screaming very loudly, (b) tipping away the rest of their drink, or (c) calling their therapist ("Hi, Dr. Goldberg? Yeah, it's back again!").

Occasionally characters in earthbound fantasy oddly refuse to rationalize magical events, even though their world is clearly as realistic as our own, and not some Faerie region in disguise. Sometimes magic just happens, without any activating device, witnessed or perpetrated by characters as blasé as Alice. In *The Tin Drum*, a little boy successfully refuses to grow up. In *Divine Intervention*, a young Palestinian blows up an Israeli tank with a peach pit. In *Orlando*, the hero/heroine's immortality and inexplicable sex change is put down to the idea that this sort of thing happens all the time in a place as weird as England.

These films may be identified as "magic realism," a term that emerged in literary criticism in the '70s and '80s, and has since become a euphemism for those who dislike the term "fantasy." Most commonly attached to the work of Latin-American authors like Gabriel García Márquez and Isabel Allende, and British intellectual fantasists like Salman Rushdie and Angela Carter, the term is still useful in describing those movies and novels that take off into fantasy while remaining grounded in political and social debate. However, magic realism is the art-house exception to the rule in earthbound fantasy, which traditionally regards magic with astonishment, so as to avoid alienating the average viewer.

While its anchoring setting restricts it from departing (at least entirely) for a fully realized secondary world, earthbound fantasy films operate under the proviso that magic underlies our world. Enchantment may manifest in the form of angels and devils, mermaids and ghosts, swapped bodies and magical artifacts, lost worlds, time-slips and sorcerers' apprentices, all of which are themselves classifiable motifs recurring throughout the fantasy genre. Earthbound fantasy is particularly useful for identifying this lexicon of fantasy symbols, since their mundane setting throws them into relief. These motifs form the ingredients of the fantasy stew, boiled up in what Tolkien describes as the "Cauldron of Story." The metaphor refers to the public consciousness, into which chunks of myth, legend, religion, history, folklore and anecdote are collected, diffusing and commingling through the ages until ladled out and served as different combinatory dishes. Paradoxically, fantasy motifs are at their most interchangeable when earthbound, when not constrained by the demands of generic story. *It's a Wonderful Life* concerns both an activating visit from an angel and a resultant hiccup in the time-stream. *Who Framed Roger Rabbit?* involves a race of fantastic creatures and hinges on a visit to an outpost of Faerie, while the *Harry Potter* movies take a magpie approach to the entire fantasy genre. Clearly such tightly packed sediment cannot be entirely segregated, but its motifs may certainly be identified.

Design in Everything: Visitors from Beyond

As objection to the *Harry Potter* phenomenon by Christian fundamentalists demonstrated in the late '90s, fantasy may be fiercely rejected when its magic shares the same world as a people's faith. Obviously fabricated secondary worlds safely quarantine the pagan magic of fairy tale, heroic and epic fantasy, clearly announcing their divorce from reality. Earthbound fantasy, however, proposes that the same forces of magic exist in the workaday (Christian) world. Here the Bible speaks of the heretical hokum of "magic," or the malignant practices of "sorcery" and "witchcraft." To the Christian, these are fabricated corruptions of the only genuine magic (so to speak), the divine miracle, the earthly manifestation of God's power and irrefutable proof of His existence. But within the fictional universe of earthbound fantasy, magic and miracles achieve essentially the same outcome, a conversion of material reality, whether turning water into wine or a broomstick into a ride to work.

Although their division (or not) depends entirely upon individual belief, the configurations of fantasy and religion remain undeniably similar. Fantasy works through the viewer's temporary acceptance of a given set of invented principles; religion works through the comparable concept of faith, through "the confident assurance that what we hope for is going to happen. It is the evidence of things we cannot yet see" (*Hebrews*, 11: 1). Within their separate spheres, fantasy and religion perform the same function, bringing about a union between the believer and a thing not physically evident or scientifically provable.

The earthbound fantasy film, in effect, plays God. Acting as "a revealer of mysteries" (*Daniel*, 2: 47), films like *Here Comes Mr. Jordan* and *It's a Wonderful Life* offer secular audiences a view of the great beyond that negates the proviso of faith. With this in mind, most films are respectful when impinging on religious terrain, their suppositions presented through a veneer of wisecracking whimsicality, which signposts the film as harmless make-believe and prevents it from exclaiming blasphemy. Few mainstream earthbound fantasies offer serious access to the world of the spirit, which many viewers believe exists outside our own in whatever form their faith decrees. Yet many films are in contact with this sphere through a figure who may be termed "the visitor from beyond." These celestial beings emanate from a given spiritual realm, from which all miracles derive. The visitor from beyond is an avatar of its native kingdom, whether Heaven, Hell or beyond, embodying that realm's principle directives and visiting the human world in order to set matters in accord.

In Alexander Hall's reincarnation fantasy *Here Comes Mr. Jordan* (1941), a key earthbound fantasy of the '40s, Heaven's equanimous registrar Mr. Jordan (Claude Rains) must find a new body for Joe Pendleton (Robert Montgomery) after a wet-behind-the-ears angel claimed the man's life years too soon. Visitors from beyond like Jordan suggest the reverse of ghosts like Cary Grant in *Topper* (1937). Instead of human beings crossing over to the immaterial "other side," beings from the spirit realm take on physical form in our world, and in so doing

Robert Montgomery takes three different roles in Alexander Hall's key earthbound fantasy *Here Comes Mr. Jordan* (Columbia, 1941). Pictured in this publicity still alongside Evelyn Keyes (who plays his girlfriend, Bette Logan), Montgomery plays deceased saxophonist Joe Pendleton, who hops into the body of murdered millionaire Bruce Farnsworth, and again into revived prizefighter Ralph "KO" Murdock.

become much like us. In *Mr. Jordan*, Joe is not greeted after his death by harp-plucking seraphs out of some gothic altarpiece, all swan's wings, white robes and tangled reams of scripture. Instead he disappointingly shakes hands with an ineffectual though officious R.A.F. type, named Messenger 7013 (Edward Everett Horton). Here on the cloud prairies of limbo, 7013 ushers souls onto an airplane bound for the next world, a comforting image that converts nebulous ideas of an unfamiliar afterlife into something reassuringly mundane. Mr. Jordan himself expresses the movie's fundamental sentiment: "Eventually all things work out. There's design in everything."

An embodiment of this solace is the figure of the heavenly angel. This visitor from beyond is the perfect device for movies to expound the tenants of Christianity without berating its audience in the language of the pulpit. Outside of Biblical adaptation, angel movies are only as direct as Scripture when patronizing their audience, like Spencer Williams' all-black musical parable *The Blood of Jesus* (1941). Here a pious churchgoer (Cathryn Caviness) dreams she is visited on her deathbed by an angel of the Lord, and is restored to waking life by drops of Christ's blood.

In the '40s, those angel movies aimed at smug white folks adopted the same

Christian worldview, but took a far less fundamentalist approach. Leslie Goodwins' musical farce *An Angel Comes to Brooklyn* (1945), Hollywood's first sustained angel comedy, takes the warm, fanciful approach to disassociate its message from the stony convention of Sunday morning church. The film distances itself even further with the notion of an afterlife reserved entirely for thespians, whose blustering chief sends Charles Kemper's newly winged stage magician to help a determined Kay Dowd achieve her dream of treading the boards.

An angel stays the hand of Abraham, the man's willingness to kill his son at God's command signifying utter devotion to His Word. Likewise, *Brooklyn*'s angel is sent to intervene because Karen has shown the utmost devotion to her calling, and because society is too insensitive to reward her itself. The same omnipotent compassion saves the world in Raoul Walsh's *The Horn Blows at Midnight* (1945), as "The Chief" orders Judgment Day be sounded by Jack Benny's angelic trumpeter, who pauses at the zero hour to rescue a suicide.

Behind these movies is the comforting notion that prayers do not go unheard and sacrifices do not go unnoticed, a view given a representative treatment in Frank Capra's humanist masterpiece *It's a Wonderful Life* (1946). Prayers to rescue archetypal nice guy George Bailey (James Stewart) are heard by euphemistic cosmic powers, who send fledgling angel Clarence (Henry Travers) to prevent him from committing suicide. Although seething with ambition, George has always been a victim of his own charitable nature. He sacrifices his dreams of becoming an architect by rescuing his father's loan company from dissolution, and gives up his wedding money when bankruptcy looms again. Like Kevin Costner in *Field of Dreams*, the Gawain-like George refuses every rational option that will save him and his family from poverty, including the Faustian offer of a well-paid job working for Lionel Barrymore's Scrooge-like villain. But unlike Costner's reluctant visionary, George is not motivated by an exterior dream-quest, but rather by his natural Samaritan urge to do what's right. He's unaware how his actions have benefited the lives of others (believing his own is only worth as much as its insurance policy), until Clarence transports him into a nightmare version of life, where his absence has brought about misery.

It's a Wonderful Life didn't find its audience on release but it's become an institution since the '70s through relentless airings on yuletide TV, and as influential as the surprise hit *Mr. Jordan*. Cary Grant's wandering angel performs the same catalytic function as *Wonderful Life*'s Clarence (albeit with more panache) in Henry Koster's *The Bishop's Wife* (1947), reconciling David Niven's unlikely clergyman with his neglected wife (Loretta Young). *Mr. Jordan*'s ineptly bureaucratic Heaven screws up again in Albert S. Rogell's *Heaven Only Knows* (*Montana Mike*) (1947), where a clerical error results in a soul never having been granted to Brian Donlevy's Wild West gambler. An angelic desk jockey (Robert Cummings) must now guide him back to the path of righteousness. Underlying these bumbling angels and their inefficient heavens is the touching notion that to humanize the divine is to make it fallible. This recalls the symbolism of the Crucifixion; only through the imperfection of Christ's earthly suffering can a perfect unknowable God cultivate the sympathy of mankind.

Uplifting: The U.S. poster for Frank Capra's *It's a Wonderful Life* (RKO/Liberty, 1946), one of America's best-loved fantasy films, based on the 1943 short story *The Greatest Gift* by forgotten fantasy-horror author Philip Van Doren Stern.

The spiritual encouragement offered by Clarence and Mr. Jordan diversified beyond the '40s, but continued to wear a sympathetic human face. The forces of romantic destiny ensure couplings that were meant to be in George Seaton's *For Heaven's Sake* (1950), Alexander Hall's *Forever Darling* (1956) and Geza von Radvanyi's *Angel on Earth* (1966). The Roman Catholic concept of the guardian angel appears in two Vincente Minnelli films, *Cabin in the Sky* (1943) and *Yolanda and the Thief* (1945), again in Vittorio de Sica's earthbound fable *Miracle in Milan* (1951), and is suggested by the airy perfection of Julie Andrews in *Mary Poppins* (1964). Other angels take pity on Mankind more indiscriminately, launching random goodwill missions in Clarence Brown's *Angels in the Outfield* (1951), Alan Bromley's *The Angel Who Pawned Her Harp* (1954) and Ján Kadár's *The Angel Levine* (1970).

By the '70s, only Disney's *Charley and the Angel* (1973) believed supernatural charity could redeem mankind. By the mid–'80s, angels were the straight men in dire teen comedies like Gary Medoway's *The Heavenly Kid* (1985) and Tom McLoughlin's *Date with an Angel* (1987). Then Wim Wenders' cerebral German arthouse movie *Der Himmel über Berlin* (*Wings of Desire*) (1987) re-evaluated a subgenre that had remained essentially unchanged since the '40s. Filmed partially in nostalgic black-and-white, the film explores the intriguing idea (first suggested by *The Bishop's Wife*) that angels may live among us.

In bleak modern-day Berlin, invisible pony-tailed angels overlook the capital, listening in on the random thoughts of its citizens. Although prelapsarian mankind is divided, this imperfect state is aspired to by the angel Damiel (Bruno Ganz). Having fallen in love with an unemployed aerialist (Solveig Dommartin), he cashes in his wings and becomes mortal. The film segues into color at this point, conveying a banal reality as vivid to the angel's eyes as the Technicolor Oz is to Dorothy's. Here Damiel meets a genial Peter Falk (playing himself), who reveals that this is not the first time an angel has relinquished immortality. ("There's lots of us," he winks.)

Damiel's gaunt companion, Cassiel (Otto Sander), also exerts his free will and becomes mortal in Wenders' nonsensical sequel *In weiter Ferne, so nah!* (*Faraway, So Close!*) (1993), but finds himself disregarded by his fellow man, and falls into a life of drink and crime at the promptings of "a satanic Willem Dafoe." The irony of such mortal angels becoming pawns in a game they once played is also realized in Brad Silberling's *City of Angels* (1998), Hollywood's surprisingly effective remake of *Wings of Desire*. A softly spoken Nicolas Cage trades immortality for Meg Ryan, who later rides her bicycle into a lumber truck, and leaves him to realize that experiencing His creation, however painful, is preferable to merely observing it.

The Christian God has a stronger presence here than in Wenders' original, whose angels are ambiguous enough to avoid the conceited proposal that one faith got it right. "Some things are true whether you believe in them or not," murmurs Cage, although we never see the duster-coated angels holding vigil over L.A. testifying to the glory of God's creation in Asia or the Middle East. Nostalgia for the Christian values of the '40s angel movies is apparent in other '90s remakes, including William Dear's *Angels in the Outfield* (1995) and Penny Marshall's *The Preacher's Wife* (1996). Old-fashioned interventions take place in two Robert Redford films, *The Milagro Beanfield War* (1987) and *The Legend of Bagger Vance* (2001), while John

Cornell's *Almost an Angel* (1990) features another *Mr. Jordan*–esque reincarnation. Here Paul Hogan's petty thief returns to Earth as an angel of good will. Even Britain contributed to the New Age fad for angels, casting them in two kitchen-sink comedies, Andrew Rajan's *Offending Angels* (2000) and Udayan Prasad's *Gabriel and Me* (2001).

One of the few films to suggest that the world's attitude may have moved on since the '40s is Danny Boyle's muddled screwball comedy *A Life Less Ordinary* (1997). Delroy Lindo and Holly Hunter are sent to Earth from Heaven's station house to bring together a poor little rich girl (Cameron Diaz) and her father's unemployed janitor (Ewan McGregor). Finding it difficult to get on with their romantic mission in an age of self-absorbed cynicism, the angels pass themselves off as ruthless bounty hunters in a bizarre attempt to bring the lovers together under duress. Hunter wallows in trash Americana, while Lindo grimly laments the days of Claude Rains and Cary Grant, when all an angel had to do was chaperone the predestined couple.

Russell Mulcahy's *Highlander* (1986) and Sally Potter's *Orlando* (1992) place angels at odds with the modern world more successfully, reversing the premise of *Wings of Desire* by elevating humans to the status of immortals. *Highlander* proposes that humanity co-exists with a race of indestructible gladiators, whose champion may redeem the world or destroy it. His divine heritage a pleasingly ambiguous possibility, a crabby sixteenth century Scot, Connor MacLeod (Christopher Lambert), struggles to come to terms with what it means to be immortal. In a clichéd but effective sequence, he refuses to desert his mortal wife as she withers into old age. A twentieth century lover summarizes his emotional isolation: "Most people are afraid to die. You're afraid to live." Tilda Swinton's angelic Elizabethan comes to the same conclusion in *Orlando*. Having lived for 400 years and weathered sexual prejudice from both sides of the fence (she inexplicably changes sex in 1710), Orlando arrives in the twentieth century where she learns the only way to begin living is to let go of the misdeeds of the past. Jimmy Somerville's kitsch angel hovers by on immobile stone wings heralding her newfound status ("at one with the human race").

These earthbound immortals crave mortality as much as the angels of *Wings of Desire* long to experience the imperfection of mortal life. For John Travolta's eponymous archangel in Nora Ephron's *Michael* (1996), this fall from grace is a gradual process. Vegging out in an Iowa motel, banging cocktail waitresses and growing an impressive paunch to offset his downy wings, Michael is practically human, and eventually reaches the Grail of any such quest for mortality, which is of course death.

Seeking to gauge how far the modern world has fallen from the ideals of Scripture, *Michael* returns to the Biblical image of the pinioned human, also used to attack modern religious hypocrisy in the smugly provocative *Dogma* (1999). Matt Damon and Ben Affleck play disgraced angels threatening to "unmake" existence by exploiting an apparent loophole in Catholic doctrine, which will allow them to re-enter Heaven. Unlike its neighboring remakes and their antecedents, *Dogma* boldly bases its eschatology not on tactful whimsy, but directly on the Bible itself. It was this fidelity, combined with writer-director Kevin Smith's outhouse humor, which upset many Catholics. A Catholic himself, Smith claimed he was out to make a film that

Looking sharp: Glowering Frenchman Christopher Lambert (pictured) plays grumpy immortal Scotsman Connor MacLeod, in Russell Mulcahy's *Highlander* (EMI, 1986); his Edinburgh-born co-star Sean Connery plays an Egyptian!

celebrated his faith, albeit in the form of "a two-hour psalm with a lot of dick and fart jokes in it." Whether optimistic, naïve or cynical, he claimed bemusement at the reaction of his peers.

Dogma challenges the fundamentalist view, questioning that if the supernatural events described in the Bible really happened, how might they have been interpreted? Quasi-Biblical visitors from beyond rant about how they've been short-changed by religion in their absence. Chris Rock's thirteenth Apostle, Rufus, complains that his contributions were edited out of the Bible because he was black. But the film ultimately confirms the humanity of Christ's story, which it believes has been forgotten by the modern church, as well as the very beings who played a part in the Savior's life.

Like *Dogma*, Gregory Widen's *The Prophecy* (1995) asks why we should think angels are on our side at all, reminding us that they are tools of God's wrath as well as His compassion. Ben Affleck voices his angelic hatred of mankind in *Dogma*, to which *The Prophecy* offers a response when Elias Koteas' failed priest-turned-homicide cop wonders, "Would you ever really want to see an angel?" Here another renegade seraph, Gabriel (Christopher Walken), follows in Lucifer's hoof-steps by giving into jealousy and seeking to instigate a second heavenly war with the help of the most evil human soul ever born. A feral Viggo Mortensen appears as Lucifer, pointing out that Walken's angel needs humanity's help to bring down Heaven because mankind naturally excels at war and deceit. This winning irony raises the question, "Would an angel ever really want to meet a human?"

Bringing uncomfortable undertones to the old-fashioned palliative that our prayers will always be answered, these films suggest that the visitor from beyond may be as much pledged to our destruction as to our preservation. Angels, of course, are the forebear of demons. Just as angel movies encourage mankind's virtue, movies starring the original fallen angel emphasize our capacity for wickedness. Since the Earth is the Devil's realm, his temptations there to test how deserving we are of a place in paradise, it's no surprise that Satan and his buddies vacation on Earth more often than God's angels. The Devil most often visits apocryphal horror films like *Rosemary's Baby* and *The Omen*, which tend to conclude with evil triumphant. The Dark One's appearances in earthbound fantasy, however, most often find him thwarted in good-natured attempts to destroy mankind.

Fantasy devil movies are almost invariably Faust tales of some kind, in which the Devil pays a visit from beyond to test the moral fiber of God's creations. In the early days of cinema, Méliès loved to see the Devil succeed and his Faustian prey damned in spectacular purgatorial fashion (*à la* Marlowe). The Frenchman's rival, Ferdinand Zecca, in his *Les Sept Châteaux du diable* (*The Seven Castles of the Devil*) (1901), preferred to relent with a last-minute redemption borrowed from Goethe, adaptations of which (and the 1859 opera by Charles Gounod) proliferate throughout the silent era.

The first important adaptation of Goethe, F.W. Murnau's *Faust* (1926) is typical of the silent adaptations in its moral outlook, with Gösta Ekman's overreaching scholar driven to sign the Devil's pact through compassion rather than ego. After the archangel Michael agrees to hand over the Earth if Faust's soul can be damned, Satan spreads his wings over an entire town and brings about a devastating plague that forces the sympathetic old alchemist's hand. Faust, restored to princely youth, dies alongside his wan consort, Marguerite (Camilla Horn), while still under contract to Satan. But Michael's faith in mankind is rewarded as he smugly points out to the irate Devil that the couple have been redeemed by love. In putting Faust's salvation down to this irresistible natural force, however, the film reneges on an earlier, more interesting assertion (made by Michael himself) that mankind can only achieve salvation by exerting their God-given ability to choose between right and wrong.

Hollywood flattered the moral sensibilities of its audience with another Goetheian ending in Faust's first modern-dress movie, D.W. Griffith's *The Sorrows of Satan* (1926). In Murnau's *Faust*, Emil Jannings' Mephistopheles wears his diabolism on his sleeve by taking the lurid forms of a repulsive goblin and a Bela Lugosi–like popinjay. The star of *Sorrows of Satan*, however, wisely chooses to conceal his true Miltonian monstrousness, a form glimpsed briefly at the ends of *The Witches of Eastwick* and the remake of *Bedazzled*. Booted out of Heaven by God Himself, the repentant Devil falls to Earth. He assumes the dapper form of Prince Lucio de Rimanez (Adolphe Menjou) and reluctantly tempts a pair of aspiring writers with promises of wealth and notoriety. The Devil retains a similarly agreeable human guise in William Dieterle's *All That Money Can Buy* (1941) as Walter Huston's "Mr. Scratch" sells seven years of prosperity to an impoverished New England farmer in exchange for his soul.

The monarch of Hell is the visitor from beyond most at home when on Earth, although his evil is often found wanting in comparison with humanity's own monsters. Long before *South Park: Bigger, Longer and Uncut* (2000) had the Devil in an abusive gay relationship with Saddam Hussein, the propagandist Hal Roach comedy *The Devil with Hitler* (1942) had Hell's board of directors agree that *Der Fuehrer* would make a much more efficient monarch than Alan Mowbray's self-important Devil.

Ever since the distributors of RKO's *All That Money Can Buy* objected to the word *Devil* in the film's original title (*The Devil and Daniel Webster*), Satan has been obliged to take on a variety of pseudonyms when visiting Earth. In *Heaven Can Wait* (1943), Ernst Lubitsch's reworking of *Don Juan in Hell* (not to be confused with the 1978 Warren Beatty movie, which is a remake of *Here Comes Mr. Jordan,* not this), he is Laird Cregar's immaculately dressed "His Excellency," lending a sympathetic ear to Don Ameche's skirt-chasing New York playboy. Claude Rains and Ray Milland both take the name "Nick" in Archie Mayo's *Angel on My Shoulder* (1946) and John Farrow's *Alias Nick Beal* (1949) respectively, while Yves Montand is "Mr. Leon" in Claude Autant-Lara's *Marguerite de la nuit* (1955). Ray Walston is the homely-sounding "Mr. Applegate" in Stanley Donen's *Damn Yankees* (1958), while Peter Cook's George Spiggott in Donen's original *Bedazzled* (1967) has a name suggestive of his own brand of banal mischief, tearing the last pages out of Agatha Christie whodunits and siccing wasps on grooving flower people. Bill Cosby in Disney's inconsequential *The Devil and Max Devlin* (1981) at least has the cool-sounding name "Barney Satin." Jeffrey Jones has to make do with "Spike" in Peter Hyams' *Stay Tuned* (1992), while Jack Nicholson's Daryl van Horne aptly summarizes his feelings towards the three women of George Miller's *The Witches of Eastwick* (1987).

From the late '50s onward, Faust's moral lesson was most commonly administered through comedy, aside from a couple of reverently direct adaptations of Goethe and Marlowe, René Clair's *La Beauté du diable* (*Beauty and the Devil*) (1950) and Richard Burton's *Doctor Faustus* (1967). The Devil now preyed almost exclusively upon marginalized losers from the working classes, rather than the middle-class lawmen and mountebanks of old. But the nature of both their near-undoing remained unchanged since the days of Adam.

Helen of Troy makes Marlowe's Faust immortal with a kiss, fulfilling the Devil's timeless promise of "Eritis sicut Deus" ("and ye shall be as gods"). Repeating the trick in *Damn Yankees,* the Devil sends one of his groupies to make sure a seducible male mortal coughs up his soul, as an aging baseball fan sells up for his team's success and a season as their star player. Liz Hurley's Devil attracts Brenden Fraser with the help of a slinky Versace number in Harold Ramis' 2000 remake of *Bedazzled*. Peter Cook's sour script for the original has Dudley Moore's contemptibly spineless loser wade through seven ironically misinterpreted wishes, all for the girl he's too self-pitying to realize loves him already. In the only marginally less misogynistic

Would you buy seven wishes from this woman? Brendan Fraser does in Harold Ramis' amusing *Bedazzled* (20th Century–Fox, 2000), with Elizabeth Hurley (pictured) as the Princess of Darkness.

The Witches of Eastwick, Jack Nicholson rants in church that women are the true serpent in Eden. During his seduction of Michelle Pfeiffer, he reveals how he wishes he were a woman himself, implying that the Devil would be all the more dangerous if he were.

Jan Švankmajer's surrealistic *Lekce Faust* (1994) realizes the inevitability in any meeting with the Devil: Whether damned or redeemed, it's a forgone conclusion that humanity will sign away its soul. In Švankmajer's film, an anonymous slob in a crumpled overcoat (Petr Čepek) enacts this cyclic tragedy, witnessing a stranger's terrified flight from damnation (a flight that later becomes his own). He assumes the mantle of Faust literally, becoming an oversized marionette exchanging lines with a polymorphous Mephisto. Švankmajer sees Faust's capitulation as endemic of the Czech Republic's own submission to the temptations of capitalism, the effects of which Otto Sander's angel experiences for himself in the post–Wall Berlin of *Faraway, So Close!*

According to the Bible, we are flawed by sin, yet surely no more so than the Devil, who, if films like Steven Brill's Adam Sandler picture *Little Nicky* (2000) are to be believed, lives a life of drudgery equal to our own. (A minion helpfully reminds Harvey Keitel's exhausted Satan, "Don't forget you're shoving a pineapple up Hitler's ass at three o'clock.") In earthbound fantasy, the Devil is a visitor from beyond as tainted by human emotion as the angels, but his mortal hatred is aimed not so much at mankind, but at God. By the end of the original *Bedazzled*, we learn that Peter

Cook's devil is on the brink of winning a soul-collecting contest with God. He returns Dudley Moore's soul as a gesture of good will, hoping to win back his wings, but God shows him the door regardless. Of course this is the Devil's tragedy; unlike the human Faust, he can never truly repent and is forever banished from the sight of God.

Paul Bogart's *Oh, God! You Devil* (1984) presents this age-old stand-off as a Manichean duel of good and evil, with George Burns playing both God and the Devil sparring through poker in a Vegas casino. It was in the first of this series that God Himself first paid His creation a proper visit, having already announced on the radio that He's on His way in William Wellman's *The Next Voice You Hear...* (1950). In *Oh, God!* (1977) and *Oh, God! Book Two* (1980), the Creator takes on Burns' stogie-puffing stage persona and confesses that He was never satisfied with the creation of the avocado. Burns is a far more genial Supreme Being than those who want to write off the Earth and start over. To avert this catastrophe in Ernest Pintoff's *Human Feelings* (1978), Billy Crystal's angel faces the task of finding six righteous souls in Las Vegas, while John Travolta and Olivia Newton-John must perform a noble sacrifice in John Herzfeld's *Two of a Kind* (1983).

The very first screen God was banned in several countries for suggesting that He was black. It didn't help that His screen debut also flirted with blasphemy at the intriguing suggestion that God may have been as much redeemed by the death of Christ as His children. Another all-black religious allegory, William Keighley and Marc Connelly's *The Green Pastures* (1936) is even more condescending to its audience than *The Blood of Jesus*. A Louisiana preacher describes Bible stories to his Sunday school class in terms of a Southern fish fry, regretfully complete with Eddie "Rochester" Anderson as Noah and Rex Ingram as "De Lawd." The idea is particularly unpleasant when regarded in the context of its time, when God was otherwise considered obvious enough a presence to remain unseen in mainstream (white) angel and devil movies.

Ironically, modern movies starring God play the same idea (albeit jokingly), allowing *Bruce Almighty* to pat itself on the back for casting Morgan Freeman in the role. But the Almighty usually remains a heavenbound entity, leaving His word to be carried out by His angels and circumscribed by the Devil, an idea given a movie of its own in Hal Hartley's *The Book of Life* (1998). Martin Donovan's designer-suited Jesus is sent to New York on New Year's Eve 1999, with his P.A. Magdalena (P.J. Harvey) and orders to bring about the end of the world by breaking the last three seals on the Book of Life (contained on a laptop). Meanwhile, in a hotel bar, a dishevelled Satan (Thomas Jay Ryan) fears the world he's worked so hard to corrupt will be wiped out. But Jesus refuses to go through with his mission, and confesses to an astonished Satan that he believes his word has been perverted and used to justify evil. ("Who do these *Christians* think they are anyway?")

The Book of Life ends on an ambivalent note, with God's reaction to His son's heresy yet to be seen, and it's just this sense of mystery that makes Him the most elusive of all visitors from beyond. On the rare occasions when God does put in a personal appearance (bearing a worrying resemblance to Charlton Heston in *Almost an Angel*), a film usually has irreverent motives for letting Him do so. In Paul

McGuigan's *The Acid House* (1998), God (Maurice Roëves) is a dishevelled barfly found drinking in a pub on a Scottish housing estate. Having nothing better to do, He turns a local wastrel into a fly. *Dogma* casts Canadian angst rocker Alanis Morrisette in the role — incidentally not the first female God, after Nancy Walker's "Mrs. G" in *Human Feelings*. Jack Baran's wilfully oddball *Destiny Turns on a Radio* (1995) takes a secular approach, with Johnny Destiny (an intensely self-satisfied Quentin Tarantino) rising out of a glowing swimming pool to dole out luck at the Vegas casinos. (It's odd how often Vegas turns up in these pictures.) But perhaps the cleverest balance between the mysterious and the defined is achieved in Terry Gilliam's *Time Bandits* (1981). God (Ralph Richardson) turns out to resemble a slightly bewildered English headmaster, who reveals the film's deadly misadventures were contrived by Him to road-test His latest creation, Evil. Pressed for the meaning why the world should be blighted with such a thing, He answers with appropriate mystery, "I think it's something to do with free will."

It's generally accepted that those from beyond are visiting the world of the One True God, which explains why His antecedents may not be entirely welcome. In Lowell Sherman's *The Night Life of the Gods* (1935), eight Greco-Roman immortals are revived from statues only to find the twentieth century has no place for them. The weakness of modern booze appalls Bacchus, while Neptune can't understand why he should have to pay for a fish supper. Venus' lack of arms prevents her from attracting a modern beau, although she finds no such trouble when similarly revived from stone as Ava Gardner in *One Touch of Venus* (1948). In *Down to Earth* (1947), Alexander Hall's partial sequel to *Mr. Jordan*, Muse Rita Hayworth receives a similarly warm welcome from red-blooded mortal men, for reasons abundantly displayed by Salma Hayek's artistically frustrated goddess turned table dancer in *Dogma*.

The Gods of the pre–Christian pantheon seem most at home when restricted to their own time and place, chilling on Olympus in epic fantasies like *Clash of the Titans*. Edwin Bower Hesser's silent *The Triumph of Venus* (1918) was possibly the first sustained dramatization of the Greco-Roman immortals' luxurious existence, before Italy's revival of the costume epic in the '60s gave dementedly askew accounts of classical myth, like Giorgio Ferroni's *The Bacchantes* (1961), Emimmo Salvi's *Vulcano, figlio di Giove* (*Vulcan, Son of Jupiter*) (1962) and Marcello Baldi's *Marte, dio della guerra* (*Venus Meets the Son of Hercules*) (1963).

Occasionally the gods can find a place on Earth, like Arnold Schwarzenegger's dopey demi-god in Arthur A. Seidelman's embarrassing *Hercules in New York* (1969). More typically they are an endangered species in the modern world, like the Wild West folk heroes of Jeremiah Chechik's *Tall Tale* (1994), who have been hiding out in the real world since the industrial revolution. In Harry Kumel's Belgian curio *Malpertuis* (1971), Orson Welles' Zeus-like patriarch discovers the last of the Greek immortals living on an island in the Ionian Sea. Having had them stuffed in living human bodies, he lets them roam the labyrinthine halls of his ancestral home. Euryale (Susan Hampshire), one of the Gorgon sisters, turns her lovers to stone while Prometheus, the fire-stealing Titan, frets about keeping the gas lamps lit and converses with a tiny tribe of squeaking humans.

The ultimate poetic conflict between man and god takes place in *Prometheus*

(1998), an ingenious update of Aeschylus' play, written and directed by acclaimed poet Tony Harrison. Written almost entirely in rhyming couplet, the film opens on a bleak Yorkshire coal town, whose last pit faces closure. ("Why you might ask should Gods come — into this world of 'Ee, by gum?'") At the misanthropic decree of Zeus, the unemployed miners are carried away like cattle inside a sealed truck and melted down into a huge golden likeness of the eponymous Titan, his right arm raised in a striker's fist. In an abandoned cinema, a defiant old man (Walter Sparrow) confronts Zeus' disdainful spin doctor, Hermes (Michael Feast, splendidly effete in his mithril boiler suit).

The gods intend to blacken humanity's name by ferrying Prometheus' golden likeness to the sites in Europe where his fire has wrought the most havoc: the bomb-sites of Dresden, the ovens of Auschwitz and the wastelands of Krakow. The irresistible power of the gods meets the immovable stubbornness of mankind. Hermes stokes the fires of human greed to bring down the ideals of socialism, while the old man doggedly argues the case for humanity's diligence and pride. The film's abstract depiction of coal-town Yorkshire, with its slagheaps, chimneys and scrap yards, is a landscape rendered as exhilaratingly mythic as anything in epic fantasies like *Jason and the Argonauts*. The Humber Bridge becomes the harp of Hermes, beneath which drift the daughters of Oceanus— miners' wives who worked at the fish market, transformed into a chorus of gaping silver mannequins on a wooden palette. ("This choir's just Zeus's little quirk — they handled scales so well at work.")

Prometheus creates an earthbound world where the gods and mankind intermingle as freely as they do in fairy tale, heroic and epic fantasy. These nostalgic genres take place before science separated mankind from magic, after which the fantastic can only return the real world through the medium of belief. Although belief remains less of a necessity when its focus is based on certainty. Our images of the Grim Reaper, the cowled, scythe-wielding skeleton who severs us from our mortal coil, is not so much our creation as a personification of an existing force. Here the visitor from beyond helps us come to terms not with a spiritual *possibility*, but a physical *certainty*.

Hailing from some negative zone between life and whatever comes after, the Grim Reaper visited Earth on film (appropriately enough) long before angels and devils. Death was ingrained in the shrill landscapes and clawing shadows of German Expressionism, but was given pallid human form in two early gothic fairy tales, *The Sea's Shadow* (1912) and Fritz Lang's *Der müde Tod* (1921). Lang also wrote a thematic quartet of silent gothic fantasies, all centering on the figure of Death. In *Hilde Warren und der Tod* (1917), the world-weary Reaper (played by Lang) urges a woman to kill her newborn child before it grows up to become a murderer. *Lilith und Ly* (1919) has Death's vampiric presence inhabit a magic mirror. *Die Pest in Florenz* (*The Plague in Florence*) (1919) reinvents Poe's Red Death as Marga Kierska's *femme fatale*. *Totentanz* (*Dance of Death*) (1919) features Sascha Gura as another female Reaper.

While these films wallow in the horror of exiting this world at death's insistence, Victor Sjöström's Swedish silent film *Korkarlen* (*Thy Soul Shall Bear Witness!*) (1920) considers the horror of what may await us on the other side. Based on European legend (and filmed again by Julien Duvivier in France in 1939 and by Arne Mattsen in Sweden in 1958), the film tells a moralizing tale similar to *It's a Wonderful Life*. A drunken reprobate becomes the last man to die on New Year's Eve, condemning him to drive a ghostly cart; the creaking of its wheels are the last thing heard by the souls he is now bound to collect. But after a friendly ghost reveals a vision of the misery he caused during life, he awakes from what was all a dream and resolves to make amends.

In Hollywood's *Death Takes a Holiday* (1934), directed by Mitchell Leisen, the Grim Reaper materializes on Earth in the form of an aristocratic Fredric March and falls in love with another man's fiancée, who willingly joins him as his consort in the spirit realm. March's Death effectively learns the value of the lives he takes. In Harold S. Bucquet's *On Borrowed Time* (1939), it's the film's mortal characters who learn to accept the inevitability of death. Cedric Hardwicke's "Mr. Brink" becomes magically ensnared by Lionel Barrymore's apple tree. As in *Holiday*, death's absence from its celestial duty means no one on Earth can die; for this same reason, Barrymore is persuaded to release Brink when his grandson is left in living agony after an accident that should have killed him. The fact that everyone must face death at some time is the bitterest pill a visitor from beyond movie can ask any audience to swallow. Few do so as candidly as *On Borrowed Time*.

Influenced by both these films, *Here Comes Mr. Jordan* is also about bereavement, as Jordan snuffs out the former identity of the hero once he has hopped into his final body. In a telling scene he also makes reference to his duty as a collector of souls, describing the gruesome manner of a man's passing with an ominously accustomed offhandedness. It becomes clear that Jordan is no mere angel, but an incarnation of Death, whose Charon-like duty it is to oversee the ferrying of souls into the afterlife. For all its merriment, *Here Comes Mr. Jordan* does not swerve from the assertion that what Jordan describes as "destiny" is irrevocable, bringing an unexpectedly portentous tone to the film's seemingly jaunty title. The film implies we can never understand death, only accept it.

While Death finds its opponent force cheerfully embodied in the baby-delivering gannet of Cyril Endfield's *Stork Bites Man* (1947), levity has always been the easiest way to convince an audience not to fear the Reaper. The solemnity of Death in Bergman's *The Seventh Seal* has lent satirical ammunition to several films. Woody Allen's hapless Napoleonic soldier is given a bony shoulder to cry on in *Love and Death* (1975), while a fearsome specter rudely interrupts dinner in *Monty Python's The Meaning of Life* (1983). While Ian McKellen's Death walks out on his own movie in *The Last Action Hero*, Bergman's film is given its most sustained ribbing in Peter Hewitt's likable afterlife comedy *Bill and Ted's Bogus Journey* (1991). "How's it hanging, Death?" Keanu Reeves and Alex Winter's deceased headbangers enquire of William Sadler's appropriately Nordic Reaper, who reveals a hilariously petulant streak when the idiotic pair beat him at Battleship.

Bill and Ted's Reaper is endearing simply because he's human enough to fall for a well-timed wedgie and boast about how many calories he burns while reaping. Alex Proyas's *The Crow* (1994) puts this humanizing process into reverse. Brandon Lee willingly accepts the mantle of Death rejected by the lost souls of the *Korkalen* films, heaving himself out of his grave to massacre the scumbags who put him and his girl-friend in the ground. Both an angel figure and an avatar of Death, Lee's unkillable zombie rocker takes a homicidal route to restoring moral order, dehumanizing himself in order to do so by ritualistically squeezing into black fetish wear and painting on a Pierrot death mask.

In *Meet Joe Black* (1998), Martin Brest's ponderous remake of *Death Takes a Holiday*, Death exchanges Brandon Lee's "mime from Hell" grin for Brad Pitt's farm boy pout. (The movie's metaphysical reassurance lies mainly in its guarantee that Death has a cute butt.) Death remains, however, implacable, no matter how personified, performing its task regardless of how we feel about it, and regardless of the faces we give it.

In the spectrum of "visitor from beyond" movies, Death stands at the perceptual divide between faith in religion and suspension of disbelief in fantasy. Since no proof is needed of its existence (or at least of the end result that defines it), believing in death in the real world is as pointless as believing in the weather. On film we accept the Grim Reaper as a fictional personification of a force existing in the real world. Depending on individual belief, a similar view may be taken regarding movie depictions of God, His angels and the Devil. A visitor from beyond like Santa Claus, however, can only be accepted as real by the other characters in his films. Not many people in the real world over the age of nine still believe in him, any more than they do in Dracula. Thus Santa occupies the same perceptual zone as the rest of fantasy; that is, he's accepted as real only within the perimeters of a given story. The exception to this rule is of course Edmund Gwenn's is-he-or-isn't-he Kris Kringle in George Seaton's *Miracle on 34th Street* (1947), an ambiguous non-fantasy that illustrates the real world issue of belief in the supernatural, in the same way as Mark Joffe's facetious courtroom drama *The Man Who Sued God* (2001).

Inhabiting an isolated polar Faerie, Santa Claus is generally portrayed as objectively as any other visitor from beyond. He featured in several silent trick films, before his screen revival in the '60s, in low budget whack-jobs like René Cardona's cult Mexican quickie *Santa Claus* (1959), in which he teams up with Merlin to save Christmas from a trick-or-treat Devil. Santa also endured self-explanatory adventures in *Santa Claus Conquers the Martians* (1964), *Santa Visits the Land of Mother Goose* (1967) and *Santa and the Ice Cream Bunny* (1972). As if teaming up with Jim Varney in *Ernest Saves Christmas* (1988) wasn't punishment enough, Santa is also forced to dole out sickly-sweet pap alongside Harry Dean Stanton's guardian angel in *One Magic Christmas* (1985), before starring in the ultimate "vs." movie, Trey Parker and Matt Stone's *Santa vs. Jesus* (1995).

A more appropriate face-off than one might imagine, this *South Park* prototype can be seen as a valid retort to Santa's biggest screen vehicle outside *Miracle on 34th Street* and its 1994 remake. Jeannot Szwarc's luxuriously nauseating *Santa Claus: The Movie* (1985) proposes that Santa was once a kindly woodcutter who froze to death in a blizzard. He was resurrected by the light of the North Star and greeted by a team of bearded gnomes (got up like shop assistants on grotto duty), who bless him with the immortality required to deliver their yearly payload of wooden toys. Even less convincing than the film's stab at mythmaking is a hypocritical scene in which Santa (David Huddleston) makes a disheartened fireside speech about the commercialization of the holiday, in a film that makes several blatant plugs for multinational sponsors.

The film's divided loyalties illustrate how the virtue of generosity celebrated by the Santa myth has been canonized to serve human greed. Even the much-loved *Miracle on 34th Street* supports this idea, as "Santa's" innate honesty brings Macy's a thriving trade in sympathetic Christmas shoppers. Santa movies suggest that perhaps all visitors from beyond are in some way man-made, created by a belief in the human virtue or natural force they embody, and summoned to fulfill our spiritual needs. The concept of the imaginary friend, a visitor from beyond resulting from individual rather than cultural belief, bears out this idea.

For an imaginary friend movie to be qualified as fantasy, the visitor's presence must be confirmed as real, in which case they are not imaginary at all. In Don Hartman's *It Had to Be You* (1947), Ginger Rogers' suppressed memory of a childhood sweetheart takes the corporeal form of a gruff American Indian, whom she introduces to her friends as "George." Henry Koster's *Harvey* (1950) boasts cinema's most famous imaginary friend, a 6'3" rabbit in a bow tie who attends a pensive James Stewart. Despite popular regard as to the ambiguity of Harvey's existence, the film slips off the rationalist tightrope and into fantasy at one point by having the invisible rabbit open a door. By contrast, Ate De Jong's bilious *Drop Dead Fred* (1991) makes the existence of Phoebe Cates' frenetic childhood pal (Rick Mayall) deafeningly obvious from the start.

The imaginary friends of Tony Scott's *True Romance* (1993), David Fincher's *Fight Club* (1999) and Woody Allen's *Play It Again, Sam* (1972) and *Mighty Aphrodite* (1995) are all confirmed to be manifestations of the protagonist's troubled psyche, visible only to their creator. Nonetheless, these underline the power of belief that enervates not only the visitor from beyond, but also fantasy itself. In Allen's films, the neurotic hero seeks romantic encouragement from a monochrome Humphrey Bogart and F. Murray Abraham's Socratic Greek. Christian Slater heeds the murderous advice of a ghostly Sun Records Elvis (Val Kilmer) in *True Romance*, while Edward Norton in *Fight Club* is driven to create an anti-heroic alter ego in the form of pugilist guru Tyler Durden (Brad Pitt). While Woody Allen wittily expresses the liberating power of fantasy, *True Romance* and particularly *Fight Club* warn of slavery to it.

The Yard Sale of the Gods: Artifact Movies

Artifacts are those odds and ends that look as though they could do a lot more than lie around looking interesting. Scattered around the Aladdin's caves, wizard's lairs and king's tombs of fantasy, these seemingly innocuous knick-knacks may be just about anything—a ring, a wand, a statue, even a car—but all of them in some way harness powerful forces, focusing them into performing a specific, repeatable feat of magic.

In fairy tale, these items are often awarded to the vulnerable young hero—Dorothy's ruby slippers for example, which protect her from the Wicked Witch and teleport her back to Kansas with three clicks of the heels. Otherwise, an artifact may be some magical totem or gadget, like the Witch's broomstick or her crystal ball. In the more realistic world of epic fantasy, such paraphernalia is more conspicuous, often motivating a quest plot in the form of McGuffins like the earth-powered sword of *Excalibur* or the malignant trinket of *The Lord of the Rings*. In earthbound fantasy, where the worlds of magic have faded to make way for the banality of mankind, the artifacts of the old world may remain in the forgotten corners of the new. Here they await recovery, when the dust of the ages will be shaken away and their ancient magic summoned into the modern world.

When *Arabian Nights* tales were in vogue during the silent era, they provided the first cohesive secondary world for movies to expound what might happen should one of fairy tale's *objet du fantastique* fall into the hands of twentieth century man. *Aladdin's Other Lamp* (1917) was the first to find out, as a young foundling (Viola Dana) dreams of buying Aladdin's lamp, which her dead father recovered during his days at sea. Having summoned the lamp's resident genie (Augustus Phillips), the ancient spirit renovates the girl's apartments, restores her guardian's missing leg and turns her disagreeable landlady into a rag doll.

The artifacts of the British *Alf* movies also made the promise of immediate wish fulfillment. In the first of these popular comedies, based on the morale-boosting WWI serial by W.A. Darlington, Aladdin's famous lamp has been melted down into a button on the uniform of a beleaguered British Tommy (Leslie Henson). But military duties are made harder rather than easier when a diligent polish summons a genie decidedly lacking in wits (James Carew). The film was remade as a talkie in 1930, with music hall duo Jimmy Nervo and Teddy Knox, before the Palladium's "Crazy Gang" made a naval-themed sequel, *Alf's Button Afloat* (1938). In *Alf's Carpet* (1929), a sequel to the silent original, a pair of London busmen fly to Arabia to rescue a kidnapped professor. A similar airborne rug headlines Columbia's desert romance *The Magic Carpet* (1951), allowing John Agar and Lucille Ball to pester Raymond Burr's evil caliph into submission.

The mysterious East continued to yield potent gizmos in western earthbound fantasy. A gargoyle-killing Tibetan dagger resolves the plot of *The Golden Child* (1986), while a Chinese amulet raises the dead, as well as granting them comic-book superpowers, in the dismal Jackie Chan actioner *The Medallion* (2003). With publicity like this, Africa became the destination of choice for Indiana Jones wannabes. Angelina Jolie's Lara Croft uncovers the embryonic cradle of life in the 2003 *Tomb Raider* sequel, while Brendan Fraser retrieves a diamond capable of transforming the world's population into chimpanzees in Joe Dante's *Looney Tunes: Back in Action* (2003). These movies either conceitedly assume the lands most likely to harbor artifacts are those apparently least civilized, or rather those cultures still in touch with their founding mythologies. Yet the natives of these lands may not regard primeval magic as entirely benign themselves. In Marshall Neilan's *The Bottle Imp* (1917), a silent adaptation of Robert Louis Stevenson's novel, a Hawaiian fisherman must rid himself of a cursed wishing bottle containing an irate volcano god.

Although such American films generally require a dramatic clash between Western culture and the atavistic past it lacks, some films find clever ways of mythologizing modern Americana. In Arthur Lubin's *It Grows on Trees* (1952), a fortune in ten dollar bills sprouts in place of leaves in the backyard of a destitute family, who are dismayed to find that (like Faerie gold) the loot crumbles to ash before they can spend it. Accurately unearthed on American shores, the eponymous Viking visor of Chuck Russell's *The Mask* (1994) turns Jim Carrey's lowly clerk into a zoot-suited, jabber-jawed hobgoblin. A shabby pair of sneakers are the relics of a modern-day god in John Schultz's *Like Mike* (2002). Donated to an orphanage and hit by lightning, they confer the gravity-defying skills of basketball legend Michael Jordan onto a scrawny 14-year-old.

Each of these artifacts confers some power or wizard-like ability on its owner, who must at some point in the film relinquish their talisman and run the story's vital last mile on their own. Even invincible superheroes like RoboCop and Brandon Lee's spooky vigilante in *The Crow* are restored to a semblance of their original humanity before their adventures conclude, illustrating Goethe's lesson that happiness will remain out of man's reach all the while he retains the stature of a god. Should these heroes not let go of that which grants them preternatural powers, they will become as damned as Marlowe's Faust or Tolkien's Gollum, who becomes as inhuman as the artifact that empowers him.

In Mark Tarlov's deluded romantic fantasy *Simply Irresistible* (1999), Sarah Michelle Gellar's aspiring chef buys (of all things) a magic crab. While never making it clear exactly what this enchanted crustacean is supposed to do (becoming an unreasoned excuse for everything, from levitating above the kitchen floor to ecstasy-inducing fog billowing out of the crème brûlée), Gellar never casts aside her magic crutch. She remains apparently unaware that her newfound cooking skills are not her own, achieving only a false sense of self-worth that itself will only last until someone decides to make a salad out of her magic pet.

Like Gellar's manipulated heroine, most artifacts have no will of their own, remaining mere plot devices. Some, however, contain so much magic they actually have a hand in the plot along with the characters. Like Sauron's ring and King Arthur's sword, the antique board game excavated in Joe Johnston's *Jumanji* (1995) possesses a life of its own. Luring new players with an ominous drumming only kids can hear, the game unleashes a stampede of destructive jungle creatures from its primeval pocket-world, even turning one player into a monkey for attempting to cheat. The ability of these artifacts to guide the plot to their preference effectively renders them characters unto themselves, like the belligerent clutter of R.W. Paul's 1901 trick film *The Haunted Curiosity Shop*, in which an antique sword, a flying skull and a nimble mummy violently upstage their human co-star.

The animated films of Jan Švankmajer explore this seeming interchange between humans and objects. In the Czech surrealist's short films *Spiel mit Steinen* (*A Game with Stones*) (1965), *Rakvičkárna* (*Punch and Judy*) (1966) and *Historia Naturae* (1967), animated objects take on a human likeness, while in his features *Alice* and *Faust* and his sex comedy *Spiklenci slasti* (*Conspirators of Pleasure*) (1996), human beings assume the appearance of objects. Švankmajer selects his junk-shop bric-a-brac carefully.

The cutlery, ornaments and furniture that litter the playroom in *Alice*, for example, have all been textured by time and use, suggesting a history as individual as the people who once owned them.

Conspirators of Pleasure also expresses secret lives through animation. We watch as several urbanites surreptitiously construct fetishistic artifacts, which come to life when their owners indulge in surrealistic perversions. A rooster costume allows a lonely man to take to the air, while his lovelorn landlady whips the cringing straw effigy of her tenant. Spiky rolling pins move of their own accord up and down the naked body of the chief of police. A news agent besotted with a female news reader succumbs to the caresses of the mechanical arms he has attached to the side of his TV. A postmistress achieves Tantric ecstasy by snorting dough-balls.

These bizarre sexual artifacts bear an unlikely similarity to the soulful Volkswagen of Disney's mawkish *The Love Bug* (1968). After "Herbie" has adopted Dean Jones as his new owner, the initially skeptical racing driver concedes that some cars may indeed run on human affection. His chubby pal (Buddy Hackett), recently returned from a spiritual sojourn in Tibet, suggests that this energizing magic may be encouraging a rebellious spirit among the machines of the world. However, the revolution feared by Hackett (and all those technophobic sci-fi movies) seems unlikely to amount to much here. Herbie restricts his independence to racing around hippie-infested San Francisco, urinating oil on people he doesn't like, getting drunk on Irish coffee, and attempting to drive off the Golden Gate Bridge in a fit of depression.

In the more colorfully benign sequel *Herbie Rides Again* (1974), he prevents the eviction of a nice old lady (Helen Hayes) who keeps company with an unruly Wurlitzer and a retired cable car that dings its bell in greeting. Herbie routs Keenan Wynn's enraged property developer by rallying a fleet of similarly sentimental VWs. These artifacts are simply another put-upon minority, but one that (provided we're nice to the Helen Hayeses of this world) may one day treat us as supportively as the gnomic freeway sign that converses with Steve Martin in Mick Jackson's *L.A. Story* (1991). These living artifacts are a far cry from the rampaging cyborgs stomping our charred bones to dust in the *Terminator* movies, although a world of hackneyed comical astonishment and insufferably chipper Mexican urchins, envisioned by *Herbie Goes to Monte Carlo* (1979) and *Herbie Goes Bananas* (1980), has nightmare implications of its own.

As a general rule, the more an artifact resembles a human being the more likely it is to come to life and behave like one. Statues in particular have a habit of doing this. While the descendents of the clay automata of the *Golem* films find unsuccessful employment guarding temples from the likes of Sinbad and Lara Croft, the goddess revived from stone in the Pygmalion myth has made a couple of appearances outside *My Fair Lady*. In William A. Seiter's *One Touch of Venus* (1948), an Anatolian marble, reputed to have had life breathed into it by Zeus, is kissed by a tipsy window dresser (Robert Walker) and becomes the gypsy-eyed Ava Gardner. Owing much to this film, Michael Gottlieb's very '80s *Mannequin* (1987) has Kim Cattrall's Egyptian feminist unfortunately reincarnated as a shop window dummy. The story is recycled even less successfully in the sequel, *Mannequin on the Move* (1991).

Nothing's gonna stop us now: Erstwhile sculptor Jonathan (Andrew McCarthy) enjoys an intimate moment with a shop window dummy (soon to become Kim Cattrall) in Michael Gottlieb's
'80s-tastic artifact movie *Mannequin* (Gladden/20th Century–Fox, 1987).

Toys have been most fruitfully exploited as living artifacts. Adults project a wilful personality onto obstinate cars and computers, just as credulous children see beloved dolls and Teddy bears as somehow sentient. The movies gave this notion credence early on in several British trick films, among them Cecil Hepworth's *The Doll's Revenge* (1907). A little boy spitefully breaks his sister's dolly, which mends itself, grows to monstrous proportions and eats him. In the American silent *The Dream Doll* (1917), a potion capable of bringing toys to life successfully turns a young girl into a doll, literalizing the idea in A.A. Milne's *Winnie the Pooh* that Christopher Robin's stuffed and stitched companions are as much children as their owner.

The disparity in size between a child and his toys, which favors the child as an adult figure, is turned into a poignant tale of responsibility in Frank Oz's *The Indian in the Cupboard* (1995), based on the books by Lynne Reid Banks. On his birthday, nine-year-old Omri (Hal Scardino) receives a mysterious medicine cabinet that brings to life a toy Indian he locks inside. This tiny Iroquois man, named Little Bear (well-played by Native American rapper Litefoot), at first regards the Brobdingnagian Omri as some kind of monster. But the film nicely reaffirms their adult/child status when Omri recoils from the tiny corpse of an elderly Mohawk, whom he inadvertently frightens to death after reviving him from plastic.

It transpires that Little Bear is not actually a living toy, but a real man, yanked out of the eighteenth century and miniaturized. In an intriguing scene we learn that the cupboard is apparently capable of taking characters out of universes other than our own. Omri eagerly converts a boxful of toys into a striking pop-culture tableau,

Young Omri (Hal Scardino) learns that life's about more than being alive as he toys with the life-giving artifact of Frank Oz's *The Indian in the Cupboard* (Columbia, 1995).

in which G.I. Joe trades blows with RoboCop, and Darth Vader fends off a *Jurassic Park* T-Rex with his light-saber. After a friend thoughtlessly converts a plastic cowboy into a soft-hearted but Indian-hating sot who threatens Little Bear's life, Omri becomes the parent forced to care for the combative Lilliputians he has brought into the world. The rites-of passage ritual that Little Bear was helping a nephew undertake before he disappeared becomes Omri's own.

Pixar's computer-animated *Toy Story* (1995) takes the Pinocchio effect of *Indian* a step further, pushing aside human characters (who are essentially narrative ballast anyway in artifact movies like *Jumanji* and *Herbie*), focusing instead on an entire race of living artifacts. Stranded at the gas station after squabbling over who has the right to accompany Andy, their child owner, on a trip to the pizza parlor, Woody, a tatty cowboy doll (voiced by Tom Hanks), and Buzz Lightyear, a space-age action figure (Tim Allen), reveal a Lilliputian world in which their utmost concern is survival. Not only must they avoid getting trampled by passing traffic or mercilessly dismantled by a toy-torturing delinquent, the toys must also remain in Andy's affections, acknowledging (as parents of the film's child audience know all to well) that today's cherished (and costly!) possessions are rejects in tomorrow's yard sale.

Artifacts in earthbound fantasy must be lost in order to be found, and an adventure begun. *Toy Story 2* (1999) explores this sense of abandonment from the view of the artifact itself. Jessie, a collectible yodelling cowgirl doll (Joan Cusack), explains to a dejected Woody that he must face up to the certainty that he will one day be forgotten, his tragedy being never to forget the parent-owners who once loved him. Yet given the choice of existing in stasis as a museum piece or living out his few remaining years with Andy, Woody bravely opts for his romantic doom. The film correctly affirms that belief, however fleeting, is the magic spark that energizes human fantasy. Without it, the imagination is just a dusty lamp waiting to unleash a genie.

Foreign Bodies: Bodyswap Fantasy

The Hindu concept of reincarnation informs one of the most popular devices of American earthbound fantasy. The idea proposes that an eternal soul revisits our world several times in several different forms, each experience further loosening that soul's grip on earthly fixations, preparing it to comprehend a vision of God. The Christian equivalent of reincarnation is purgatory, like the 16-year stretch endured by Charles Boyer's disreputable circus barker in Fritz Lang's *Lilliom* (1935). Having suffered in order to purge himself of pride, the eponymous Lilliom earns a single day of earthly parole, his behavior determining his future quality of afterlife.

All four film versions of Ferenc Molnár's 1909 play (Lang's, Frank Borzage's in 1930, the 1921 silent *A Trip to Paradise* and Henry King's 1956 musical *Carousel*) hide a thoroughly Christian morality beneath their whimsical eschatologies. Yet all are ostensibly governed by the Eastern concept of karma, the moral law of cause and effect, which states that our actions in one life will affect our future in the next. Like Lilliom, murdered mobster Eddie Kagle (Paul Muni), in *Angel on My Shoulder* (1946) is also given a chance to reform, when the Devil (Claude Rains) fuses his soul with the body of an incorruptible judge. Although Eddie eventually has to return to Hell, his earthly exploits in the judge's body bring him a step closer to redemption, as he nobly refuses to take revenge on the double-crosser who did him in. Similar steps to spiritual healing are taken in Emile Arddino's weepy *Chances Are* (1989), as a grieving widow (Cybill Shepherd) comes to terms with the death of her husband, reincarnated as her daughter's teenage boyfriend (Robert Downey, Jr.). Similarly, Troy Miller's placid family comedy *Jack Frost* (1998) has a departed dad (Michael Keaton) return from beyond to spend a final winter with his son in the form of a cuddly CGI snowman. Wistful reincarnation dramas like these concern essentially Christian souls granted time and a physical form in which to settle their earthly affairs before moving on. However, the majority of bodyswappers are not ready to take the plunge into the next world just yet.

In Warren Beatty and Buck Henry's marshmallow *Heaven Can Wait* (1978), the first remake of *Here Comes Mr. Jordan*, Beatty's Joe Pendleton (like Robert Montgomery's before him) is the victim of a Heavenly glitch and therefore not officially dead. Upon finding out that Joe's mortal remains have been cremated, Mr. Jordan (played here by James Mason) allows him to take up temporary residence in the body of a billionaire scheduled to be bumped off by his adulterous wife. Unlike Eddie in *Angel on My Shoulder*, Joe lives out his new life not for the benefit of a karmicly determined future, but to re-evaluate his present condition. Produced in the Watergate era, *Heaven Can Wait* briefly explores an angle that goes untouched in *Mr. Jordan*, as the bemused Beatty becomes the voice of the common man suddenly elevated to a position of authority. Exposing the suspect politics of the '70s with the downhome honesty of the '40s, Beatty reveals the corruption within the company belonging to his host body. But since Beatty's remake re-casts Joe as a celebrity quarterback, the class divide between him and the billionaire's body he assumes is significantly narrower than before.

Lending a voice to the blue-collar underdog by way of reincarnation was first achieved in the silent *The Spirit of the Conqueror* (1914), in which the souls of historical dignitaries settle an earthly labor dispute by the unusual method of reincarnating Napoleon Bonaparte as the son of a corrupt financier. Eight decades later, in *Mr. Jordan*'s second flyweight remake, the Weitz brothers' *Down to Earth* (2001), the working class wish to be king for a day is interestingly fulfilled by making its reincarnatee a black man (Chris Rock). But the film scuppers its own good idea by retaining the narrative rules of the first two movies. Like Montgomery and Beatty before him, Rock retains his own features in the eyes of the audience, while everyone else sees him as the crusty old white guy he has become, albeit with the moves and banter of a sharp young black man. This makes it difficult to see the funny side when Rock provokes horrified gasps at an all-black comedy club, or gets his lights punched out for waving gang signs to the tune of *DMX*.

To walk a mile not only in someone else's shoes but in their entire body, a character doesn't have to be dead or even half dead; in fact, most bodyswap fantasies are upbeat comedies that prefer to keep their protagonists alive as much as possible. The trick of transferring someone into a body they were not born in is often achieved in movies through the agency of a magical artifact. In Disney's *The Shaggy Dog* (1959), a glowing scarab ring sucks a teenage nerd into the body of a nearby sheepdog. In the first *Vice Versa* movie (1948), the eye of an Indian jackal god misgrants wishes in the tradition of W.W. Jacobs' horror tale *The Monkey's Paw*, while in Tom Bradley's rather sleazy *The Hot Chick* (2002) a pair of Abyssinian earrings switch the bodies of Rob Schneider's petty thief and Rachel McAdams's high school cheerleader. But whether contrived through a magical artifact, reincarnation after death, or for no reason at all, the purpose of the bodyswap remains the same, to literally see the world through the eyes of another.

Awaking one morning from troubled dreams to find oneself transformed into an animal is a Kafkaesque premise whose full potential remains unexplored in movies. Such interspecies bodyswapping rarely makes an exchange beyond the canine. In Lou Breslow's *You Never Can Tell* (1951), Dick Powell plays a faithful Alsatian murdered after inheriting a fortune and reincarnated as a P.I. Joe Camp's *Oh, Heavenly Dog* (1980) reverses the premise by reincarnating Chevy Chase's murdered P.I. as Jane Seymour's pet pooch. At least the poster for *The Shaggy Dog* had a witty exploitation tagline ("I Was a Teenage Boy!"), while its sequel *The Shaggy DA* (1976) employs doggy mayhem to poke fun at post–Watergate politics even less successfully than *The Werewolf of Washington* (1973). Carlo Carlei's farcical revenge-thriller *Fluke* (1995) is another man-becomes-dog movie. Derived somehow from James Herbert's bleak horror novel, the film has a murdered Matthew Modine seeking grim recompense while in the unhelpfully adorable form of an abandoned puppy.

Horror movies like *The Fly* (1986) and *Ginger Snaps* (2000) afflict their protagonists with bestial degenerations, while fantasy films have yielded few comparably compelling results beyond Rene Auberjonois turning into a bird while narrating *Brewster McCloud* and the nerd-to-mythical beast conversion of *Flight of Dragons*. The genre's most entertaining man-to-beast makeover takes place in Steve Barron's dry absurdist comedy *Rat* (2000). Pete Postlethwaite plays Dublin deliveryman Hubert Flynn, who spends more time with Guinness and betting slips than he does with his family. One afternoon he emerges from his empty shirt collar in the appropriate form of a rat. Much to the annoyance of his shrewish wife (an outstanding Imelda Staunton), her rodent husband refuses to speak to the devious journo (David Wilmot) who plans to write an exploitative bestseller based on the Flynns' predicament. While a know-it-all uncle comes up with a number of sensible suggestions ("He'll have to give up the job. People doesn't want their bread delivered by a rat!"), the rest of the family are unsure whether Hubert's humanity is still intact.

The film scores most of its laughs while maintaining this ambiguity, before Hubert learns his lesson and returns to normal, describing life as a rat as preferable to being human. In the meantime, his family have become rather like animals themselves, discussing the pros and cons of murdering and exploiting him. The film's suggestion that a man may find peace if he were an animal implies that man's own beastliness is perfectly natural. Disney's eco-friendly animated feature *Brother Bear* (2003) takes this idea to its logical conclusion, as a transformed Native American decides to remain in his adopted animal form. Perhaps this is why the animal bodyswap genre is so undernourished — because there is little dramatic friction to be had in returning to so natural a state. Those bodyswaps that set up the most intriguing conflicts are usually those perceived as the most unnatural.

Before the sexual revolution, swapping one's gender for another was considered a daring affront to notions of conformity. Even when contrived through make-believe rather than surgery, movies had to negotiate such exchanges with extreme caution. Set in a coastal hotel, Sidney Drew's *A Florida Enchantment* (1914) is a silent farce that makes the audaciously modern suggestion that the sexual orientations of its characters are as variable as the bodies they exchange. A woman exacts revenge on her philandering husband using a seed from the "Tree of Sexual Change" to turn herself into a man. Without bothering to change out of her summer dress, she willingly takes to flirting with women, and turns a hapless maid into a horny bellhop. The movie absolves its rampant gender-bending with the get-out clause of an it-was-all-a-dream ending. The punchline of Hal Roach's husband-and-wife-switching *Turnabout* (1940), based on Thorne Smith's novel, offended the censors by leaving the husband pregnant after his transformation back into a man.

By the '60s, Vincente Minnelli's sour *Goodbye Charlie* (1964) was considered less subversive, but more misogynistic. Harry Madden's philandering playboy returns from his own murder in the form of Debbie Reynolds. Charlie takes to new sexual avenues as keenly as the transformed wife of *A Florida Enchantment*, seducing a millionaire mommy's boy, while sadistically blackmailing his previous conquests. His best friend (Tony Curtis) struggles with his own confused feelings towards Charlie's attractive new form. Is he merely lusting after the body of an eye-catching woman, or is he realizing hidden feelings he has had towards his friend all along? We never find out as Charlie is killed a second time and reincarnated as a vodka-drinking mutt.

Blake Edwards' obnoxious *Switch* (1991) updates this premise with Ellen Barkin as the misogynist reincarnated as a woman at the suggestion of the Devil. This feminist backlash was elegantly parried by Tilda Swinton's immortal Elizabethan in *Orlando*. Having failed his masculine duty of killing his fellow man in a foreign war, Lord Orlando inexplicably changes sex and suffers the prejudices espoused by her ignorant former self. Her new sex prohibits her by law from owning property, while the pretentious buffoons of the literary salons inform her that without the guidance of a father or a husband she is lost. Such imposed gender conformity is cleverly exceeded in Norman René's *Prelude to a Kiss* (1992). Here spiritual love transcends gender (as it does in the same-sex embrace of *Ghost*) and Alec Baldwin falls into a passionate soul-transferring clinch with the cancer-riddled old man who has stolen the soul of his wife (Meg Ryan).

Unlike the bodyswappers in man-to-beast or age-exchange films, characters in sex-switching fantasy rarely express the wish to change their bodies or explore new gender roles. But their subsequent transformations may fulfill some subconscious desire, a reluctant jaunt into a body of the opposite sex taking place in order to prevent a psychological schism. Many bodyswaps result from this unrealized desire for change, as the body mutates of its own accord.

Among female characters, this transformation is usually psychological, as a desire to take on a different identity becomes a form of mental vampirism. Like the ambiguous personality exchange that takes place between Bibi Andersson and Liv Ull-mann at the end of Bergman's *Persona* (1966), Robert Altman's equally enigmatic *Three Women* (1977) has Sissy Spacek absorb the personality of a self-obsessed Shel-ley Duvall. In Paul Aaron's *Maxie* (1985), the ghost of a failed starlet who died in the '20s takes another shot at stardom by periodically possessing the body of a young secretary (Glenn Close). David Lynch's *Mulholland Drive* (2001) also evokes the ghosts of old Hollywood, as an aspiring actress (Naomi Watts) falls in love with an amnesiac beauty (Laura Elena Harring) and inexplicably absorbs the life of the woman's dead twin.

Since men are supposedly less aware of the ebb and flow of their own bodies, any revolt from within will most likely be portrayed as malignant. The devilish alter ego of Roger Moore's repressed businessman in Basil Deardon's *The Man Who Haunted Himself* (1970) takes over his life and eventually chases him to his death. Moore's is a more malevolent doppelganger than the one mourned by Irene Jacob in Krzysztof Kieślowski's ambivalent *The Double Life of Véronique* (1991) or the help-ful double in the British comedy *The Man in the Mirror* (1936). In Bruce Robinson's panic-stricken *How to Get Ahead in Advertising* (1989), Richard E. Grant's increas-ingly unstable ad exec discovers a talkative boil, which eventually grows to substi-tute his own head. These castration anxieties are aggressively refuted, however, by Jamaa Fanaka's psychedelic blaxploitation movie *Welcome Home, Brother Charles* (*Soul Vengeance*) (1975). A convicted pimp (Marlo Monte) learns from a mystically inclined cellmate how to use his penis to hypnotize women and strangle anyone who gets too close to him in the prison showers.

Other films play male bodily distortion for laughs. In John Pasquin's *The Santa Clause* (1994), Tim Allen is subpoenaed by magical law to assume the mantle of St. Nick. Having gained 45 pounds overnight, as well as a craving for milk and cookies and an unshaveable white beard, Allen visits his doctor, who is perplexed to hear his patient's heart beat to the tune of *Jingle Bells*. Considerably less endearing is Tom Shadyac's mawkish Jim Carrey vehicle *Liar Liar* (1996), in which a child's birthday wish renders Carrey's bustling lawyer unable to speak anything but the truth for 24 hours. Most astute of these comedies is Woody Allen's ingenious mockumentary *Zelig* (1983), which observes a Jewish clerk, Leonard Zelig (Allen), who supposedly became a cultural phenomenon in the '20s as "the human chameleon." Devoid of personality himself, Zelig changes his personality and physical appearance to satisfy his own neurotic need to fit in (Allen's self-depreciating summary of his own diffident *oeuvre*).

In Carl Reiner's meandering screwball comedy *All of Me* (1984), the male body becomes a battleground for the war of the sexes. Eccentric lawyer Roger Cobb (Steve Martin) becomes half-possessed by the spirit of a dead client, Edwina Cutwater (Lili Tomlin), who controls one side of his body and frowns back at him whenever he looks in the mirror. Like *Liar Liar*, *All of Me* recognizes that the courtroom is the best place for a character who cannot shut his yap, but the movie's best joke takes place in the bedroom. As Roger tries to make it with Edwina's stable girl (Victoria Principal), her mortified employer intervenes, filling Roger's head with thoughts of elderly nuns and dead kittens. The joke is so funny the film cracks it twice, this time with the disembodied Edwina a willing participant, although her intrusive fantasizing puts Roger off his stroke. ("She's got the whole cast of *Gone with the Wind* humping in my head.")

Spike Jonze's ruthlessly inventive black comedy *Being John Malkovich* (1999) is the last word on this inter-body sex war, and perhaps on bodyswap fantasy itself. Unemployed puppeteer Craig Schwartz (John Cusack) crawls through a magic portal behind a filing cabinet and enters the mental cockpit of actor John Malkovich (sportingly playing himself). From here, Craig can view the world through the other man's eyes for 15 minutes before being spat into a ditch beside the New Jersey turnpike.

Charlie Kaufman's script relentlessly builds on this bizarre though simple premise, and goes one step further than the kinky two-in-a-body threesome almost perpetrated by *All of Me*. Craig's dowdy wife, Lotte (Cameron Diaz with frizzy mane and sagging stretch pants), falls in love with her husband's sardonic colleague, Maxine (Catherine Keener). Repulsed by Craig's own pathetic advances, Maxine lusts after Lotte, but only when she's encased in Malkovich's body. Craig jealously takes Lotte's place during one of the girls' bodyswapping liaisons and refuses to leave Malkovich's head, taking over the actor's life and using his fame to live out his own dreams. In a sarcastic comment on the shallow cult of celebrity, the same pretentious puppet shows that earned Craig a smack in the teeth on the streets of Manhattan win him worldwide adoration when he performs them as Malkovich.

The modern world presented in *Malkovich* is as weird and mutable as the pocket universe that opens out inside the actor's head. Here Lotte and Maxine make a gravity-defying scramble through the actor's suppressed memories, while a curious Malkovich himself enters a nightmarish bistro where diners and staff all wear his face. The film suggests the real world has caught up with bodyswap fantasy. Science now enables us to assume whatever form our neuroses desire, a prospect expressed as a fear of what our bodies may become in *Malkovich* and Maurizio Nichetti's Italian sex comedy *Volere, Volare* (1991), in which a dubbing artist (Nichetti) metamorphoses into a cartoon character.

Robert Zemeckis's ghoulish black comedy *Death Becomes Her* (1992) takes a righteous swipe at the destructive culture of plastic surgery. Two conceited showbiz rivals (Goldie Hawn and Meryl Streep) sip an immortality-conferring tonic that prevents them from dying, even after they are both gruesomely murdered. Much of the movie's shallow fun comes from watching a respectable actress like Streep totter about on broken legs, while her dislocated head flops from her neck like a football in a sock. Through the medium of CGI, her body becomes as amusingly pliable as the live-action cartoon characters of *The Flintstones* and *The Mask*. As Bruce Willis' spineless mortician vainly tries to repair Hawn and Streep's rapidly decaying though still mobile bodies, the search for immortality becomes a gross cosmic comedy. Hollywood's promise of everlasting life is mistakenly perceived as an everlasting body, rather than an everlasting image.

The body's most natural revolt against the mind, the aging process is the one most fiercely contested, not least because it concludes with death. It is perhaps overreaching to suggest a fear of decease lies at the heart of age-exchange pranks like the *Freaky Friday* movies, but the lesson they teach is one of acceptance, of submission to life's natural course, which must be taken at its own pace.

Based on F. Anstey's 1882 novel, Peter Ustinov's *Vice Versa* (1948) first established the now-familiar set-up. A stuffed shirt (Roger Livesey) idly wishes he could escape the attentions of a gold-digging chorus girl by returning to his school days, and is summarily transformed into a likeness of his son (Anthony Newley), who wishes in turn to take his father's place. Their uncomfortable experiences in each other's social spheres remind them of the futility of pursuing greener grass. Aleksandr Ptushko poetically reverses this idea in *A Tale of Lost Time* (1964), in which those adults who cherish their time on Earth become young, while the young who allow youth to be wasted on them become prematurely old. Most films after *Vice Versa*, however, merely employ an age-exchange as a chance to let their actors goof around in the manner of a rejuvenated Cary Grant and Ginger Rogers in Howard Hawks' sci-fi comedy *Monkey Business* (1952).

One of the two most influential movies in this subgenre is also the only movie to deal with the age gap between females. In Disney's *Freaky Friday* (1976), 13-year-old tomboy Annabel Andrews (Jodie Foster) and her exasperated mother (Barbara Harris) magically trade lives for a day. The results are predictable though occasionally amusing, with Mom almost pulling a Mrs. Robinson on the boy next door, while Annabel regards Dad's new secretary with icy disapproval. When the film reaches its moral conclusion, Annabel has learned to behave like a proper young lady, while Mom now appreciates the stresses of being a teenager (although her brief taste of youth's freedom fails to prompt her into re-evaluating her own domestication).

The sophisticated 2003 remake of *Freaky Friday* appeals simultaneously to the women who saw the first film when they were girls, as well as the daughters they have since raised. This time Disney ensures their mother and daughter double-act is as empowered as possible, with Mom a celebrity therapist and daughter an assertive rock chick. Movies like these rely heavily on their lead performers, typically with showier roles for the childish adults than for the suddenly responsible kids. As game as Barbara Harris in the original, Jamie Lee Curtis is well-matched by young Lindsay Lohan, whose fussiness and middle-aged dance moves are as funny as Curtis' teenage gait and morning-after shriek ("I'm like the Crypt Keeper!").

The other important age-exchange movie appeared in the middle of a brief cycle that sprang up in the late '80s, following TV's rediscovery of the original *Freaky Friday*. Penny Marshall's poignant *Big* (1988) emerged as a flower amid a field of weeds, including Rod Daniel's *Like Father, Like Son* (1987), Paul Flaherty's *18 Again!* (1988), Brian Gilbert's remake of *Vice Versa* (1988) and the Corey Feldman sci-fi comedy *Dream a Little Dream* (1989). Unlike its dud contemporaries, *Big* narrows its focus to the metamorphosis of a single body. At Coney Island, 12-year-old Josh Baskin discovers a creepy mechanical swami named Zoltar that grants his dejected wish to be "big." The next day, he wakes up in the body of an adult (Tom Hanks).

Eschewing the special effects that attend the transformations of so many other bodyswaps, *Big* works well primarily because its fantasy conceit is depicted so realistically. Josh's mom (Mercedes Ruehl) mistakes her terrified adult son for an intruder and chases him out of the house with a kitchen knife. A desperate appeal for help is misunderstood by Josh's streetwise best friend, Billy (Jared Rushton), who thinks he's being propositioned by a child molester. Josh's vulnerability and

Having found this spooky artifact tucked away at a travelling fair, 12-year-old Josh Baskin (David Moscow) makes a wish in Penny Marshall's moving bodyswap comedy *Big* (20th Century–Fox, 1988).

terror at his abandonment in the adult world is convincingly realized as he takes refuge in New York, tearfully cowering in the grubby bedroom of a sleazy hotel, amid a cacophony of gunshots, screams and sirens.

Until City Hall can track down Zoltar's carnival, Josh must remain in the adult world for six weeks, innocently showing up the pretense of the adult world in the meantime. He bluffs his way into working for a toy firm and makes friends with the company's gruff chairman (Robert Loggia), who, like Josh, finds the middle-age world of '80s yuppie culture bewilderingly meaningless. They have a tremendous scene together in FAO Schwarz, nimbly dancing out the tune of "Chopsticks" on an over-sized keyboard, a moment that captures the spontaneity of childhood better than anything in the contrived likes of *Toys* or *Santa Claus: The Movie*. Hanks' sensitive comic performance as the adult Josh renders entirely credible the effect his childishness has on those around him, particularly upon predatory career woman Susan (Elizabeth Perkins). At first attracted by Josh's success, Susan is disarmed by his apparent interest in her for reasons other than her body, and finally submits to his candid sincerity in a daring though delicate love scene.

A model age-exchange movie, *Big* achieves the trick of speaking directly to young and adult audiences alike. Although it views childhood through the gauze of nostalgia, the film refuses to underline the lessons learned by its older characters. Susan and her spiteful boyfriend (John Heard) are left to struggle on with their lives. Theirs is the world which young Josh's rites-of-passage has prepared him for. It is only when he commits to this complex sphere that he reaches the mature conclusion that he is not ready for it. In a touching finale, the child Josh and the adult Susan return to their separate worlds.

The Eighth Wonders of the World: Fantasy Creature Features

The possibility that strange creatures from a distant past may have survived into the twentieth century or beyond has long been a dominant theme of fantastic cinema. *The Lost World* (1925), based on the Arthur Conan Doyle bestseller, and the seminal *King Kong* (1933) were among the first sci-fi movies in which modern man discovered a long-extinct species existing somewhere in the unmapped reaches of the world. Later films drew upon contemporary reports of supposedly genuine prehistoric survivals, lending them credence in movies like *Bigfoot* (1969), *Baby: Secret of the Lost Legend* (1985) and *Loch Ness* (1994).

The creatures of fantasy, however, do not derive from provable prehistory, or from the laboratory of some latter-day Frankenstein. The mythical Hippogriffs, Jabberwocks and Manticores that escape into our world do so from a point in time that never was. The bygone imaginary worlds supposed by folklore and legend not only remain the source of inspiration for every ghoul and were-beast that ever stalked a horror film, but also furnish the generic secondary worlds of fairy tale, heroic and epic fantasy.

Among the first creatures native to these worlds found hiding out in the modern were the shape-shifting spirits of Middle Eastern folklore collectively known as genies. Having stowed away down the centuries inside various artifacts, these ethereal beings were first summoned to perform modern-day wish grantings in the silent *Aladdin's Other Lamp*, the British *Alf* movies and Gregory Ratoff's propagandist time-slip comedy *Where Do We Go from Here?* (1945). The only genie to rise above his traditionally schematic station was a bumbling Dick Shawn in George Sherman's spoof desert romance *The Wizard of Baghdad* (1960). Demoted to the rank of mortal, Shawn is sent to Earth from the spirit realm to sort out the usual business of the grand vizier usurping the caliph's throne. Equally unremarkable, but more respectable by dint of its source novel by F. Anstey, is Harry Keller's *The Brass Bottle* (1964), starring Burl Ives as the genie who emerges from the titular container to make life difficult for Tony Randall.

The idea of employing a wish-granting manservant inspired a male chauvinist spin a year later in TV's long-running *I Dream of Jeannie* (1965–70), with Barbara Eden as Larry Hagman's obedient bimbo. As if TV movie spin-offs *I Dream of Jeannie: 15 Years Later* (1985) and *I Still Dream of Jeannie* (1991) were not embarrassing enough for genie-kind, Geoffrey Lewis's dispossessed (Irish) djinn stumbles around L.A. searching for his lost bottle in Michael Marvin's execrable *Wishman* (1991). After Disney restored him to his former fairy tale glory in *Aladdin*, the god-awful *Wishmaster* series drove the genie into bargain-bin horror with the help of Andrew Divoff's wish-granting psycho.

Descendents of Hans Christian Andersen's Little Mermaid have enjoyed a more fruitful career in earthbound fantasy. These creatures surfaced as early as the genies in several silent fairy tales, including *Undine* (1916) and *Queen of the Sea* (1918), as well as Herbert Brenon's *Neptune's Daughter* (1914) and Captain(!) Leslie T. Peacocke's *Neptune's Bride* (1920). Conceived by maritime folklore as an alluring young woman sporting an impenetrable fish's tail, the mermaid clearly symbolizes the carnal frustrations of sailors too long out of port. Yet most mermaid stories are sensitive, often wonderfully tragic affairs about irreconcilable love.

Drawing upon one such tale (a Cornish yarn known as *The Mermaid of Zennor*), Peter Blackmore's source-play forms the basis of Ken Annakin's *Miranda* (1948), the first major mermaid movie. A fish-tailed Glynis Johns plays the brazen Miranda Trewella, who drags overboard a respectable physician named Paul (Griffith Jones) while he is fishing off the coast of Cornwall. Agreeing to her demand for a three-week stay in London, Paul passes her off as a patient, using a bath chair to hide her twitching tail from Clare (Googie Withers), his suspicious wife. Starved of male attention beneath the waves, the ingenuous Miranda causes flushed cheeks all round as she enchants Charles the butler (David Tomlinson) and Paul's politely bohemian chum Nigel (John McCallum).

The film's quaint British exterior belies a subversive feminist spirit worthy of Angela Carter, with the wanton Miranda coming ashore not for love but for sex. The film concludes on the ambiguous image of Miranda cradling a newborn child, suggesting that her canoodlings with Charles and Nigel concluded with more than a kiss and a discreet fade-to-black. (Since Miranda never loses her tail we're left to imagine how such an inter-species union was ever achieved.) Unlike Andersen's muted sea maid, Miranda snares admirers with a persuasive silver tongue, while Johns' husky tones have a way of turning innocent lines into dirty double entendres. "It's quite pretty when it's wet, isn't it, Paul?" she coos in front of Clare (referring of course to the loveliness of her concealed tail).

Released the same year as *Miranda*, Irving Pichel's American comedy *Mr. Peabody and the Mermaid* (1948) features a less proactive heroine, but one whose affections prove far more dangerous. William Powell plays the aging Arthur Peabody who deals with his midlife crisis by enjoying a brief fling with the mute young mermaid (Ann Blyth) that he reels in while on vacation in the Caribbean. Bewitched by the siren song of the creature he names Lenore, Peabody is compelled to elope with her into the sea, where an underwater embrace nearly drowns him. Here the mermaid's attractiveness becomes an innocently predatory lure. Like Miranda, Lenore possesses the siren song of legend spoken of by Shakespeare's Oberon, who recalls, "the rude sea grew civil at her song and certain stars shot madly from their spheres to hear the sea-maid's music." Yet this talent is tempered by its effect on human ears, as *Henry VI*'s Richard III boasts he'll "drown more sailors than the mermaid can."

This balance of the innocent and the poisonous agrees with the suggestion of legend, underlined by Andersen's fairy tale, that the mermaid does not possess an immortal soul, a vacuum in her persona that likens her to the sex objects of male fantasy. While the mermaid's carnal receptivity is trumpeted by the title of *Miranda*'s sequel, Ralph Thomas' *Mad About Men* (1954), the mermaid's innocent exhibitionism is exploited by John Lamb's cheesecake adventure movie *The Mermaids of Tiburon* (1962), which casts skinny-dipping "Queen of the Nudists" Diane Webber. Most screen mermaids, however, drape their long hair artfully to avoid landing their films with an R-rating, a practice that amused one reviewer of *Mr. Peabody*, who described the seaweed covering Ann Blyth's modesty as "a triumph of the Johnson office over the ichthyologists, and a rather humorous commentary on American movies in itself." The mermaid's credentials as the ultimate male fantasy is also pointed out by *Mad* magazine's parody of Ron Howard's *Splash* (1984), as the film's lovelorn hero, Alan (Tom Hanks), is reminded that Daryl Hannah's naïve mermaid is the girl every man dreams about: a dynamite blonde nymphomaniac who hardly speaks.

As a literal fish-out-of-water comedy, *Splash* is amusing enough. While Miranda consumes cockles by the bucketful, honks like a sea lion and catches sardines in her mouth, Madison (named after Manhattan's avenue) performs similarly embarrassing party tricks. She destroys the TV showroom at Bloomingdale's with a sonic squeal and offends diners at a swish restaurant by chowing down on an entire lobster. As a neat twist on mermaid lore, Madison's fins become legs on dry land, but revert to fins whenever she gets wet. This prompts the striking image (also seen in *Miranda* and *Mr. Peabody*) of the mermaid soaking herself in salted bathwater, draping a huge set of fins over the rim of the tub. "I'm just changing," Madison calls while struggling to dry herself and revert to human form before Alan can open the bathroom door. The scene actually originates from a family legend of the Counts of Luxembourg, an ancestor of whose is said to have wedded a beautiful girl on the Bluebeardesque condition that he must never see her bathe on a Sunday, the day she indulged in reverting back to her true form.

The heroine of *Miranda* avoids exposure in an aquarium by diving into the Thames, while *Splash*'s Madison is publicly doused by Eugene Levy's raving scientist and subsequently carried away by the Feds. Once rescued from the lab, where like E.T. she is probed half to death by uncaring scientists, Madison escapes into the sea with Alan (who unlike Mr. Peabody can breathe underwater so long as he's with his mermaid lover). Madison surfaced again (played by Amy Yasbeck) to rescue a captive dolphin in a made-for–TV sequel, *Splash, Too* (1988). Lest the romantic scenario of boy-meets-fish become too familiar, the mermaid sprouts claws and fangs in *She-Creature* (2001) before returning to fairy tale for a similarly sinister turn as a shoal of web-fingered succubae in P.J. Hogan's *Peter Pan*.

When animals chat as freely with humans in earthbound fantasy as they do in fairy tale, the conversation usually leads the human onto a psychiatrist's couch. In earthbound fantasy, the animal kingdom is a separate magical world, which only wizards like Dr. Dolittle or hybrid creatures like mermaids are privileged to cross. When Donald O'Connor's dimwit G.I. hears the voice of Chill Wills issuing from a mule in Arthur Lubin's *Francis* (1950), he immediately considers himself a candidate for the laughing academy. This one funny joke is pounded flat by the rightfully loathed series that followed, consisting *Francis Goes to the Races* (1951), *Francis Goes to West Point* (1952), *Francis Covers Big Town* (1953), *Francis Joins the Wacs* (1954), *Francis Joins the Navy* (1955) and *Francis in the Haunted House* (1956). By now audiences were praying for *Francis in the Glue Factory*, but series director Arthur Lubin had

All woman ... well, nearly. Husky-voiced siren Glynis Johns plays the titular sex-starved mermaid in this publicity still from Ken Annakin's saucy British picture *Miranda* (Gainsborough, 1948).

yet to conclude his crimes by transferring the idea to TV with *Mister Ed* (1961–65). When not gassing amongst themselves in movies like the *Dr. Dolittle* remakes or the science-fantasy *Cats and Dogs* (2001), garrulous or otherwise enchanted beasts wisely stick to fairy tale, although MTV's earthbound fantasy *Joe's Apartment* (1996) wrings genuine laughs out of lodging college boy Jerry O'Connell in a rancid East Village apartment occupied by a swarm of singing cockroaches.

Before the movies opened the Pandora's Box of CGI, puppets were the most common form of anthropomorphized animal to converse with humans in earthbound fantasy. *The Muppet Movie* (1979), *The Great Muppet Caper* (1981) and *The Muppets Take Manhattan* (1984) all charmingly bend reality to the degree where talking frogs, singing pigs and inquisitive things (whatever Gonzo is) are allowed to interact as freely with the human world as the riverbank wildlife of *The Wind in the Willows*. The mocking parallels such puppets draw between humans and animals was put to more misanthropic use in two 1989 films following on from pornmeister Gerard Damiano's *Let My Puppets Come* (1977). Peter Jackson's grotesque one-joke Muppet parody, *Meet the Feebles*, graphically proposes that puppets can behave as bestially as the venal humans they imitate. More elegant in its puppet debauchery is Henri Xhonneux's dirty comedy *Marquis* (1989). This tells the story of De Sade's incarceration in the Bastille, with the famous pornographer cast as a wistful half-human spaniel who spends his days talking to Colin, his own loquacious penis.

Interacting with humans as seamlessly as physical caricatures like Jim Henson's Muppets, the "Toons" of Robert Zemeckis' frenetic *Who Framed Roger Rabbit?* (1988) are free to play a deeper role in the human story than are allowed the decorative sidekicks of Disney fluff like *Pete's Dragon*. The film's inspired premise integrates the golden age of American cartoons with the neighboring age of film noir. Cuckolded cartoon star Roger Rabbit (voiced by Charles Fleischer) pairs up with an embittered P.I., Eddie Valiant (Bob Hoskins), himself as much a genre caricature as Roger. This synthesis of worlds is revealed as an irate human director calls *cut* on the film's opening cartoon and the camera pulls back to reveal exhausted cartoon actors stomping off a three-dimensional set and into the human world.

In his review of *Roger Rabbit* in *The Encyclopaedia of Fantasy*, author John Grant sees the Toons as a kind of fairy derived not from ancient folklore but modern technology. Their bodies composed of living ink and paint, the Toons possess the fairy-like ability to shape-shift, allowing them to shake off dropped anvils with nothing more messy than a revolving halo of stars. According to folklore, fairies may be repelled by objects made of iron, an equivalent of which is here revealed by malevolent lawman Judge Doom (Christopher Lloyd), whose turpentine concoction "The Dip" is capable dissolving Toons out of existence.

Like the Muppet movies and cartoon-meets-reality films like *Volere, Volare, Cool World, Last Action Hero, The Adventures of Rocky and Bullwinkle* and *Looney Tunes: Back in Action, Roger Rabbit* understands that if such outrageous creatures are to thrive harmoniously among humans, then the reality of the rational world must be tweaked in order to accommodate them. In its cleverest sequence, the film takes this idea a step further by having Eddie venture into the Faerie outpost of Toontown. In this lunatic animated suburb the inflexible human becomes as elasticized as Roger. Eddie is flattened into an irate puddle on the floor of a speeding elevator and unwittingly steps off an apartment building, hanging in mid-air just long enough to register a horrified expression before he grabs his hat and plummets.

The Toontown sequence of *Roger Rabbit* recalls those tales of travellers who wander into the kingdom of the fairies, suddenly becoming beholden to their laws over time and space, a manipulation of reality carried over when the fairies themselves enter the human world. True to folktale, films depicting these various pixies, sprites, gnomes and goblins (collectively known as fairies) have them delighting in vexing cloddish humans with parlor tricks, as they did in early silents like Ferdinand Zecca's *La Fée des roches noires* (*The Fairy of the Black Rocks*) (1904), James Williamson's *Gabriel Grub, The Surly Sexton* (1904), Theo Bouwmeester's *Mischievous Puck* (1911) and J. Searle Dawley's *Little Lady Eileen* (1916), starring Marguerite Clark. Like the Toons, the fairies appeal to mundane humanity for the very light of their world, which they bring into our own. Edwin S. Porter's *A Good Little Devil* (1914) depicts this idea at its most simple-minded, with Mary Pickford playing a blind girl who escapes into a dainty imaginary world swarming with fairies.

Owing to the apparent variety of their species, fairies are the fantasy creatures who have received the most on-screen exposure outside their world of origin, with the Irish Leprechaun managing to distinguish himself from the host and generate his own modest subgenre. Himself can be seen spinning yarns in Edward Buzzell's *Three Wise Fools* (1946), and plying his traditional trade as a cobbler in Henry Koster's *Luck of the Irish* (1948). The latter film also employs the folkloric device of the Leprechaun's pot of gold, to which humans are entitled should they ever succeed in capturing its owner, as does Albert Sharpe's eponymous rogue in Disney's surprisingly scary *Darby O'Gill and the Little People* (1959). Francis Ford Coppola's *Finian's Rainbow* (1968) is fairly typical of Leprechaun movies in its brand of plastic blarney, although it manages unusually to work impassioned socialist rhetoric into a whimsical plot about a wish-granting crock of gold sought after by a hyperactive Tommy Steele.

One imagines that the Leprechaun's miserly guile would go far in the modern world. But aside from the animalistic Pooka, identified as James Stewart's invisible pal in *Harvey*, and the lonesome gnome who gets his tiny hands on a Rolls-Royce in Disney's *The Gnome-Mobile* (1967), the only film to propose the idea of fairies living among us is Roddy McDowall's regretfully obscure arthouse movie *The Devil's Widow* (*Tam-Lin*) (1971). Based on a Robert Burns poem, the film is an interesting update of the folk ballad in which a young man is held in thrall by the queen of the fairies and rescued Orpheus-fashion by his human lover. Ava Gardner plays aging socialite Michaela Cazaret, a fading Titania smitten by the one sincere member of her swinging '60s retinue, a photographer named Tom Lynn (Ian McShane), who is himself in love with Janet (Stephanie Beacham), a minister's daughter. Cazaret refuses to dismiss Tom from her service, despite his pleas; when he tries to escape from her Scottish country retreat, she playfully selects him as the stooge in a lethal hallucinogenic parlor game.

The Devil's Widow is an effective reminder that fairies are not all as nice as Tinkerbell. In many ways a more faithful depiction of fairy behavior can be found in the vicious activities of Warwick Davis' psychopathic goblin in the schlock horror *Leprechaun* movies, or the little monster found in the basement by a boy called Harry Potter in John Carl Buechler's kid's movie *Troll* (1986). Yet the image of fairies as benign little tree-huggers persists, epitomized in their benevolence by the archetype of the fairy godmother, who pops up to lend a hand outside of fairy tale in *A Simple Wish* (1997) and *The Santa Clause 2* (2002). An equine Pooka also performs a very fairy godmotherly service for a family of Dublin travellers in Mike Newell's social-realist fantasy *Into the West* (1992).

This romanticizing of pagan folklore brought about two films in 1997 (one American, one British) based on a celebrated real-life fairy encounter. In the case of the Cottingley fairies, two little girls from Yorkshire managed to fool investigators for over 70 years with a collection of faked photographs that appeared to show them conversing with several fairies. The ambiguity of the facts in the case, which allowed its appeal to endure for so long, is entirely lost on Charles Sturridge's erroneously subtitled *Fairy Tale: A True Story*, which cannot resist showing off its swattably precious CGI fairies from the outset. Infinitely better is Nick Willing's *Photographing Fairies*, which plays a tantalizing perceptual game and cleverly uses the Cottingley case as a springboard for its own complex ideas.

Skeptical Edwardian photographer Charles Castle (Toby Stephens) is hired by a seemingly gullible woman, Beatrice Templeton (Frances Barber), to examine several photographs that appear to show her two young daughters gambolling with fairies. When Charles concludes that the pictures are genuine, he visits Beatrice, who dies falling from the tree where her daughters took the pictures. It seems the fairies are indeed real, appearing as grotesque elfin sprites that could have fluttered out of a Richard Doyle painting, but which can only be seen after ingesting a mysterious star-shaped flower. Charles succeeds in capturing the results of his trip on camera, although we are never sure his evidence sways anyone but himself.

"These are dark times," says Edward Hardwicke's sympathetic but non-committal Sir Arthur Conan Doyle (the author who publicly verified the authenticity of the Cottingley case). "We must cultivate hope like a precious flower." Symbolized by the vision-inducing blossoms, this hope is itself ambiguous and Charles' visions may be nothing more than a personal fantasy induced by the trauma of losing his wife. Taking on board Doyle's suggestion that fairies, should they exist, may be some form of earthbound angel, Charles concludes that proof of their existence is by extension proof of God's. "What if the next world is a place as real as Clacton-on–Sea?" he asks, acknowledging that proof of supernatural creatures, however small, existing in our world would call into question our entire perception of reality.

Moving On: Ghost Stories

Horror and fantasy feel differently about death. Compare these two exquisite ghost stories, Alejandro Amenábar's horror film *The Others* (2001) and M. Night Shyamalan's fantasy *The Sixth Sense* (1999). In *The Others,* a tightly wound Nicole Kidman plays the matriarch of a gloomy island mansion, who realizes that she and her two children are dead, yet clings fearfully to her lost life with an anchoring mantra ("This house is ours"). The anxious nine-year-old psychic of *The Sixth Sense*, Cole Seer (Haley Joel Osment), encourages just such phantoms to move on, and overcomes his terror of the anguished souls who haunt him. His retrieval of Excalibur in a school production of *The Sword in the Stone* symbolizes this triumph. The degenerative spiral of *The Others* places it as horror, while the optimistic healing arc of

The Sixth Sense identifies it as fantasy. Granted, fantasy's ghosts are usually of a friendlier disposition than many of those in *Sixth Sense*, whose agitated presences embody the same terrified rejection of death as those of *The Others*. But as Cole learns to recognize their humanity, they become as approachable as the playful spooks of *Topper* or *Blithe Spirit*, whose cheerfulness in the face of death denotes a healthy acceptance of the inevitable.

The Others and *Sixth Sense* reveal close similarities to Charles Dickens' seminal nineteenth century ghost story *A Christmas Carol*. Several versions of this now over-familiar tale appeared long before Brian Desmond Hurst's austere British production *Scrooge* (1951), best remembered for a splendidly doleful Alistair Sim in the title role. Several silent versions appeared before Seymour Hicks grumbled the first audible "Bah, humbug" in Henry Edwards' *Scrooge* (1935) and Reginald Owen followed suit in Edwin L. Marin's *A Christmas Carol* (1938). However, like H. Rider Haggard's equally significant earthbound fantasy novel *She: A History of Adventure*, Dickens' story has yielded its most interesting results outside the field of its own adaptations.

Although now considered pushy, Dickens' moral urgency popularized the concept of ghosts intervening in human affairs. The idea informed early angel movies, notably *It's a Wonderful Life*, although ghost movies had already set the idea to work, albeit with particular and often prejudiced morals in mind. Harry Pollard's *The Miracle of Life* (1915) puts a downright evangelical spin on the Scroogean reformation, as the ghost of a "Child-That-Might-Have-Been" deters a young woman from undergoing an abortion by showing her a vision of her soul's impending damnation. Dixie National Pictures' monstrosity *Lucky Ghost* (1942) believes those most in need of spiritual improvement are African-Americans in general. Other films took a less bullying approach by identifying the intervening ghost as a deceased family member who (like Lilliom) returns to amend a present wrong, like the elderly uncle in the two versions of David Belasco's play *The Return of Peter Grimm* (Victor Schertzinger's in 1926, and George Nicholls, Jr.'s, in 1935).

A different strain of ghostly fantasy allows earthbound spirits the opportunity to escape their wretched existence by attending to unfinished business. In T. Hayes Hunter's *Earthbound* (1920), the ghost of a godless adulterer must atone for past sins by reconciling his former mistress with her cuckolded husband. Just in case the story's moral message needed clarifying, Irving Pichel's 1940 remake introduced an evangelist from beyond named Mr. Whimser (Charley Grapewin), who chides the hero for not paying enough attention to the Bible. Similarly didactic, the tearful conversion to piety undergone by the ghost of a caddish publisher (Noël Coward) in Hecht and MacArthur's *The Scoundrel* (1935) leaves one nostalgic for the days when he dismissed a rejected author's suicide as a "foolish effort to call attention to bad writing."

Directed by René Clair for producer Alexander Korda, *The Ghost Goes West* (1935) leaves moralizing to the past, gently contrasting old world mysticism with new world modernism and establishing several now-familiar set-ups of ghostly comedy. Robert Donat's dashing eighteenth century highlander, Murdoch Glourie, finds himself refused entrance to Heaven by his ancestors for chasing comely milkmaids instead of upholding the honor of his clan. Murdoch haunts his ancestral castle for two centuries, waiting to find a rival McLaggan out of whom he can bully an apology for a long-standing insult. Then his wastrel descendent, Donald (Donat again), is forced to sell the old place to a vulgar American entrepreneur, who transports the gloomy pile brick by brick to sunny Florida. As in later comedies like *Here Comes Mr. Jordan*, the film ignores the mysteries of the universe laid open by the presence of the supernatural. Clair's film instead plays as frothy absurdism, with the disapproving Murdoch, still bound to his ancestral home, forced to immigrate to the new world, which welcomes him with a ticker tape parade.

More immediately influential, the Hal Roach–produced *Topper* (1937), based on the comic novel by Thorne Smith and directed by Norman Z. McLeod, re-routes the Anglo-American face-off of *Ghost Goes West* and turns the moral reform of Scrooge on its head. Constance Bennett and Cary Grant play Marion and George Kerby, frivolous American sophisticates who drive into a tree after a heavy night's drinking, and arise nonplussed from their dead bodies as transparent phantoms. Realizing they cannot enter Heaven until they have performed a good deed, they resolve to tutor their meek English friend Cosmo Topper (Roland Young) in the ways of hellraising. The Kerbys' need to conserve ectoplasm periodically necessitates they become invisible, inciting a now wearingly routine farce as apparently one-sided conversations provoke head-scratching, double-takes and offended misunderstandings. Romance threatens to blossom between the flirtatious Marion and the appreciative Topper, whose marriage is thus endangered in the sequel *Topper Takes a Trip* (1938), and again by the wisecracking ghost of Joan Blondell in *Topper Returns* (1941).

But such intriguing potential had already been realized by earlier, more serious ghost fantasy. While the vivacious life forces of Murdoch Glourie and the Kerbys earmark them for a ghostly return, undying love forms the silver cord that tethers parted lovers in Sidney Franklin's irresistibly melodramatic *Smilin' Through* (1932). Leslie Howard plays the bereaved John Carteret, who sadly converses with the ghost of his bride, Moonyean Clare (Norma Shearer), accidentally killed on her wedding day by her jealous admirer, Jeremy (Fredric March). History threatens to repeat itself when he has to care for Moonyean's niece (Shearer again) and she falls in love with Jeremy's son (March again). When war threatens to part the young lovers, Moonyean's ghost urges John to heal their rift, and rewards him for doing so by taking his hand after he dies in his sleep. *Smilin' Through* does not have to work hard with such melancholy material, while the sentimental old gent who returns in A. Edward Sutherland's *Beyond Tomorrow* (1940) less effectively intervenes to ensure a romantic match as boringly predestined as those enforced by the angels of *The Bishop's Wife* and *Forever Darling*.

Intrinsic to all the devices of ghostly fantasy — interventions, moving on and romance — is the idea of adjusting to the natural flow of life and submitting fearlessly to its conclusion in death. For this reason, ghost fantasy (along with visitor-from-beyond and afterlife movies) took on a special significance during the Second World War. Produced in the years immediately following America's commitment to the conflict in Europe, the ghosts in Stuart Heisler's *The Remarkable Andrew* (1942) and Charles Lamont's *That's the Spirit* (1945) symbolize the intervening

The ghost of eighteenth century highlander Murdoch Glourie (Robert Donat) turns his considerable charm on Peggy Martin (Jean Parker), whose father is about to transport the ghost's ancestral home to Florida in René Clair's *The Ghost Goes West*. (London/United Artists, 1935).

character of the nation. In *Andrew*, the ghost of President Jackson (Brian Donlevy) saves an honest accountant (William Holden) from taking the rap for an embezzlement scam. In *Spirit*, Jack Oakie's turn-of-the-century vaudevillian heroically surrenders himself to an angel of death in lieu of his ailing wife. Meanwhile, Irving Pichel's *Happy Land* (1943) accounts for the real cost of America's intervention with a story remarkably similar to *It's a Wonderful Life* (1946). After the war in Europe claims his son, small-town pharmacist Lew Marsh (Don Ameche) falls into despair, until the ghost of Lew's dead grandfather takes him on a time tour to illustrate how much his son's compassion benefited the lives of others before he gave his own.

One of the most accomplished fantasy films of the war years, Victor Fleming's wrenching *A Guy Named Joe* (1943) made its consolatory stance explicit on its release (almost exactly two years after the Japanese raid on Pearl Harbor) by including a written dedication to the armed forces and their families. The film's title refers to air force slang for a "right chap," which flying ace Pete Sandidge (Spencer Tracy) must become after he dies heroically in a raid on a German aircraft carrier. He wakes up in the same cloudy prairie as Robert Montgomery two years earlier in *Here Comes Mr. Jordan*; there Pete meets a dead friend who cheerfully informs him of his death. Introduced to his new commanding officer (Lionel Barrymore's Mr. Jordan–like

"The General"), Pete learns that all airmen (American ones at least) are invisibly mentored by the imperceptible ghosts of former flyboys, and is himself sent to tutor skittish rookie Ted Randall (Van Johnson).

The Calvinist sense of design in everything that dictates Pete's death (foretold by his intuitive sweetheart, Dorinda [Irene Dunne]) also has a hand in his afterlife, as Ted is stationed in the same South Pacific base as Pete's grieving ex. In the face of Ted falling in love with Dorinda and life carrying on without him, Pete must relinquish his meaner feelings and the love he still feels for Dorinda. Having jealously goaded Ted into a dangerous flying display, Pete is rebuked by The General with the film's key speech about the importance of freedom, faith and the future, which simultaneously reminds Pete of his mission and the film's original audience of what their loved ones were dying for. In a supremely moving moment, Pete finally lets go ("the only kind of love worth having is the kind that goes on living"), yet Dorinda has yet to move on herself and goes to fly to her death on a suicide mission from which Pete talks her down and lets her run into the waiting arms of Ted.

A Guy Named Joe explicitly confronts issues of death and loss, while the ghost fantasies immediately following the war are tactfully dishonest. When mobsters gun down Danny Kaye's nightclub crooner in H. Bruce Humberstone's *Wonder Man* (1945), his soul does not die, but instead absorbs the mild-mannered personality of his "superidentical" twin. The elderly Sam Griggs (Frank Morgan) is old enough for us not to grieve unduly over his becoming a helpful ghost in S. Sylvan Simon's *The Cockeyed Miracle* (*Mr. Griggs Returns*) (1946), while the only real ghost in George Blair's haunted house farce *The Ghost Goes Wild* (1947) manifests in a schematic supporting role.

David Lean's well-titled *Blithe Spirit* (1945), based on Noël Coward's play, ignores the war entirely, taking place within the self-absorbed social circle of well-to-do novelist Charles Condomine (Rex Harrison) and his wife Ruth (Constance Cummings). Holding an after-dinner séance, Margaret Rutherford's indomitably dotty medium summons the envious green ghost of Charles' dead first wife, Elvira (Kay Hammond). While Charles is only mildly irritated by his ex-wife's acid remarks about the new furniture, Ruth cannot tolerate the intrusion (an unusual *ménage à trois* that reaches its natural conclusion in the cheeky Brazilian comedy *Dona Flor and Her Two Husbands* [1977], remade by Hollywood in 1982 as *Kiss Me Goodbye*). *Blithe Spirit*'s ghostly comedy relies on dextrous wit rather than *Topper*-esque slapstick and assumes audiences of its time would laugh more readily at the prospect of losing a sarcastic wife, rather than a husband, brother or son. Yet the movie reassuringly maintains that death does not change those it claims. Rather than take a sudden interest in donning sheets and rattling chains, the film's phantoms remain as petty as they were in life.

Jokey films like Jules Dassin's Anglo-American morale booster *The Canterville Ghost* (1944) and Abbott and Costello's *The Time of Their Lives* (1946) feature ghosts of the ancient rather than recent dead, reassuringly terrified by the trappings of the modern world. Turning the tables on the spirits that frightened audiences in chillers like *The Uninvited* (1944) and *Dead of Night* (1945), these movies switch the lights on and expose ghosts to mortal ridicule. Doing likewise, Vernon Sewell's *The Ghosts of Berkeley Square* (1947) makes the prospect of ghostly life seem merely dull rather than painful. Xenophobic English phantoms Bulldog (Felix Aylmer) and Jumbo (Robert Morley), once officers in the army of Queen Ann, suffer constant affronts to their dignity, as a parade of foreign types take up residence in their haunted address. Otherwise, life goes on pretty much as it did before, spending eternity leafing through *The Daily Spectre*, or the impenetrable guidebook left for them to make sense of the afterlife (an idea borrowed by *Beetlejuice*).

Most ghost fantasies of this period make light of the lingering trauma in which they are rooted, and which only a thoughtful minority attempt to examine. Less sentimental than the dead serviceman who reassures his living wife that he is in God's keeping in Rudolph Mate's *Miracle in the Rain* (1956), Joseph L. Mankiewicz's *The Ghost and Mrs. Muir* (1947) simultaneously acknowledges and short-changes the feelings of bereaved war widows. Although engaged in a genteel courtship with the ghost of Rex Harrison's blustering sea captain, Gene Tierney must honor her commitment to her dead husband (whom, Harrison observes, she never loved anyway) and not move on with another man until after she is dead.

Tempestuous seas and dead lovers also feature heavily in William Dieterle's *Portrait of Jennie* (1948) and Albert Lewin's *Pandora and the Flying Dutchman* (1950). In the former, Joseph Cotten's artist realizes he has fallen in love with a girl (Jennifer Jones) who drowned 20 years ago; in the latter, James Mason's hexed seafarer cannot rest until he has found the reincarnation of his murdered wife (Ava Gardner). Like Mrs. Muir, who literally ghost-writes her dead suitor's life story, both men attempt to salve psychic wounds through creative activity. Each are busy with a portrait of their missing love, now as inaccessible to the living present as the perceived innocence of the years before the war.

Following on from these artistically successful (if undervalued) mainstream films, Kenji Mizoguchi's masterful (if over-praised) *Ugetsu Monogatari* (1953) similarly realizes the rich symbolic potential of ghostly fantasy. Based on an eighteenth century collection of Japanese ghost stories, this elegantly mundane depiction of the unearthly sees ambitious peasant Genjuro (Masayuki Mori) take to profiteering during a civil war. Seduced by an opalescent noblewoman (Machiko Kyo) who confesses to being a lonely phantom, a repentant Genjuro is welcomed home by the dutiful wife who died in his absence. The film evokes an atmosphere of the uncanny almost completely without falling back on gothic paraphernalia, subtly implying the cosmic administration that Western movies invariably depict in the flesh.

Now that ghostly fantasy had been embraced by arthouse fare, the knockabout antics of ghosts like those in *Topper* seemed embarrassingly gauche. The only comedy throwback to appear before the '80s was Disney's blandly wholesome *Blackbeard's Ghost* (1967), with Peter Ustinov as the sad-sack pirate redeeming himself by saving a trio of old ladies from eviction. Otherwise, ghosts chiefly materialized in respectable European films, conjured by Giulietta Masina in Fellini's *Giulietta degli spiriti* (*Juliet of the Spirits*) (1965), bewitching Corin Redgrave in Eduardo de Gregorio's tortuously enigmatic *Sérail* (1976) and evoking memories past while vomiting into a little boy's ear in Bergman's *Fanny and Alexander* (1982).

While these intellectual movies shape ghosts to meet the symbolic needs of their *auteurs*, Lionel Jeffries' modest children's film *The Amazing Mr. Blunden* (1972) successfully readdresses ghost lore on its own terms. The enigmatic Mr. Blunden (Laurence Naismith) arranges for the destitute Allen family to move out of their Edwardian slum by giving them a caretaking job at a derelict country mansion. The Allen children, Jamie and Lucy (Garry Miller and Lynne Frederick), meet orphans Sarah and Georgie (Rosalyn Landor and Marc Granger), who lived in the house a hundred years ago. In an intriguing extension of the theory implied by *A Christmas Carol*, these "ghosts" are not actually dead, but reaching out to the Allen siblings across the gulf of time. By means of a magic potion, Jamie and Lucy become temporal phantoms themselves and travel back in time to save Sarah and Georgie from the cruel stepparents who will eventually cause their deaths.

Elsewhere, ghost fantasy's founding text was fast becoming the stuff of greetings card kitsch, with the help of two more numbly adherent adaptations, Ronald Neame's musical *Scrooge* (1970), with Albert Finney on Grinch duty, and Clive Donner's leaden *A Christmas Carol* (1984), featuring George C. Scott as a rather overfed miser. Thank goodness Richard Donner's droll update *Scrooged* (1988) acknowledges how crass the tale's seasonal sentiment has become. Bill Murray's ruthless TV exec proposes that we might as well celebrate Christmas with a show about Santa and his elves letting off automatic weapons alongside Lee Majors. Such sarcasm is unfortunately lost on the makers of both *The Muppet Christmas Carol* (1992) and *A Diva's Christmas Carol* (2000).

Ingeniously reduced to the level of household pests in the hugely successful science-fantasy *Ghostbusters* (1984), fantasy's spooks had lost their mainstream appeal by the early '80s. Most only manifested in low-rent fluff like *O'Hara's Wife* (1982), in which Ed Asner is made to feel better about pulling the plug on his ailing spouse when she returns to annoy him in slapstick fashion. The ghost of Bruce Lee helps a devoted fan kick the crap out of Jean-Claude Van Damme in *No Retreat, No Surrender* (1985), while *School Spirit* (1985) gives a ghostly teen the chance to spy on showering cheerleaders. Later entries *Ghost Chase* (1987) and *Ghost Dad* (1990) have even less to recommend them.

As colorful as Hong Kong's *A Chinese Ghost Story* (1987) Tim Burton's impish black comedy *Beetlejuice* (1988) successfully reenergized fantasy's spooks and allowed them to get back at the living after the indignities inflicted upon them in *Ghostbusters*. Alec Baldwin and Geena Davis play the Maitlands, a gentle young dead couple appalled to find the beloved New England home to which they are bound has been bought by a family of grotesquely hip New Yorkers. When the Maitlands' hopelessly passé attempts to scare away the living are met with applause (their idea of scare tactics is to possess a dinner party into performing Harry Belafonte's *Day-O*), the couple hire freelance "bio-exorcist" Beetlejuice (Michael Keaton). Summoned by calling his name three times, this sleazy ghoul explodes like a maddened Toon upon the living, just as they were thinking of turning their ghostly housemates into a tourist attraction.

Following on from comedies like *The Ghosts of Berkeley Square*, and upping the visual ante, *Beetlejuice* undercuts the seriousness of being dead, the film's gaudy impertinence becoming one of its more influential factors. Like the modish family who regard the quaintly despondent Maitlands as nothing more than bankable curios, '80s Hollywood no longer had the patience for ghosts unless they were of the wild and woolly variety. Neil Jordan's *High Spirits* (1988) began life as a quietly odd little film, a sort of ghostly *A Midsummer Night's Dream*, in which the inhabitants of a haunted Irish castle are paired off with a busload of rich American tourists. But the studio disastrously reconfigured the film into a raucous sub–*Beetlejuice* carnival.

By the late '90s, Hollywood became even more forgetful of the fact that fantasy's ghosts were once people, treating its spectral characters more and more like Beetlejuice. For all his volatile energy, Burton's prankster is ultimately no more than a plot device, like the unstoppable Headless Horseman of *Sleepy Hollow* (1999) whose appearances in the real world are also regulated by human will. The epitome of this way of thinking is to reduce spooks to sideshows in a funfair, as Disney does literally in the "adaptation" of its own theme park ride, *The Haunted Mansion* (2003), a film essentially no different from silent novelty reels like *The Ghost's Holiday* (1907).

Before the age of dehumanizing CGI, however, ghosts tickled the sense of spiritual nostalgia that also resulted in those sentimental remakes of old angel movies. Jerry Zucker's *Ghost* (1990) stands at the top of a cycle of straight-faced ghostly fantasy, preceded by Lloyd Fonuielle's *Gotham* (*The Dead Can't Lie*) (1988), an unsuccessful attempt to fuse a modern ghost story with vintage noir, and instigated by Spielberg's *Always* (1989), a superficial remake of *A Guy Named Joe* replacing fighter pilots with firefighters. The plot of Zucker's box office hit is conventional enough: Nice-guy New York banker Sam Wheat (Patrick Swayze) is killed by a mugger and subsequently displaced as an insubstantial spirit, who must set earthly matters to rights before he can move on. The film's effectiveness derives from treating its hackneyed material with complete seriousness. Far from the mildly flummoxed Spencer Tracy ("Well, howdya like that..."), poor Sam reacts with vivid terror. Unable to contact his endangered lover (Demi Moore), he finds himself locked in an alien dimension, authentically freaked out by the presence of his unsympathetic fellow phantoms.

While dexterously exploiting white middle-class paranoia about losing everything one has worked to achieve, the film also reassures its audience that anything so terrible could never happen without a reason. Sam's death, we learn, was no accident, but part of a money laundering scam contrived by his former best friend (Tony Goldwyn). This is the same cosmic government that orders the universes of *Here Comes Mr. Jordan* and *A Guy Named Joe*, and to an even more overtly Christian degree. Tunnels of light and luminous beings welcome the virtuous deceased, while scary groaning shadows peel themselves off the walls and drag screaming bad guys to Hell.

Making up in part for the movie's troubling nervousness about ethnic minorities, the lovable Whoopi Goldberg plays Oda Mae Brown, a sassy charlatan as surprised as Sam to find that her psychic powers are for real. In a clever scene, she puts her talents to honest use in her back-street parlor, now crowded with hopeful clients and impatient souls. Dispensing with the histrionics, Oda Mae communicates between the two worlds with all the weary irritability of a telephone operator at the end of her shift. Like the prosaic phantoms of *Blithe Spirit* and *Ugetsu Monogatari*, the scene reminds us that, contrary to popular expectation, most departed loved ones are less likely to cry "murder most foul," as to comment on a loved one's new hairstyle.

Alan Rickman in Anthony Minghella's conceited but undeniably moving *Truly, Madly, Deeply* (1990) eloquently recalls life as a ghost "like standing behind a glass wall, while everybody got on with missing me." The suggestion that we co-exist with an invisible community of the dead is essentially as exploitative a scheme as the sham service provided by Oda Mae in *Ghost*. Since we all must eventually confront death, and no certainty exists as to what awaits us on the other side, the proposal perhaps stands one step closer to the credible than the attentive congregation of angels in *Wings of Desire*.

Suggesting the dead have any interest at all in the living is an idea that works because it flatters mortal vanity, but it also eases the sting of bereavement. In *Truly, Madly, Deeply*, Jamie (Rickman) moves in with his partner, Nina (Juliet Stevenson), only after his death. But he quickly annoys her, rearranging her apartment and inviting his creepy friends over for all-night video marathons. His return serves to ease her grief at his departure, but also proves she no longer needs him. She moves on into a new life with an irritatingly demonstrative "art therapist" (Michael Maloney).

While another low-budget British film, Peter McKenzie-Litten's dreadful post–AIDS spin *To Die For* (1994), brought the ghostly romance cycle to a close, Brad Silberling's surprisingly poignant *Casper* (yet another spook from the '40s) looked towards ghost fantasy's effects-heavy future. Although ostensibly a vehicle for the cleverest Toon-meets-reality special effects since *Who Framed Roger Rabbit?*, the 1995 film effectively retains the emotional baggage of *Ghost* and *Truly, Madly, Deeply*. Its baby-faced phantom develops a doomed crush on the teenage girl (Christina Ricci) who comes to live in his seafront mansion, which her psychologist father (Bill Pullman) has been hired to exorcise of Casper's three obnoxious uncles. With its widowed counsellor and all his gentle talk about "the living impaired," *Casper* explicitly aligns ghost fantasy with therapy.

The dead also encourage the living to press on with the ambitions of life in Phil Alden Robinson's *Field of Dreams* (1989). "If you build it, he will come," sighs a ghostly voice, prompting Iowa farmer Ray Kinsella (Kevin Costner) to dig up his cornfield and build a baseball diamond. Months pass, bills mount and disgraced baseball legend "Shoeless" Joe Jackson (Ray Liotta) appears in the field looking for a game, having wandered out of time like the ghostly children of *The Amazing Mr. Blunden*. He is later joined by his roughneck teammates, whom only Ray and his supportive family can see. Prompted by further instructions, the incredulous Ray (his predicament superbly realized by the perceptive Costner) acts to heal the pain of both the living and the dead. He tentatively befriends an embittered '60s activist (an awesome James Earl Jones), and fulfills the dream of rookie batter Archie "Moonlight" Graham (played in old age by a twinkly Burt Lancaster), who died never having stared down a big-league pitcher.

Although rather self-conscious, *Field of Dreams* is nonetheless one the great American fantasy films, worthy of a place alongside *The Wizard of Oz* and *It's a*

Ray Kinsella (Kevin Costner), wife Annie (Amy Madigan) and daughter Karen (Gaby Hoffman) witness a ghostly flowering in Phil Alden Robinson's key modern American fantasy *Field of Dreams* (Universal/Gordon, 1989).

Wonderful Life. Like George Bailey, Ray Kinsella is a modern-day Gawain, but one who not only succeeds in his trial of spirit (unlike the legendary Arthurian knight) but becomes a Grail-like savior, whose selfless actions heal the souls of others. Like that of all those conversant with the dead, Ray's own reward lies in reconciliation with the departed, playing catch with the father who died before his son could take back hurtful parting words.

The Sixth Sense's Cole Seer is as reluctant a psychic as Ray Kinsella, *Ghost*'s Oda Mae Brown, or even Cosmo Topper, in a film just as much about communicating with the living as with the dead. Putting *Ghost*'s idea of a haunted world to terrifically scary effect, *Sixth Sense* administers therapy not only to Cole's attendant counsellor (Bruce Willis), but also between Cole and his fraying single mom (a superb Toni Collette). While counselling Cole, Willis realizes that he himself is just another of the sad phantoms haunting his young patient. Meanwhile, Cole's mother struggles to grasp her son's apparent instability. In a reconciliation more plangent that the final goodbyes of *Ghost* or *Truly, Madly, Deeply* combined, Cole reaches out to his mother while they are stuck in traffic, coming clean about his incredible gift by relating a message of love from his late grandmother.

Films like *The Sixth Sense* propose the rich irony that the dead can teach the living how to live. The ghosts of fantasy do not haunt our present like forbidding scarecrows (although they do in *Ugetsu Monogatari*), or else drag us into the past like the specters of *The Shining*. Rather they are fragments of the past that urge us to look to the future.

Frontier Incidents: Lost World Fantasy

The idea that Darwin was wrong is a common precept of earthbound fantasy cinema. These films imply that the magic described in myth and folklore once flourished on our planet like a primeval forest, but gradually deteriorated under the rationalizing advance of science. Whether an undiscovered enclave, a secret community or a gateway into a parallel universe, the few islets of magic remaining in the modern world are the only places left where the gods and monsters of old continue to thrive.

In his 1886 bestseller, *She: A History of Adventure*, imperialist scribbler H. Rider Haggard had two Victorian explorers uncover one of fantasy's archetypal lost worlds. The setting for a ripping yarn of cannibalism, reincarnation and death, the savage prehistoric land of Kôr is located in the uncharted plains of Africa and governed by its immortal matriarch Ayesha (known to her quailing subjects as She-Who-Must-Be-Obeyed). She preserves her irresistible beauty by showering in a column of magic fire. Bubbling with Freudian significance, the book inspired a literary vogue for lost world fiction still popular in the days of Méliès, who first adapted the genre's founding novel with *La Colonne de feu* (*The Pillar of Fire*) (1899).

The story was never more popular than in the silent era. American film pioneer Edwin S. Porter produced an adaptation in 1908, followed by a 1911 film from the Thanhouser Company, starring Marguerite Snow. A British version appeared in 1916, starring Henry Victor, followed by Fox's film of 1917, starring vamp Valeska Suratt. Haggard himself wrote the inter-titles of the British 1925 version, starring Betty Blythe, before he died later that year. In keeping with the more paleoecological lost world of his own *King Kong*, Merian C. Cooper explained away the powers of Ayesha's preservative flame as something to do with natural radioactivity, in the 1935 RKO production. He also relocated her kingdom to the freezing Arctic tundra and cast Richard M. Nixon's future Congressional rival, Helen Gahagan, in the title role.

Among the many rip-offs and imitations of Haggard, only Pierre Benoît's *L'Atlantide* (1919) made it onto film. Here two French Foreign Legion officers crossing the Sahara uncover the lost city of Atlantis, ruled over by the insatiable Queen Antinea, who enjoys turning surplus lovers into gold statues. The story was first filmed as a rambling French epic in 1921 and again in 1932 (by G.W. Pabst) as *Die Herrin von Atlantis*, starring Brigitte Helm. However fanciful their plots, lost world escapades like these retained a whiff of credibility in an age when the documentary travelogue was still a novelty, uncovering worlds audiences had only read about in Haggard and Burroughs.

"In these days of wars and rumors of wars," reads the opening captions of Frank Capra's box office hit *Lost Horizon* (1937), "haven't you ever dreamed of a place where there was peace and security, where living was not a struggle but a lasting delight?" In the film, based on the novel by James Hilton, Ronald Colman plays intrepid British consul Robert Conway, whose plane crashlands in the Himalayas. Rescued by Sherpas, Robert and the other passengers are led to the hidden valley of Shangri-La, an idyllic civilization (resembling a health resort) where a centuries-old lama (Sam Jaffe) wants Robert to take over as spiritual manager. The old man foresees a time when civilization will self-destruct and the spirit of brotherly love cultivated by Shangri-La will smugly set about healing the wounds of the world. Strangely enough for a Buddhist, he concludes his prophecy with "and the meek shall inherit the earth."

Essentially a communal variation on Ayesha's "Flame of Life," Shangri-La is miraculously free of any form of conflict, allowing its spaced-out citizens to live fantastically long and (one imagines) fantastically dull lives. To live permanently cut off from time is to live cut off from life; in other words, Shangri-La is a nice place to visit, but who would want to live there? For this reason, stories of such utopian lost worlds require dissidents, like Robert's apprehensive brother George (John Howard), who finds the prospect of succumbing to everlasting beatitude just a little too creepy, and temporarily convinces Robert (with good reason) that there is something rotten in the state of Shangri-La.

A figure of anarchy also threatens the lost world of Vincente Minnelli's musical *Brigadoon* (1954), whose bucolic Scotch village, fearing incursions of witchcraft, vanishes into Scotch mist a century at a time. The village beauty's jealous suitor sees life in Brigadoon as a cursed existence and threatens to cross the bridge between the village and the outside world, thus breaking the spell over all. Skirting their own ironic suggestions that a utopia must be preserved in blood, both *Brigadoon* and *Lost Horizon* do their lost worlds' dirty work for them, contriving accidents to befall their dissident characters before they can be murdered by their fellows. (However, there is evidence to suggest *Lost Horizon* originally came to a more ambivalent conclusion, before Columbia recut the film prior to its release.)

Before Charles Jarrott unwisely remade *Lost Horizon* as a 1973 Burt Bacharach musical, the more exciting lost worlds of Haggard and Benoît exploited their kitsch credentials on entering the '60s. Bollywood contributed its version of *She*, Muhammad Hussein's *Malika Salomi*, in 1953, before Hammer put a radiantly wooden Ursula Andress in a feathered robe for *She* (1965) and Olinka Berova in a miniskirt for the sequel, *Vengeance of She* (1967). The queen of the B films, Maria Montez, starred as Benoît's Antinea in Gregg Tallas' *Siren of Atlantis* (1949), while the Italians parked her kingdom beneath a nuclear testing site in Edgar G. Ulmer's *Antinea, l'amante della città sepolta* (*The Lost Kingdom*) (1961).

As the real world's mysterious continents yielded to Western tourism, the sea still seemed a viably inscrutable location for a lost world. Ray Harryhausen worked another of his monster-infested islands into Jack Sher's *The 3 Worlds of Gulliver* (1960), as a pygmy crocodile and a carnivorous squirrel menace Kerwin Mathews on the Arthurian isle of Brobdingnag. The rancid setting of Walerian Borowcyzk's disposable fable *Goto, l'île d'amour* (*Goto, Island of Love*) (1968) leaves a crumbling surrealistic society to its own devices, while the hidden island of Paul Anderson's

Ursula Andress (center) plays the fair, the chaste, the unexpressive She, admiring the view of her lost world alongside visitors Horace L. Holly (Peter Cushing, left) and Leo Vincey (John Richardson) in Robert Day's plush adaptation *She* (Hammer/Associated British/Warner-Pathé, 1965).

far more enjoyable *Mortal Kombat* (1995) gives a group of inter-dimensional martial artists the privacy needed to kick each others' teeth out. Recalling King Arthur's Avalon, the craggy fairy-haunted island of John Sayles' *The Secret of Roan Inish* (1993) is a destination, not a setting, as the atavistic taint of fairy blood forces an Irish family to retreat from the modern world and return to the timeless island fastness of their forefathers.

The motif of the secret island symbolizes the lost world's isolation and sense of retreat from the modern (Western) world, yet worlds of magic can still flourish even when obscured from view. Constituting a secondary world (that possibly threatens to marginalize the primary), the wizards' society of the *Harry Potter* movies prospers invisibly right under our noses. Here a lost world is not a boat trip but a footstep away, if you know where to look. One has only to tap a sequence of bricks in a London street to uncover a thriving wizard's bazaar, or walk through an illusory wall at King's Cross to catch a secret train to wizard school.

Peter Weir's achingly atmospheric *Picnic at Hanging Rock* (1975) suggests another such veiled world, where the reality of Alice's golden afternoon is only a tenuous caul on the other side of which lurks Wonderland. In turn-of-the-century Australia, a party of schoolgirls take tea in the shadow of Hanging Rock near Mount

Macedon. As though enraptured by a siren song, several of the party wander off among the crags and vanish. A search party reveals no clues, although several days later one of the girls is recovered, bruised but miraculously unharmed and with no memory of what happened. The film is based on a true story.

With its inscrutable central mystery revealed only by teasing intimations (one of the girls prophesizes her own disappearance, and everyone's watch stops at the stroke of 12), the film hovers on the brink of what Cocteau described as "frontier incidents between one world and another." It is in elaborating this point of contact that becomes the *raison d'être* of earthbound fantasy, but remains skillfully closeted in *Picnic*.

Contact with a world of pagan mysticism threatened with extinction by the onset of Christianity or science is often conceitedly seen as the reserve of "primitive" cultures like the endangered Navaho shapeshifters of *Wolfen* (1981) or the secretive Aborigines of Peter Weir's *The Last Wave* (1977). When not patronized by the Western world, these sensate cultures can provide a playful contrast between the two. In John Carpenter's incontinent *Big Trouble in Little China* (1986), Kurt Russell's loudmouth trucker pulls into San Francisco's Chinatown and stumbles into an incomprehensible gang war waged by rival triads, bristling storm gods and a sinister demon sorcerer. While Russell's good ol' boy machismo dithers in the face of rampant Taoist magic, Eddie Murphy in Michael Ritchie's tad sharper *The Golden Child* (1986) doesn't have the same problem. Persecuted by a Tibetan demon cult, the streetwise Murphy confounds Charles Dance's glowering warlock by evoking nothing so extraordinary as a mundane customs law.

As in *Harry Potter*, Peter Hewitt's unusually confident British fantasy *The Borrowers* (1997), based on the books by Mary Norton, utilizes worldly skepticism as the cloak of ignorance beneath which a lost world survives. Secretly mountaineering around our homes in search of provisions, the tiny Borrower family (like the diminutive protagonists of *Toy Story* and *Chicken Run*) disclose a Lilliputian perspective on our world, transforming it into a landscape as unfamiliar as any faraway Kôr or Shangri-La. Inventively constructed from humanity's clutter, the miniature lost world of the Borrowers is a place where mislaid credit cards form bedroom doors, retractable tape measures turn into makeshift elevators, and light fixtures and empty milk bottles become death traps.

When lost worlds are completely eclipsed by earthly rationality, the secondary worlds of fairy tale, heroic and epic fantasy may be accessed in their stead. In *Prisoners of the Lost Universe* (1983), Terry Marcel's mercifully obscure follow-up to *Hawk the Slayer*, a jobbing kung fu expert (Richard Hatch) is teleported to the low-budget heroic fantasy world of Vonya, while a bespectacled physics professor (Urbano Barberini) discovers his inner-barbarian on the "counter-earth" of the *Gor* films. Elsewhere, epic fantasy provides imperiled lost worlds for insecure Earth children to save in Ronny Yu's *Warriors of Virtue* (1996) and in the *Neverending Story* series. Such rare lapses in border control within traditionally hermetic secondary worlds usually result in movies as bad as these, although the revolving door system that operates between Faerie and the real world can expel the same volume of crap. Trans-Faerie mismatches include *Troll*, the *Beetlejuice*-derivative *Little Monsters*

(1989), the depressing *The Pagemaster* (1994) and the stunningly misconceived *Thomas and the Magic Railroad* (2000).

The appeal of Faerie as the ultimate children's playground was realized early by Gaumont's irresistibly titled *Daisy's Adventures in the Land of the Chrysanthemums* (1904), and later (definitively) in the *Alice* and *Oz* films. But when Faerie is depicted as a lost world parallel to our own, its escapist qualities are often overemphasized, allowing earthbound travellers to ditch the real world for a realm of unbridled wish fulfillment. These day trips to Faerie are often at their most childish when adults make the crossover. Only Henry Hathaway's *Peter Ibbetson* (1935) bucks the trend by wringing genuine tears from its boldly self-indulgent premise, as Ann Harding and Gary Cooper (playing her incarcerated lover) communicate unto death through a shared dream-world.

Steven Spielberg's excruciating *Hook* (1991) is more typical. It represents a nadir in regressive fantasy by turning Neverland into a primal-therapy resort for over-worked yuppies. Robin Williams' Peter Pan, now an earthbound grown-up, returns to the world of his immortal childhood to rescue his children, abducted for no particular reason by Dustin Hoffman's Captain Hook. Refusing to acknowledge, let alone confront, the real world neuroses the Peter Pan story sets out to resolve, Spielberg's film sees fantasy as nothing but a magic tonic for the soul, erasing dilemmas without confronting them. Barrie's pungent archetypes are reduced to clowns, and anything so abrasive as meaningful drama is subverted into an over-budgeted soufflé of sentimental escapism. Stories like these, in which life's difficulties are happily resolved with the wave of a magic wand, are fantasy of the very worst kind.

Ingeniously avoiding the pitfalls blundered into by *Hook*, Pixar's computer-animated *Monsters, Inc.* (2001) presents a parallel world as banal as our own. The film reveals that the monsters lurking in children's closets actually rely on terrified screams to power their homeworld ("We Scare Because We Care" is their corporate slogan). To shriek-harvesting Joes like Sully and Mike, a blue yeti and a cycloptic apple (voiced by John Goodman and Billy Crystal), theirs is just another world of blue-collar grind, shop-floor rivalry and locker room banter. Differences between their world and ours are superficial. Both worlds have need of janitors, except theirs have to mop up their own slime trails. They have sushi bars too (reverently named "Harryhausen's"), and their tabloid headlines are no less unbelievable. ("Baby Born With Five Heads. Parents Delighted.")

Like the industrialized subterranean fairyland of Edouard Nammour's *Tooth* (2003) and the North Pole assembly lines of Santa movies like Jon Favreau's *Elf* (2003), *Monsters, Inc.* gives its lost world a kind of credence by partially rationalizing the fantastic as a form of science. The effect is underlined by the film's CGI animation, a scientific advance conversely given to bolstering the realism of invented worlds like those of *Shrek* and *The Lord of the Rings*. When such patently artificial worlds exist within the real world (like the animated Toontown of *Who Framed Roger Rabbit?*), the technology bringing that secondary world into being (in this case animation) becomes a form of magic, whose author is as mysterious as our own.

In this way, Woody Allen's bittersweet comedy *The Purple Rose of Cairo* (1985), John McTiernan's action movie spoof *Last Action Hero* (1993) and Gary Ross' dizzying

Pleasantville (1998) all create lost worlds out of the science of moving pictures. *Purple Rose* has lyrical pith-helmeted adventurer Tom Baxter (Jeff Daniels) stride out of a movie screen and into Depression-era New Jersey, where he falls in love with adoring cinemagoer Cecilia (Mia Farrow). Although bemused by life in the real world (where he finds a passionate clinch doesn't end with a fadeout), Tom is delighted to be free of the dictates of movie narrative. The other characters in the titular Lubitschean comedy he once inhabited are left to mill about on screen, like the displaced creations in Pirandello's *Six Characters in Search of an Author*.

An expensive flop in its day, but an interesting film nonetheless, *Last Action Hero* reverses the premise of *Purple Rose*, as a magic ticket allows young movie addict Danny Madigan (Austin O'Brien) access to the violent screen world of destructive supercop Jack Slater (Arnold Schwarzenegger). In a world dictated by the conventions of cheesy action pictures (the sort in which Schwarzenegger and McTiernan specialize), Danny uses his off-screen foreknowledge to help crack a murder case, while rather too pointedly underlining the clichés on display. The best jokes are those allowed to work for themselves, like the appearance of the duty sergeant responsible for all those odd-couple cop movies ("You're pulling duty with the animated cat"). In Slater's world, spectacular explosions result from even the smallest caliber bullets, while Danny tries to convince Schwarzenegger he exists in a PG–13 movie by encouraging him to use an R–rated cuss-word.

The sprawling *Pleasantville* begins as though preparing to open out into the same predictable comic territory as *Stay Tuned*. Teen siblings (Tobey Maguire and Reese Witherspoon) squabble over a magic remote control (lent them by a TV repairman from beyond) and accidentally zap themselves into the sitcom world of Pleasantville, an impossibly wholesome TV series from the '50s. Assuming the identities of Bud and Mary-Sue Parker, offspring as impeccably apple-pie as their mom and pop (Joan Allen and William H. Macy), the kids find themselves in Shangri-La by way of Norman Rockwell, a black-and-white utopia where rain never falls, neighbors always wave and firemen never do anything more dangerous than rescue stranded cats. The film only briefly exercises its most obvious potential as a fish-out-of-water comedy, before moving on to challenge its own premise to breaking point. Mary-Sue sparks a sexual revolution among the Brylcreemers and bobby soxers by willfully deflowering the chaste captain of the basketball team, after which this uniformly monochrome world gradually blossoms into vivid color, heralding the advent of free will.

Allowed greater freedom than the dissident serpents neatly done away with in *Lost Horizon* and *Brigadoon*, Bud and Mary-Sue prompt the inhabitants of Pleasantville to question the limits of their fictional universe, which unfolds in obedience to their every answered query. What we are seeing is nothing less than the birth of a secondary world, one that rejects the hermeticism of nostalgia and embraces the uncertainty of the present.

The Purple Rose of Cairo and *Last Action Hero* are similarly positive in their espousal of the real world, if not quite so optimistic. By the end of *Purple Rose*, Cecilia rejects the fictional Tom Baxter for Gil Shepherd, the actor who plays him, sent by the film's producers to track down his runaway creation. But her decision brings the film to a realistically crushing conclusion, as Tom's self-absorbed alter ego flies back to Hollywood without her. *Last Action Hero* also underlines the fact that life isn't what it is in the movies. Charles Dance's one-eyed screen hitman gets hold of Danny's magic ticket and enters the real world, a place, the film cynically asserts, where the good guys never win.

These parallel screen worlds, like the lost worlds of the *She* movies and *Lost Horizon*, offer sanctuary from time and ultimately death, for as long as one remains within their protective borders. Ayesha transgresses the laws of her own lost world by taking one flame bath too many, and rapidly withers into a mummy. Similarly, the dissident Russian girl of *Lost Horizon* sets foot outside Shangri-La for the first time in decades and is devoured by time as it suddenly catches up with her. When Jack Slater enters the real world in *Last Action Hero*, he suddenly comes under the jurisdiction of the Grim Reaper (Ian McKellen), who looms out of the screen during a Bergman festival when Arnold's formerly bulletproof action man is mortally wounded in a gun battle.

Lost world fantasy explores our trepidation of crossing over into the ultimate undiscovered country, the one that awaits us after death. Movies set in Hell delight in describing its horrors, while films concerning Heaven rarely take their newly departed souls further than the pearly gates, focusing instead on what happens once they get there. Often characters are offered a second chance at life, like the reformed circus barker of the *Lilliom* films and the star-crossed lovers of Jean Delannoy's *Les Jeux sont faits* (*The Chips Are Down*) (1947). The jovial Englishman of Irving Reis' *Three Husbands* (1950) is allowed to peer down at his living friends and observe the results of an edifying posthumous prank.

If departed souls have to hang around in limbo for any length of time, they are usually undergoing some form of appraisal. In Robert Milton's *Outward Bound* (1930) and Edward A. Blatt's *Between Two Worlds* (1944), based on the same Sutton Vane play, a group of bewildered souls find themselves on board a ghostly passenger ship where they receive judgment for their earthly conduct. Otakar Votocek's reworking of the same story, *Wings of Fame* (1990), and Albert Brooks' comedy *Defending Your Life* (1991) put up their souls in luxury hotels, the former for as long as their celebrity endures on Earth, the latter until they appear at a court hearing that will decide whether they move on to Heaven or reincarnate. New arrivals in Hirokazu Koreeda's *After Life* (1998) effectively judge themselves, led away to interview rooms and encouraged to choose the most precious memory of their lives. After reliving this experience in the form of a short film put together by the staff of limbo, the souls move on, taking the bliss of that moment with them into eternity.

Afterlife movies assuage our fears of oblivion more explicitly than any other kind of lost world fantasy. "You didn't disappear," Cuba Gooding, Jr.'s, missionary soul assures Robin Williams in *What Dreams May Come*. "You only died." Like the comfortingly human form of the visitor from beyond, the familiar surroundings that furnish afterlife movies like Michael Powell's *A Matter of Life and Death* (*Stairway to Heaven*) (1947) serve to humanize and quantify otherwise nebulous spiritual concepts. This convention offered obvious comfort during the war, the idea that lost loved ones did not wake up in some frighteningly alien world, but were welcomed by a friendly face and ushered into new surroundings not so shockingly dissimilar from those they had just left.

Following the example of Mr. Jordan in his R.A.F. duds and Spencer Tracy's doomed daredevil turned angelic mentor, Powell's postwar afterlife fantasy continues the wartime tradition of likening gallant Allied airmen to heavenly angels. Bailing from his stricken Lancaster, Captain Peter Carter (David Niven) is washed up on the coast where he meets June (Kim Hunter), the plucky American radio operator who heard his valiantly upbeat swan song the night before. Unknown to Peter, he was due for arrival in Heaven's lobby, where freshly wrapped angel wings are handed out to new arrivals in a setting somewhere between The Ritz and a dry cleaner's. Having lost him in the fog, Conductor 71 (Marius Goring, as an effeminate dandy who lost his head during the French Revolution) is sent to get him back. But Peter refuses to leave Earth, having fallen in love with June, who believes Peter may be hallucinating (the film skillfully maintains ambiguity throughout).

Originally commissioned as a propaganda piece to cement Anglo-American relations, the cultural grievances of both nations are aired in an almost transcendent sequence. Peter's recently deceased physician (Roger Livesey) argues his ex-patient's case for remaining on Earth against a baleful Revolutionary soldier (Raymond Massey), who hates the British since he was the first American killed by one of their bullets. Powell throws such cosmic force behind Peter's struggle for life (the camera pulls back from the celestial courtroom to reveal a public gallery the size of a supernova) that the lack of a convincingly unbreakable bond between Peter and June is easily forgiven.

Jean Cocteau's *Orphée* (1950) is less visually overpowering, but just as tangible in its sense of a connection between this world and the next. Its love story has far greater gravity as Death herself, an icy young woman known as The Princess (Maria Casarès), falls in love with Jean Marais' eponymous Left Bank poet. Like the painter in Poe's *The Oval Portrait*, Orpheus becomes so consumed by his art that he barely notices the death of his muse, Eurydice (Marie Déa). As Marais remorsefully pursues her into the underworld, Cocteau reveals an afterlife (referred to as "The Zone") consisting of nothing so unearthly as a series of blackened corridors inside a bombed building. But here the laws of physics startlingly defy our own. Orpheus and his Hermes-like chauffeur flout gravity as they clamber and slide across vertical walls, while mirrored glass quivers like mercury at a touch.

Connecting Cocteau and Powell is the idea that the word of a cosmic dictatorship may be contested. The heavenly bureaucracies established by the first two *Lilliom* films did not make mistakes regularly until the '40s (confirming a wartime suspicion that the universe had gone mad). While motivating plot and allowing characters to be more than stooges of the cosmos, the convention of the celestial mistake also humanizes through fallibility the concept of Heaven, whose perfection otherwise makes it as boring as Shangri-La.

Beetlejuice traces the clerical errors of *Here Comes Mr. Jordan* onwards to the incompetent administrations that must have made them. Burton's film envisions a government as hellishly inscrutable as our own, with maddening muzak-filled waiting rooms crowded for eternity with souls arriving in the same mutilated condition

No love lost: June (Kim Hunter) and deceased RAF Capt. Peter Carter (David Niven) appeal to the court of Heaven in Powell and Pressburger's cosmic romance *A Matter of Life and Death* [*Stairway to Heaven*] (Archers, 1946).

as when they expired. Despite their mangled appearance, a football team is slow to realize they didn't survive that crash, while a magician's assistant sawn in half eternally waits her turn alongside a drowned scuba diver with the shark that killed him still clamped to his leg. Skeleton secretaries type away in chaotic offices, while suicides and road-kill dangle from the ceiling and limply scatter documents. Refuting the underlying promise of escape made by most afterlife movies, *Beetlejuice* suggests that life after death (perhaps by virtue of its being "life") may be no less aggravating than it was before.

On the other side of the secretary state of limbo, Heaven presumably provides an escape from all troubling Earthly complexities, yet films rarely let us know for sure, since to define Heaven is to impose limits and values on the indefinable. In *Down to Earth* (2001), Heaven is an exclusive nightclub, on whose doorstep God's consigliore (Chazz Palminteri) welcomes the virtuous and tells the sinful to go to Hell. Alan Rudolph's futile *Made in Heaven* (1987) depicts paradise as a decidedly white middle-class affair, a sunny suburbia where everyone blissfully glides after the cultured pursuits of classical music and literature. During their *Bogus Journey*, Bill and Ted get past the doorman by quoting *Poison* lyrics, sneaking into a Heaven resembling a brilliantly lit convention hall, where dead celebrities pass eternity playing charades.

In *Heaven Can Wait*, the officious I.R.S.–type who greets Warren Beatty explains his way around the film's concession that there exists more than one faith in the world: "The rules of this way station are your own. They are a product of your image and of those who share your image." Vincent Ward's *What Dreams May Come* (1998) expands this idea by making its afterlife entirely subjective. The film states that the Buddhists had reincarnation figured, while the Catholics got right the bit about suicides being damned. Otherwise, Heaven (and Hell) is whatever you want it to be. Here the deceased occupy their own private universe, a *Matrix*-like world obedient to their every whim. Yet this has little to do with leaving Earthly fixations behind, as Robin Williams revels in the mortal thrill of swooping like a condor around his own malleable paradise.

Field of Dreams suggests you can exert a similar degree of control over your surroundings without having to die first. Raising interesting questions about the plane of existence they inhabit after disappearing into the cornfield, the ghostly jocks whose lives are fulfilled by playing in Kevin Costner's ballfield ask before departing if this is Heaven. "No. It's Iowa," says Costner, as if it were easy to mistake the two. The experience of bliss supposedly only achievable in a lost world is merely a state of mind, the film suggests. Not only Heaven and Hell, but life itself is what you make it. Reconciled with his departed father, Costner's character himself asks if Heaven exists. "Oh, yeah," is the wisely indefinite reply. "It's the place dreams come true."

Browsing Through Time: Time-slip Fantasy

You know where you are with "Once upon a time." It points a big "You Are Here" sign at a place well outside the chronology of the real world. But the perception of time in other types of fantasy is treacherous, as treacherous in fact as any realistic narrative. All stories (and of course all films) maintain a sense of purpose, of design in everything, by manipulating recorded time, arranging and conducting the otherwise inflexible gauge that ticks away the moments of our lives.

Time-slips are glitches on this cosmic calendar, and most frequently occur in fantasy as earthbound stories, where they are usually the only leap of imagination the film and the audience have to make. Heroic and epic fantasies rarely wish to draw attention to the artificial structure of their worlds, or threaten it with rips in the fabric of time. Similarly, storytellers who navigate the elasticized time and space of fairy tale have enough to think about without negotiating the byways of quantum physics as well.

In this way, stories about hiccups in the space-time continuum are tied to the personalities who cause them. In earthbound fantasy, these are most often the work of cosmic forces out to teach us a lesson, like the altered version of James Stewart's present that Clarence the angel uses to illustrate his point in *It's a Wonderful Life*. More easygoing day trips out of time are usually brought about by the time traveller himself. The eponymous tourists of the *Connecticut Yankee in King Arthur's Court* movies and their variants guzzle unpredictable potions, enlist the services of mystics wise to the ways of time, or simply don't look where they are going and blunder into open wormholes. Like the Frankensteinian scientists of sci-fi, who harness time through technology, mortals who assume the mantle of Chronos magically must also shoulder the blame when the inevitable mishaps occur.

Unlike those of its more expeditious cousin sci-fi, time-slips in fantasy rarely send their protagonists into the future, staunchly asserting that the answers to their problems can only be found in the past. Fantasy's few glimpses of the future invariably direct their onlookers back to the present. In Herbert Blaché's silent Dickens adaptation *The Chimes* (1914), a pauper becomes a prophet as he dreams of the calamitous future that awaits his daughter should he continue to forbid her from marrying.

Intimidating mortals with the same kind of visions that ensure the reform of Scrooge, the cosmic enforcers of early time-slip fantasy betray a decidedly chauvinistic streak. Like *The Chimes*, Albert Parker's silent *Eyes of Youth* (1919) also believes that the course of a woman's life is best decided for her. A young woman (Clara Kimball Young), undecided whether she should marry one of two men, or else fulfil her dream of becoming an opera singer, is reassured by an Indian yogi that she will die as damaged goods should she choose any path other than that of marrying the man who loves her.

In Alfred Werker's *Repeat Performance* (1947), Joan Leslie plays a Broadway actress who murders her abusive husband (Louis Hayward). Her repentant wish to relive the past year is anonymously granted, but fate conspires against her to reach the same outcome. Her attempts fail a second time when she tries to save her marriage by keeping hubby away from a predatory floozy. Victims of a patriarchal fate, the best these women can hope to do is stand by their man no matter what the future brings.

Released several years before the war, Frank Lloyd's time-slip romance *Berkeley Square* (1933) spookily prefigures the separation motifs of post-war ghost movies like *The Ghost and Mrs. Muir*, similarly stressing that the perfect wife should be faithful beyond death. Lloyd's film is based on the play by John L. Balderston (itself inspired by Henry James' unfinished novel *The Sense of the Past*). Leslie Howard plays Peter Standish, a neurotic American architect living in 1933, who switches places with his identical eighteenth century ancestor. Stepping into the past through a wormhole (walking through the door of his Berkeley square residence exactly 149 years after his ancestor), Peter falls in love with his great great great aunt, Helen Pettigrew (Heather Angel). But their amor ends sadly as the nostalgic Peter becomes disillusioned with the unromantic realities of the eighteenth century. Helen finally convinces him to return to his own time, where he is pleased to learn that she chose to die a spinster and now waits for him in the afterlife.

Given the advance of World War II, such fatalism is understandable, although many films of this time fail to realize the narrative hazards posed by concrete prophecies. By assuming the future can never be changed, René Clair's disastrous *It Happened Tomorrow* (1944) kills its own terrific premise. A ghostly librarian hands rookie reporter Larry Stevens (Dick Powell) a copy of tomorrow's newspaper. Instead of heroically preventing disasters or putting all his savings on a winning horse, the unimaginative Larry uses his foreknowledge to beat his colleagues to the hottest stories. (A TV series, *Early Edition* [1996–2000], made a better fist of the same premise.)

Consequently the film telegraphs its every climax and quickly becomes a bore. Stories foretold are no fun to tell, and for this reason movies like *Here Comes Mr. Jordan* hinge their predestined plots on some kind of cosmic error, giving humanity the chance to answer back to their heavenly governors.

Thirty years later, Derek Jarman's nihilistic (and terribly dated) *Jubilee* (1978) used the inflexibility of its foreknowledge more sensibly. Queen Elizabeth I (Jenny Runacre) orders Shakespeare's Ariel to transport her to the England of the future. Here the film spits in the face of its modern audience by revealing the "No Fewcha!" apocalypse of the Sex Pistols, which it is now too late to prevent. Drawing the earliest ironic comparison between past and present, the silent *The Dawn of Freedom* (1916) gives a similar caution. Undergoing hypnosis and awakening 100 years in the future, a Yankee war hero (Charles Richman) leads a worker's revolt against his own tyrannical ancestor, suggesting contemporary America would do well to remember the Revolutionary spirit on which it was built.

The founding text of such stranger-in-a-strange-time movies is another key earthbound fantasy novel. Mark Twain's *A Connecticut Yankee in King Arthur's Court* (1889) has concussed nineteenth century engineer Hank Martin wake up in the epic fantasy England of King Arthur (technically making this a journey through space rather than time, but never mind). The book was directly adapted as a silent in 1920 by Emmet J. Flynn, a talkie in 1931 by David Butler (with Will Rogers in the lead), and a musical in 1949 by Tay Garnett (with Bing Crosby crooning *I'm Busy Doin' Nothin'* in the court of Cedric Hardwicke's King Arthur). Twain's story segues from Arthurian parody to bleak satire, as both Hank and Arthur fall victim to the supposedly reasoned principles of modern America. The films are more cheerful, however, and keep the satire one-sided. Preferring to poke fun at the stuffy British affection for monarchy and chivalry, the films select only scenes from the book that flatter Hank's character and emphasize triumphs of American ingenuity over British pomposity. Hank's humiliation of Arthur's champion on the jousting field using pistol and lasso, and his cowing of the superstitious natives by successfully predicting a solar eclipse with his pocket almanac, are among the most popular scenes on film.

Another scene, featuring in the first two *Yankee* films, reveals the underlying tension of all such time-slip fantasy. Instigating the Industrial Revolution at least three centuries too early, the enterprising Yankee renovates Arthur's ancient realm with plumbing, electricity, factory-made goods and the advertising needed to sell them. Progressive technology becomes a yardstick measuring the span between past and future. But for Twain, this ultimate expression of man's reason is also an expansion of his capacity for destruction. None of the *Yankee* films include the scene from the book where Hank almost single-handedly massacres an army with electrified wire and machine-guns.

The first *Berkeley Square* film shared Twain's trepidation. The eighteenth century lady Helen Pettigrew sees in her modern lover's eyes reflections of the Great War, Tommy guns and industrial smoke, horrors she will thankfully never live to see. Roy Ward Baker's British remake *The House in the Square* (*I'll Never Forget You*) (1951) recasts Peter Standish (Tyrone Power) as an atomic scientist, whose attempts to facilitate the Industrial Revolution almost win him a ticket to Bedlam. Similarly, Meg Ryan sees the eighteenth century as preferable to the present in James Mangold's time-slip romance, *Kate and Leopold* (2001). She finally concedes that passion is dead in the modern world and runs away through time with a dashing English duke (Hugh Jackman).

The time-slip in Vincent Ward's figurative epic fantasy *The Navigator: A Medieval Odyssey* (1988) spells out fantasy's common objection to technology by putting the world of superstition into a before/after perspective. Reversing the premise of the *Yankee* films, *The Navigator* tells the *Watership Down*–like story of a band of twelfth century peasants compelled by a psychic's visions to tunnel to the other side of the world, emerging in modern-day New Zealand. Their native time, for all its vulnerability to the ravages of disease and famine, is a sensate place of community and compassion, eminently favorable to the technophile world that eclipses it and threatens to make human life obsolete.

David Warner's politely malicious cyborg airs the feelings of the opposition in Terry Gilliam's kaleidoscopic *Time Bandits* (1981), ranting about the supremacy of digital watches over God's pointless creations (like men's nipples). "Are we not in the hands of a lunatic?" The film cleverly has us inclined to agree. Young Kevin (Craig Warnock) is bundled away by a sextet of fugitive dwarfs (who used to work for another of earthbound fantasy's cosmic bureaucracies) and learns that the fabric of reality is dangerously unstable; the dwarfs' ex-employer only had seven days in which to make it.

Like the titular *City of Lost Children* and Christopher Lee's technophile wizard in *Lord of the Rings*, the presumptuous villain of *Time Bandits* embodies the spiralling application of logic that threatens to cut humanity off from the spiritual. Yet he possesses an imagination superior to anyone else in the film (besides that of the director, who surely stands alongside Méliès and Cocteau as one of the most significant imaginations in cinema). Having stolen the Supreme Being's map of the universe, the best the dwarfs can decide to do with it is scuttle through the fraying seams of time and mug historical celebrities. Even the good-hearted, history-obsessed Kevin only wants to escape from his loveless parents, who are like machines themselves in their robotic obsession for consumer goods. In a climactic sequence, the boy's toy-littered bedroom becomes a magnified battlefield playing out technology's eternal conquest of romance, as Evil casually dismantles the knights, cowboys and tanks rallied from the annals of time. But his victory is cut short by a visit from God, who refuses to let on whether He has a design in everything, or is just making it up as He goes along.

Although *Time Bandits* has just as much fun upsetting Napoleon (Ian Holm), Robin Hood (John Cleese) and King Agamemnon (Sean Connery) during its more conventional visits to the past, time-slip comedies are not usually rooted in complex statements about life, the universe and everything. Harry Watt's *Fiddler's Three* (1944) is as trivial as the *Yankee* films it rips off, as lightning strikes wartime entertainers Tommy Trinder and Sonnie Hale on Salisbury Plain, transporting them back to the time of Nero. Ignoring a wealth of opportunity is another terrible British film, Paul Matthews' *Merlin: The Return* (2000). Traditionally the villainous henchman

The long and the short of it: In this publicity still, Robin Hood (John Cleese, top) poses along-side (from left to right) Fidget (Kenny Baker), Vermin (Tiny Ross), Og (Mike Edwards), Randall (David Rappaport), Strutter (Malcolm Dixon) and Wally (Jack Purvis), the eponymous rogues of Terry Gilliam's extraordinary *Time Bandits* (HandMade Films, 1981).

of Morgan Le Fay in the *Yankee* films, the celebrity wizard (Rik Mayall) wakes up in present-day England to prevent the evil Mordred (Criag Sheffer) from empowering himself through science. Gil Junger's *Black Knight* (2001) has even less of an idea what it's doing with its own provocative contrasts. The movie sends an African-American (Martin Lawrence) to medieval England, letting him do nothing more interesting than play to racial stereotypes when he gets there.

Although equally low comedies, *Army of Darkness* (1992) and Jean-Marie Poire's *Les Visiteurs* (1993) at least have something in common with Twain in their urge to overturn the twentieth century's sense of superiority. Sam Raimi's slapdash conclusion to his *Evil Dead* movies dumps cowardly, chainsaw-wielding screwball Ash (Bruce Campbell) in medieval England. Here he proves himself an incredible jerk, treating the peasants like damn dirty apes, deflowering Embeth Davidtz's token princess and raising an army of rowdy skeletons when he fluffs a magic spell. Remade by Hollywood as *Just Visiting* (2001), *Les Visiteurs* again reverses the *Yankee* premise. Jean Reno's brutish French knight and his revolting vassal, Jacquasse (Christian Clavier), are wrenched out of the feudal past and have to make their way in the Republican present, where social hypocrisy remains unchanged. Reno's loutish aristocrat is regarded as a bum by the film's buffonish *nouveau riche*, while Jacquasse becomes a millionaire by retrieving a fortune he stashed a thousand years earlier. He threatens to remain in the modern world, where his vulgarity is tolerated only because of his wealth.

For the sake of comedy, all these films largely ignore the concept of the time paradox, the theory that altering the events of the past will change the course of the future. But this idea becomes central to time-slip movies like Francis Ford Coppola's *Peggy Sue Got Married* (1986). Kathleen Turner plays Peggy Sue, the depressed divorcee who passes out at her high school reunion and wakes up as her teenage self in 1960. As she revisits her formative years with the consciousness of her adult self, the film asks whether or not she should attempt to change the unhappy outcome of her future by rejecting the advances of her philandering husband-to-be, Charlie (a superbly gawky Nicolas Cage). Unlike the heroine of *Repeat Performance*, Peggy Sue's life is open to change, but the film flounders through its inability to explain exactly how she slipped through time. (The concussion device so many of these films fall back on almost never explains how their time travellers are transported bodily through time. The idea worked for Twain because Hank Martin travels to a point in history that only exists in his head.)

Thrillingly suggesting that to a degree any perceptible design in everything is of our own making, *Peggy Sue Got Married* underlines the import of one's actions, the consequences of which define our future. Few films outside of *The Man Who Could Work Miracles* and *Bruce Almighty* lend anyone direct control over their destiny. But the prospect that life may similarly be a result of our own doing overwhelms many a time-slip movie, as the film steps in like an over-protective parent and runs the characters' lives for them. As though ironically commenting on the contrived plotting of the *Harry Potter* series itself, head wizard and walking plot mechanic Dumbledore (Michael Gambon) lends the boy wizard a time bauble so he can ensure his own rescue in *Harry Potter and the Prisoner of Azkaban* (2004).

Time-slips offer characters the chance to win their lives back from fate, but some films refuse to let it pay up. Brett Ratner's *Family Man* (2000) subjects Nicolas Cage to narrative bullying throughout. Don Cheadle's visitor from beyond sends him into a version of the happy but destitute life he would have lived had he not dumped his high school girlfriend (Téa Leoni) and pursued a career on Wall Street. Once Cage returns to his regular lonely life and determines to seek out his old flame, she conveniently turns out to be loaded. James Orr's *Mr. Destiny* (1990) also tries to have it both ways. Corporate schmoe James Belushi whines about how his life turned out ever since he struck out at the high school baseball game in 1970, and visitor from beyond Michael Caine gives him a vision of life had he hit a home run. Learning that all rich people are soulless fiends, Belushi returns to his regular life so he can re-appreciate what he already has. That is, until the film lets him win a promotion by punching out his scumbag boss and revealing an illicit takeover in front of the board. Like the *Back to the Future* trilogy, these films arrange their characters' lives like plumbing, with time-slips giving the chance to sort out any psychic blockage causing problems further down the line.

Exploring the other extreme, time-slip fantasy may abandon its characters to chaos. Peter Howitt's existential romantic comedy *Sliding Doors* (1997) suggests that the merest flutter in a certain direction may cause a disastrous tsunami in one's future. The movie divides the secure middle-class life of a P.R. girl (Gwyneth Paltrow) into two streams: one in which she misses her train and ends up finding the man of her dreams (John Hannah), the other in which she catches it and winds up dead. Like *Time Bandits*, *Sliding Doors* revels in life's seeming randomness. In Tom Tykwer's *Run Lola Run* (1998), Franka Potente experiences the same exhilaration, pounding down the streets of Berlin in three separate versions of her life, trying to recover a bag of dirty cash in all three. However, neither film is true fantasy, belonging instead to the same branch of the perceptual "uncanny" as *Amélie* and *Moulin Rouge*. These time-slips are purely the result of tricky editing, and the primary navigators of time within the films are the directors themselves.

Disney's *The Kid* (2000) could have achieved a balance between contrived fatalism and freewheeling entropy. Revisiting the confrontation with his inner child that formed the conclusion of Terry Gilliam's *12 Monkeys*—itself inspired by Chris Marker's *La Jetée* (*The Pier*) (1962)—Bruce Willis plays an irascible middle-aged image consultant reformed by a visit from his chubby eight-year-old self (Spencer Breslin). It transpires that Willis' character has orchestrated this encounter without even knowing it. At the very end he is visited by his 70-year-old self, who reveals that he tinkered with the past so he could achieve his dream of becoming a pilot and starting a family. A fine twist, if the film could explain how it worked. Like *Peggy Sue Got Married*, *The Kid* is a realistic fantasy that never engages in its own mechanics and ends up floundering on its pretensions to magic realism.

In determining whether or not time is there to be done with as we please, time-slip fantasy (like all fantasy) echoes religion in its attempt to understand the world and how we might live within it. The conversion by coercion of determinist films like *The Chimes* and *Family Man* clearly resemble fundamentalism, threatening damnation should the characters not do as they are told. Ironically, atheist films like *Sliding Doors* and *Run Lola Run* most positively endorse the liberty of choice needed to make a "freewill offering" of one's life to God. *The Kid* opts for easygoing humanism without resorting to value judgments on the actions of its main character.

Harold Ramis' *Groundhog Day* (1993) skillfully weaves ideas from all three doctrines around the Buddhist concept of reincarnation. Bill Murray plays Phil, an ambitious TV weatherman sent to cover a springtime festival. On Groundhog Day, the people of Punxsutawney, Pennsylvania, ceremonially awaken the titular rodent from hibernation to find out if it can see its own shadow, thus prophesizing six more weeks of winter. Phil undergoes a similar awakening when stranded in town by a blizzard and forced for unknown reasons to relive the same maddening day for eternity. Every morning as he wakes, the radio mockingly announces his everlastingly clean slate with Sonny and Cher's *I Got You, Babe*.

Marooned in time like the hotel guests of Alain Resnais's *L'Année dernière à Marienbad* (*Last Year at Marienbad*) (1961), Murray achieves a conversion more convincing than the one he underwent in *Scrooged*. But the forces navigating his fate are never formally identified. The film is ambiguous enough to suggest that Phil's time-trap could just as much be self-imposed as enforced by some celestial do-gooder. After briefly questioning his sanity, and accepting his fate, Phil realizes he can live with impunity and has lots of deadpan fun baiting cops, stealing money and seducing women he has pumped for information the day before. He also uses his accumulated knowledge to charm his producer, Rita (Andie MacDowell), although he always fails to consummate their relationship by the end of the day.

Driven increasingly insane, he tries to break the cycle by killing himself. Several successful attempts later, he reaches the ultimate selfish conclusion that he is some kind of god. Having exhausted his own egotism, Phil becomes a good Samaritan, using his time to educate himself and help others. But even this moral path leads to a dead end, as the elderly derelict whose life he makes numerous attempts to save, seems fated to die by the end of the day. Only when Phil realizes the truth of his personal feelings for Rita is he allowed to move on.

Groundhog Day cracks a grand metaphysical joke about time-slip fantasy's assertion that the present is inescapable. The future, which Phil yearns to escape to, can never be attained since it becomes the present on point of arrival (as would the past if ever reached by a time-slip). Yet the present is also the focal point of life, like the burning gate of a film projector through which life flashes past at 24 frames per second. *Groundhog Day*, like all relevant time-slip fantasy, comes to the wise conclusion that life can only really be lived as though there is no time *but* the present.

Priests of the Invisible: Wizards and Witches

Wizards are the clergy of fantasy, those with a hotline to whatever godly forces govern their world. Such humans are gifted with a degree of magical power enabling them to manipulate reality, a privilege usually only the reserve of the infinite and its attendant visitors from beyond.

Most familiar as the archetypal Merlin and his bearded chums, who potter about secondary world fantasy in robes and pointed hats, fictional wizards are drawn from the real-life shamans and druids of ancient cultures. Before Christianity declared open season on every wart charmer and wise woman in medieval Europe, shamanism continued as an acceptable feature of rural life. These self-ordained hierophants performed their "magic" for the benefit of the community. On their behalf, the shaman conversed with the spirits of animals and the dead, made prophecies and encouraged favorable weather for crops ... or just gave people something for their lumbago.

Although the Newtonian enlightenment put a stop to anti-witchcraft hysteria in the eighteenth century, ending 400 years of sanctioned genocide (predominately directed at women), a fragment of that cultural misogyny survives. The wizard's female counterpart, the witch (derived from the Old English "wicca") owes much of her diabolic reputation to religious propaganda. Typecast in the role of the child-munching ogre of fairy tale, the witches of earthbound fantasy have become a reservoir of male anxieties.

The first significant fantasy of its type, René Clair's genteel supernatural comedy *I Married a Witch* (1942), based on another Thorne Smith tale, reveals the genre's typically nervous attitude towards feminine power. Forties sex bomb Veronica Lake plays Jennifer, an ingénue witch burned at the stake by New England puritans, and released into twentieth century society when her ashes are disturbed. Fredric March plays the poor flustered sap who stands no chance against her silken charms.

But Jennifer's powers are limited to parlor tricks, like slamming doors from a distance and sliding up the banisters like a slinky Mary Poppins. More like a bottle of expensive perfume than a human being, her character functions solely to radiate all the feminine charms (and how) that reduce men to intoxicated nitwits. She spends most of the film pining for her beau after accidentally downing a love potion, and lets her domineering father (Cecil Kellaway) boss her around. The film's focal villain, Kellaway's malicious warlock punishes his daughter with mortality by confiscating her powers. Despite Jennifer's wizardly status, her abilities are not hers to control, and she happily trades them for domestic bliss by the end.

For witches there is no hex after marriage, echoing the folklore that states that wizards must remain celibate in order to retain their magical powers. But witches make this sacrifice for love, for that which makes them human. While aspiring to this status, self-reliant witch Gillian Holroyd (Kim Novak) casts a love spell over publisher Shep Henderson (James Stewart) in Richard Quine's *Bell, Book and Candle* (1958). Believing herself bound by witch lore never to relinquish her powers and fall in love, Gillian confides in her dizzy aunt Queenie (Elsa Lanchester), "It might be pleasant to be humdrum once in a while."

Just as much as Clair, Quine delights in exposing the vulnerability of men to the almost magical sensuality of women, but Quine's film is easily more hip than its predecessor. Leaving behind the cauldrons and broomsticks of puritan New England, Gillian lives in the big city, haunting its basement jazz clubs and mingling with its pretentious clientele. Like the backbiting bloodsuckers of Neil Jordan's *Interview with the Vampire* (1994), the witch glides unnoticed through regular human society, while existing somewhere below its surface, in a secret supernatural world that operates (deliberately in both cases) like a closeted gay community. Not that *Bell, Book and Candle* sees the presence of this world as a threat to the male ego, as does *I Married a Witch*. Rather, Gillian emerges as more of a danger to herself and the women who challenge her, earning the film some delectably catty humor. "A witch?" exclaims Shep's jilted fiancée (Janice Rule). "Shep, you just never learned how to spell."

Her newfound humanity confirmed as she sheds her first tear in striking close-up, Gillian follows Veronica Lake's Jennifer by exchanging her powers for the love of a good man. Leaving their sisters cloistered for most of the Sexual Revolution, Gill and Jen ensured the domestication of witchkind. In *Bewitched* (1964–72), TV's unofficial continuation of Clair and Quine's films, newlywed Samantha Stephens (Elizabeth Montgomery) approaches magic like a woman unable to resist maxing out her husband's credit cards. Over a monumental 250 episodes she demonstrated how embarrassing power in a woman's hands could be for a man, constantly exerting the magical powers she promised long-suffering husband Darrin (Dick York [1964–69] and Dick Sargent [1969–72]) she had given up.

While a woman's potential to defy the patriarchy is traditionally quelled in wizard movies, the same power in men is allowed free rein. Such films instead propose how these abilities may be used responsibly and whether they might benefit the

Witchcraft charms thee! Posing in this publicity still, with goldfish bowl and fishing rod in lieu of cauldron and wand, Veronica Lake demonstrates exactly why bewitched beau Fredric March never stands a chance in René Clair's bubbly *I Married a Witch* (Masterpiece/United Artists/Cinema Guild, 1942).

world. In Lothar Mendes' British film *The Man Who Could Work Miracles* (1936), based on a script and story by H.G. Wells, a trio of whimsical gods conduct a cosmic experiment to test the worth of mankind, granting awesome cosmic powers to George McWhirter Fotheringay (*Topper*'s Roland Young), a timorous shop assistant from Essex.

After amusing himself and others by ordering the shop floor to tidy itself, turning a broken walking stick into a tree, and teleporting a bothersome bobby to Hell and back, George's display of power quickly attracts profiteers. His domineering employer (Edward Chapman) tries to persuade him to use his powers for the benefit of the business. A shop-floor lothario (Robert Cochran) advises him to be selfish, although George cannot interfere with free will and therefore cannot make his colleague, Ada (Joan Gardner), reciprocate his pale affections. A priest (Ernest Thesiger) urges him to banish human misery forever, while the blustering Colonel Winstanley (Ralph Richardson) takes offense at the idea of a commoner possessing power over his world and tries to blow the little man's head off.

George's power seems of no positive use to anyone. Blinded by greed, the educated classes are in their own way as blinkered as the proletariat, who are either hopelessly unimaginative or distracted by sentimentality. When the worm finally turns, George creates himself an ivory tower from which he voices the frustrations of the common man. Naively threatening to wipe out all the world's leaders unless they agree to put an end to war, he stops the world turning on its axis to give them time to think — and, by doing so, almost inadvertently destroys the planet. Making his only really sensible wish, George reverses time to the point before he ever got his powers, sacrificing them for the good of mankind and suitably impressing his cosmic benefactors.

Possibly conceived as a swipe at George W. Bush's America, Tom Shadyac's Jim Carrey vehicle *Bruce Almighty* (2003) puts a flailing clown in charge of the most powerful nation in the world. Convinced that God (Morgan Freeman) has it in for him, unlucky TV journo Bruce Nolan (Carrey) is summoned by the man in white and lent the entirety of His powers. Like George Fotheringay, Bruce goofs off for a while before realizing the import of his authority. He tiptoes across water and parts his soup like the young Moses in that *Far Side* cartoon. He also fulfills James Stewart's promise to lasso the moon for his sweetheart (Jennifer Aniston), inadvertently causing tidal floods across the third world and doomsday hysteria across America. Like the cozy British outlook that constrains *The Man Who Could Work Miracles*, the focus of *Bruce Almighty*'s godly powers is curiously myopic. God underlines the shallowness of Bruce's vision when He asks what His subject really cares about, dismissing a prayer for world peace as, "That's great, if you want to be Miss America."

With its cathartic power tripping and confirmation of the existence of God, the film clearly attempts to provide balm for American audiences in the wake of the unconscionable terrorist attacks of 9/11 (the film was a huge success at the domestic box office). In so doing, *Bruce Almighty* perhaps says more than it means to. Largely ignoring the overseas catastrophes brought about by his egotism, Bruce answers the whispered prayers of America alone. After riots erupt when he grants everyone a winning lottery ticket (resulting in 17 bucks apiece), Bruce digs deeper into his in-box of prayers and realizes that true power lies in the ability to overcome whatever life may throw at you.

Like Dorothy returning from Oz newly aware that she doesn't need the magic she yearned for after all, or Frodo bringing about an apocalypse of sorts so that for better or worse mankind can start to think for itself, the neophyte wizards of *Miracles* and *Bruce* affirm the worth of mundane humanity. Yet the wish that is granted in order to prove that one does not need it teaches a paradoxical lesson. While confirming the obvious futility of yearning for something that doesn't exist, it implies that there is some cosmic design out there that knows we will do okay without it.

Often a wizard's power serves to prove Lord Acton right about mankind's fallibility. Power does tend to corrupt and absolute power does corrupt absolutely, a tragedy played out in misanthropic wizard movies like Jerzy Skolimowski's unsettling *The Shout* (1978). Alan Bates' charismatic sorcerer can deliver the "Terror Shout" (a roar like the take-off of a jumbo jet, striking dead anyone within earshot). Having learned this trick and others during an 18-year stay with the Australian aborigines, Bates uses his power to intimidate a philandering church organist (John Hurt) and seduce his wife (Susannah York). The Rasputin-like healer of Simon Wincer's dismal *Harlequin* (1980) also uses his gift to ingratiate himself into a household before destroying it.

Just as dangerous are those wizards with no ill intentions swayed by ordinary folk with plenty. In the William Castle exploitationer *Zotz!* (1962), Tom Poston's professor unearths an ancient coin giving him the power to kill with a word (the film's title). Washington dismisses his talent, while the Commies show tremendous interest. William H. Macy's infectious loser in Wayne Kramer's *The Cooler* (2002) becomes hopelessly entangled in the schemes of the vicious Vegas casino boss (Alec Baldwin) who employs him to jinx his customers' winning streaks.

Witches are rarely so irresponsible. Set in a dilapidated Welsh Bingo hall, Julian Kemp's charming Ealing-style comedy *House!* (1999) has an usherette (Kelly McDonald) use her power to dictate the course of a game, not to earn herself a fortune, but to save her workplace and the community of oddballs whose lives depend upon it. Such maternity is not unusual in movie witches, whose powers are invariably inherited (as are McDonald's in *House!*) rather than bestowed or learned, like those of the destructive male wizards of *Bruce Almighty*, *Zotz!* and *The Shout*. The witch's role in earthbound fantasy is more sharply defined than that of the wizard. She embodies the apparent natural mysticism of women, at least as perceived by men, for whom women appear closer to nature by dint of their ability to produce life seemingly out of nothing. Womb-envious men must therefore repress any similar expression of power on the woman's part.

Witches rarely have to learn the lessons of responsibility that movies like *Bruce Almighty* teach their wizards, whose masculine powers naturally err on the more aggressive and overreaching side. So much so that men who manage to control rather than relinquish their magic (or indeed die in the course of refusing) may cease to be considered human at all. The point made here is that mankind cannot possibly hope to assume the mantle of God, and only a guy would be dumb enough to try. Should George Fotheringay or Bruce Nolan have ever learned to command their powers responsibly, they may have ended up as inhuman as carnies like Dr. Lao (Tony Randall) in George Pal's *7 Faces of Dr. Lao* (1964) and Mr. Dark (Jonathan Pryce) in Disney's *Something Wicked This Way Comes* (1983). Both characters command powers so absolute and moralities so commanding they are more like angels than human beings.

Humanity also becomes the price paid for supernatural power in Robert Altman's strange black comedy *Brewster McCloud* (1970). An owlish teenager (Bud Cort) secretly constructs a pair of Leonardo–style wings in the fallout shelter of the Houston Astrodome. His neutered angel assistant (Sally Kellerman) insists that Brewster must retain his virginity if he is to achieve his dream of flight. Ignoring her advice, Brewster falls in love with a ditzy tour guide (Shelley Duvall) and consequently only manages a few triumphant circles in his pedal-powered contraption before, exhausted, he plummets to his death.

The ability to fly here becomes an apt metaphor for the composition of fantasy itself. Brewster's ritual celibacy becomes one of the narrative rules that must be adhered to in order for his fantasy to work. Boundaries are crossed at the risk of the endeavor falling apart. Alain Tanner's *Les Années lumière* (*Light Years Away*) (1981) ritualizes the process even further. Trevor Howard plays another Icarus, a bird-obsessed old coot who owns a derelict country garage. He initiates a young drifter (Mick Ford) into his friendship by setting him symbolically futile tasks, manning dry petrol pumps and polishing wrecked cars, while the old man tinkers in his garage. After unveiling a pair of functional wings, he ritualistically daubs himself in birds' blood, matter-of-factly skips into the air and flies away. He later crashes to earth, his eyes pecked out in symbolic punishment.

Despite what the woolly-minded escapists think, all flights into fantasy are tethered and temporary. The dreamer will always return to Earth; he can either land or he can crash. Thus the corny climax of Nick Castle's otherwise surprisingly touching *The Boy Who Could Fly* (1986) rings desperately false. An autistic orphan (Jay Underwood), whose powers remain a nicely sustained ambiguity until the end, joyously takes flight above a crowded funfair. Suddenly inspiring everyone to turn their lives around, he flies away into the clouds forever, a spurious embodiment of the indomitability of the human spirit.

Even more introverted than those who dream of flight are those wizards whose powers are chiefly mental. Unlike more gregarious wizards, this sheltered assembly of anguished telepaths, modern-day shamans and misunderstood prophets find themselves at the mercy of the state, their psychic powers disclosing revelations that must be relayed to a skeptical outside world.

In describing just such an attempt to reconcile the idealist and the realist, Joseph Losey's controversial anti-war fable *The Boy with Green Hair* (1948) ironically landed its director on the Communist blacklist. A young Dean Stockwell plays a prickly little boy named Peter, whose hair turns bottle-green the day he discovers he is a war orphan. The local doctor is mystified, while the rest of the town ostracize the boy for fear of contagion, despite his grandfather's best efforts to stand up for him. Peter then has a vision of children like himself from around the world. They sadly assure him that his hair symbolizes a hope for peace, of which he must become a delegate. Peter tells the whole town of his pacifist mission, but everyone assumes sinister intentions and forces him to shave his head. The ghostly war orphans remind Peter that he can relinquish his responsibility at any time, but the boy defiantly assures the world his hair will grow back green.

The dramatic tension of whether or not the psychic will convince the world of his vision also drives Kwesi Owusu's magic realist *Ama* (1991), in which a computer disc prophesies a tragedy that a young African Londoner must avert. Like Peter, Ama becomes a Cassandra and fails in her mission. Here the heedless skepticism of the real world rings true, but not in Terry Hughes' limp romantic comedy *The Butcher's Wife* (1991). A badly miscast Demi Moore plays a sort of mystic Forrest Gump, a barefoot clairvoyant of trite romantic prophecies to which everyone seems willing to lend an ear.

Like the "ancestral messengers" of *Ama* and Peter Weir's *The Last Wave* (1977), Eddie Murphy in the fun remake *Dr. Dolittle* (1998) becomes an urban shaman, re-establishing a line of communication between two worlds. Unlike Rex Harrison's loud and proud English eccentric, Murphy is a dedicated San Francisco M.D. who spends most of his life trying to suppress his powers and fit in. Harangued by his daughter's motor-mouthed guinea pig (voiced by Chris Rock), Dolittle finally realizes what he sees as his destiny, and secretly takes on an alcoholic monkey, a depressed tiger and a prima donna circus bear that upstages him in the 2001 sequel.

Not attuned to his mystic frequency, Dolittle's family believe he is suffering a breakdown and have him committed after catching him giving mouth-to-mouth to a dying rat. The film quietly reinforces the psychic's struggle to make his voice heard above the din of reality by recasting Dolittle as a black man. Like Whoopi Goldberg's misunderstood medium in *Ghost*, Dolittle has a harder time than most psychics being taken seriously by his white peers.

Frank Darabont's otherwise agreeable *The Green Mile* (1999) practically spells out this problem in flashing neon. Based on Stephen King's serialized novel and set in a Depression-era penitentiary, the film describes the long walk made by John Coffey—note the initials (played by Michael Clarke Duncan)—a hulking though childlike black man with miraculous healing powers and the tormenting ability to "see" the sins of others. Convicted with prejudice for murdering children he was actually trying to save, he awaits a symbolic crucifixion in the electric chair.

Of all earthbound wizards, psychics easily have the least fun. They may be persecuted by the very people they are trying to help, or find themselves isolated from the rest of humanity by their privileged perception of the world. Taking up at the point when the psychic discovers his powers, M. Night Shyamalan's icy *Unbreakable* (2000) draws attention to the psychic's struggle to connect with his new identity. A train derails, killing everyone on board except morose college security guard David Dunn (Bruce Willis), who walks away miraculously unharmed. David is soon contacted by the shock-haired Elijah Price (Samuel L. Jackson), a cultivated comic-book entrepreneur, whose diseased bones are as fragile as crockery (earning him the playground nickname "Mr. Glass"). Elijah believes that superhero comics exaggerate a cosmic truth, a surviving link to a Manichean belief system. He also believes that David is gifted with powers that single him out as mankind's champion.

David does his best to ignore the increasingly apparent truth, while his son (Spencer Treat Clark) touchingly begins to idolize his father for the very gift that threatens to push them apart. Standing in a crowded train station, psychically detecting the evil deeds of those brushing past him, David commits to his new life as a superhero, rescuing two children from a psychopathic intruder in the film's most unsettling scene. His assimilation ends in triumph, but also serves to define that of the outcast Elijah, whose horrifying confession assures David's future commitment to life as a psychic crimefighter.

Greenhorn wizards can rarely turn away from their new identities, not that those of the post–*Bewitched* generation wanted to. Aside from Angela Lansbury's apprentice witch nonsensically turning skeptic by the end of Disney's *Bedknobs and Broomsticks* (1971), a new wave of witch movies saw wiccans eager to find their place in the parliament of sexual politics. Very loosely based on John Updike's novel, *The Witches of Eastwick* grants the collective wishes of Cher, Susan Sarandon and Michelle Pfeiffer, who conceive their perfect man during a sort of margarita-fueled sabbat. Jack Nicholson's devilish playboy answers their prayers, his presence quickly persuading them to stop seeking fulfillment in men. His offers of consummation turn sour as he exploits their bodies and drives Veronica Cartwright's bedevilled puritan to death amid a torrent of regurgitated cherries.

The movie subscribes to Angela Carter's controversial theory that women are attracted to men for the very qualities that may morally repulse them. Nicholson certainly limns a magnetic beast, but the film's fantasy logic is too vague to make much sense of him. He seems to be some kind of feminist joke, a malignant phallic god who only fulfills the wishes of others so that he might fulfill himself. All three women find themselves pregnant with the Devil's sons, whom he hopes will corrupt the world in his stead, while he puts up his hooves and is looked after by a good woman (or three).

While *The Witches of Eastwick* reaffirms the ecclesiastic myth that a witch's life revolves around the Devil, Nicolas Roeg's *The Witches* (1990) and Disney's *Hocus Pocus* (1993) conclude they *are* the Devil. A feverish horror movie for kids (adapted from Roald Dahl), *The Witches* abandons all sympathy for witchkind. Re-establishing witches among the ogre elite, the film lays down its ground rules as fussily as though it were dealing with vampires or werewolves. Living among us like they do in *Bell, Book and Candle*, Roeg's witches are undetectable but for their purple-tinged eyes, lack of toes, scabby baldpates and bad wigs. An orphaned American boy (Jason Fisher) discovers a crowd of these monsters holding a convention at an English seaside hotel. Planning to turn the nation's children into mice, Angelica Huston's imperious Slavic dame provides the horror high point by peeling off her human face to reveal the beak-nosed crone beneath.

These vicious parodies of womanly maternity are driven by an unquenchable hatred for children. We learn that witches literally regard children as excrement, a nasty Freudian touch. *Hocus Pocus* also takes the side of the torch-waving mob, but is much more conventional in going about it. Revived in the twentieth century, a trio of New England witches blandly embody all the traditional feminine sins of vanity, spite and greed. Bette Midler plays the ringleader, whose cackle alone makes one wish for Judy Garland and a bucket of water.

Andrew Fleming's *The Craft* (1996) and Griffin Dunne's *Practical Magic* (1998) make a much more interesting contrast. The former is a disposable teenybopper horror movie, the latter a grown-up "chick flick." Both films posit witchcraft as a ritual of sisterhood, yet the teenagers of *The Craft* definitely have the advantage over their older sisters. New girl Sarah (Robin Tunney), gifted with mystic potential

The Devil (Jack Nicholson) enjoys more than the best tunes in this publicity still from George Miller's *The Witches of Eastwick* (Warner/Guber-Peters/Kennedy Miller, 1987), but his glamorous groupies Alex (Cher), Jane (Susan Sarandon) and Suki (Michelle Pfeiffer) are not quite as compliant as Old Nick would like.

inherited from her mother, falls in with a coven of high school wiccans, known by their detractors as "the Bitches of Eastwick." They are led by trailer-trash gothette Nancy (*Return to Oz*'s Fairuza Balk, whose bristling performance is one of the best things about the film).

Here the powers harnessed by witchcraft are neutral, but governed by karma. The girls have lots of harmless fun glamming each other up with magic, but when they start placing vengeful hexes on those who piss them off, they also must suffer the consequences. Nancy summons a powerful pagan spirit, but uses it to fuel her own self-loathing. In the film's showdown, Sarah defeats her by summoning the same force and dishing out only what the other girl has brought upon herself. Nancy fails her initiation by getting drunk on her own power, thereby becoming power itself, as much a non-human entity as Dr. Lao or Mr. Dark.

She ends up strapped to a bed in the booby hatch, while Sarah ends the film in full control of powers that prove too much for the witches of *Practical Magic*. Orphaned by an ancestral curse that does away with any man with whom an Owens woman falls in love, sisters Sally (Sandra Bullock) and Gillian (Nicole Kidman) live in New England with their witchy maiden aunts (Stockard Channing and Dianne Wiest, patently dotty old birds without a game line between them). Earth mother

Young, angry and Wiccan: Clockwise from top, Nancy (Fairuza Balk), Rochelle (Rachel True), Bonnie (Neve Campbell) and Sarah (Robin Tunney) star as "the Bitches of Eastwick" in this publicity still from Andrew Fleming's potent little witch picture, *The Craft* (Columbia, 1996).

Sally loses her husband to the family curse and renounces magic, while fiery tear-away Gillian makes the Hollywood mistake of enjoying sex and has to be punished. The girls are forced to kill Gillian's swarthy foreign attacker (twice), but his leering specter continues to haunt them.

In *Practical Magic*, witchcraft is the cause of everyone's misery, and has to be put away under the kitchen sink, as it was in the days of Veronica Lake. The film's tagline is telling: "There's a little witch in every woman," the operative word being "little," as though feminine power is a forbidden vice to be indulged in as occasionally as a box of chocolates, rather than something transformative, elemental and frightening, and all the more attractive for it.

This self-empowerment theme is even more pronounced in films featuring magically endowed children. Just as *The Craft* refutes the vulnerability of teenage girls, Danny DeVito's *Matilda* rejects the helpless babes-in-the-wood archetype of the child in fairy tale. The young heroine wields her intelligence far more readily than her telekinetic abilities, equating true power not with forcing the world to do your bidding, but in cultivating natural confidence and self-control. This potent message also bolsters the appeal of the wizard movie series that is presently the most successful franchise in fantasy cinema.

The plea for child literacy made by Michael Ende in *Die unendliche Geschichte* (*The Neverending Story*) (1979) was finally answered in 1997 by British author J.K. Rowling's phenomenally successful *Harry Potter* series. The books delighted readers of all ages the world over, and became the most popular fantasy fiction since *The Lord of the Rings*. Coincidently *Harry* and *Rings* were adapted for film at the same time, although it was harder to see how Harry—the geeky schoolboy wizard (as indelibly British a hero as James Bond)—would emerge from the other end of the Hollywood machine. Unwilling to tamper with a successful formula, Warner Brothers played it safe. Never making good on their rumored threat to cast Haley Joel Osment in the lead, the studio hired sure-bet director Chris Columbus to transplant the story from page to screen with the minimum of creative interference. Aside from a nonsensical trans–Atlantic title change (to *The Sorcerer's Stone* in the U.S.), *Harry Potter and the Philosopher's Stone* (2001) surprisingly emerged as English as tea and cricket.

With British stage talents in full pantomime flight, *Philosopher's Stone* exudes a charming BBC quaintness, far removed from the knowing brashness of most American kid's fare. Destined to become one the greatest wizards of all time, young Harry (Daniel Radcliffe) grows up in a monotonous London suburb, barely raised by the detestable Dursleys, his fastidiously normal aunt and uncle (Fiona Shaw and Richard Griffiths). On his eleventh birthday, giant groundskeeper Hagrid (Robbie Colrane) spirits him away from the world of "muggles" (wizard slang for non-magical folk) to the gothic funhouse of Hogwarts School of Witchcraft and Wizardry. Here Harry meets carrot-topped loser Ron (Rupert Grint), bookish know-it-all Hermione (Emma Watson) and snivelling rival Draco Malfoy (Tom Felton).

The film plays a similar narrative game to *Star Wars*, unrolling before the audience like a length of fabulous carpet, disclosing an ever-expanding secondary world. The actual plot regards some vague conspiracy concerning baleful potions teacher

Prof. Snape (Alan Rickman) and dotty headmaster Dumbledore (Richard Harris, who died shortly after making the second film and was replaced by Michael Gambon). Somewhere behind all this lurks the malevolent shadow of Voldemort, the corrupt necromancer who murdered Harry's parents and left their infant son with a portentous lightning-bolt scar on his forehead.

Far more compelling than the plot are the various phantasmagoria of Harry's world: goblin accountants, dozy trolls, baby dragons, spectral mascots, magic cloaks, chocolate frogs, earwax jellybeans, violent chess sets and broomstick polo (a swift, incomprehensible game known as Quidditch). *Philosopher's Stone* falls over itself in snagging the book's every ingredient, terrified of disappointing the fans. But in so doing, the film gorges itself, and waddles from scene to scene, with Hagrid dishing out clues whenever the kids hit a wall in the plot ("I shouldn't have told you that," he mumbles, quite rightly).

Harry Potter and the Chamber of Secrets (2002) and *Harry Potter and the Prisoner of Azkaban* (2004) follow much the same pattern. Adapted from the weakest of the books, *Chamber of Secrets* is probably the most balanced and enjoyable of the three films so far. A goblin dogsbody warns Harry not to return to Hogwarts as another mysterious something threatens the welfare of its students. Luckily for Harry, a term spent languishing at the Dursleys' is avoided thanks to Ron, who provides his getaway in the form of a levitating Ford Anglia. Amusing sidelines disguise the over-cryptic plotting. An origami letter bellows a mother's disapproval over the dinner table, while Kenneth Branagh goes for it as Gilderoy Lockhart, the vaingloriously incompetent Defense Against the Dark Arts teacher.

With a zesty new talent (Mexican director Alfonso Cuarón) replacing Chris Columbus, *Prisoner of Azkaban* should have been the most remarkable film so far. Insane criminal Sirius Black (Gary Oldman), who apparently betrayed Harry's parents to Voldemort, has escaped from the wizard prison of Azkaban, and is hunted through the grounds of Hogwarts by a flock of soul-sucking wraiths known as Dementors. By now, however, the Potter formula feels mechanical, despite boasting sharper special effects (Harry tames an impressive Harryhausen-esque Hippogriff) and keeping up with its rivals by adopting a spooky rainswept ambiance (Hogwarts now looks as though it has teleported to New Zealand).

So absurdly faithful to their source books as to be practically interchangeable, the *Harry Potter* films fail to discriminate Rowling's shortcomings. While the author excels at invention, her plotting is remarkably weak. Like Michael Ende, she appears to subscribe to the fatal "anything goes" school of fantasy, with thudding contrivances regularly passed off as the arbitrary work of "magic," which acts as a narrative cure-all whenever the story paints itself into a corner. *Chamber of Secrets* is the worst offender, with Harry literally pulling solutions out of a hat during his battle with the Chamber's Basilisk (a monstrous serpent, whose gaze turns living things to stone). The all-knowing Dumbledore's pet phoenix turns up in time to claw out the creature's lethal eyes, and to dish out magic swords and medicinal tears as needed.

But these failings do little to diminish the importance of the *Potter* series, which possibly qualify as the first thoroughly post-modern fantasy films. The source books

Let the boy win his spurs: Daniel Radcliffe swaps broomstick for sword in this publicity shot for Chris Columbus' *Harry Potter and the Chamber of Secrets* (Warner/Heyday/1492, 2002).

meld *Tom Brown's Schooldays* with Neil Gaiman's graphic novel *The Books of Magic*, along with borrowings from the Grimms, Andersen, Dickens, Baum, Tolkien, C.S. Lewis, Dahl and Terry Pratchett. With such an eclectic range of sources, the films can locate themselves comfortably in just about any fantasy subgenre. The primary world of the muggles is one of fairy tale hyperbole, where the social services never swoop on the Dursleys for keeping their nephew locked in a cupboard. Both the mundane and the magical world constitute an epic fantasy secondary world, threatened with corruption by the dark lord Voldemort and redeemed by the vulnerable hero Harry. But the films are most usefully discussed within the context of wizard movies, since they deal ultimately with the predicament of a rational child faced with the discovery that he commands magic.

As Harry decides whether to use his powers for good or ill, the films take a braver moral stance than most children's fantasy. They acknowledge the fast-track advantages of doing wrong, rather than enforcing the deceit that virtue is the only road to success. After Harry unknowingly selects Voldemort's twin-wand, John Hurt's creepy salesman in *Philosopher's Stone* confides in Harry that his nemesis "achieved great things. Terrible, but great." These sentiments are echoed when the school Sorting Hat (an animated bonnet that gauges the potential of each pupil and sorts them into classes) declares Harry could achieve his ambitions far quicker in the unscrupulous house of Slytherin than he ever could in Samaritan Gryffindor.

Harry's choice is that of most children: Should he do what he is told is right or what he knows is wrong? The *Potter* films assert that despite the guidance and expectations of parents, of teachers, of class, creed and gender (Hogwarts commendably opens its doors to all), the child himself ultimately decides how his life is lived. This empowering sentiment constitutes much of Harry's appeal, underlined unintentionally by Daniel Radcliffe's rabbit-in-headlights performance. Although the actor relaxes more with each film, and wields a formidable smile, he never quite musters anything befitting the consequence of his role.

This positive tackling of the idea of destiny is the *Potter* films' only winning card over *The Lord of the Rings*. While Harry successfully refuses to bow to fate, Middle-earth's nascent king Aragorn (Viggo Mortensen) must accept his calling whether he likes it or not (making it something of a relief that his intentions are noble). In *Philosopher's Stone*, Hermione points out Harry's natural affinity for magic after he wins his spurs on the Quidditch field. "It's in the blood," she says, indicating a trophy won by his father. In *Chamber of Secrets*, Harry learns that when Voldemort scarred him as a baby, the sorcerer left a splinter of his powers behind, manifesting as the boy's sinister talent for conversing with snakes. Although good-natured, Harry has the potential to become as evil as the one who murdered his parents, and since destiny has no hold over him he must be cautious. But (in his customary post-climax explanation) Dumbledore assures the boy that one's nature or past need not decide one's future. "It is not our abilities that show us what we truly are. It is our choices."

In proposing that the mundane and magical spheres of *Harry Potter* should co-exist, Rowling presents a potent metaphor for the way children perceive the world. For the child at play, a world of magic is similarly only a heartbeat away, the imagination becoming a magic wand transforming the everyday into the fantastic. This author remembers how the chicaning pattern on a hallway carpet was transcended through imagination into the hi-tech corridors of the Death Star, traversed by handfuls of grubby Star Wars figures. Similarly at night, the creak of a floorboard became the tread of a vampire, and the unlit stairs a bottomless well.

For children, life seethes with half-believed wonders, since the real world is largely unknown and imagination fills in the gaps. The powers commanded by *Bruce Almighty* are directed at returning the adult world to this plastic state. Similarly, the interior magic of movies like *Unbreakable* transform concrete notions of the self, and return adult characters to the uncertainty of adolescence. Directed at a secondary world, the magic of the *Harry Potter* films confirms what children already know, that to a degree they are the gods of their own world.

Magic realist movies take place in the same playground of the mind, where the imagination gives shape to the agenda of the adult just as it forms the whims of the child. In Alfonso Arau's *Como agua para chocolate* (*Like Water for Chocolate*) (1991) a sheltered Mexican girl (Lumi Cavazos) transfers her embittered emotions onto others, as she cries into the mixture of her sister's wedding cake. In Clare Peploe's lesser film *Rough Magic* (1995), an intrepid magician's assistant (Bridget Fonda) lays an egg, turns a man into a sausage and disgorges her own heart. These free-floating phenomena matter-of-factly underline the invented nature of all narrative, as well as announcing the presence of an *auteur* at work. The storytelling filmmaker becomes the ultimate wizard, plunging shaman-like into the spirit world of his imagination and relating wisdom back to the real world.

Although the visions of the storyteller in Tim Burton's *Big Fish* (2003) are almost insufferably egocentric, they do illustrate how the fantasist has the power to transcend mortality, becoming his own tale and living on through the people he leaves behind. Compulsive yarn-spinner Edward Bloom (played by Albert Finney, with Ewan McGregor in flashback as Bloom the younger) is dying of cancer in his Alabama home. Having not spoken to his father for three years, level-headed William (Billy Crudup), his only son, returns to his father's side. In their final days together, William tries to reconcile the fictions he has grown up with and the actual truth of his father's life.

Another Munchausen figure (and another of Burton's "Edward" proxies), Bloom unravels the events of his life through a repertoire of tall tales. After shooting out of his straining mother's womb like a bar of soap, he grew to boyhood and met a one-eyed witch (Helena Bonham Carter), whose glass eye disclosed a vision of his death. Armed with this foreknowledge, Edward lives fearlessly knowing he cannot die until his appointed hour. He befriends a giant named Karl (Matthew McGrory), discovers the eerily peaceable lost world town of Spectre, and works for Danny DeVito's lycanthropic circus master, who pays him with nuggets of information about the girl Edward has fallen in love with. After marrying her, he is drafted and steals plans to a secret Communist weapon with the help of Siamese twin showgirls.

Unlike the timid children of *Edward Scissorhands* and *The Nightmare Before Christmas*, Bloom succeeds in sharing his creative gift with the world. At the point of Edward's death (in an exultantly moving scene), William ends the tale of his father's life himself. He describes how they escape from the hospital to the river, where the characters from Edward's tales give him a send-off as he turns into a giant catfish and swims away. Back in the real world, a hospitalized Edward dies peacefully.

Bringing the wizardly storytellers of fantasy to task, *Big Fish* challenges (if only nominally) the accusation that fantasy betrays an inability to cope with the truth. For Edward, a life without make-believe is "only the facts and none of the flavor." For William (unbelievably his only critic), his father's tales are nothing but "amusing lies." Although the film makes its bias clear and is too diffident to let the audience decide for themselves, it does maintain a true principle of its genre: No matter how elaborate, all fantasy stems from reality. When Edward insists that his neurotic fantasizing is just his way of seeing the world, he does have a point. No matter how far from the consensus view, one person's perception is no less valid than anyone else's. Fantasy is not a lie, only another way of perceiving the truth.

5

Heroic Fantasy

Heroes at Large

In the introduction to his landmark pulp anthology *Swords and Sorcery* (1963), editor L. Sprague De Camp explains, "The tales collected under this name [sword and sorcery] are adventure fantasies, laid in imaginary prehistoric or medieval worlds, when (it's fun to imagine) all men were mighty, all women were beautiful, all problems were simple, and all life was adventurous. In such a world, gleaming cities raise their shining spires against the stars; sorcerers cast sinister spells from subterranean lairs; baleful sprits stalk crumbled ruins; primeval monsters crash through jungle thickets; and the fate of kingdoms is balanced on the bloody blades of broadswords brandished by heroes of preternatural might and valor."

The story goes that in 1961, British author Michael Moorcock requested a term to describe this conventionalized subgenre of fantasy fiction, whose axe-straining barbarians later achieved iconic status on the covers of countless rock albums and sleazy paperbacks. Writing in George Scither's fanzine *Amra*, fellow fantasy author Fritz Leiber suggested the phrase "sword and sorcery," most likely prompted by the phrase "sword and sandal" (the term describing the Italian costume epics enjoying a revival at the time). Unfortunately, this nickname quickly became a slur, describing the kind of hackwork that arguably constitutes much of the form, reaching an artistic nadir in the late '70s. Attempting to sidestep the genre's own reputation, some anonymous marketing suit suggested an even more fitting alternative.

"Heroic fantasy" crystallized as a literary form in dustbowl America, just before the Depression, roaring into life within the short stories of eccentric Texan scribbler Robert E. Howard. From the flurry of yarns that Howard drove out for the pulps before his suicide in 1936, the genre's first superstars strode forth. King Kull the Atlantean, reluctant dictator of Valusia, summarized his straightforward take on politics in *By This Axe I Rule!* With rapier and flintlock, Elizabethan puritan Solomon Kane stood fast against tides of the supernatural. Conan the noble Cimmerian savage, Howard's most famous creation and the archetypal heroic fantasy protagonist, fought, drank and whored his way through life in the primeval Hyborian age.

Howard wasn't exactly D.H. Lawrence. He wrote not for the airy joys of prose, but for fistfuls of cash (when he got it), and did so at breakneck speed, hammering out stories for half-a-cent a word, without wasting time on the niceties of grammar and syntax. Howard's singular and much-imitated style is often crudely cavalier, but he writes with such furious conviction that the best of his tales fairly tear themselves off the page. His swashbuckling prose characterizes both the writing and the movies he inspired. Although heroic fantasy cinema did not flirt directly with its literary antecedents until the '80s, earlier movies tapped the same narrative vein.

Heroic fantasy's chief convention is its endorsement of a superhuman central character, otherwise known as the superhero. The superheroes of heroic fantasy mainly concern themselves with magic and mysticism, leaving the pseudo-scientifically rational to the superguys of sci-fi (like Batman or Superman). The forces of magic taking precedence in a heroic fantasy story usually assume one of two forms, either a secondary world full of bizarre and mystical goings-on, or magical powers demonstrated by the superhero him/herself. In movies, a heroic fantasy superhero may exhibit inhuman strength like that of Hercules, or he may inhabit a world as infested with magic and monsters as Conan's Hyboria. A heroic fantasy superhero may even inhabit an earthbound primary world, where mysticism seeps through the cracks and has to be held at bay by the likes of Indiana Jones.

One step away from the primary world of earthbound fantasy, heroic fantasy's secondary worlds conduct themselves with a degree of realism similar to the matter-of-fact worlds of epic fantasy. Even though heroic and epic fantasy may be rife with fantastical monsters, their fictional worlds still adhere to the basics of physics. Reality-defying magic exists, but simmers below the surface rather than soaking the very fabric of existence itself, as in the fairy tale. In effect, the forces of magic in heroic and epic fantasy are more "realistic" than those of the more elastic fairy tale. Heroic and epic fantasy rationalize their magic to an extent, usually harnessing it within appropriate vessels, like wizards, artifacts or lost worlds. These must be deployed carefully or else they risk drowning the story, which has to be realistic to the degree that it engages the audience. When the secondary worlds of heroic or epic fantasy become as anarchically fantastical as Faerie, they inevitably topple into parody or fall apart altogether.

Both heroic and epic fantasies traditionally take place in similar, autonomous, quasi-historical secondary worlds, but the genres differ significantly in two ways. Firstly, heroic fantasy worlds are necessarily less detailed than those of the epic fantasy. The antics of the superhero take priority; their worlds are essentially backdrops. The secondary worlds of epic fantasy tend to be more precise in their geography and history because (secondly) their heroes inextricably sympathize with the world they inhabit. Frodo in the epic fantasy *The Lord of the Rings* is a courageous everyman striving to save an entire world and its people, prepared to sacrifice his own life in order to do so. A heroic fantasy superhero, like Schwarzenegger's Conan, remains detached from his surroundings. He is the adolescent solipsist, fighting for nothing beyond his own interests. His superheroic abilities are limited by their serving only to change the lives of those immediately surrounding him, the princess he rescues, the loved one he avenges or the fiefdom he liberates. The heroic fantasy superhero is the lonely pioneer of the wild fantasy frontier. He is Gilgamesh, Beowulf, Achilles and Monkey, fighting to tame a pagan landscape with might or cunning, ridding its unexplored quarters of monsters, paving the way for civilization, which in epic fantasy becomes another battleground, fought upon by more humble heroes like Frodo.

The concept of the superhero is central to an understanding of heroic fantasy, since heroic fantasy movies comprise part of the broader superhero genre. Although the term "superhero" is most commonly associated with cape-and-costume movies like *Superman* (1978), *Batman* (1989) and *Spider-Man* (2002), the term can apply just as accurately to characters outside the sphere of comic adaptations. The usually eponymous lead character of the superhero movie embodies outrageous physical or mental powers far beyond the ken of regular movie heroes like Charles Foster Kane, Michael Corleone or Thelma and Louise. If not specifically magical in origin, the superhero's powers are certainly extraordinary, if not downright unbelievable. Consider the incredible mental agility of Basil Rathbone's Sherlock Holmes, the enviably effective sexual magnetism of Sean Connery's James Bond or the precision firepower and pugilistic fury of Angelina Jolie's Lara Croft. The defining talents of the superhero, though utterly beyond our grasp, are precisely what attract us to them. They are another form of fantasy wish fulfillment, iconic embodiments of our values and desires; they are us as we wish we were, more potent, more beautiful, more in control of themselves and their world. But we must not take their ideals literally, as did Hitler. The moral and physical perfection of the superhero is a target to aim for, not a destination to be reached.

The "super" prefix also usefully emphasizes a clear but often unacknowledged division among the characters we collectively regard as heroes. Non-superheroes are those compelled to embark upon some kind of restorative quest, undergoing various trials and betrayals, finally experiencing some form of spiritual transformation. A key figure in the development of the fantasy genre, anthropologist Joseph Campbell believed the hero's urge to change (that is, his urge to embark upon his quest) is born of Man's separation from God. "Whenever one moves out of the transcendent, one comes into a field of opposites. One has eaten of the tree of knowledge, not only of good and evil, but of male and female, of right and wrong, of this and that, and of light and dark. Everything in the field of time is dual: past and future, dead and alive, being and nonbeing." In Western mythology, when Man comes to the realization that the world is contradictory, he seeks to reinstate a sense of wholeness, that childlike sense of unity when one saw the world as undivided. But the superhero does not undergo the evolution suffered by the hero. The superhero hails from a period before Campbell's "field of time."

If the hero's sense of duality is born the moment Man leaves the Garden, then the superhero would appear to operate from within the Garden itself. The stories of the superhero take place within a prelapsarian adventure playground. Here battles are continuously fought but neither combatant gives ground, like the ying/yang of Peter Pan and Captain Hook, existing in a bubble of conflict sealed off from the complexities and ambiguities of the adult world. Herein lies the superhero's immortality. He is like some earthbound god, not only ageless but also immune to death. After all, to die is to change — and change is what the superhero can only ever achieve for others. The price the superhero pays for the extraordinary powers he enjoys is an imprisonment within the cycle of his own adventures. The only way he can escape is by dying in the line of duty (and no producer worth his salt will let go of a lucrative franchise) or else he can attempt to give up adventuring altogether, relinquishing his superpowers in exchange for mortality. But as George Lazenby's Bond finds to his cost, as he sobs over the body of his murdered wife at the end of *On Her Majesty's Secret Service* (1969), the fate of the superhero is not easily escaped.

It took over 50 years for the front ranks of heroic fantasy superheroes to reach the cinema. By that time, the other fantasy subgenres had laid down significant groundwork with the likes of *Die Nibelungen* (1924), *The Wizard of Oz* (1939) and *The Thief of Baghdad* (1940), whose quest plots and imaginative monsters provided a recognizable playing field for the arrival of the heroic fantasy superhero. Not that there was a dearth of other superheroes before the '50s. Action men like Tyrone Power in *The Mark of Zorro* (1940), Errol Flynn in *The Adventures of Robin Hood* (1938) and Johnny Weissmuller in *Tarzan, the Ape Man* (1932) and its sequels embodied their superheroes indelibly. Although all derived from non-fantasy sources, these movies cast considerable influence over heroic fantasy swashbucklers like Indiana Jones and Conan.

But as popular as these features were, a different format proved particularly accommodating to the pre-heroic fantasy superhero. The Saturday afternoon serials of the '30s and '40s, fondly remembered as the "cliffhangers," enthralled generations of under–15s, doling out stories comic-book fashion in weekly 20-minute installments. Spanning every popular genre from the Western and jungle adventure to sci-fi and crime drama, the serials proved as uniquely suited to tales of superheroism as the comics and pulps they plundered from the mid–'30s onwards. Their brisk running time only had room for dynamic plot-driving stuff like car chases, punch-ups and heroic posturing.

Since the superhero is the proverbial rolling stone, never gathering enough moss to bring his adventures to a close, his immutable nature naturally lends itself to franchise. Universal bought the rights to a package of comic strips owned by King Features Syndicate, releasing a string of successful serials chronicling the delirious exploits of Alex Raymond's dashing spaceman. Struggling to dethrone Charles Middleton's Ming the Merciless in *Flash Gordon* (1936), Larry "Buster" Crabbe never spares a thought for giving up his dangerous adventures by settling down with either Jean Rogers' wilting journalist Dale Arden or Priscilla Lawson's foxy Princess Aura. Instead he hurtles on to confront the unvanquishable Ming again in *Flash Gordon's Trip to Mars* (1938) and *Flash Gordon Conquers the Universe* (1940).

Unlike the primal sword-swingers favored by Howard and his literary heirs, the serials prefer to chronicle the adventures of less morally ambiguous types, like Ralph Byrd's incorruptible detective in *Dick Tracy* (1937), the mysterious upstanding avenger of *The Lone Ranger* (1938) and Allan Lane's clean-cut Sgt. King in *King of the Royal Mounted* (1940). Like the urbane sorcerers Howard pits against his brutish superheroes, the villains opposing the serial action-men are most often well-heeled brainiacs out to conquer the world. Applying equivalent devices to the magic crystals and fabled trinkets employed against Conan, serial bad guys tote fearsome-sounding gewgaws like Bela Lugosi's "Devisualizer belt" from *The Phantom Creeps* (1939), the "Lunarium"-powered "Interceptor ray" of *Brick Bradford* (1947) and the intriguingly named "sonic vibrator" of *Captain America* (1944).

Saturday matinee superheroes owing their abilities to insubstantial mystic forces rather than technology are a notable rarity. The serials and thrillers of the time take a hard-headedly rational approach to superheroics, usually purging their characters of mysticism. In Walter B. Gibson's original pulp stories, the Depression-era crime-fighter The Shadow could render himself effectively invisible. In his '30s radio show he had the hypnotic ability to "cloud men's minds." When the character made his first feature appearance in *The Shadow Strikes* (1937), starring Rod La Rocque, he left his magical talents at home. As in the Columbia serial that followed, *The Shadow* (1939), Victor Jory's superhero is merely a resourceful detective and a master of disguise. Monogram's feature *The Shadow Returns* (1946) demystifies him further, as Kane Richmond's mild-mannered businessman-crimefighter promises his ditzy girlfriend (Barbara Reed) that he will give up sleuthing and settle down just as soon as he has recovered a bag of stolen jewels.

One superhero slipped through this rationalist net on a technicality. In the first installment of Republic's rollicking 12-chapter serial *Adventures of Captain Marvel* (1941), callow newsboy Billy Batson (Frank Coghlan, Jr.) tags along with an archeological expedition into a forbidden Siamese tomb. The kid wanders into a forgotten chamber and bumps into an immortal mystic, who grants Billy extraordinary powers not from the scientific future but the legendary past. Combining Solomon's wisdom, Hercules' strength, Atlas' stamina, Zeus' power, Achilles' courage and Mercury's speed into the spoken acronym "SHAZAM!," the mystic magically transforms the whiny-voiced Billy into Tom Tyler's manly Captain Marvel, charged by his ancient mentor with protecting humanity from the curse of the Golden Scorpion. This antique device can transmute base metals into gold, but the hooded criminal mastermind called The Scorpion intends to convert it into a "Solar Atom Smasher."

Exemplifying the ramshackle exuberance of the serial in its heyday, *Captain Marvel* also establishes several conventions of the heroic fantasy movie. Like gold medal–winning swimmers Buster Crabbe and Johnny Weissmuller before him, *Captain Marvel*'s burly Tom Tyler was a championship athlete before he turned to acting. Casting body beautifuls from the world of pro sports, notably in seminal movies like *Hercules* (1958) and *Conan the Barbarian* (1981), has remained a practice in heroic fantasy movies ever since. Casting directors shrewdly surmise that their star's limited ability to emote will be compensated by their looking great in as few clothes as possible, and at a much lower rate than any member of Equity. In *Captain Marvel*, Tyler balances his undeviating blank expression with a forceful presence and considerable physique, hurling himself (and others) across the set with infectious abandon.

A former coal miner, lumberjack and prizefighter, Tyler's pre-acting résumé reads like something out of a Howard yarn, while his Captain Marvel displays tendencies at times as casually homicidal as any Conan. He thinks nothing of pummelling unarmed wrongdoers, throwing them off the tops of buildings or even machine-gunning them in the back as they run away. The serial absolves such amoral heroics by implying that villains and foreigners deserve what they get at the hands of American justice.

Revelling in physical power is another facet of heroic fantasy's appeal, almost

The conquering hero: Tom Tyler poses in this publicity shot as the manly hero of William Witney and John English's madcap *Adventures of Captain Marvel* (Republic, 1941), one of the few superhero serials that qualifies as heroic fantasy.

invariably adopting the dramatic ying/yang of brawny hero versus brainy villain. (In epic fantasy, the reverse typically occurs, as physically vulnerable heroes must resort to their wits and courage against opponents of outrageous physical power.) Appealing especially to children (and the childish, many have argued), this formula dispels feelings of displacement in a world of adult complexity by relating to the empowerment figure of the indestructible superhero, who overcomes with fist or sword what he cannot overcome with his mind. Heroic fantasy movies offer a fantasy of escape into a body more potent and powerful than the viewer's own, a notion made flesh in *Captain Marvel* as the teenage Billy physically transforms into the imposing adult Tyler.

While TV killed the serial, evicting its resident superheroes into programming or features, the essentially juvenile appeal of heroic fantasy remained a problem, particularly when its superheroes developed explicit adult propensities in the '80s. But for the first few years of his eventual emergence into mainstream cinema, the heroic fantasy superhero gambolled through his adventures with the same innocence as his forerunners in the serial. In this idyllic age, justice packed thews of iron and wore a frighteningly short skirt.

Men as Men Should Be: The Peplum Strongman

"Everyone hated it, except the public," recalled independent distributor Joseph E. Levine in an *American Film* interview in September 1979. He refers to a modest Italian costume epic that he purchased the American rights to for a pittance some 20 years before. After lavishing $1 million on an unprecedented advertising campaign, the film reaped a gargantuan profit, grossing 900 million lire in Italy alone, as well as raking in a fortune at the American drive-in.

Despite its title, Pietro Francisci's *Le fatiche di Ercole* (*Hercules*) (1958) is an adaptation of Apollonius of Rhodes' four-volume epic poem *Argonautica* ("Third Century B.C.," the film's credits point out). Hercules himself takes a back seat in a sober quest for the Golden Fleece mounted by Jason (Fabrizio Mioni). The callow Mioni's dominance over the plot and his performance of the film's pivotal hero-deed technically qualify *Hercules* as epic fantasy, but the picture beefs up the role of its heroic-fantasy guest star with added labors and bits of *The Odyssey*. Although arguably nor far from "terrible" (as Levine himself regarded it), this enjoyably naive romp is of prime historical importance as the movie that instigated the revival of the Italian costume epic, which in turn established the first superhero of heroic fantasy cinema.

Flexing his fantasy credentials in the very first scene, Hercules (played by former Mr. Universe Steve Reeves) rescues Princess Iole (Sylva Koscina) from her runaway chariot, helpfully uprooting a tree and hurling it in the path of the fleeing horses. Showing off in front of Iole's stepfather, King Pelias (Ivo Garrani), Hercules bends an iron spear like a pretzel, landing himself a job training the king's soldiers. The men adore him as he poses atop a rock, struts around the athletics field in a skirt and offhandedly mops the floor with the poor dope who challenges him to track and field. The polished magnificence of Steve Reeves set the standard among the strongmen who followed, although departing considerably from the "Herakles" of legend, an earthly prole with an uncontrollably violent temper (a character closer to the barbarian long-hairs of Robert E. Howard).

In the 1950s, Italian cinema was living *la dolce vita*. Rossellini and De Sica's neo-realist films attracted international acclaim, and Rome's Cinecittà studios thrived on international productions. American producers filmed their most expensive ventures in this "Hollywood on the Tiber," taking advantage of local color and cheap labour. American costume epics like *Quo Vadis* (1951) and *Ben-Hur* (1959) inspired the Italians to reclaim a genre they had made their own back in the silent days with Luigi Maggi's *Gli ultimi giorni di Pompei* (*The Last Days of Pompeii*) (1908) and Giovanni Pastrone's *Il caduta de Troia* (*The Fall of Troy*) (1910). Following the international success of *Hercules*, Italy reeled off a torrent of cut-price follow-ups between 1958 and 1965. Valued today as kitsch artifacts in the same vein as the Japanese *Godzilla* movies, these muscle pictures were generally deplored by critics, although an enthusiastic French cult christened them "les pepla" (plural), from the Latin "peplum," denoting the skimpy linen kilt sported by the strongman lead.

Unlike the Italians, American audiences may not have been as aware of the peplum strongman's classical heritage, but knew what he stood for when Joseph Levine had his name spread across every billboard in letters of stone. "Hercules" was already a byword for superhuman strength to kids raised on comics in the '40s, when Mystic, Blue Ribbon, Hit, Marvel and Quality all published the strongman's exploits. Aside from the circus strongmen in both versions of *The Unholy Three* (1925 and 1930), the name appeared most frequently amid the supporting casts of several Hollywood movies, denoting eugenics-obsessed types in lightweight comedies like Jimmy Durante's *Student Tour* (1934), Jack Benny's *College Holiday* (1936), Abbott and Costello's *Little Giant* (1946) and Sterling Holloway's *Man or Mouse* (1948). The only Hollywood feature to attempt anything like a classical portrayal of the ancient Greek superhero was Walter Lang's *The Warrior's Husband* (1933). Set in 800 B.C. this gender comedy sets Amazon matriarch Hippolyta (Marjorie Rambeau) against an army of chauvinistic Greeks led by Theseus (David Manners). Laurel and Hardy's burly comic foil "Tiny" Sandford turns up amid the Greek ranks as their drastically unfit champion.

Italy's national cinema had installed the archetype of the strongman long before *Hercules*. Counterbalancing the iconic female *diva* or "goddess" of romantic "frock-coat films" like Mario Caserini's *Ma l'amour mio non muore!* (*But My Love Does Not Die!*) (1913), the strongman first appeared as Nero's muscular Roman slave, Ursus, in Enrico Guazzoni's *Quo Vadis?* (1913). Giovani Pastrone's monumental *Cabiria* (1914) featured another noble slave, Maciste (pronounced variously as Ma-cheest-ee and Ma-chee-stay). Played by ex-docker Bartolomeo Pagano, Maciste became Italy's own Superman in a long-running series of silent action pictures, transposing the hero from the distant past to the present day in Pastrone's *Maciste* (1915), Vincenzo Denizot's *Maciste atleta* (*Maciste the Athlete*) (1918), and Ramono Luigi Borgnetto's *Maciste in vacanza* (*Maciste on Holiday*) (1921). Other silent strongmen emerged in competition in now all but forgotten movies like Luciano Albertini's *Sansone* (*Samson*) (1917), Raimondo Scotti's *Ajax* (1921), Domenico Gambino's *Saetta più forte di Sherlock Holmes* (*Saetta Against Sherlock Holmes*) (1922) and Mario Restivo's *Ultime avventure di Galaor* (*The Last Adventure of Galaor*) (1921). Although clear precursors of the heroic fantasy strongman, these heroes lacked any explicitly superhuman qualities, remaining extraordinary among their peers, but equally mortal.

These strongman capers expired by the mid–'20s and remained absent from Italian screens by the time the blackshirts marched on Rome and seized power for their own self-styled Maciste. *Uomo del blocco* to Hitler's *Übermensch*, Benito Mussolini advocated the ultimate Italian leader as a man of Herculean proportions, "ruthless and energetic enough to make a clean sweep." Heroic fantasy films and fiction regularly come under fire from critics accusing them of cryptofascism. (The genre comes under its most sustained and entertaining assault in Norman Spinrad's novel *The Iron Dream* [1972], which posits failed politician Adolf Hitler as a writer of Conan-esque pulp.)

The *totalitario* state promoted by Mussolini and a heroic fantasy film like *Hercules* certainly invite comparison. The regime would certainly have approved of the movie's promotion of a sportsman as its central character. (Mussolini hailed championship wrestler Primo Carnera as a particularly inspirational figure, and the performer appears as Antaeus the earth-giant in *Hercules'* sequel *Hercules Unchained*.) They would also have smiled upon the hero's policy of intervention and restoration, exerting power and control over a people significantly weaker than himself. Italy's fling with fascism arose out of disillusionment with insipid government and a desire for assertive leadership. The fantasy of the sculpted strongman arises from a similar impulse, out of dissatisfaction with one's own body and a perceived failure to govern it to an ideal.

Yet *Hercules*, and the peplum cycle that followed, presents itself as avowedly anti-fascist. Jason and Hercules wish to rid the land of the usurping Mussolini-figure of King Pelias, who murdered the previous monarch, Jason's father. Pelias is goaded into action by the whispers of his Adolf-like sidekick, Eurytus (Arturo Dominici), who disguises himself among Jason's crew and does his best to hinder the hero's quest. Jason spears a guardian Tyrannosaurus (of the stuntman-in-a-suit variety) and grabs the Fleece (which looks like a grubby hearthrug), but Eurytus steals it and sneaks back to Pelias. Playing second fiddle to Jason until now, Hercules steps up to sort things out. Snapping his chains and twirling them around his head at the palace guards (in what became a signature pose of the Italian strongman), he literally brings the house down. Such images of rebellion and liberation persist throughout the peplum. Subjugated villagers take up arms against dictators, chains are wrenched out of dungeon walls and swung defiantly at oppressors, and strongman heroes parade bodies unfettered by clothing.

Finally Hercules kills the treacherous Eurytus, while the usurper Pelias poisons himself in shame. Jason claims his rightful throne, reinstalling a benevolent monarchy, while Hercules sails away into the sunset with Jason's sister. Critic Richard Dyer, in his piece *White Man's Muscles*, concurs that the peplum strongman movies reject fascism, but notes an underlying tension: "[I]n its address and narrative organization it [the peplum] also shows continuities with fascism, or perhaps with even longer continuities, which fascism fed on as much as it promoted. Rather than attempt to side the peplum (and by implication its audience) either with or against fascism, it should be seen as an imaginary working through of the shameful momentousness of the period, shameful because it was fascist and/or because it was defeated."

In *Hercules*, Steve Reeves' strongman barges into social affairs wielding a power too great for anyone to contest. But unlike *Il Duce*, the heroic fantasy superhero rarely rules over those he has conquered, leaving such tiresome state affairs in the hands of whoever he has restored to the throne, while he wanders off into the sunset in search of further adventure. Those who choose to settle down and rule will either degenerate into tyrants (staple bad guys for other superheroes to oust), or else will mature into an epic fantasy hero, fighting no longer for himself but to protect his people's way of life. Either way, the superheroic cycle is brought to an end. Howard's King Kull stories suggest the heroic fantasy superhero is perhaps incapable of ruling a kingdom, implying that if a man is savage enough to claim a throne by brute force alone, then he clearly has no place within civilization.

Unlike the heroic fantasy superheroes that followed, revenge or wealth do not interest the strongman. His fantastic strength literally god-given, the strongman only ever addresses his benefactors directly in Alberto De Martino's lively *Il trionfo di Ercole* (*The Triumph of Hercules*) (1964), as Dan Vadis pleads for Zeus to return his strength, nullified as punishment for killing a friend in a fit of rage. The strongman is a single-minded force of nature, a finger of God who interferes in human affairs with the entire moral aforethought of a hurricane, sweeping away the forces of evil so the common man can make a fresh start. The strongman is literally the superhero as earthbound divinity, earning his ticket to Olympus through noble deeds.

The peplum strongman is never so tragic as the Hercules of legend, who had to atone for murdering his wife and children while in the throes of a blind rage. The strongman is an immaculate figure of worship, with adoring female (or only very slightly less adoring male) companions doting over his sculpted bod. This veneration of male flesh is understandable coming from the country that gave us Donatello and Michelangelo, but intriguing when one considers the popularity of strongman movies abroad. In the west, open adoration of the male nude was limited to mail-order-only "physique photography," which came in under the censor's radar next to the "naturist" movies of the '60s.

There is an interesting scene midway through *Hercules*, when the Argonauts stumble upon an island inhabited by a tribe of leggy Amazons. Unwisely condescending to his aggressive and clearly dangerous female captors, Jason falls in love with their queen (Gianna Maria Canale), while the men are happily entranced by her dancing girls and unwittingly drugged in preparation for their own bloody sacrifice. Having missed out on all the fun by opting to stay on board ship with the guys, Hercules ventures ashore to rescue the Argonauts and threatens them with a suggestively oversized club when they protest.

Whereas epic fantasy considers the abstracts of courage, heroic fantasy glorifies the physical. Setting themselves in an age when it was natural to wear next to nothing, these movies have a better excuse than most to showcase the physical attributes of their stars. Unlike the barbarian swordsman who relies on cold steel, the strongman's signature weapon is his body. As immaculate and devastating as Toshiro Mifune's *katana* or Dirty Harry's .44 Magnum, the power of the strongman's armoring muscle is showcased in displays of brute strength, as he bends prison bars, topples stone columns and lobs boulders across the sky. (He also loves hefting marble

Nothing to lose but his chains: Steve Reeves is about to be the cause of a hefty insurance claim as Hercules in Pietro Francisci's *Le fatiche di Ercole* [*Hercules*] (Oscar/Galatea, 1958).

coffee tables into ranks of huddled soldiery, who never seem to have the sense to get out of the way or shoot arrows into his vulnerable kneecaps.) The camera stresses the muscular exertion of these activities, with loving close-ups of straining thews. But as Steve Cohan asks in *Masked Men, Masculinity and the Movies in the Fifties,* "straining for *whose* benefit?"

The homosexual appeal implicit in the strongman archetype is even more forthright in *Ercole e la regina di Lidia* (*Hercules Unchained*) (1959). Picking up directly after events in the first film, and again directed by Pietro Francisci, Steve Reeves' Hercules and his companion, Ulysses (Gabriele Antonini) come between a pair of feuding warlords, the effeminate Eteocles (Sergio Fantoni) and his brother Polynices (Mimmo Palmara). Charged with delivering a vital message that will prevent war between the two, the heroes are diverted from their course when a parched Hercules sips the Waters of Forgetfulness. He becomes enthralled to flame-haired enchantress Omphale (Sylvia Lopez), who (similar to the Bluebeard-like Antinea of *L'Atlantide*) hides a gallery of embalmed former lovers in her basement.

Like *Hercules* (and indeed the entire peplum cycle), *Hercules Unchained* adopts a very Catholic stance with regard to its females, who fall into one of two categories: (a) the virgin (usually fair and winsome), or (b) the temptress (usually dark and wanton, and whom the noble strongman has to be drugged into falling for). While the film scorns the feminine underhandedness of Omphale and Eteocles, and regards the puny Ulysses as an everyman, it places Hercules on the highest pedestal of masculinity, and then proceeds to undermine the sexual identity of all.

Reversing the Amazons scene from *Hercules*, *Hercules Unchained* has the superhero himself in need of rescue from a straight man's paradise, surrounded by giggling dancing girls, and indulging in a carnal relationship we never imagine him enjoying with his prim wife Iole (Sylva Koscina). During their regular massage sessions, Ulysses (pretending to be a mute halfwit in order to ingratiate himself in Omphale's palace and rescue his friend) tries to remind the bewildered Herc of his true identity, relating the danger of losing him to a man-swallowing womb of embalming fluid. Omphale plies the strongman with goblets of memory-erasing water, and in a naughty Freudian touch Hercules symbolically loses his manly strength after repeatedly "drinking from the cup." Ulysses finally brings him back to the gay fold. "At last I know who I am," the strongman declares to the spurned Omphale.

Gay parables within strongman movies are rarely as explicit as in *Hercules* and *Hercules Unchained*, the only two Hercules films starring Steve Reeves that can be considered true fantasy. Although he cuts a truly dynamic figure, Reeves is laughably wooden, but it is this very inexpressiveness that lends his Hercules a sense of enigmatic sexuality. Reeves' Hercules always distances himself from the action, remaining as aloof and unknowable as a Rodin sculpture. The strongman movies that followed cast more vividly earthy types, like the cuddly Reg Park, the gallant Gordon Scott or the hatchet-faced Gordon Mitchell, none afraid to engage the offer of a fight or a woman.

The archetype of the strongman reaffirms the worth of a powerful male body. Popular in Italy during a period of national industrialization, strongman movies regularly find their protagonists in contest with forms of machinery. In Antonio Leonviola's *Maciste, l'uomo più forte del mondo* (*Mole Men Against the Son of Hercules*) (1961), Mark Forest is strapped to a weighted yoke that will drive blades through the bodies of his comrades chained beneath, unless he can withstand the weight of stone piled on his shoulders. His symbolic triumph echoes the victory of American folk hero John Henry over the steam drill, which similarly threatens to eradicate his human worth.

In the driving seat: U.S. championship muscleman Steve Reeves avoids the morning traffic as the king of peplum strongmen in Pietro Francisci's *Ercole e la regina di Lidia* [*Hercules Unchained*] (Oscar/Galatea, 1959).

In 1960, the past-worlds of the peplum realized their potential for the fantastic. Previously the peplum justified the use of overt fantasy by adapting specific mythological texts, like Mario Camerini's epic fantasy peplum *Ulisse* (*Ulysses*) (1955), or else confining it to asides within otherwise (reasonably) down-to-earth historical dramas, like the wobbly Tyrannosaurus in *Hercules* and the memory-erasing Waters of *Hercules Unchained*. Encouraged by the success of Ray Harryhausen's monster mash *The 7th Voyage of Sinbad* (released in 1958, the year before *Hercules* hit the U.S.), peplum filmmakers worked outlandish monsters into their plots as tacky showstoppers. Strongman Brad Harris shoves a splintered mast through the head of a floppy giant iguana in Guido Malatesta's *Golia contro i giganti* (*Goliath Against the Giants*) (1960). Silvio Amadio's epic fantasy *Teseo contro il Minotauro* (*Theseus Against the Minotaur*) (1960) features a monster that looks less like a bull and more like a cross between the lovable troll of *Labyrinth* and one of Maurice Sendak's *Wild Things*. The starring beastie of Alberto De Martino's *Perseo l'invincibile* (*Medusa Against the Son of Hercules*) (1963) resembles some kind of shuffling Lovecraftian shrub.

Successive fantasy peplums depict more realized secondary worlds, in which magic extends beyond the body of the super-powered strongman, or the inclusion of a monster or two. In Vittorio Cottafavi's *La vendetta di Ercole* (*Goliath and the Dragon*) (1960), Mark Forest's strongman descends into a maze of monster-infested caves to retrieve a magical Blood Diamond, stolen from the forehead of his deity's idol. Of course the implications of his holy quest are secondary to monster-bashing, as he throttles Cerberus, a three-headed fire-breathing dog, beats up a moth-eaten bat-man (clearly suspended from a wire) and pokes out a dragon's eye as it wags its head at him through a hole in the wall. Hungarian Mr. Universe Mickey Hargitay faced a stumpy three-headed hydra in Carlo Ludovico Bragaglia's *Gli amori di Ercole* (*The Loves of Hercules*) (1960) before Jayne Mansfield's Queen Hippolyta leads him into a forest comprising former lovers, transformed into agonized trees. These films suggest a milieu more akin to the exotic pulp worlds of *Weird Tales* than the refined mythological settings of Greek legend. Wonders similarly lurk around every corner and the superhuman abilities of the strongmen become just another expression of the magic infusing their world.

The strongman's implausible vigor remains a constant feature of the peplum, although many of these films should not be regarded as fantasy. Strongman Ed Fury's impossible strength in Carlo Campogalliani's non-fantasy *Ursus* (1961) is a generic convention, enabling the hero to habitually uproot trees, wrench chains out of the brickwork and reduce sets to rubble like a diminutive King Kong. Such feats function as mere hyperbole unless the strongman's powers are specifically referred to as of divine or magical origin, or else set in the context of an explicitly fantastical world. Strongman movies like *Ursus* operate in a quotidian historical world where, stylistically speaking, the inclusion of a performer with a build as imposing as that of Fury would appear arbitrary if he could *not* perform feats far beyond the capabilities of those around him.

Strongmen like these can be likened to the "flying swordsmen" of the Asian sword opera. The protagonists of Chang Cheh's *Dubei dao* (*The One-Armed Swordsman*) (1966), King Hu's *Long menke zhen* (*Dragon Gate Inn*) (1967) and *Xia Nü* (*A Touch of Zen*) (1970) can leap a hundred feet in the air, tear out an opponent's heart and shove it in his face, or prance from tree limb to tree limb as delicately as Peter Pan. Such reality-bending feats are not concrete manifestations of magic, but stylistic flourishes fancied by the filmmaker.

Several pepla expand the idea of the strongman in a secondary world. Antonio Leonviola's *Maciste nella terra dei cyclopi* (*Atlas Against the Cyclops*) (1961) sets itself up as a promising sequel to *The Odyssey*. Circe places a curse on the descendants of Ulysses, which will endure until the last living descendent of Homer's voyager is devoured by a Cyclops. Gordon Mitchell has to save Ulysses' infant heir and his mother (Vira Silenti) from Chelo Alonso's despotic Queen, who has them thrown to a giant *Krull*-style Cyclops in the last reel.

Giacomo Gentilomo's science-fantasy *Maciste contro il vampiro* (*Goliath and the Vampires*) (1961) begins straightforwardly enough as barrel-chested Gordon Scott (world-famous for his *Tarzan* pictures) sails to the Arabian isle of Salmanak to dispatch a fearsome vampire lord. An increasingly crackpot tale unfolds, involving a Flash Gordon–attired sheik (Jacques Sernas) and his subterranean army "the Blue Men." A crash-helmeted vampire (Guido Celano) wishes to use Scott as the basis for an alchemically created army of "robots with blood," and orders his brain be "destroyed by sound waves." His minions attempt this by covering Gordon with a giant bell and walloping it with sledgehammers. Fortunately, the hero has the foresight to plug his ears with wax.

Antonio Leonviola's *Mole Men Against the Son of Hercules* (1961) is much less fun, as strongmen Mark Forest and Paul Wynter (the only black strongman) rescue their women from Moira Orfei's evil queen and her grass-skirted minions, who dissolve into bones at the touch of a sunbeam. In Amerigo Anton's similarly lackluster *Il trionfo di Maciste* (*Triumph of the Son of Hercules*) (1961), Kirk Morris for some reason displays a pair of weird Vulcan eyebrows while facing up to Ljuba Bodin's Cleopatra-like seductress, her insatiable fire god and a race of razor-taloned troglodytes.

Although heroic and epic fantasy movies comprise only around ten percent of the entire peplum cycle, they remain among the best remembered. One of the most cohesively silly is Vittorio Cottafavi's heroic fantasy *Ercole alla conquista di Atlantide* (*Hercules and the Captive Women*) (1961), which boasts both a credible fantasy setting and an appealing Hercules in the form of British bodybuilder Reg Park. Sent to investigate overseas, Park's genial strongman has to bring a mutiny to heel, dragging his fleeing ship ashore by its anchor chain. Embedded in the cliffs of misty Atlantis, he finds Laura Altain's princess left by her people as a sacrifice to Proteus (*The Odyssey*'s seal-loving water god). When the grumpy deity appears and tells Hercules to mind his own business, the strongman gets him in a headlock. As they wrestle, the old man turns himself into a wall of fire, a glowing-eyed iguana, a clearly tranquilized lion and a disgruntled vulture (hurled at Park from off-screen). "Today's dedicated to Uranus," Altain tells Hercules without a trace of a giggle, taking him to meet her resplendently disdainful mother Queen Antinea (Fay Spain), who plans to transform her slaves into a world-conquering clone army.

Cottafavi's flamboyant direction lifts *Captive Women* above the herd, but more so does Reg Park's gregarious Hercules, who, like some kind of steroid-abusing Hobbit, would much rather be napping or eating than getting involved in exertive adventures. An opening tavern brawl establishes the film's playful tone, as extras smash pots over each other's heads and make love to the serving maids under the tables. Oblivious to the riot, Hercules quaffs a mug of wine and munches on a leg of mutton.

Bold enough to term the peplum a "movement," Cottafavi came up with the term "Neomythologism," referring to Italian cinema's reclamation of the historical spectacle, and its celebration of everything romantic, heroic and extravagant. The neomythologist peplum became the object of a fleeting critical fad among young French and British critics, who detected an attempt to counterbalance Italian cinema's tendency towards introspection. Raymond Durgnat, writing for British film journal *Motion*, was particularly vocal. "These films are doing for the general public almost exactly what the Renaissance painters did for the noblemen and intellectuals of their day — appealing to the classical tradition, with its sensuality and worship of physical beauty, against the Christian strain."

Durgnat praised the peplum for the sensual purity of its brightness and color, qualities hardly apparent when viewing the films today. Surviving prints are invariably damaged, blinkered by pan-and-scan, drained of their succulent Eastman Color. Most also carry the scars of the re-dubs and re-edits inflicted upon them when they crossed continents. As a rule, pepla were shot practically silent, then redubbed from country to country. The name of the starring superhero changed to correspond to native familiarities, plucking suitably bellicose titles out of the history books, the Greek Titan Atlas, the Biblical giant Goliath, the Old Testament strongman Samson, as well as the more familiar Ursus, Maciste and Hercules.

When Joseph Levine released a package of peplum movies directly to American television in 1964, he tried to explain away the trans–Atlantic difference in titles by collectively pronouncing his strongmen "The Sons of Hercules." (Each *Sons of Hercules* movie opens with a hearty title song, which to the frantic twangs of a Spanish guitar describes how "The mighty sons of Hercules were men as men should be! They took the world and shook the world, the sons of Herculeeeeeeeeees!") Shorn of mythological significance, the strongmen themselves remain practically identical but for the bodybuilders playing them. As well as re-dubbing, these movies also suffered re-editing to fit theater running times. *Goliath and the Dragon* (1960) and *Atlas Against the Cyclops* (1961) are notable sufferers of this practice. Clearly neither are great films, but possibly more enjoyable in their original Italian form than in the almost unintelligible versions slapped together by their American distributors. *Ercole al centro della terra* (*Hercules in the Haunted World*) (1962) is the most illustrious of these trans–Atlantic casualties.

Directed by Italian horror auteur Mario Bava, who won critical favor with flamboyantly sadistic horror movies like *La maschera del demonio* (*Mask of the Demon*) (1960), *Haunted World* is unusually well-regarded among critics (although English-language prints have been truncated by distributors and censors, excising several scenes that remain unwatched outside Italy). In this otherwise successful combination of heroic fantasy and Hammer horror, Hercules (Reg Park — who manages to land himself in two of the best heroic fantasy pepla) must retrieve a living stone from the land of the dead in order to cure his wife Deianira (Leonora Ruffo), presently under the spell of diabolical statesman Lyco (Christopher Lee). As Hercules journeys through the underworld, Lyco plans to somehow ensure his everlasting rule over the land by drinking Deianira's blood at the coming lunar eclipse. Hercules battles his way through constricting cavern walls, fends off flying zombies and finally crushes Lyco and his undead cohorts beneath a volley of polystyrene boulders.

Bava's inventive handling makes *Haunted World* probably the best of all the heroic fantasy peplums, cleverly playing the film's obvious lack of budget to his advantage by evoking as unreal an atmosphere as possible. Shot in Technicolor with livid reds, greens and blues like neon against black backgrounds within a theatrical *mise-en-scène*, the movie's secondary world radiates a delirious grandeur. In what could have been another routine strongman outing, Bava concocts some inspired flourishes. A woozy sea voyage takes place under a sky of blood red and swirling black. The gigantic roots of the tree of the Hesperides twist as if in agony, bathed in icy blue and flashes of white. In the subterranean realm of Hades (all dry ice and *papier-mâché* stalactites), moaning vines drool blood from severed stems. Cobwebbed tombs grind open, disgorging undead tenants, and rotten hands burst through the soil to rake the super-hero's legs. It feels as though Hercules has wandered into the pages of an EC horror comic.

Haunted World, like its fellow fantasy peplums, has as little regard for mytho-logical fidelity as the non-fantasy peplum has for historical fact. Bava's movie rea-sons that sticking to classical plots only gets in the way of the fun. Why settle for only one of Hercules' labors (retrieving the Apples of the Hesperides), when it can work in the gory tale of Procrustes (the evil human innkeeper of the Theseus leg-end), and throw in Christopher Lee's Dracula persona and a squadron of airborne zombies for good measure? The peplum loves playing mix-and-match with the sto-ries of legend, but as the cycle drew to a close in the mid–'60s, it displayed an almost surreal regard for logic.

The last few heroic fantasy pepla display what can be described as either the last gasps of a cycle approaching burnout, or else a playful disrespect for genre conven-tion. Neomythologist Riccardo Freda wanted his audience to believe the latter, although his patchwork *Maciste all'inferno* (*The Witch's Curse*) (1961) does nothing to convince. Without a word of explanation, Kirk Morris's loinclothed Mediterranean strongman gallops into the freezing highlands of seventeenth century Scotland to save a woman wrongly accused of witchcraft. Reg Lewis sports a *Johnny Bravo* pom-padour in the prehistoric ice age of Guido Malatesta's amusingly silly caveman pic-ture *Maciste contro i mostri* (*Fire Monsters Against the Son of Hercules*) (1962). More jerry-rigging took place in the editing room on Alvaro Mancori's *Ercole l'invincibile* (*The Son of Hercules in the Land of Darkness*) (1964), enabling Dan Vadis' strongman to fend off the same Tyrannosaurus that Fabrizio Mioni's Jason killed six years before in *Hercules*. Piero Regnoli's *Maciste nelle miniere de re Salomone* (*Samson in King Solomon's Mines*) (1964) has nothing to do with Haggard's novel. Instead, Reg Park's Tarzan-esque strongman strides around South Africa in a Greek skirt and leopard-skin sweatbands, taking in stock footage of native dances and grazing wildlife. Park also appears on the Russian steppes in Antonio Margheriti's *Ursus, il terrore dei Kirghisi* (*Hercules, Prisoner of Evil*) (1965) with the added gothic twist of a curse that periodically transforms him into a rampaging Mr. Hyde.

In Sergio Leone's *Per un pugno di dollari* (*A Fistful of Dollars*) (1964), Italy's national superhero shed his muscle and his conscience in exchange for a six-shooter. In the *Western all'italiana*, the human body, so prized by the peplum, is as cheap as trail dust, heaped onto Clint Eastwood's cart like racks of beef and counted up as bounty at the end of Leone's sequel *Per qualche dollari in più* (*For a Few Dollars More*) (1965). The superhero no longer needed stacks of muscle when he had a weapon and the ability to wield it faster and with more precision than any unfortunate bravo who crossed his path. His world changed also, reducing the azure firmament, blossom-ing woodland and frothing waterfalls of the peplum to an arid, sepia wasteland, as deadly and inhospitable as the protagonists that haunted it. Italy quickly forgot all about the strongman and now rattled off assembly-line Westerns like rounds from Django's Gatling gun.

By the '70s, another superhero archetype adopted the manly physicality of the peplum strongman. Endorsing the power and beauty of the unarmed male body just as much as Steve Reeves, Bruce Lee immortalized the figure of the kung fu avenger. In the movies that launched his international career, *Tangshan Daxiong* (*The Big Boss*) (1971) and *Jingwu Men* (*Fist of Fury*) (1972), Lee's scowling avenger transcends bodily limitations, with blurring punches, soaring kicks and unearthly squawks. Like the strongman, the avenger is his own magical weapon, although he brings a cerebral dimension to the table by drawing upon the seemingly magical reserves of Asian mysticism. Western audiences generally have less patience for all that stuff about the oneness of being, but endless enthusiasm for gymnastic ass-kicking. For all David Carradine's gentle attempts to bring the Wild West round to the idea of contemplation, the real reason so many people tuned in to watch *Kung Fu* (1972–75) was to watch him beat the stuffing out of each week's wrongdoer.

In Richard Moore's oafishly pretentious *The Silent Flute* (*Circle of Iron*) (1978), Carradine plays a sightless beggar prompting a pugnacious martial artist (Jeff Cooper) across ancient China in search of the Book of Enlightenment, kept on an island commune full of hippies (led by the ever-game Christopher Lee). Passing through a fishing village, Carradine breaks a handsome boy's face, smugly excusing himself by saying the boy's narcissism would cause him to grow up a tyrant. In Western hands, the spiritual superiority of the kung fu avenger gives him license to exert the physical, interfering in the affairs of commoners and busting civilian heads in a way that seems unconscionable in the halcyon days of the peplum strongman. Clearly the heroic fantasy superhero was giving in to urban paranoia.

Sailing the Seas of Fate: Sinbad

Temporarily stranded on a rocky island, surveying the sun-bleached bones of other shipwrecked mariners, Robert Malcolm's irascible Sinbad grumbles, "This is why I hate the sea," in *Simbad e il califfo di Bagdad* (*Sinbad and the Caliph of Baghdad*) (1973), directed by Pietro Francisci of *Hercules* fame. One imagines Sindbad the Sailor of the *Arabian Nights* tales echoing a similar sentiment. During the course of his seven famous voyages, as described by his chronicler Scheherazade, this hapless seafarer finds himself shipwrecked on an inhospitable island almost every time he puts to sea. He nearly drowns when his shortsighted captain mistakes a dozing whale for an island. Pygmies sacrifice him to a band of ravenous Cyclopes. A native king forces him to marry his daughter, then has his new son-in-law buried alive when the girl dies. In another episode, the Roc (a huge predatory bird) dumps a boulder on his ship after its hungry crew make breakfast out of the monster's hatchlings. Given Sindbad's reputation for attracting calamity, it remains one of the many mysteries of the *Arabian Nights* how he convinced anyone to sail with him.

The most striking dissimilarity between Sindbad (as spelled in *Arabian Nights*) and Sinbad (as most commonly spelled by the movies) is that the former remains less romantically depicted than the situations he finds himself in. Modelled on Persian traders who sailed the seas between Basra, the East Indies and China in the eighth century, Sindbad remains nothing more dashing than a particularly hapless merchant, whose intelligence and inventiveness help him out of the circumstances dumped in his lap by capricious *kismet*.

Sinbad, on the other hand, has become a heroic fantasy archetype in his own right. Distant cousin to Fairbanks and Flynn, Sinbad is the dashing Marco Polo of the fantasy world, advance scout of burly monster-stompers like Hercules and Conan. Scrawny in comparison to the strongman or the barbarian swordsman, and of a cheerful decadence antithetical to the austere discipline of the kung-fu avenger or the samurai swordslinger, Sinbad wields worldly cunning and a devilish grin as his signature weapons, but holds in reserve a swift Arabian scimitar. Aside from a similar measure of guile, the Eastern Sindbad and the Western Sinbad have little in common.

Sinbad's buccaneering image is entirely an invention of the cinema, established in 1958 with the success of the Harryhausen monster movie *The 7th Voyage of Sinbad*. Films prior to this took inspiration directly from the exotic literary exploits of Sindbad. Disregarding an alleged 1919 Universal single-reeler of the same name (whose existence this author has so far been unable to verify), Sinbad embarked on his first screen voyage in 1935 in Ub Iwerks' eight-minute ComiColor cartoon *Sinbad the Sailor*. This has Sinbad captured by treasure-hunting pirates and tied to a tree, which turns out to be the leg of a giant Roc. Sinbad unties himself when the beast takes to the air, drops onto the pirates' ship and sails away with their treasure. The monstrous bird of the Sindbad tales makes a second appearance in the Fleischer brothers' 20-minute musical cartoon *Popeye the Sailor Meets Sindbad the Sailor* (1936). Played by Popeye's hirsute nemesis Bluto (voiced by Gus Wickie), Sindbad spots Popeye's tug from his island kingdom and sends his pet Roc to trash the ship and kidnap Olive Oyl (Mae Questel). But the spinach-guzzling sailor (Jack Mercer) rescues the gangling maiden, fending off a two-headed Yiddish giant in the process.

The first live-action Sinbad appears in Universal's *Arabian Nights* (1942). This trivial yet popular non-fantasy stars the alluring and famously untalented Maria Montez alongside the bright-eyed and very talented Sabu as circus performers. Together they help Jon Hall's deposed Caliph reclaim the throne of Baghdad from his treacherous brother (Leif Erickson). Long retired from seafaring and reduced to a tiresome slapstick routine with John Qualen's Aladdin, Sinbad turns up in a minor role, played by Shemp Howard of the Three Stooges.

Powell and Pressburger's 1940 *The Thief of Baghdad* stimulated public enthusiasm for Arabian *fantastique*, eagerly exploited by movies like *Arabian Nights* and 1944's *Ali Baba and the 40 Thieves*, another of Universal's Hall-Montez pictures. This led to a cycle of desert romances (or "tits and sand" pictures as producers liked to call them). An offshoot of the '30s swashbuckler, this popular but mostly uninspired body of film relocates the conventions of *The Prisoner of Zenda* (1937), *The Man in the Iron Mask* (1939) and *The Sea Hawk* (1940) to an exotic Technicolor Arabia crammed to the minarets with dancing girls in little more than yashmaks, and which bore about as much resemblance to the Middle East as Disneyland.

One of the most successful films of this cycle is also the most significant Sinbad movie of the pre–Harryhausen era, not least because it is the first feature in which the character takes the lead role. RKO's *Sinbad the Sailor* (1947) is an indifferent non-fantasy, in which a head-scarfed and hoop-earringed Douglas Fairbanks, Jr., woos the radiant Maureen O'Hara's gold-digging Kurdish princess, while seeking the fabulous treasure of Alexander the Great. Flinging himself across the stagy chiaroscuro sets with as much gusto as his father in the silent *Thief of Baghdad* (1924), Fairbanks, Jr., prances around the campfire regaling his disbelieving audience with tales of his fantastic encounters. An amalgam of the yarn-spinning everyman of the *Arabian Nights* and the roguish adventurer he was to become in *The 7th Voyage*, Fairbanks, Jr.'s, Sinbad emerges as something of a Munchausen figure, a teller of self-aggrandizing tales believed by no one. Doug the younger's portrayal carried enough dash to cast Sinbad's raunchy name in the public mind as a romantic rascal in the mould of Zorro and Robin Hood, superheroic roles that Doug the elder previously made his own.

The ethos of the Fairbanksian swashbuckler feeds into heroic fantasy cinema through the Sinbad movies, but was already ingrained in heroic fantasy fiction. The swaggering novels of Dumas and Sabatini, which provided the basis for seminal swashbucklers like Fairbanks' *The Three Musketeers* (1921) and Flynn's *Captain Blood* (1935), also cast an influence over Robert E. Howard's sword-and-sorcery tales. Naturally enough, the swashbuckler and heroic fantasy share a number of conventions: historical settings, an emphasis on combat and a central superhero. In *Swordsmen of the Screen*, Jeffrey Richards describes the model swashbuckler, and could just as easily be outlining the ideal heroic fantasy movie. "[A]t its best, [the swashbuckler] is an exhilarating excursion into pure style, a heady blend of male beauty and agility, the grace and color of historical costume, the opulence and splendor of period sets and the spellbinding legerdemain of horseback chases, chandelier-swinging and dazzling swordplay."

The vital difference between the two genres is the social class of their protagonists. The code of the swashbuckler is, as Richards puts it, "the code of the ruling class," to which the heroic fantasy superhero rarely belongs. "The typical swashbuckling hero is the gentleman hero, well born, comfortably off, a man of breeding and polish." Sadly, the vagabonds and sweaty sorts who make up the majority of heroic fantasy archetypes may regularly rub shoulders with troubled kings, erudite wizards and sheltered princesses, but remain members of the earthy proletariat, contracted to perform heroism on behalf of an ineffectual ruling class.

The Sinbad archetype, established as a dashing adventurer in *Sinbad the Sailor*, reappears in RKO's belated follow-up *Son of Sinbad* (1955). This supposedly spicy Arabian farce stars a turbaned Dale Robertson (complete with Texan drawl) as Sinbad's licentious offspring, and a poetic Vincent Price as his Cyrano-like sidekick. As in its predecessor, no fantasy is in evidence in *Son of Sinbad*, and the same rational attitude prevails in the movies that rattled off the desert romance assembly line, which Columbia and Universal started up in the '40s.

Following on from *Arabian Nights*, the character (or at least the name) of Sinbad regularly features in the desert romance, usually next to Aladdin as part of a comic double-act. In Universal's *The Desert Hawk* (1950), Richard Greene's gallant outlaw romances Yvonne De Carlo's haughty Princess Scheherazade, while Sinbad (played by another Stooge, Joe Besser) trades slapstick blows with Jackie Gleason's

Aladdin. Sebastian Cabot's Sinbad lingers in the background of Edward J. Danziger's *Babes in Bagdad* (1952), an Arabian Nights spoof starring Paulette Goddard and Gypsy Rose Lee; as the wisecracking inmates of John Boles' harem, they lead a campaign to emancipate the women of the city and resign the men to a life of monogamy. Columbia's *Thief of Damascus* (1952) features a poker-faced Paul Henreid as the general who defects from the army of John Sutton's tyrannical sultan and helps restore the rightful ruler of Damascus. A sad-sack Lon Chaney, Jr., lends comic support as another retired Sinbad, this one with nothing to show for his adventures but a naughty tattoo and a tiresome clowning routine alongside Robert Clary's whinging Aladdin. Like Doug the younger's skeptical campfire audience, these films see themselves as too level-headed to be taken in by Sinbad's embroidered accounts of his adventures, although they bandy the fairy tale names of Scheherazade, Ali Baba and Aladdin in much the same way as the peplum juggles the mythological names of Hercules, Samson and Atlas.

The desert romances that do set themselves out as fantasy do so without any mention of Sinbad. The characters of the *Arabian Nights* had become just another part of the desert romance's non-fantasy formula, which heroic fantasies like Columbia's *The Magic Carpet* (1951) and Universal's *The Golden Blade* (1953) attempt to convert by lending desert outlaws John Agar and Rock Hudson magical assistance with a flying rug and a sword of invulnerability. One slapdash Italian heroic fantasy, Antonio Margheriti's *La freccia d'oro* (*The Golden Arrow*) (1962), starring Tab Hunter, manages to rope in a plot device from the Fairbanks *Thief*, along with an enchanted arrow that returns to the archer's hands after hitting its target, a magic carpet, a trio of unfunny genies and a brace of fire demons (or rather stuntmen in burning asbestos suits).

The turning point in Sinbad's screen career came in 1958, the year the peplum strongman won a new following in Italy. *The 7th Voyage of Sinbad* was the first stab at fantasy taken by the producer–stop-motion animator double-act of Charles H. Schneer and Ray Harryhausen, who previously enjoyed a fruitful run of sci-fi films with *It Came from Beneath the Sea* (1955), *Earth vs. the Flying Saucers* (1956) and *20 Million Miles to Earth* (1957). In their first film to feature Harryhausen's toplining "Dynamation" system (in which live performers act in concert with stop-motion models), Schneer and Harryhausen target a much younger audience than the drive-in crowds who went for their sci-fi pictures. *The 7th Voyage*'s vivid Technicolor palette (this was also their first color film), elaborately attired American actors and blandly un–Arabian setting, mark it as a product of the desert romance cycle, while its director, Nathan Juran, had previously helmed 1953's *The Golden Blade*.

The wholesome Kerwin Mathews plays Sinbad, who lands on the desert island of Colossa in time to save a bald magician, Sakurah (Torin Thatcher), from Harryhausen's hungry cloven-hoofed Cyclops. The wizard's magic lamp falls into the monster's paws, while Sinbad and his betrothed, Parisa (Kathryn Grant), return to Baghdad, where the Caliph banishes Sakurah from the city for prophesizing its destruction. Eager to retrieve his lamp, the vengeful wizard reduces the sleeping princess to the size of a chess piece and convinces Sinbad to return to Colossa, where he can restore her with a potion.

Back on the island, Harryhausen's stop-motion set pieces take over. The Cyclops finds Sinbad's men rummaging through its cave of treasures and licks its lips while roasting one of the trespassers on a spit. The men later turn the tables on the island's monsters by making a meal of a newly hatched two-headed Roc, only to have their repast interrupted by its furious mother. Sakurah eventually restores Parisa to her normal size and makes a dangling lab skeleton drop from the ceiling and have at Sinbad with a scimitar. Finally, in a *King Kong*–style wrestling match (which inspired similar bouts in the *Godzilla* movies of the '60s), Sakurah's pet dragon tussles with the Cyclops, before Sinbad's men shoot it through the heart with an oversized crossbow bolt and it collapses on top of its evil master.

Harryhausen's beautifully rendered creations, the remote coastal locations and Bernard Herrmann's lush Arabian score evoke a pleasingly other-worldly atmosphere, despite a slightly mechanical feeling overall. Richard Eyer's child-genie, released from the lamp after Parisa speaks his real name and appearing at her side like a surrogate son, makes for a decidedly soppy ending, while Kerwin Mathews' sword-at-the-ready Sinbad shows little enthusiasm.

The 7th Voyage cemented Sinbad's adventures in Harryhausen's monster-infested world, where several films attempted to take on the animator at his own game, including Edward Small's brazen *7th Voyage* rip-off *Jack the Giant Killer* (1961). AIP also took a shot when they acquired Aleksandr Ptushko's Russian epic fantasy *Sadko* (1952) released in the U.S. in 1962, recut (by a young Francis Ford Coppola) and redubbed under a new title, *The Magic Voyage of Sinbad*. Two years later the studio picked up Senkichi Taniguchi's heroic fantasy *Daitozoku* (1964), starring Toshiro Mifune as a shipwrecked pirate who saves a princess with the help of an incompetent wizard. The latter film was retitled *The Lost World of Sinbad* and released in 1965 on a double-bill with Giuseppe Vari's heroic fantasy peplum *Roma contro Roma* (*War of the Zombies*) (1963).

MGM released Byron Haskin's patchy *Captain Sindbad* (1963), the only post–Harryhausen Sinbad movie to retain the original spelling of its hero's name. An awkward Guy Williams plays Sindbad, whose ship is destroyed by not just one but an entire squadron of boulder-hefting Rocs. With her sweetheart left for dead, Princess Jana (Heidi Bruhl) falls into the hands of jolly despot El Kerim (Pedro Armendariz), who (when Sindbad runs him through) pulls the sword from his chest and politely hands it back. A resonant touch this, borrowed from the Russian folktale of *Koshchei the Deathless*; Kerim has stashed his mortal heart safely outside his body, effectively rendering him immortal. The film saves a couple more dreamlike touches for the climax, as Sindbad ascends a gigantic length of rope inside a hollow tower and grapples with a huge disembodied hand.

Aside from casting Dan Harrison in the title role of their non-fantasy peplum *Simbad contro i sette saraceni* (*Sinbad versus the Seven Saracens*) (1964), the Italians were too busy ransacking world mythology for their own heroic fantasy epics to bother with Sinbad. By 1973, the indefatigable Pietro Francisci finally got around to it with *Sinbad and the Caliph of Baghdad*. The movie is a crude non-fantasy costume farce, but remains possibly the only live-action movie to come close to the *Arabian Nights'* portrayal of Sinbad as a resourceful unfortunate at the mercy of the winds of fate. Robert Malcolm is enjoyable as the cantankerous mariner, charging about in his underpants, a false beard and a flamboyant '70s hairdo. This unlucky adventurer finds himself roughed up by tax collectors, robbed by camel thieves, shanghaied by slavers, fondled by an amorous tailor and left to drift at sea in a dinghy.

In the same year, Schneer and Harryhausen produced the greatest Sinbad movie yet, and one of the best titles on their collective resumé. Based on an astute screenplay (by *Avengers* scriptwriter and co-producer Brian Clemens), *The Golden Voyage of Sinbad* is a muscular adventure yarn set in a tangibly real fantasy world, albeit frustratingly constrained by Gordon Hessler's non-committal direction. The early scenes among the bazaars of Arabia subtly establish the urban shores of Sinbad's secondary world with its hot, dingy streets packed with haggling merchants and lounging hashish smokers. Leagues ahead of Kerwin Mathews' well-scrubbed role model, John Phillip Law's swarthy Sinbad, although never allowed to outshine the special effects, makes a robust hero and certainly the most Arabic of all screen Sinbads. Like his scruffy crew, he wears a turban (although he takes it off when he goes to bed), manages to keep up a Middle Eastern accent, and is full of Arabic aphorisms ("Trust in Allah, but tie up your camel").

Law's adventure begins as a butter-fingered little gargoyle drops part of an ancient talisman onto his ship. The captain keeps it around his neck as a trinket, but finds it sought after by the diabolist Koura (played with grinning malevolence by a pre–*Doctor Who* Tom Baker). In a neat catch, the magician ages every time he invokes the forces of darkness, providing a credible balance to his powers. On meeting Douglas Wilmer's disfigured vizier, his face encased in an golden mask, Sinbad learns the talisman is part of a map leading to the Fountain of Destiny, which grants power and riches to whoever throws all three pieces into it. With Koura in pursuit, Sinbad sets sail with Caroline Munro's bosomy slave girl draped over one arm.

This time the stop-motion sequences feel more like part of a coherent narrative than preconceived set-pieces for the rest of the plot to revolve around. One of the most effective scenes, involving an encounter with a goatish djinn and an ingenious escape plan, gets by without any stop-motion contributions. Elsewhere, Harryhausen animates a creaking figurehead that rips itself free of the prow, a winged homunculus spy that Koura brings to life with his own blood, and a living statue of Kali, which sprouts a tulwar from each of her six hands and engages in a spectacular swordfight with Sinbad and his crew.

Golden Voyage plays fast and loose with mythology. The green-skinned savages of imaginary Lemuria (a setting borrowed from Lin Carter's *Thongor* novels) revere a multi-cultural grab-bag of monsters, comprising the Hindu Kali, a Greek Cyclopean centaur and a Middle Eastern Griffin. Following an anticlimactic duel between Sinbad and an invisible Koura, Sinbad runs the villain through, turning the Fountain's gushing waters a sickly red, and passes the crown of riches to the vizier, restoring both the monarch's scarred features and his blighted kingdom. The epic fantasy hero often gives up his life to further a cause, whereas the heroic fantasy superhero

Full of Eastern promise: The dashing John Phillip Law shows 'em how it's done as the heroic lead of Gordon Hessler's ***The Golden Voyage of Sinbad*** (Morningside/Columbia, 1973), the second and the best of Harryhausen and Schneer's Sinbad trilogy.

makes an equivalent sacrifice, relinquishing his opportunity to lead a comfortable, adventure-free life.

Golden Voyage made so much money for Columbia that the studio rushed a sequel into pre-production while its predecessor was still in release. Reportedly, respected director Sam Wanamaker became frustrated by the contrived script and the precedence Harryhausen's special effects seemed to take over all else, resulting in a miserable shoot and expensive delays. Wanamaker later refused to discuss the film. Schneer and Harryhausen's third and final Sinbad feature, Sinbad and the Eye of the Tiger (1977) reaped even more at the box office than Golden Voyage, despite its vast inferiority.

Eye of the Tiger's mishandling perhaps makes it the more interesting of the two. With a lack of authentic atmosphere and anemic romantic leads (Patrick Wayne and Jane Seymour), Eye of the Tiger subverts the achievements of the previous film and regresses back to the days of the desert romance. The strident American accent and toothpaste grin of Wayne's Sinbad are almost as absurdly out of place as his Day-Glo orange turban. Seymour is equally unremarkable as a simpering Arabian princess with an English accent.

Seymour's brother, Prince Cassim (Damien Thomas), is about to be crowned Caliph when he is turned into a stop-motion baboon by his short-tempered step-mother, Zenobia (Margaret Whiting, looking like a Turkish madam), who hopes to get her son crowned in his place. Sinbad embarks on a lengthy voyage to seek Patrick Troughton's Greek scholar Melanthius. The ex–Doctor Who's dotty performance steals the film as he and his grouchy daughter (Taryn Power) accompany Sinbad beyond the Arctic Circle to the lost world of Hyperboria (another literary name-poach, this one from Clark Ashton Smith). Inside an ancient pyramid, the simian Prince Cassim is dangled in the middle of a crackling aurora and restored.

Eye of the Tiger demonstrates the importance of recognizing the fantasy subgenres, as Beverley Cross' contradictory script tries to articulate fairy tale, heroic and epic fantasy as though they were all the same. The film is clearly intended as a hero-centric narrative along the same lines as its heroic fantasy predecessors (even though Patrick Wayne's inexpressive Sinbad looks insipid even next to Kerwin Mathews). At the same time, it strains for epic fantasy's grandeur, which it never grasps since the consequences of failure do not match the scale of Sinbad's quest. The 7th Voyage and Golden Voyage wisely restrict adventuring to a couple of islands, in keeping with the modest goals of their plots, while Eye of the Tiger spans half the globe when all Sinbad needs to do is restore the regent of a single kingdom within it. The film also cheats by cutting from the collapsing pyramid, straight to Cassim's crowning, with no mention of the arduous homeward journey that must have taken place in between. Eye of the Tiger's thrust, to restore a human transformed into an animal, is a common fairy tale motif (recurring throughout the Arabian Nights), giving the film a further uncertainty of tone.

The sheer length of this misconceived quest also means that Tiger lags far behind 7th and Golden in terms of pace. The whole film feels cheap and shoddy, and most incidents are less than enthralling. In the one episode everyone remembers with a chuckle, Zenobia turns herself into a seagull in order to spy on Sinbad, but runs out of potion as she turns herself back, leaving her with a huge bird's paddle in place of a foot. Harryhausen tries to keep the story afloat with another batch of stop-motion creations. By now the wow-factor of his Dynamation had begun to pale. The film's over-familiar monster parade includes a trio of chittering bug-eyed skeletons, a killer bee (which a decidedly un-wise old Melanthius feeds a size-increasing potion), a surly walrus and an amiable one-horned troglodyte, who steps in for a wrestling match with a defrosted saber-toothed tiger. A bronze minotaur brought to life with a clockwork heart is more interesting, but gets the least to do.

The importance of Harryhausen's role in the development of special effects remains incontestable, but his contributions to the fantasy genre, made most consistently through his Sinbad features, may have been overestimated. Since his films are so warmly regarded by commentators who embraced them as children (this author being one of them), many resist the urge to criticize. But Peter Nicholls is bold enough to point out the problem in his review of *7th Voyage* in *Fantastic Cinema*: "although they have devoted much of their lives to the craft, Harryhausen and Schneer seem to have no more than a novice's appreciation of what elements constitute true fantasy. For one thing, *7th Voyage* never suggests anything by implication, by creating subtleties of atmosphere. The whole point of animated fantasies of this sort is typically to *show* the fantastic straight on — and in this case, in color."

By contrast, movies like Powell and Pressburger's *Thief of Baghdad* (which echoes throughout the Harryhausen Sinbads) understands that a sense of willing engagement in a fabricated world cannot be evoked solely through a pageant of special effects. Too often this knuckle-headed literalism exhibits itself in fantasy films like *The Mummy Returns* (2001), in which barnstorming special effects swallow the story (what little there is). Secondary worlds can be evoked far more effectively "by implication," by the characters making casual references to locations and events taking place elsewhere in their world. The original *Star Wars* (1977) does this constantly, with throwaway references to "the Kessel Run," "Womp Rats" and "the Clone Wars," inferring a universe that lives and breathes beyond the parameters of the given story. Harryhausen's best films testify that a palpable sense of wonder is not entirely absent from the Schneer-Harryhausen oeuvre. Nicholls rightly concludes, "[T]here is no denying that Harryhausen contrived to bring a lot of sparkle, excitement and fun back into the world of fantastic cinema, which was beginning to lose sight of these qualities."

Following his final voyage under the auspices of Schneer and Harryhausen, Sinbad had become so identified with stop-motion monster movies that when the Dynamation maestro announced his retirement following the epic fantasy *Clash of the Titans* (1981), the character found himself unemployed for the next ten years. For the duration of the '80s, Harrison Ford's Han Solo and Indiana Jones assumed Sinbad's mantle, cornering the market in globe-trotting daredevilry. Due to the expense of recreating Sinbad's secondary world, with its galleons, lost worlds and monsters, the sailor put in less regular appearances in substantial features than he did in animated TV series and short films.

Two more Ray Harryhausen creations, a defrosted saber-toothed tiger (left) and the lumbering Trog (right), take part in another monster smack down at the climax of Sam Wanamaker's turgid *Sinbad and the Eye of the Tiger* (Columbia/Andor, 1977). Human protagonist Prince Kassim (Damien Thomas), Princess Farah (Jane Seymour), Dione (Taryn Power) and Melanthius (Patrick Troughton) cower in the background.

Most of these depicted him in a far more whimsical fairy tale fashion than in his heroic fantasy features. In episode three of his portmanteau ballet film *Invitation to the Dance* (1954 — released in Britain in 1955 as a separate short entitled *The Magic Lamp*), Gene Kelly appears as Sinbad wearing white Navy duds and dancing through an animated Arabian wonderland. Japan produced two animated Sinbad fairy tales, Taiji Yabushita's feature *Shindbad no bôken* (*Adventure of Sinbad*) (1962) and a 52-episode cartoon series, *Arabian Naito: Shindobaddo no bôken* (*Arabian Nights: The Adventures of Sinbad*) (1975).

The American cartoon series *Sinbad Jr.* (1964–65 — previously titled *The Adventures of Sinbad the Sailor* until Hanna-Barbera took over production in 1965) features a scrawny seafaring tyke (voiced by Tim Matheson) who becomes a red-haired strongman in sailor togs whenever he tightens his magic belt. The Czech Karel Zeman contributed an animated 14-minute short, *Dobrodružství Námorníka Sindibáda* (*The Adventures of Sinbad the Sailor*) (1971), later re-edited into Zeman's animated feature *Pohádky Tisíce a Jedné Noci* (*Tales of 1001 Nights*) (1974). Sinbad's last hurrah before his '80s exile was in the 1978 Filmation superhero cartoon *Freedom Force*, in which he fought alongside the Egyptian goddess Isis, the Super Samurai, Merlin and Hercules.

Sinbad found life after Harryhausen tough enough without suffering the ignominy of appearing as Magilla Gorilla in *Scooby-Doo in Arabian Nights* (1994). He resurfaced in the early '90s, in a pair of mistimed movies that yet again regressed the character back to his days in the desert romance. Philippe de Broca's lavish timeslip fantasy *Les mille et une nuits* (*A Thousand and One Nights*) (1990) features Catherine Zeta-Jones' Scheherazade escaping her cheerfully murderous husband with the help of Gérard Jugnot's time-hopping genie. Sinbad turns up as Vittorio Gassman's aquaphobic sailor.

The sailor's lowest live-action ebb came with Enzo G. Castellari's *Simbad il marinaio* (*Sinbad of the Seven Seas*) (1989), starring woolly-haired muscleman Lou Ferrigno. This made-for-TV rip-off of Powell and Pressburger's *Thief* was reportedly shelved for two years by its financiers Menahem Golan and Yoram Globus. (Back then, it said something about the quality of a movie when even Cannon refused to release it.) After a misinformed opening scrawl tells us that Edgar Allan Poe penned the *Arabian Nights* in 1845, Ferrigno lumbers like a tranquilized moose after four magic Christmas tree baubles that will save the city of Basra from John Steiner's goggle-eyed vizier. The film offers the kind of impoverished lunacy in which Italian heroic fantasy seems to specialize. Imprisoned in the palace dungeons, Sinbad ties a swarm of rubber snakes together to form a getaway ladder (surely the most novel use of a serpent since James Earl Jones fired one from his bow in *Conan the Barbarian*).

The advent of CGI largely banished the budgetary restrictions glaringly apparent in *Sinbad of the Seven Seas*, presenting Sinbad with a prime opportunity for exposure and hopefully some measure of reinvention. Live-action TV series *The Adventures of Sinbad* (1996–98) sold itself on the back of *Hercules: The Legendary Journeys* and *Xena: Warrior Princess*, but never attempted anything like the same heroic fantasy overhaul. Zen Gesner's airbrushed Sinbad embarked on two dismal seasons of adventure that merely recycled the conventions laid down by Harryhausen. He was accompanied by an ensemble crew reminiscent of an AD&D gathering and given to banal patter of the I-got-a-bad-feeling-about-this variety.

Aside from Richard Grieco's live-action turn in Alan Mehrez's negligible timeslip fantasy *Sinbad: The Battle of the Dark Knights* (1998), in which he takes a young time traveller under his wing, Sinbad has presently found a home in two expensive animated features. The first of these, Evan Ricks and Alan Jacobs' woefully animated CG feature *Sinbad: Beyond the Veil of Mists* (1997) opens with an evil wizard (voiced by Leonard Nimoy) tricking the king of Baghdad (John Rhys-Davies) into exchanging bodies. The king's daughter (Jennifer Hale) convinces the pony-tailed Sinbad (Brendan Fraser) to take her through the fabled Veil of Mists to find a cure. Amid a horribly stilted script that cannot resist the odd anachronistic wisecrack, Sinbad is described as a sentimental free spirit, but remains an even greater emotional blank than he was under Zen Gesner. The film gives him little to do on his adventures, but provides some nice landscapes for him to pass by. When they descend into an Atlantean city, Joe Alves' production design offers a mechanical Manta Ray that swallows Sinbad and the princess (its steel innards threatening to grind them into sushi) and a submarine race of fish-men seen harvesting huge anemone-like mushrooms.

DreamWorks' infinitely better-animated *Sinbad: Legend of the Seven Seas* (2003) offers similarly pretty scenery, but a secondary world just as lacking in wit and excitement. This, Sinbad's final voyage to date, avoids any reference to the character's literary homeland (unsurprising given recent events involving the Middle East), locating its secondary world safely in Syracuse (the chief Greek city of ancient Sicily). Here Sinbad (voiced by Brad Pitt) is as romantic as he was in *Veil of Mists*, although DreamWorks assign him a morally ambiguous career as a pirate. Eris (Michelle Pfeiffer), the slinky goddess of chaos, frames him when she steals the Book of Peace, an artifact that somehow brings harmony to the 12 kingdoms of the world.

Marina (Catherine Zeta-Jones), a Thracian politician who yearns for adventure, accompanies Sinbad on his voyage to steal back the book, and together they carry on a routinely argumentative love affair. "Are you a thief or a hero?" she asks, as Sinbad struggles with the possibility that his heart may actually be as black as that of Eris. Of course, he finally learns the true meaning of heroism, but in the interim emerges as a fairly unlovable sort. Perfectly willing to abscond to Fiji and risk letting his boyhood friend die in his place, Sinbad changes his mind when Marina promises him wealth.

Brad Pitt's doughy tones let the vocal side down, although visually this Sinbad is the most energetic of them all, swooping through the rigging and acrobatically laying out all comers. He is also probably the only fantasy Sinbad who spends more time at sea than on dry land. The difficulties in incorporating water effects with stop-motion meant that Sinbad's adventures in the Harryhausen pictures had to take place on terra firma. But this movie's emphasis on monster-centric set-pieces, including a scrape with a ship-hugging kraken and a shoal of watery sirens, a helter-skelter escape from a gigantic snow hawk and a brush with a mountainous anglerfish, prove that 26 years after *Eye of the Tiger*, Sinbad is still finding it hard to escape the ghost of Harryhausen.

Days of High Adventure: The Barbarian Swordsman

From the mid–1960s onwards, pulp anthologies, heavy metal albums, Marvel comics and tattoo parlors popularized the rock 'n' roll imagery of heroic fantasy. Previously, the pristine Steve Reeves-ian strongman and his forebears leapt most readily to the public mind at any suggestion of pre–Biblical derring-do, and thus found its way into some of the earliest illustrations of Robert E. Howard's Conan.

In the '30s, while Howard was still alive, *Weird Tales* illustrator Margaret Brundage depicted the barbarian in pastel, describing an airy Valentino-like buccaneer. In the '50s, independent publishers Ace Books and Gnome Press reprinted a number of Conan stories with covers presenting him as a Brylcreemed Victor Mature type. Most illustrators had trouble envisioning Howard's grasp of the fantastic, usually settling on images borrowed from the Italian epics or the Hollywood Arabias. Cover artists like Ed Emshwiller, Wally Wood, Norman Saunders and Frank Kelly Freas drew a discreet veil over the image of the uncouth savage who lurks in the actual stories, until the 1966 publication of Lancer Books' hugely successful paperback *Conan the Adventurer.*

Bruised in oils by the legendary Frank Frazetta, this Conan was no pec-flaunting pretty boy, but a dread brute with a lank mane of black hair, his knotted torso garlanded with scars, veins and weaponry. He stands ankle-deep in a mire of corpses, a blood-streaked sword thrust into the ground, and a nude woman wound about his leg. Frazetta reworked this image for nine more of Lancer's 12 *Conan* titles, defining the signature archetype of heroic fantasy fiction, which itself underwent a popularity explosion in the '60s. Early in the decade, working under Fritz Leiber's newly coined banner "sword and sorcery," editors like L. Sprague De Camp and Lin Carter raided the pulp archives, forming popular anthologies that recovered the work of Howard successors like Catherine L. Moore, Henry Kuttner and Clark Ashton Smith.

With the 1968 publication of *The Lord of the Rings'* hefty omnibus edition (since the mid–'50s the book had been whetting the public's appetite for all things fantasy as three separate volumes), enthusiasm for heroic fantasy skyrocketed. A veritable horde of literary barbarians descended upon the bookshelves shielded with Frazetta-styled covers. Ironically, their common front cover come-on ("In the tradition of Conan") proved depressingly accurate as the deluge wore on. Meal-ticket barbarians like John Jakes' *Brak*, Lin Carter's *Thongor* and Gardner F. Fox's *Kothar* and *Kyrik* gradually outnumbered more considered creations like Fritz Leiber's droll *Fafhrd and the Grey Mouser*, Michael Moorcock's revisionist *Eternal Champion*, Jack Vance's witty *Cugel* and Karl Edward Wagner's traditionalist *Kane*.

The movies caught up in 1977 with the optioning of Conan, and a wave of secondary world fantasies broke in the early '80s, by which time sales of their equivalent books were in decline. Although regarded at the time as a gestalt "fantasy" boom, most of these films concern themselves with the sundered kingdoms, callow heroes and transformative quests of epic fantasy, as in *Dragonslayer, Excalibur, Clash of the Titans* (all 1981), *The Dark Crystal* (1982) and *Krull* (1983). Heroic fantasy made up a smaller, low-budget contingent, represented by *Hawk the Slayer* (1980), *The Sword and the Sorcerer* and *The Beastmaster* (both 1981), but boasted among its ranks one of the most significant fantasy films of the '80s. John Milius' *Conan the Barbarian* (1981) was the first direct adaptation of a heroic fantasy text, and remains easily the best film adapted from or inspired by the writings of Howard. This includes Dan Ireland's well-acted but otherwise not very good biopic *The Whole Wide World* (1996), starring a well-cast Vincent D'Onofrio as the troubled author and Renée Zellweger as his posthumous biographer, Novalyne Price Ellis.

Conan the Barbarian brought to the screen the archetype of the barbarian swordsman, as conceived by Howard and popularized by Frazetta. In many ways a bitter reflection of the peplum strongman, the barbarian swordsman is human, not some immaculate progeny of the gods. He is not blessed with the powers of an immortal, though his physical capabilities are wildly romanticized. He represents the courage and tenacity of humble mankind, a noble savage skeptical of civilization and yet often pitting his trademark sword (although axes and bows are favored by some) against the magical beings who threaten to overwhelm it. With his rock-star mane he is a sour product of the '70s anti–Establishment, which took over from the '60s flower culture that revered Tolkien.

The ongoing financial onslaught of George Lucas' *Star Wars* trilogy (demonstrated by its secondary salvo, Irvin Kershner's *The Empire Strikes Back* [1980]) made studios more inclined to consider fantastical material that set itself in times long ago or in worlds far far away. But it is a mistake to assume that cinema's sudden interest in fantasy was merely a by-product of the success of *Star Wars*. Cinema's interest in fantasy fiction by the mid–'70s was quite possibly strong enough to have sparked off an influx of adaptations, regardless of Lucas.

According to an interview in the British genre magazine *Starburst*, London-based producer Milton Subotsky acquired the film rights to Lin Carter's Conan clone Thongor in 1976. He apparently had a mind to adapt the property into a Harryhausen-style adventure movie for kids, along the same lines as his own Burroughs-adapted *At the Earth's Core* (1976) starring Doug McClure and Peter Cushing. Subotsky wrote a script based on Carter's first Thongor novel, *The Wizard of Lemuria* (1965), and assembled a package that United Artists picked up at Cannes in 1978 and suddenly dumped six weeks after *Screen International* announced *Thongor in the Valley of Demons* was good to go. Reasons for the studio's cold feet remain unclear, although rampant over-funding of Michael Cimino's epic Western *Heaven's Gate* (1980) was dragging them into financial turmoil.

In 1975, Subotsky looked into acquiring the rights to Conan, before realizing that Howard's tales contained far too much raunch and bloodshed for the cheerful kid's matinee he had in mind. Filmmakers always run into this problem (and rarely emerge out of it) when adapting heroic fantasy fiction for the cinema. Adult readers enjoy the rough sex and bloodthirsty violence embraced by the genre, while kids love the magic and monsters. This leaves filmmakers in a quandary that almost always wins out to the promise of a younger, wider audience.

Adult heroic fantasy movies are exceptionally rare. Most producers handed a property full of wizards and ogres immediately regard it as one for the kids, and encourage their directors to keep the leading lady buttoned up and to padlock the lid on the Karo syrup. Films based on Howard stories notably suffer from such thinking. Over-fanciful adventures like *Red Sonja* (1985) and *Kull the Conqueror* (1997) hit resounding bum notes, while *Conan the Destroyer* (1984) presents a fairly straightforward adaptation, but has trouble taking its barbarian hero seriously. Many such films find themselves in trouble with the distributors come release time, when the final cut proves too violent for children and too ridiculous for adults.

With the collapse of *Thongor in the Valley of Demons*, Subotsky rallied with a barely passable horror omnibus, Roy Ward Baker's *The Monster Club* (1980), a co-production between Subotsky's company, Sword and Sorcery, and ITC's Chips, the latter which ironically had just released a heroic fantasy of its own. Terry Marcel's low-budget *Hawk the Slayer* (1980) was first out of the gate during the early '80s fantasy boom, pre-empting Hollywood's *Conan* where Subotsky's *Thongor* had failed. This earnest fantasy film hails from traditionally skeptical Britain, ranking it as a distinctly left-field effort. Unfortunately, memories of the film ensure that no British filmmaker will take another crack at the genre for a very long time to come. Based on an original script by Marcel and Harry Robertson, *Hawk* sets itself in a secondary world owing more to the Anglo pastorale of Tolkien than the Middle Eastern wastelands of Howard.

The story centers on the Cain and Abel feud between two brothers: Jack Palance's villainous, one-eyed Voltan and John Terry's noble adventurer Hawk (a sort of Robin Hood cum Man With No Name). When Hawk inherits his ancestral Mind-Sword, Voltan murders their father and runs amok, ransoming the abbess of a nearby nunnery (Annette Crosbie). Hawk is summoned to her rescue and, with the help of a blind witch, recruits a team of former comrades, each the last of their Tolkien-inspired race: a mallet-hefting giant (Bernard Bresslaw), a diminutive elf bowman (Ray Charleson) and a whip-cracking dwarf (Peter O'Farrell). After a number of repetitive skirmishes, Hawk kills Voltan in a slow-motion duel and finally rides off in search of further adventure.

In outline the film sounds serviceable, but its reputation as a cheeseball classic remains well-deserved. Marcel (at least recognizing the roots of the genre he is working in) apes the mode of Leone's Spaghetti Westerns, adding a strangely catchy Morricone-Does-Disco score. Palance overacts appallingly as the kind of default bad guy who turns up all the time in lazy fantasy like this. He dresses like a weird Vegas magician, laughs his head off whenever engaged in acts of villainy, bellows "Silence!" whenever people annoy him, and cannot refrain from murdering his own employees whenever he needs to illustrate a point. John Terry compensates for his co-star's excesses by not acting at all. The dopey giant and snack-obsessed dwarf offer excruciating comic asides, while the brooding elf adopts a robotic monotone in an effort to come off as aloof and mysterious.

Lovers of risible dialogue have much to savor ("The hunchback will have something to say about this," is everyone's favorite), while budgetary constraints reduce a "whirlpool of flying firebolts" to a barrage of Day-Glo ping-pong balls. Elsewhere, an inquisitive sentry is immobilized with green Silly String. Like Courtney Solomon's epic fantasy *Dungeons and Dragons* (2000), *Hawk the Slayer* is truly awful, but somewhere, beneath layers of stunning ineptitude, one cannot help sensing an affection for their genre. *Hawk* actually makes an effort to imply the unseen sprawl of its secondary world, although lines like, "The wizards are gathering in the south," hardly convince when Hawk's world seems to reach no further than the same clearing in Epping Forest.

Weapons like *Hawk the Slayer*'s Mind-Sword are often a central motif of heroic and epic fantasy, in this case signifying the world-saving destiny of the hero, an association more common among epic fantasy types like *Excalibur*'s Arthur and *Lord of the Rings*' Aragorn. In most heroic fantasies, the hero's sword symbolizes his masculine power and his competence when it comes to hacking the enemy to bits. The rule of thumb among barbarian swordsmen is the bigger and more fanciful, the better. Schwarzenegger's Conan goes for reliability and refinement, opting for an unmagical but magnificently crafted double-handed broadsword. John Terry's levitating pigsticker in *Hawk* sports an Elfin Mind-stone, which glows green at appropriately dramatic moments. Lou Ferrigno's tin prop in Luigi Cozzi's science-fantasy *Hercules* (1983) spouts multi-colored flames, while Richard Hill's in *Deathstalker* (1983) can chop stone. None can top the Swiss Army monstrosity Lee Horsley waves about in *The Sword and the Sorcerer* (1982): It boasts not one but three blades *and* doubles as a harpoon gun.

Without these grandiose weapons, the likes of Conan would be little more than a grubby cousin of the peplum strongman. The mystic bond between warrior and weapon forms the opening sequence of *Conan the Barbarian*, ritualizing the forging of the sword that Conan will later use to dispatch a monstrous father figure. *Conan* is unusually sensitive (perhaps too sensitive) to the totem of the sword; most barbarian swordsman movies see their signature weapons simply as a way of dispatching bad guys, advertising their proficiency with names like the Slayer, the Destroyer, the Conqueror, the Annihilator and so on.

The undeniable potential of the '80s barbarian swordsman to satisfy public appetite for sadism had already been exhausted by the fantasy-publishing boom of the previous two decades. Critics detected a disturbing trend pandering to readers' most reptilian desires. Michael Moorcock sums up the opposition most reasonably in his 1987 survey of fantasy literature *Wizardry and Wild Romance:*

> Unfortunately the majority of imitators who came in recent years to fulfill the demands of publishers sensing a commercial market were attracted to what is presumably a compensatory fantasy of homicidal barbarians and grunting rapists. As a result they produced characters even more terrifyingly simple-minded than Conan himself. The appeal was never easy for me to understand, but I was given a clue some years ago when, as a guest of a fantasy convention, I appeared on a panel with a group of sword-and-sorcery writers who told the audience that the reason they wrote such fantasy was because they (and, they implied, the audience) felt inadequate to cope with the complexities of modern life. "Where today," asked one, "can you put an arm hold around a man's throat and slip a knife into him between the third and fourth ribs and get away with it?" The answer was, of course, that the Marines were still looking for recruits. But maybe he meant, "Where can you do that and not have someone retaliate?" If that's the main appeal of such stories it probably explains why most people over the age of eighteen stop reading them.

Heroic fantasy movies adapted from and inspired by such sources generally restrain themselves. However, Jack Stokes' and John Bruno's segments *Den* and *Taarna*, from Gerald Potterton's animated sci-fi–heroic fantasy omnibus *Heavy Metal* (1981), along with *Conan* and *The Sword and the Sorcerer*, were accused of glorifying violence in the same way as sleazy slasher films like *Friday the 13th* (1980). British authorities even deemed two Italian *Conan* knock-offs, Lucio Fulci's *Conquest* and Franco Prosperi's *Invincible Barbarian* (both 1983), brutal enough to warrant attention during that year's great video nasty scare. Milius' *Conan* actually takes a responsible approach to its violence (although this was possibly imposed by the American censors), while most of its immediate followers depict the same world of casual brutality as the Spaghetti Western.

Cobbled together from Kenji Misumi's first two movies in the *manga*-adapted *Lone Wolf and Cub* series of the early '70s, Robert Houston's outrageously bloodthirsty *Shogun Assassin* (1980) provides an interesting contrast to the hack-'em-up violence that upset critics of the '80s barbarian movies. Released by Roger Corman's New World to simultaneously appeal to the kung fu and slasher crowds, the film also cashed in on the anticipated vogue for fantasy sword-slinging. Tomisaburo Wakayama's portly samurai wanders feudal Japan pushing his infant son along inside a bamboo pram, which is rigged with an array of diabolical weaponry that springs out to impale argumentative passersby. Wakayama scythes through a parade of stunningly choreographed encounters, ending with casualties ejecting blood with the ferocity of a burst water main.

Like most Japanese sword operas (known in Japan as *chambara*), the film features no magical elements, although its world is archly stylized. Warriors seem capable of hearing an eyeball moving in its socket and react with superhuman speed, splitting heads in perfect symmetry, hurling shuriken with impossible precision, even leaping out of their own clothing to avoid the sweep of a blade. The film renders this delirious, almost childlike invention with ritualistic severity, its bursts of combat conducted as formally as a Zen tea ceremony. Like the innate surrealism of fairy tale, this overt stylizing views violence with a degree of detached irony, never indulging quite so vicariously as straightforward hack-and-slashers like *The Sword and the Sorcerer* and *Deathstalker*.

Their producers sensing a potentially lucrative genre in heroic fantasy, *Hawk the Slayer*, *Conan* and *Sword and the Sorcerer* were all ambitiously planned as the first in a projected series. Producer-director-writer Nicholas Corea offered *The Archer: Fugitive from the Empire* as the pilot of a never-happened TV series. This dire telefeature is even worse than *Hawk the Slayer*, but received some theatrical exposure outside the U.S. under the title *The Archer and the Sorceress*. Broadcast for the first time on NBC in 1981, the film opened with a statement anticipating the fantasy boom to come: "This summer, five motion pictures will be about swords and sorcerers. Tonight you will see the first."

Of course *Hawk the Slayer* got there the year before (even if it had yet to reach American shores), but *Archer and the Sorceress* was indeed the first of many such tacky American heroic fantasies. Opening with possibly the best-worst scene-setting lines ever written ("Once, in a world that was or never was. In a time that might have been or could yet still be."), the movie has Toran of the Hawk Clan (Lane Caudell) framed for the murder of his father, Chief Brakus (*Airport*'s George Kennedy, looking shameful in Teutonic blonde pigtails). Banished, Toran inherits from his aged mentor the half-sentient "Heart-Bow," a weapon capable of firing explosive arrows, as well as moving solid objects using only the power of the mind. With the help of Belinda Bauer's bikinied sorceress and Victor Campos' avaricious rogue, Toran squares off against a black-armored axe-man and his squad of snake-men storm troopers.

Unlike *Hawk the Slayer* and *Archer and the Sorceress*, *Conan* did not need to borrow from *Star Wars*. Yet the film proved unpopular among Howard's fans since it owes little to anything the author ever wrote. With the continued popularity of

Down and dirty: Arnold Schwarzenegger prepares for a night on the town in John Milius' much-misunderstood *Conan the Barbarian* (Dino De Laurentiis/Edward R. Pressman, 1981). Compare this vision of Robert E. Howard's sword-slinger to the still from its sequel, *Conan the Destroyer* (page 208), to see how all its predecessor's good work was undone.

sword-and-sorcery fiction in the '70s, Marvel Comics made the canny move in 1970 of buying several Howard properties and adapting them for children, a previously untapped market that responded enthusiastically. Marvel's *Conan the Barbarian* (1970–93), along with examples of Frazetta's artwork, convinced producer Edward R. Pressman to buy the film rights to Howard's character in 1977. The fact that the film retains the title of Marvel's comic rather than any of Howard's stories testifies that the film was sold as an offshoot of the comic from the very beginning; the first draft of the film was even co-written by the comic's scripter, Roy Thomas. Oliver Stone wrote a second draft in 1978, apparently a hallucinatory vision set in a mutant-infested post-apocalyptic future. The project was turned down by every director and finally sold off to Italian mogul Dino De Laurentiis, who felt the script far too violent for a movie based on a kid's comic and demanded a rewrite. De Laurentiis hired movie brat John Milius, who also had little interest in Howard and knew Conan primarily through Frazetta's artwork. The director rewrote Stone's script, excising most of its phantasmagoria, envisioning the film not as "fantasy" with all the high-flown trappings associated with it, but as a historical picture with supernatural trimmings.

The resulting film invents the origin of Howard's superhero, while peppering the plot with events and names from the original stories. Opening with the murder of his parents at the hands of James Earl Jones' charismatic warrior-priest, Thulsa Doom, the story charts Conan's rites-of-passage transformation from boyhood to manhood (or rather into Arnold Schwarzenegger)—from his violent apprenticeship as a gladiatorial pit fighter, to his years as a wandering rogue and finally on a quest for revenge that leads him to rescue a princess from Doom's Manson-esque snake cult.

Conan's functional secondary world is its most commonly overlooked achievement. Like *Lord of the Rings*' Middle-earth and the original *Star Wars* universe, *Conan*'s mythical realm of Hyboria resonates by visually echoing earthbound history. Conan's wintry homeland of Cimmeria resembles the Scandinavia of Viking saga, while the barren plains of the South exude a convincing Middle Eastern exoticism; even the swordplay is choreographed to recall the grace of the samurai. Ron Cobb's baroque production design, Basil Poledouris's operatic score and Spain's forbidding vistas all lend substantial weight to Milius' secondary world.

Unusually for an American secondary world fantasy, *Conan* attempts to recreate a foreign world on its own ground, populating its crowd scenes with European and Asian extras, not the jobbing Californians of later barbarian movies. It also casts seasoned athletes in the lead roles, where they look convincingly at ease amid the vigorous action. Dancer Sandahl Bergman gives a dashing performance as Valeria, Conan's Valkyrie-like lover, as does surfing legend Gerry Lopez, as his glowering sidekick. Schwarzenegger poses rather than acts, but his sheer presence is enough to fill the role, embodying the implacable fury of the kung fu avenger, the martial discipline of the samurai sword-slinger and the amoral self-interest of the Spaghetti gunman.

Conan the Barbarian stands as a benchmark for heroic fantasy. All the more frustrating, then, that Milius cripples his own achievement by approaching the film from an over-considered psychological angle, creating a superhero closer in spirit to

Joseph Conrad than Robert E. Howard. Opening with a quote from Nietzsche (which encouraged critics to level further accusations of latent fascism at the genre), the director expects his audience to watch in patient awe as Conan is forged by adversity, like the glowing hunk of metal beaten into a magnificent sword in the opening sequence.

Rather than get on with any kind of ripping yarn, which would have revealed its own symbolic subtexts, Milius stalls the narrative with painterly tableaux. In a ridiculously protracted ending, the acolytes of the beheaded Thulsa Doom symbolically extinguish their torches and depart, while Conan holds an introspective pose and broods for hours over the meaning of it all. The movie's pace is wearyingly sluggish, possibly a result of Milius having to cut over 20 minutes of violent action from the film after American censors repeatedly condemned it to a commercial death with an "X" rating.

If ever a movie warranted a director's cut, it is *Conan the Barbarian*, which remains an absorbing, but ultimately frustrating film. In a way, it reverses the kind of schizoid thinking that usually blights secondary world fantasies by being too ponderous to satisfy as an adventure movie, too rooted in pulp culture to interest the intellectuals it adjures. It presently enjoys cult status among fans too young to have discovered Howard in the '70s and looms large on the fantasy film landscape, albeit as the most distinguished casualty on the heroic fantasy highway.

Sex, Violence and the Hyborian Way: The Sons of Conan

Although too wrapped up in its own gloomy concerns to have any fun with it, *Conan the Barbarian* established the default secondary world of heroic fantasy, enjoyed by other barbarian swordsmen for the rest of the '80s. The strongman and Sinbad inhabit secondary worlds as idealized as those of fairy tale, neatly bisected by good and evil. *Conan*, meanwhile, offers a more pragmatic vision, a brutal quasi–Iron Age, where civilization is in its infancy and mankind barely evolved from living in caves. The men of this world are mostly statuesque brutes, its women invariably voluptuous, and everyone depends on brute strength or animal cunning to survive. This world proposes a sort of pre–Biblical equivalent to the unruly terrain of the Spaghetti Western, where morality is of little concern, even among its heroes. This world is necessarily cruel; else its stories would not work. The barbarian swordsman needs the moral elbow room to literally get away with murder, an idea repulsive to the civilization of Arthurian and Tolkienean romance.

By the early '80s, the cults of Tolkien and Howard, and the rising popularity of fantasy role-playing games like *Dungeons and Dragons* and *Runequest*, had become part of an established subculture. But even mainstream audiences recognized a default "fantasy" world when they saw it in the movies. After *Conan*, they knew what to expect from heroic fantasy, although few successive films attain the required balance of fluid storytelling and a convincing secondary world.

Filmed and released at the same time as *Conan*, Albert Pyun's independently produced *The Sword and the Sorcerer* (1982) was made entirely in Los Angeles, for apparently less than it cost to build Thulsa Doom's mountainside temple. Ironically, Pyun's film features exactly the kind of galloping narrative Milius' film lacks; many Howard fans even prefer it. Having disposed of the eons-old demon sorcerer who helped him usurp the throne, scowling King Cromwell (Richard Lynch) rightly suspects that the vengeful monster still lives. Lee Horsley plays the rugged Talon (a rather puny barbarian swordsman padded out with furs and a mane of over-styled hair) hired by Kathleen Beller's spunky rebellion leader, who in return for a night's pleasure wants him to rescue the rightful king (Simon MacCorkindale) from Cromwell's dungeons.

Lighting its acres of bare-naked flesh and gracelessly gory swordfights with a lurid comic book glow, the movie then disregards the lot with the good-humored abandon of an Errol Flynn swashbuckler. The advances in special effects made in the early '80s by superstar makeup artists like Dick Smith and Rick Baker allow a couple of effectively grisly set-pieces. In the opening sequence, the sorcerer rises from his blood-swamped tomb, its walls encrusted with living faces, and induces a witch's heart to burst out of her chest; at the climax, he gruesomely sloughs off the disguising flesh of Cromwell's snaky counsellor (George Maharis).

Colorful components like these convey a spirit closer to Howard than anything in *Conan*, but the similarity is hardly accidental since Pyun's movie poaches just about every idea it has from Howard. It all ends true to superheroic tradition, with a triumphant Talon riding off towards further adventure with a rousing cry to his comrades that sums up the ethos of the heroic fantasy superhero: "We've a battle in the offing, kingdoms to save and women to love."

Although *The Sword and the Sorcerer* gets it right where *Conan* gets it wrong, the movie's secondary world gives the game away with ludicrous wigs, phony beards and cod-antique dialogue. Twitches like these characterize the American *Conan* imitators that followed. Don Cascorelli's *The Beastmaster* (1982), notionally based on the 1959 sci-fi novel by Andre Norton, is the most expensive and respectable.

Here the drastically uncharismatic Marc Singer plays errant prince Dar, a barbarian Dr. Dolittle able to command the animal kingdom and see through its eyes, as a result of being magically born through a cow. After pillaging horsemen murder his foster parents and he is sent forth with vague instructions about meeting his destiny, Dar befriends a pair of thieving ferrets, rescues a black tiger from a group of nasty hunters and chances upon an escaped slave girl (Tanya Roberts). Vexed priest Maax (Rip Torn) hears a prophecy stating that Dar will kill him, although in the climactic swordfight atop an Aztec pyramid, one of Dar's ferrets contravenes this cosmic decree by nibbling on the not-quite-dead bad guy's neck until he tumbles into his own sacrificial pyre. The young ward of a friendly pilgrim (John Amos) concludes the story by inheriting the throne in Dar's place. Heroic fantasy employs such "dormant monarch" characters often, allowing the superhero to ride away into another adventure without the baggage of responsibility.

Beastmaster is cheerfully silly, with as many jazzy touches as one would expect from the writer-director of the imaginative *Phantasm* movies (a signet ring bearing an inquisitive eyeball, berserkers in *Mad Max* fetish-wear, mouthless bat-creatures who liquefy their prey). But as with most American heroic fantasies, the movie lacks flavor. Like the ersatz Hollywood Arabias of the early Sinbad pictures, American secondary worlds usually balk at assimilating their own imaginary cultures. In this way, the monosyllabic names, contemporary hairdressing, elaborate hats, Californian accents, dry-cleaned peasant garb and scorched desert locations contrive to make the world of *Beastmaster* typically implausible. Unlike the rocky bruisers and earthy wenches of *Conan*, the airbrushed lovelies of *Beastmaster* look less ready to crush the jeweled thrones of the earth beneath their sandaled feet, and more like they are just killing time until the gym opens.

Beastmaster launders the iconography of heroic fantasy fiction for American audiences, while *Fire and Ice* (1982), an animated collaboration between Ralph Bakshi and Frank Frazetta, retains a muddy European fatalism. Conceived before but released after *Conan*, *Fire and Ice* tells a much narrower tale than Bakshi's adaptation *The Lord of the Rings* (1978). For the most part it accomplishes its own modest ambitions, with a script by Conan comic writers Roy Thomas and Gerry Conway.

In a primeval wilderness somewhere between Edgar Rice Burroughs and Clark Ashton Smith, listless ice-wizard Nekron (voiced by Sean Hannon) uses telepathically shifted glaciers to steamroll neighboring kingdoms. Fire Keep, the last outpost of humanity, stands defiant, until Nekron's Neanderthal dogsbodies kidnap the improbably endowed princess Teegra (Cynthia Leake). With only three silk hankies to cover her modesty, Teegra escapes several times until she falls into the muscular arms of Larn (Randy Norton). This now-homeless tribesman finds himself with little to do in the movie until he joins forces with a jaguar-masked axeman named Darkwolf (Steve Sandor). After a *Star Wars*–style aerial assault on Nekron's icy stronghold (with pterodactyls in lieu of X-Wings), Darkwolf executes the necromancer, while Fire Keep destroys the oncoming glaciers with a bellyful of molten lava.

Fire and Ice celebrates the kind of hairy-chested iconography that had only then made it from print into film. Its rotoscoping dwells lovingly on Teegra's every jiggle, while relishing the tactile thunk of steel hitting flesh in its brutal combat scenes. Rabid wolves and giant lizards inhabit primordial swamps and vine-strangled ruins, along with a Morlock-like troll, and a shrieking witch who returns from the dead to pass on a vital plot point. The film is superficial certainly, but serves as a substantial last hurrah for the atmosphere and pulp dynamism of heroic fantasy fiction, which later films obscured.

In the '50s, Steve Reeves' peplum strongman inflamed Hollywood's love affair with the male body. In the '80s, Arnold's barbarian swordsman rekindled this affection, and the hard-bodied superhero traded swords for firearms in cartridge carnivals like *Rambo: First Blood, Part II* (1985), *Predator* (1987) and *Die Hard* (1988). The Italians welcomed *Conan* as a return to the giddy days of the old school peplum. Video producers repackaged forgotten non-fantasy costume epics with flashy Frazetta-style sleeve art, attempting to pass them off as part of the Hyborian new wave. Thus Sergio Grieco and Franco Prosperi's *La schiava di roma* (*Slave of Rome*) (1960), starring Guy Madison and Rossana Podesta, became *Slave Warrior*, Antonio Leonviola's *Taur, il re della forza bruta* (*Taur, the King of Brute Force*) (1962) became

Man is the hunter: Primeval poster boy Larn (voiced by Randy Norton) argues the case for heroic fantasy in Ralph Bakshi's animated *Fire and Ice* (20th Century–Fox/Producers Sales, 1982).

Tor, Mighty Warrior, and Ferdinando Baldi's Romans vs. Visigoths epic *Il massacro della foresta nera* (*Massacre in the Black Forest*) (1967) somehow became *Arminus the Terrible*.

Exploitation filmmakers like Aristide Massaccesi, Franco Prosperi, Teodoro Ricci, Ruggero Deodato and Lucio Fulci had only just exhausted the zombie/cannibal cycle kicked off by George A. Romero's *Dawn of the Dead* (1979). Now they employed a confounding array of pseudonyms to distance themselves from the cinematic crimes they committed in the name of heroic fantasy.

Massaccesi's entertainingly awful *Ator l'invincibile* (*Ator, the Fighting Eagle*) (1982), first of the Italian *Conan* copycats, epitomizes the mindboggling inanity of the movies that followed. Kitted out in yeti boots, a *Fame* headband, a luxuriant Bon Jovi coiffure and a brass dinner plate strapped to his chest, American heartthrob Miles O'Keeffe plays barbarian swordsman Ator. With dim-bulb sincerity he asks his sweetheart, Sunja (Ritza Brown), why they cannot marry, and has to be gently reminded that she is his sister. Undeterred, Ator asks their father for his consent and happily discovers he was adopted. But horsemen in the employ of the lounging Spider King (Alessandro Barrera) ruin everything by trashing Ator's village, slaughtering his family and kidnapping his bride.

Handed an auspicious toy sword by his Genghis Khan–wigged mentor (Edmund Purdom), Ator teams up with a flaxen-haired swordswoman, Roon (played by Sabrina Siani, a gamine exploitation regular who appears in just about every Italian barbarian movie hereafter). Together they sneak into the cave of the Blind Warriors, who live by their highly developed sense of smell. Having enthusiastically attacked his own shadow in a bid to retrieve "the Mirror of Mordor," Ator reveals the artifact before the Spider King, who goes up in a puff of pink smoke like the Wicked Witch of the West. Roon dies in another playground swordfight before Ator does earnest battle with a flailing puppet spider. Stock footage of an erupting volcano denotes the collapse of evil's reign and an horrendously off-key power ballad wails over the closing scenes as Ator and Sunja triumphantly frolic through a field.

Ator's tumbledown production values, mismatched dubbing, methodical swordfights, non-acting and dilapidated special effects typify the straight-to-video fodder that Italy produced on spit and Scotch tape during its heroic fantasy revival. Massaccesi followed up with a dreary sequel, *Ator l'invincibile 2* (*The Blade Master*) (1983), made on the fly with no script, primarily to give the fairly bankable O'Keeffe something to do while he was still under contract. Now living in a cave with a mute Kato-like Chinaman named Thong (Chen Wong), O'Keeffe's Ator must stop a mincing Mongol warlord (David Cain Haughton) from pestering a weary alchemist for the secret to the atom bomb. Highlights include Ator rolling around with a flaccid rubber python and attacking a Swiss chateau with a hang glider built out of twigs.

Other films are no less stunningly ridiculous and Teodoro Ricci's *Thor il conquistatore* (*Thor the Conqueror*) (1982) is perhaps the worst of them all. Shaggy-haired Italian muscleman Luigi Mezzanotte plays a knuckleheaded barbarian taken in by a Merlin-like mentor (Christopher Holm) who periodically transforms himself into an owl and narrates the movie straight to camera. After cannibal warriors poke his eyes out with a stick, Thor restores his sight with drops of snake venom. His master helps him get his own back by conjuring a white stallion. "Centuries from now, he'll be called a horse," the wizard explains. "And a horse adds to your force." Thor then frightens away his enemies with some hostile cantering.

Although these movies chiefly pillage *Conan*, the Italians borrowed from just about everything proving popular at the time, including *Raiders of the Lost Ark, The Empire Strikes Back, Superman II* and *Quest for Fire*. Franco Prosperi's *Gunan il guerriero* (*The Invincible Barbarian*) (1983) even steals Harryhausen's stop-motion dinosaurs from *One Million Years B.C.* (1966) for a cosmic prologue explaining man's evolution. The rest of the movie has Pietro Torrisi's muscleman fighting his brother for the right to wield Excalibur against a Herod-like tribal chief, whose horsemen burnt down Torrisi's village in the first reel.

Pernicious horsemen did this again in the opening scenes of Prosperi's *Sangraal, la spada di fuoco* (*Sword of the Barbarians*) and *Il trono di fuoco* (*The Throne of Fire*), made back to back in 1983, and both starring the oddly simian Torrisi and the ever-affordable Sabrina Siani. In *Sword of the Barbarians*, Torrisi is crucified and made to watch as yet another unfortunate village is vandalized and the womenfolk hurried off for sacrifice before a topless goddess of fire. Siani turns up as a guffawing witch guarding the Ark of the Sun, from which Torrisi retrieves a giant crossbow and does away with some bothersome cannibal cavemen. Prosperi made even less of an effort with *Throne of Fire*, in which Harrison Muller's acid-blooded sadist (weirdly resembling a young George Lucas) plans to rule the land by seating himself on Odin's flammable seat of office during the next solar eclipse, or as he puts it, "on the day of the night in the day." Torrisi plays Siegfried the homeless barbarian clod who spends most of the film tied up and tormented by bad guys (using props left over from *Sword of the Barbarians*), while the sinuous Siani gets on with some passably spirited combat, as bikini-wearing swordswoman Princess Valkyrie.

The only halfway sane stab at heroic fantasy made by the Italians at this time was Lucio Fulci's comparatively well-considered *Conquest* (1983), a Spanish-Mexican-Italian co-production that adds some unusual kinks to the standard barbarian caper. Andrea Occhipinti's callow youth is ritually armed with a sacred bow that fires laser bolts (a similar device appeared the same year in the animated TV series *Dungeons and Dragons* [1983–87]) and befriends a craggy barbarian scout (seasoned Spanish actor Jorge Rivero). Together they battle clay-smothered savages, swamp zombies, Rivero's doppelganger and a tribe of warbling, cobweb-spitting mummies, before Occhipinti is unexpectedly beheaded and Rivero smothers himself in his dead companion's ashes in order to absorb his strength.

Fulci's slurred direction snuffs any spark of promise. Compounding the errors made by *Conan*, *Conquest* attempts to combine Milius' primordial mysticism with that of *Quest for Fire*, employing gauzy photography, dawdling lap dissolves and billows of obscuring smoke. The only moments of clarity are when the camera zooms in on a squirting flesh wound (the film in its original form is exceedingly gruesome, but most copies are heavily cut). Sabrina Siani turns up yet again as the sorceress whom the guys are prophesized to destroy. Wearing nothing but a gold mask and a metal thong, she writhes ecstatically, fondles a huge python and roasts her coke-snorting werewolf minions over a giant hotplate.

Siani, the perpetually unclothed queen of Italian barbarian movies, is afforded more deference in *Conquest* than in her previous outings. In *Invincible Barbarian* she is tortured with stakes and otherwise disregarded by both sexes, first by a tribe of Amazons ("Get her ready for copulation") and later by a group of bandits who squabble over who has the right to rape her first. *Thor the Conqueror* sums up the generally repulsive mindset of these films, as Luigi Mezzanotte is chided by his mentor for molesting a woman too gently, later discovering domestic bliss after raping Maria Romano's "Queen of the Warrior Virgins."

Aside from a handful of female authors (Catherine L. Moore, Leigh Brackett, Marion Zimmer Bradley, Elizabeth Moon and Storm Constantine) and one movie directed by a woman (Gabrielle Beaumont's negligible *Beastmaster III* [1995]), heroic fantasy is almost exclusively dreamed up by men for men. As such, the genre can be read as symbolic sexual fantasy, which has generally found darker expression in print than in film. Howard's writing admires strong women, while weaker members of the sex are generally exchanged like currency among the men. More progressive than most movies of its kind, *Conan the Barbarian* aligns itself with Hong Kong action cinema in the way it never makes a fuss about Sandahl Bergman's swordswoman being on an equal martial footing to her man. Jack Hill's lurid comedy *Sorceress* (1983) was the first heroic fantasy to place a female (or rather two females) in superheroic roles, although the movie is just as unenlightened as its Italian cousins. Lynette and Leigh Harris's telepathic twins jiggle for the camera and exchange rude jokes with Bob Nelson's bare-chested prince, as they struggle to recall the magic word that will unleash a menagerie of shabby monsters and do away with their evil undead foster father.

Matteo Ottaviano's Spanish non-fantasy barbarian movie *Hundra* (1983), though irredeemably corny, pleasingly pokes fun at the barbarian swordsman's machismo. Emerging as the first true barbarian swordswoman and a genuine Xena prototype, Laurene Landon's titular Amazon returns to her village to find it trashed (those marauding horsemen again) and seeks a suitable man with whom to carry on the tribal bloodline. In between hacking bloody divots out of leering sexist scumbags to the sound of her Xena-esque yodel, she makes a play for Ramiro Oliveros' abashed young healer, although her primitive advances appall him. Having finally had her way with him, Hundra neatly subverts the eternal bachelor image of the male superhero by leaving her man to look after their baby and riding off into the sunset alone. A gravelled voiceover concludes, "The seed of Hundra is in all women, so let all men beware."

As well as swapping its heroes' genders, heroic fantasy movies began shuffling its iconography with that of sci-fi, many not recognizing the differences between the two. *Heavy Metal* (1981) did so first with a compilation of genre stories adapted from the anthologized comic of the same name. Antonio Margheriti's scrappy but enjoyable science-fantasy *Il mondo di Yor* (*Yor: The Hunter from the Future*) (1982), based on the '70s comic by Juan Zanotto and Ray Collins, features Reb Brown as a typical heroic fantasy barbarian. We first find him gorily dispatching a rampaging Triceratops and hang-gliding into his enemies' lair on a giant bat to the strains of his Europop anthem. In a neat Tarzan-like twist, we learn that as a child this noble savage was brought to this prehistoric planet to escape the nuclear war devastating his home world, and now has to exchange laser fire with the stomping android hordes of John Steiner's Overlord.

A fellow nuclear refugee, the Overlord wishes to repopulate this miserable planet with a strain of androids derived from the genetically perfect DNA of Yor and his buoyantly permed girlfriend (Corine Clery). Yor stops him in time, but not without help from an elderly but still feisty caveman (Luciano Pigozzi), who saves the hero from an explosive end with some energetic trapeze work. Quite unusual behavior this, for an oldtimer, in a genre whose senior citizens are typically relegated to the role of the beautiful girl's father, the doddery magician or the wise old geezer who tags along with the band of heroes and bashes bad guys on the head from the sidelines whenever a fight breaks out.

Working for Menahem Golan and Yoram Globus's every-expense-spared Cannon Films, Italian filmmaker Luigi Cozzi combines sci-fi and traditional myth-and-magic much less successfully in his attempts to revive the peplum strongman. Starring Lou Ferrigno, Cozzi's sub–basement-budget *Hercules* (1983) and *Hercules II* (1984) tackle the mythological character from the same science-fantasy perspective as

Superman, but play rather like demented peplums infused with the laser-disco kitsch of TV's *Buck Rogers*. Created by the gods out of cosmic light, Ferrigno's ursine Hercules is tormented with mechanical monsters sent by Sybil Danning's conniving goddess of the underworld. Later he shoves apart the continents of Europe and Africa and flies through space while tied to a boulder.

Hercules II is even loonier, as Ferrigno retrieves the thunderbolts of Zeus, extracting each from a variety of monsters, including a fire demon which the hero launches into space with a Popeye-style uppercut. Ferrigno fares no better in another American heroic fantasy directed by an Italian, Bruno Mattei's *The Seven Magnificent Gladiators* (1983). Dan Vadis' moustachioed demi-god terrorizes the peasants until Ferrigno's Roman charioteer magically barbecues him with the sword of Achilles.

While the Italians quickly lost interest in heroic fantasy (abruptly moving on to churning out *Mad Max* and Indiana Jones clones instead), American filmmakers persevered, finding ways around the prohibitive costs in recreating the Hyborian landscape. Just as '60s Hollywood realized it could make its epics look even more spectacular by filming on the cheap in Italy, so legendarily resourceful exploitation producer Roger Corman took advantage of cheap labor and favorable exchange rates by filming a string of heroic fantasy micro-epics in Argentina. With the help of *Beastmaster*'s assistant producer Frank K. Isaac, Jr., Corman's newly founded company New Horizons entered into a fruitful partnership with Buenos Aires–based producers Alex Sessa and Hector Olivera.

Throughout the '80s, this joint venture produced barbarian swordsman capers (*Deathstalker* [1983], *The Warrior and the Sorceress* [1984], *Deathstalker II: Duel of the Titans* [1987]), sleazy boobs-and-battle flicks (*Barbarian Queen* [1985], *Amazons* [1986] and *Stormquest* [1988]) and child-friendly epic fantasy (*Wizards of the Lost Kingdom* [1984], *Wizards of the Lost Kingdom II* [1988]). Based on original scripts that plunder ideas from big-budget fantasies just as much as the Italian movies, these mostly negligible cheapies were produced primarily for a home-viewing audience. The distinctively polished sleeve art (by Peruvian fantasy artist Boris Vallejo) depicted familiar muscle-bound conquerors rescuing fantastically endowed girls from the clutches of bestial demons. None of it bore the faintest resemblance to anything the film had the budget or imagination to offer.

John Watson's *Deathstalker* (1983) delivers its sleazy payload more efficiently than anything the Italians produced, and displays a far more cynical sensibility overall. This crude knockabout stars gimlet-eyed lug Richard Hill as the titular mercenary, a laconic, amoral outlaw clearly modelled on Clint Eastwood's Man With No Name. The thatch-haired superhero refuses to help rescue Barbi Benton's princess from Bernard Erhard's tattoo-headed court magician, who has usurped the throne, until unwillingly charged by a pantomime witch with retrieving the Three Powers: the Sword of Justice, which makes its wielder unsurpassable in combat, the Amulet of Life, which renders its wearer invulnerable, and the Chalice of Magic, which is, well, magical.

He obtains the sword from a grizzled Muppet and enters a gladiatorial tournament held by the wizard who reasons this will wipe out every warrior in the land strong enough to oppose him. On the way, Deathstalker teams up with Richard

Brooker's treacherous brigand and Lana Clarkson's bare-breasted swordswoman, who like every other woman in the picture gives in to the hero's advances within minutes of meeting him. Though generally barren, *Deathstalker* does display the odd flash of dumb humor. A pig-faced ogre beats an opponent to death with his own detached arm, and one of the wizard's unfortunate male minions is transformed into a likeness of the captured princess and sent on a seduce-and-destroy mission.

These Argentinean-American heroic fantasies only took their material seriously once, in John C. Broderick's dreary *The Warrior and the Sorceress* (1984). Here David Carradine's morose sword-slinger wanders into a frontier town and plays a pair of feuding warlords against each other in an uninspired homage to *Yojimbo*. Various heroic fantasy elements are grafted onto Kurosawa's plot, including a magic sword, a tentacled dungeon monster and a quadruple-breasted slave girl with a venomous tongue between her legs. Other than this, the Corman pictures surmise that audiences cannot possibly be taking this stuff seriously, so they go about sending it up themselves.

Critic Yvonne Tasker pinpoints this reaction to the absurdities of heroic fantasy in *Spectacular Bodies*, specifically citing heroic fantasies *Conan the Destroyer* and *Red Sonja* and the science-fantasy *Masters of the Universe*, a trio of movies that treat their genre with a derision they believe it deserves: "Humour is derived from the juxtaposition of the barely clad heroes and heroines (so clearly offered as sexual spectacle) with the intense earnestness of the mock mythologies constructed for these fantasy worlds. Thus, there is a doubleness operating in these films around a tacit acknowledgment of the hilarity with which the narratives, which take themselves seriously, are actually received. Minor characters constantly comment on the action, acting to undercut the overblown figures of the heroes and heroines." What Tasker fails to recognize is that the "intense earnestness of the mock mythologies" is precisely necessary if a secondary world fantasy does not wish to distance its viewers with the irony she implies we must regard them all. Serious fantasy films like *Conan the Barbarian*, *Excalibur* and *The Lord of the Rings* are only received with "hilarity" when the viewer intellectually dismisses them.

Filmmakers themselves often dismiss such material before the audience has a chance to do it for themselves. Just such a course was taken by Italian producer Dino De Laurentiis, who prepared to reaffirm the supremacy of the genre's flagship hero with the official sequel to his *Conan the Barbarian*. Correctly deducing that a combination of sex, violence and pretension had limited the appeal of the first film, the mogul demanded the barbarian clean up his act for his second outing, undercutting the hero's dignity and defusing the violence with an air of self-awareness.

Critics and audiences found the tongue-in-cheek approach to Hyborian barbarism taken by *Conan the Destroyer* (1984) easier to swallow than the dour self-importance of its predecessor, although this family-friendly sequel actually undoes all of Milius' good work. In the first film, Arnold's barbarian swordsman is as grubby and functional as the surrounding landscape; when he returns in *Destroyer,* he gleams like a brand-new bathroom set. Reinstating the male body-worship of the peplum, old hand Richard Fleischer irreverently recalls the high-camp heyday of the strongman, implying we should not take his descendent any more seriously.

Opening with Mako's half-hearted voiceover and Basil Poledouris' unenthusiastic score, the movie sees Sarah Douglas' sorceress queen promising to resurrect Conan's dead lover if Conan accompanies winsome Princess Jehnna (Olivia D'Abo) on her travels to retrieve the jeweled horn of the Lovecraftian god Dagoth. More of an ensemble piece than *Barbarian*, *Destroyer* features a lineup of eccentric characters, each lending a particular quirk to the scheduled quest. Stan Laurel lookalike Tracey Walter gives a slightly creepy performance as Conan's irksome jewel-gulping sidekick. The film's two black performers emerge as far more engaging: Former basketball star Wilt "The Stilt" Chamberlain is the princess's towering dreadlocked bodyguard, and '80s funk diva Grace Jones (clearly taking the film much more seriously than anyone else) gives an astonishingly feral performance as a crazy-eyed Amazon. The return of Mako's grimacing shaman pays inconsistent lip service to the original film, while Arnold's appallingly stilted Conan is a laughable lummox, retaining none of his former dignity as he goons about, oblivious to the coy advances of his pubescent ward.

Whereas *Barbarian* takes pains to create an authentically grungy milieu for its superhero, *Destroyer* creates an unrealistically hygienic world (shot in the Mexican desert), which despite its bigger budget gloss looks decidedly cheap, with costumes and props evidently cannibalized from the first film. *Silent Flute* screenwriter Stanley Mann turns in a brisk script, based on an original story by *Fire and Ice* writers Roy Thomas and Gerry Conway, containing a couple of sequences that recapture the flavor of Marvel's comic. In a neat visual homage to Frank Frazetta's cover to the 1967 Lancer paperback *Conan*, Schwarzenegger wrestles a red-cloaked demon which can only be wounded by attacking its reflection. During the finale, the resurrection ritual is botched and the dreaming god Dagoth mutates into a giant reptilian sloth, which Conan subdues by tearing out its jeweled horn.

Although Fleischer treats Conan as lightly as Milius treats him seriously, the sequel's greater popularity gave heroic fantasy a second wind in the '80s. De Laurentiis, Fleischer and Schwarzenegger returned to sword and sorcery a year later with the dreadful *Red Sonja* (1985), which so embarrassed Arnold, whose image dominated the film posters over that of its star (21-year-old Danish model Brigitte Nielsen), that he reportedly tried to pull out of his contract and later refused to promote the film. Conceived as a coattail rider in much the same way as the '70s Marvel comic from which it derives (which plucked the heroine's name from the supporting cast of Howard's tale *Shadow of the Vulture*), *Red Sonja* suffers the same obtrusive wisecracking, impractical costumes and K-Mart props as *Conan the Destroyer*.

Sonja's theatrical cut begins with Nielsen's pokerfaced heroine refusing the lesbian advances of lascivious Queen Gedren (Sandahl Bergman), and her subsequent rape at the hands of Gedren's guards. Bound by self-imposed chastity, Sonja's martial prowess is an expression of her vengeful fury in much the same way as the exploitation heroine of Abel Ferrara's *Ms .45* (1980). *Red Sonja*'s video release, however, cut the instigative rape scene (so the film could obtain a more kid-friendly rating) and inserts an absurd Cinderella prologue in which an unidentified fairy godmother bestows Sonja's strength in the form of a blessing. Either way, the most

O polished perturbation! Arnold Schwarzenegger stands to attention in this publicity still from Richard Fleischer's tongue-in-check sequel *Conan the Destroyer* (Dino De Laurentiis/Edward R. Pressman, 1984), which sends the barbarian swordsman back to the high-camp days of the Italian peplum.

popular reading of the film is that Sonja's mission of vengeance against Gedren is actually a repression of homosexual desire.

Otherwise, *Red Sonja* is not very interesting, and predictably betrays its own nominal concession towards feminism. It begins by portraying Sonja as a Hundra-like swordmistress (even if her abilities have to be granted by an outside agency) and an independent spirit who refuses the attentions of men and the stereotypical gender roles they offer (unlike her heroic contemporaries, Sarah Conner in *Terminator* [1984] and Ellen Ripley in *Aliens* [1986], who conversely embrace traditional roles and became super-moms). Although Sonja sneers at Ernie Reyes, Jr.'s, bratty boy prince when he offers her a job as his royal cook, the film turns tail as she succumbs to her maternal instincts and teaches him to swordfight. She also realizes the importance of having a man around, relying on Arnold's robotic adventurer to bail her out of trouble, do any heavy lifting and engage her in a passionless clinch before the end credits.

Despite Sonja's return to the straight and narrow, Nielsen's heroine became a lesbian pin-up like her successor Lucy Lawless's Xena (the first true advocate of feminist heroic fantasy). Lanky, square-jawed and hard-eyed, both women have more physically in common with the men of their genre than a typical heroic fantasy damsel like *Fire and Ice*'s Teegra, whose round curves, soft bosom and wanton eyes betray a masculine ideology in her creation.

Women in heroic fantasy movies divide broadly into three categories: the damsel, the seductress and the swordswoman. The damsel is the most common, usually found decorating a Hercules or a Sinbad, or elegantly recoiling behind a barbarian swordsman as he tussles with his latest foe. The seductress often appears as some kind of evil queen (peplum goddess Moira Orfei built a career on such roles). This hero-seducing succubus uses a combination of magic and feminine guile to achieve her aims. The swordswoman is an aggressive rejection of such yielding femininity. With the exception of Sandahl Bergman's Valeria, Laurene Landon's Hundra and Grace Jones' snarling androgynine in *Conan the Destroyer*, most swords-women amount to no more than a sexy mannequin groping a phallic weapon.

Such poseurs topline the non-fantasy swordswoman movies that dribbled onto video after *Red Sonja*, including Hector Olivera's salacious *Barbarian Queen* (1985) and its even more awful sequel, Joe Finley' s *Barbarian Queen II: The Empress Strikes Back* (1988), pornmeister Chuck Vincent's Sibyl Danning vehicle *Warrior Queen* (1987) and a pair of post-apocalyptic Amazon movies, Avi Nesher's belated *She* (1983), starring Sandahl Bergman, and Robert Hayes' *Phoenix the Warrior* (1988). Olivera's typically awful *Amazons* (1986) is the only fantasy film of this tawdry bunch. Just like its kin, this purports to be an empowerment tale while indulging in scenes of skinny-dipping, slap-and-tickle and mild bondage. Ex-porn star Lisa Berenger's barbarian swordswoman must retrieve a sacred weapon that will save her fellow Valeria-alikes from the lightning bolts of Joseph Whipp's smirking magician.

Amazons features more backbiting, hugging and feminine mysticism than the boisterous *Deathstalker* movies that share its sets. Similarly the mini-skirted heroine of *She-Ra: Princess of Power* (1985–86), the animated *He-Man* spin-off series, has to make do with powers rather less dynamic than those of her strongman brother. While He-Man gets to ride around on a rearing green tiger, all She-Ra gets is a dainty, winged unicorn, her adventures revolving around wimpy powers of healing and telepathy.

British press handouts for Ed Friedman and Lou Kachivas' *He-Man and She-Ra: The Secret of the Sword* (1985), an animated feature conceived solely to launch the She-Ra series and the toy range that followed, emphasized the contributions of the film's "Educational and Psychological Consultant," whose task it was to provide "specific, positive morals interwoven within the story." However, the moral lessons aimed at the film's young female audience do not progress further than Sunday school, as the weak-willed Princess Adora falls under the spell of shape-shifting cyborg Hordak, finding herself in need of rescue by the strongman alter ego of her brother, Prince Adam. Mattel Toys' She-Ra is probably the only instance of a heroic fantasy heroine conceived solely to appeal to a female audience. Most heroic fantasies sensibly acknowledge that grown women are not their bread-and-butter, and don't really care whether their superheroines are liberated or not, so long as they show enough thigh and cleavage to keep the guys (and maybe some of the girls) interested.

She-Ra's parent show, *He-Man and the Masters of the Universe* (1983–85), is notable for the way it thoughtlessly picks over Howard's heroic fantasy tales as much as the movies. The image of its blue-skinned, skull-faced villain Skeletor (easily the most vivid character in the show's entire dismal ensemble) comes directly from that of Thulsa Doom in the Lin Carter–Robert E. Howard Kull tale *Riders Beyond the Sunrise*. If it were not little more than a string of 20-minute commercials for Mattel's toy line, the series could almost advance a parody of the heroic fantasy superhero. Its Aryan bodybuilder He-Man flaunts a German Cross of Iron on his S&M harness, while his indolent alter ego, in his hot pink waistcoat and lavender tights, looks like he's on his way to a Pride march.

Thanks to his two successful features, He-Man's progenitor Conan proved recognizable enough a character to warrant his own Universal Studios theme tour, whose designer, Gary Goddard, directs the redundant live-action He-Man feature. *Masters of the Universe* (1987) jimmies a barbarian swordsman into its science-fantasy storyline, while reinforcing the fascist associations that have haunted heroic fantasy since the peplum. Acting somewhere beneath his lumpy makeup as the emaciated sorcerer Skeletor, Frank Langella booms endlessly about power and mastery over all, while the insensible Dolph Lundgren's muscular blonde warlord battles legions of goose-stepping, black-armored troops. The movie also includes a sequence of peplum-esque kinkiness, as Lundgren's time-travelling barbarian throws down his sword before Skeletor and submits to slavery. Skeletor parades him around his throne room bare-chested then has him thrashed with a laser-whip. A female henchman raises an eyebrow in kinky approval, while Skeletor clutches his staff in apparent ecstasy.

Heroic fantasy appears tailor-made for the fetishist. Howard often gets carried away into fervent sub/dom terrain, which John Norman's reprehensible *Gor* books elaborated to a misogynistic degree in the '70s (remaining largely responsible for the accusations of sadism levelled at heroic fantasy writing at the time). The peplum had already realized the genre's fancy for whips and chains, and by the '80s barbarian swordsmen were tied up and gloated over by members of both sexes with notable frequency. But heroic fantasy cinema very rarely reaches the nadir of sexual brutality fathomed by writers like John Norman, whose first two Gor books, *Tarnsman of Gor* (1966) and *Outlaw of Gor* (1967), remain the only heroic fantasy texts outside Howard and Andre Norton that have made it to the screen so far.

Fritz Kiersch's *Gor*, shot back to back in South-West Africa's Namib Desert in 1987 with its sequel (John Cardos's *Outlaw of Gor*), is surprisingly dry considering its source material, playing on the book's best-selling name rather than its content. A bespectacled physics professor, Tarl Cabot (Urbano Barberini), is summoned to the desert world of Gor. Playing Cabot's nemesis with earnest camp, poor Oliver Reed distressingly flaunts more bare flesh than any other male in the film. Restraining its own emphasis on bondage, *Gor* is another casualty of the dilemma "is-this-for-kids-or-adults?" Kiersch's camera never really leers at events the way one expects, leaving the audience feeling so detached it's hard to get worked up about the offensiveness of the film's conceit that true masculinity is only achieved when men resort to barbarism.

Closer to the sheer awfulness of the books, *Outlaw of Gor* is more decidedly adult in tone. This time Barberini's Cabot is accused of murdering the king by a treacherous slave girl (Donna Denton) and Jack Palance's loitering high priest. A subdued Palance foregoes the *Hawk the Slayer* histrionics, playing second fiddle to Denton's evil queen, who overacts him off the screen. This time the sadism is more pronounced, as characters are regularly pushed around, beaten up and humiliated by a variety of drooling tormenters. Unlike kinky fantasy peplums like *Samson in King Solomon's Mines* (1964), American heroic fantasies rarely overemphasise the bare flesh of their male stars. A definite sense of not wanting their audiences to get the wrong idea pervades, and the sexual accent most often remains on the scantily clad women. The *Gor* and *Deathstalker* movies all cast former centrefolds (Rebecca Ferrati, Barbi Benton and Monique Gabrielle) in lead roles, while tavern scenes feature nubile dancing girls gyrating over appreciative mercenaries and ripping each other's tops off in mud-wrestling pits.

After the debacle of *Red Sonja*, Hollywood packed its bags and left secondary world fantasy to the exploitation vultures. The Italians added a deliriously dire third installment to their *Ator* series with Alfonso Brescia's *Iron Warrior* (1987). Again played by the pitiable Miles O'Keeffe (by now surely giving serious thought to firing his agent), Ator rescues a purple-eyebrowed princess from the murderous attentions of his heavy-breathing cyborg brother. This was filmed in 1985 under the working title *Echoes of Wizardry*, completed in 1987, but shelved until 1991, by which time a fourth and thankfully final *Ator* had been filmed, Aristide Massaccesi's *Quest for the Mighty Sword* (1989), starring muscleman Eric Allen Kramer as Ator's son.

By now no one was taking heroic fantasy seriously; filmmakers had realized this was a genre easier (and cheaper) to send up than to attempt getting right. Ruggero Deodato's Italian-American co-production *The Barbarians* (1987) is a good example of the nearly agreeable silliness that took over. *Sword and the Sorcerer*'s Richard Lynch plays a villain with another flamboyant hairdo who steals a magical ruby and gets his fingers bitten off by a pair of young orphans. Growing to colossal proportions as they slave in a quarry, sibling bodybuilders David and Peter Paul (billed as the "Barbarian brothers") are almost likeably idiotic as they squabble over weapons, bray like donkeys and call each other "bonehead." After recovering the ruby by hacking their way into the guts of a marsh dragon, they restore it to its apparently rightful place, in the belly button of Eva La Rue's chirpy thief.

Much funnier is Jim Wynorski's cheeky *Deathstalker II: Duel of the Titans* (1987), which employs the anachronistic gags that later wallpapered the jokey secondary worlds of TV's *Hercules* and *Xena*. Freely cannibalizing footage from the first *Deathstalker*, this enjoyably crude caper has John Terlesky's lantern-jawed hero rescue Monique Gabrielle's whiny princess, and reclaim her throne from treacherous alchemist Jerak (John La Zar, with wardrobe from Siegfried and Roy and the bad guy's standard line in urbane sarcasm). Boasting a surprisingly funny script, *Deathstalker II* has plenty of fun at the expense of heroic fantasy conventions. The hero relishes his encounter with yet another tribe of sex-mad Amazons, but finds himself put on trial for crimes against womanhood. Forced to go ten rounds with real-life wrestler Queen Kong in an over-long fight scene, the hero is reduced to screaming, "Not the hair."

In the approaching light of the oh-so-ironic '90s, heroic fantasy was itself becoming a joke not even the exploitation hacks found funny. The *Deathstalker* series threw up two more installments, Alfonso Corona's *Deathstalker III: The Warriors from Hell* (1988) and Howard R. Cohen's *Deathstalker IV: Match of the Titans* (1990), both straightforward heroic fantasy romps and both utterly meritless. Sylvio Tabet's dreary time-slip comedy sequel *Beastmaster 2: Through the Portal of Time* (1991) makes a more straightforward attempt to hold up the antiquated pomposities of heroic fantasy to twentieth century ridicule. A spoiled senator's daughter (Kari Wuhrer) drives her Porsche through a portal into the desert realm of Marc Singer's Beastmaster. Accompanying her back to present-day L.A. with his animal posse, Dar must prevent his sarcastic warlord brother Arkon (Wings Hauser) from stealing a "neutron detonator" with which he will somehow rule their homeworld. Watching these barbarian swordsmen navigate a predictable fish-out-of-water schtick involving blaring car stereos, flummoxed cops and gay shop assistants demonstrates just how low their archetype has sunk since the days they swashbuckled with earnest vigor through *Conan the Barbarian* and *Sword and the Sorcerer*.

The sword-slinging violence and sexual roughhousing that come with the heroic fantasy territory have no place in big-budget family films, while the exploitation merchants who would welcome them usually have neither the skill nor the patience to construct a world cogent enough to contain them. Filmmakers also have yet to realize that there is more to heroic fantasy fiction than Howard. The literary barbarian swordsman has moved on since the '30s, while his cinematic cousin remains trapped in his own Hyborian past.

Into the Unknown with Hat and Bullwhip: The Neopulp Adventurers of Heroic Fantasy

Whereas the barbarian swordsman emerged from the pen of a penniless Texan pulp-smith, the neopulp adventurer resulted from a collaboration between two of the twentieth century's most commercially successful filmmakers. Producer George Lucas and director Steven Spielberg's serial-pulp refurbishment *Raiders of the Lost Ark* (1981) proposes a new addition to the heroic fantasy pantheon, namely Harrison Ford's bespectacled archeology professor, who spends his spring break in pursuit of ancient magical treasure. Lacking the enviable physique of the peplum strongman and the barbarian swordsman, Indiana Jones more resembles a modern-day Sinbad. Trekking to forgotten reaches of the world and encountering the agents of fantasy that reside there, he arms himself with nothing so mystical as a bullwhip, a mean right hook and a bellyful of good ol' American grit. The world of Indiana Jones is not the secondary world of Hercules, Sinbad and Conan, but our own. Modern technology has eclipsed the world of magic that the heroic fantasy superheroes of the legendary past take for granted. As in earthbound fantasy, only isolated enclaves of the fantastic survive. It is these and the wonders they reserve that lure superheroes like Indy into commencing their exploits.

The sense of nostalgia implicit in all heroic fantasy especially concerns the concept of the neopulp adventurer. Indiana Jones' adventures are characterized by the same spirit of all–American derring-do that infused the Saturday matinee serials, although Lucas and Spielberg shrewdly choose to evoke the memory of how good they were, not the reality of how good they actually are. Offering an even greater degree of sex, violence and adventure than the serials that fed on them, the American pulp magazines of the F.D.R. years provide another touchstone, which Spielberg tipped his hat to again with his TV anthology series *Amazing Stories* (1985–87). The world of neopulp recalls an early twentieth century America marked not by the Great Depression and a gradual slide into war, but by a happy childhood curled up in the crowded front row of the Rialto, mesmerized by the breakneck exploits of *Tailspin Tommy* (1934) and *King of the Mounties* (1942), or else hidden beneath the bed covers engrossed in a flashlight reading of *Weird Tales* or *Spicy Adventure Stories*.

Lucas and Spielberg's Indiana Jones was not the first modern-day movie explorer to set an adventurous foot on forgotten ground, although his forebears mostly did so in pursuit of non-fantastical treasure. In the series of Victorian potboilers by H. Rider Haggard, the great white hunter Allan Quatermain flirts with earthbound goddesses, travels through time, and engages in fisticuffs with native sorcerers. On screen he resigns himself to the more grounded search for a forbidden diamond mine, as described in Haggard's most popular novel *King Solomon's Mines* (1885).

Like Howard's Conan, Haggard's Quatermain has yet to receive a fair crack of the cinematic whip. A safari-suited Cedric Hardwicke is presentable enough in Robert Stevenson's *King Solomon's Mines* (1937), as is Stewart Granger, smooching Deborah Kerr in a tree in Compton Bennett and Andrew Marton's *King Solomon's Mines* (1950). In Kurt Neumann's *Watusi* (1958), the Granger film's quickie sequel, George Montgomery plays Quatermain, Jr., retracing Dad's treasure-seeking footsteps. Alvin Rakoff's *King Solomon's Treasure* (1978), adapted from the later novel *Allan Quatermain* (1887), has John Colicos encountering some decidedly rubbery dinosaurs drafted in from an Edgar Rice Burroughs picture.

Burroughs' lost world novels feature similarly stuffy adventurers trekking across prehistoric landscapes, and receive a colorfully impoverished treatment in Kevin Conner's *The Land That Time Forgot* (1974), *At the Earth's Core* (1976) and *The People That Time Forgot* (1977), all starring an anti-conservationist Doug McClure taking pot shots at innocuous prehistoric wildlife. Allan's adventures are too full of levelheaded imperialism to dabble much in hocus pocus, while the Burroughs films are too much in love with their Muppet dinosaurs and Vernean pseudo-science. Neither contains any dint of fantasy, which *Raiders* was first to bring to the treasure-hunting table. As such, not all neopulp adventurers warrant consideration as heroic fantasy, only those in touch with the forces of magic.

In *Raiders*, set in 1936, Indiana Jones is enlisted by U.S. military intelligence to retrieve the lost Ark of the Covenant, the ceremonial chest which the Hebrews used to transport the fragments of the Ten Commandments. "If you believe in that sort of thing," says Jones, conversely acknowledging that fundamentalist Christians may not consider this a fantasy film at all. The Ark, believed to render unstoppable any army that carries it into battle, is also sought by a group of Nazis, led by Paul Freeman's urbane Gallic treasure seeker, Belloq. Like Belloq, Indy is driven by an unhealthy zeal for adventure and an urge to thumb his nose at the awesome Forces-Men-Were-Not-Meant-to-Disturb. Although he threatens to blow up the Ark when it falls into Nazi hands, Indy finds he cannot go through with it, since he wants to behold the artifact's consummate vision as much as the enemy. "I am a shadowy reflection of you," remarks Belloq. "It would take only a nudge to make you like me."

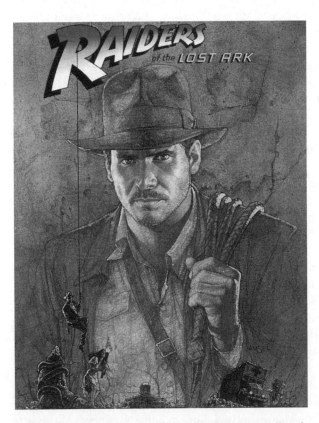

Indy eventually steps back from the brink when the Ark's powers (fore-shadowed by eerie asides throughout the movie) erupt at the climax in a special effects hoopla of shrieking ghosts, lightning bolts and liquefied faces. This destroys Belloq and his transfixed Nazi pals, while Indy (like faithful Lot of the Old Testament) averts his eyes. By the time the authorities have the Ark hidden away in a bottomless warehouse, the agnostic

History repeats itself ingeniously in Lucas and Spielberg's *Raiders of the Lost Ark* (Paramount/Lucasfilm, 1981). This is the U.S. poster art for the movie starring Harrison Ford.

Indy has witnessed irrefutable evidence of the existence of God (or at the very least some higher power) and emerges a believer, although he resigns himself to this revelation with nothing more than a shrug and a quiet drink. Surely a more believable outcome would be his exchanging hat and bullwhip for a monk's habit and a life of prayer. But we accept Indy's spiritual indifference. He is a superhero, after all, and this is a movie that by design amounts to not much more than a brilliantly directed cascade of action set-pieces.

The picture opens as it means to go on, midway through a previous adventure. Indy effects a breathless escape from a trap-infested dungeon somewhere in the jungles of South America, dodging tarantulas, spring-loaded spears, poison darts, pit falls, descending slabs, a rumbling boulder and offended natives. Once the Nazis recover the Ark in Egypt, the roller coaster plunge commences. Indy gets punched, pummelled, shot in the arm and dragged in the dirt. His constant physical punishment is the movie's cruel running gag; the inspired punchline comes when Indy's former lover (Karen Allen), who herself welcomes him with a fearsome right hook, nurses him once the action is over, then accidentally chins him with a swing mirror. Apart from being very funny, the hero's suffering reminds the audience of his humanity, that his adventures take place in a real world as bloody and painful as Conan's Hyboria.

Conan and Indy are not clean-cut types like Hercules or Sinbad, and they don't win every battle; they sweat, they bleed, they bellow in pain, get covered in dirt, forget to shave and fight dirty when they need to. The ophiophobic Indy also has a touchingly neurotic streak (played down in later films), which counterbalances the mounting absurdity of his relentless adventures.

Spielberg's second venture into neopulp, *Indiana Jones and the Temple of Doom* (1984), lays down its mission statement during an opening homage to Busby Berkeley and Cole Porter's hymn to excess "Anything Goes." And so it does, as Jones' skepticism at the outset of *Raiders* is disregarded by a prequel that ends with the superhero undergoing another understated spiritual conversion. *Temple of Doom* is appallingly and brilliantly manipulative of the child audience which *Raiders* disregards, offering lurid excess where the first film is all lean economy. It also recalls the spirit of the serials more deliberately, renovating specific scenes from old favorites like *Zorro's Fighting Legion* (1939), *Drums of Fu Manchu* (1940), *Perils of Nyoka* (1942) and *Manhunt of Mystery Island* (1945).

Temple of Doom begins in Shanghai a year before the events in *Raiders*, as Indy escapes from a near-fatal exchange with the triads along with his orphaned Asian ward Short Round (Ke Huy Quan) and a shrill American nightclub singer (Kate Capshaw). Forced to abandon their sabotaged plane, the three crash-land somewhere in India, where they chance upon a starving village. Jones learns that a sacred fertility stone protecting the people from famine has been stolen, along with the village children, by the inhabitants of the local maharajah's palace, who have succumbed to the vile Kali-worshipping cult of the Thugee. Opening with easy laughs at the expense of Capshaw's displaced party girl (terrorized by jungle fauna, revolted by wriggling cuisine and doused in live bugs), the movie segues into a genuinely horrific second half, which somehow gets away with heart extraction, living human sacrifice, creepy voodoo dabblings and a generally Dickensian regard for children (which brought the

censors down heavily on the film in the U.K.). This is one of the most willfully sadistic children's movies ever made.

Indy emerges as less of a two-fisted adventurer, more a parody of the Bondian
super-spy. He appears in an immaculate tuxedo in the opening nightclub scene, but
proves himself much less the gentleman by accidentally punching a matchbox girl
during a hands-and-knees scramble for a poison antidote. Like Bond, he is wined
and dined by the bad guy (albeit with live eels, beetle pâté and monkey brain sor-
bet), before failing to bed his female companion, grappling instead with a tenacious
Thugee assassin. Spielberg has long expressed his wish to direct a Bond film and
Temple of Doom seems a covert attempt to do so, granting Indy's opponents dark
and ancient magic in lieu of the fiendish technology most Bond villains command
in their bid to conquer the globe. Elsewhere, a sense of the supernatural is quietly
evoked. The village elder suggests divine forces contrived Indy's plight, while the
restored stone brings life back to the village as miraculously as the dead trees that
blossom at the passage of a reinvigorated King Arthur in *Excalibur*.

In what could easily form the prologue to artifact movies like *One Touch of
Venus* and *Jumanji*, Indiana Jones' quests to retrieve mystic knick-knacks provided
a model for the inevitable Italian rip-offs. Antonio Margheriti saddled David Warbeck with the dashing titles of Bob Jackson and Rick Spear and sent him on separate
quests for a magical snake idol, in *I cacciatori del cobra d'oro* (*The Hunters of the
Golden Cobra*) (1984), and the mystic scepter of Gilgamesh, in the *I sopravvissuti
della città morta* (*The Ark of the Sun God*) (1986). Ferdinando Baldi's 3-D *Treasure
of the Four Crowns* (1982) casts its own pokerfaced producer (Tony Anthony) as J.T.
Striker, looking less like a soldier of fortune and more like a Grand Prix mechanic.
He searches for the last crown of the Visigoths, which at the end causes his head to
whiz around like Linda Blair's and temporary turns him into a human flame thrower.
Elsewhere, a snake monster pops out of a swamp for absolutely no reason whatso-
ever.

Other exploitation stabs at neopulp stick to the non-magical diamonds and gold
routine pioneered by the Allan Quatermain movies, as in Matteo Ottaviano's *Yellow
Hair and the Fortress of Gold* (1984), starring *Hundra*'s Laurene Landon; René Cardona's *Treasure of the Amazons*; Mino Guerrini's *The Mines of Kilimanjaro*; and Uli
Lommel's *Revenge of the Stolen Stars* (all 1985). With their pitiful one-two of J. Lee
Thompson's *King Solomon's Mines* (1985) and Gary Nelson's *Allan Quatermain and
the Lost City of Gold* (1986), both starring a bumbling Richard Chamberlain, Cannon Films thought they were being clever by plundering Spielberg through Indy's
predecessor.

Hong Kong filmmakers are rather more inventive, lending their adventurers the
talents of the kung fu avenger. But the magical Macguffin at the center of Teddy
Robin Kwan's nonsensical *Wai Si-Lei Chuen Kei* (*Legend of the Golden Pearl*) (1985)
turns out to be the "solar piloting computer" of a homesick alien, while Jackie Chan's
Long Xiang Hu Di (*Armor of God*) (1986) completely forgets about its mystical relics
by the end. The terrifying daredevilry of Chan's gum-chewing tomb raider proves
far more interesting anyway. He climactically belly-flops off a mountain ledge onto
a hot air balloon, a stunt that would make even Indy blanche.

High as an elephant's eye: Harrison Ford takes the bus to work as Indiana Jones in Steven Spiel-berg's sadistic sequel *Indiana Jones and the Temple of Doom* (Paramount/Lucasfilm, 1984).

The non-magical neopulp tradition continued in the mainstream with Robert Zemeckis's *Romancing the Stone* (1984); its sequel, Lewis Teague's *The Jewel of the Nile* (1985); and Richard Donner's *The Goonies* (1985). These exotic adventures staunchly avoid contact with the magical, for fear of riding the Indiana Jones band-wagon too obviously. By now, Indy's adventuring had become familiar enough to parody, as Lucas and Spielberg do themselves in *Indiana Jones and the Last Crusade* (1989), a bored comic rehash of *Raiders*, directed for the most part on autopilot by Spielberg.

This, the third and hopefully final Indiana Jones adventure, takes Indy's Bondian heritage literally by casting Sean Connery as Dr. Henry Jones, the superhero's obstinate father. The old boy livens up the film considerably, cramping his son's swashbuckling ego and even sleeping with his girlfriend. After a largely irrelevant prologue starring River Phoenix as Indy in his Eagle Scout days (contrived solely as a warm-up for Lucas's future TV series *The Young Indiana Jones Chronicles* [1992]), the main story opens in 1938 and concerns the quest for the Holy Grail, another Biblical relic, this one bringing everlasting life to whoever drinks from it.

Jeffery Boem's idiot-proof script loses control over its fantasy elements, taking the inherent absurdities of Indy's adventures as a license to allow lapses in common sense logic and some shocking plot contrivances. Accompanied by Alison Doody's femme fatale, Indy wades through a petroleum-filled tomb bearing a flame-dripping torch that doesn't ignite the place until the story wants it to. Meanwhile, John Rhys-Davies's rotund Egyptian turns up in time to greet Denholm Elliott's museum curator, even though the two have never met. A faintly ridiculous ending in the Grail chamber comes perilously close to Monty Python territory as Indy meets a doddery old knight who has been guarding the place for centuries and falls over with the weight of his own sword. Nor does Boem have enough of a handle on the rules to confirm whether or not Indy and his father are now immortal, having both drunk from the Grail (surely a great excuse for bringing them into the modern world in future films).

Easily the weakest of the Jones films, *Last Crusade* is a big-budget endorsement of the kind of mishandling heroic fantasy suffered later in Stephen Sommers' *Mummy* films. But for now, Indy's wartime adventuring sparked an interest in other pulp-era superheroes. *Doc Savage: The Man of Bronze* (1975), Michael Anderson's camp take on Lester Dent's eugenic sci-fi strongman, is the first and best-forgotten crack at pulp renovation. The success of *Temple of Doom* led to the revival of a band of pulp, serial, comic-strip and comic-book superheroes worthy of their own wartime chapter of the League of Extraordinary Gentlemen. W.E. Johns' dashing WWII aviator meets his American twin in John Hough's time-slip fantasy *Biggles* (1986). Norman Pett's clothing-repellent secret agent does little of interest in Terry Marcel's *Jane and the Lost City* (1987). The Joker upstages Bob Kane and Bill Finger's caped crusader in Tim Burton's *Batman* (1989). Chester Gould's hardboiled detective romances Madonna in Warren Beatty's *Dick Tracy* (1990). And Joe Johnston's *The Rocketeer* (1991) salutes the jet-propelled stars of Republic's *King of the Rocket Men* (1949) and *Radar Men from the Moon* (1952). Only Batman was enough of an icon to shed his pulp trappings and reinvent himself for a modern audience. The other films stage their adventures in the comparatively quaint recreations of their own bygone heyday, as does Russell Mulcahy's *The Shadow* (1994) and Simon Wincer's *The Phantom* (1996), the only two of these nostalgic adventures that dabble in fantasy.

After languishing in serials and B-pictures that granted him neither the capacity to walk unseen nor the ability to hypnotize, Mulcahy's film grants the Shadow his full complement of fantasy powers. Alec Baldwin fills the role with an understated magnetism similar to Harrison Ford's, struggling against his meaner urges so convincingly as to make one wonder why he was never cast as Bruce Wayne. After a neat prologue that allows a glimpse of the superhero's salad days as a taloned opium baron, Baldwin terrorizes the New York underworld at night, falls for Penelope Ann Miller's telepathic society dame during the day, and faces off against Genghis Khan's swaggering descendent (John Lone), who boasts the same hypnotic powers as himself.

With its vertiginous swoops over the benighted, rain-drenched canyons of Manhattan, and the gothic shadow of its menacing superhero reaching for evildoers across art deco sets, *The Shadow* is little more than a stylistic ride on the cowl-tails of *Batman*. But at least Baldwin looks a formidable superhero, with his billowing cloak, black fedora, ball-bearing stare and a gleaming automatic in each hand. If only the same could be said for the unfortunate Billy Zane in *The Phantom*. Charged with preventing Treat Williams' media magnate from bringing the world to heel with a set of magic skulls, Zane's superhero is forced to go about his heroic duty in broad daylight wearing a lavender body-stocking and a pained expression.

Zane's Phantom, like Harrison Ford's Indy, goes after fabulous treasure without the benefit of magic powers like Baldwin's Shadow. Emphasizing their superheroes' human qualities and making their eventual triumph all the more admirable, most fantasy neopulps leave magic at the disposal of the artifacts their superheroes hunt for. Like the central artifact of *Lord of the Rings*, the Ark of *Raiders* is almost a character unto itself, so full of malevolent energy it is capable of turning the plot on its own.

About the only original idea in Stephen Sommers' lively but undernourished *The Mummy* (1999) was in casting the bandaged star of Universal's horror pantheon in the role of the sought-after treasure. Brendan Fraser's soldier of fortune, Rick O'Connell, leads a 1926 expedition to the lost city of Hamunaptra, where Rachel Weisz's klutzy librarian foolishly reads aloud from an ancient grimoire. She revives the withered corpse of a philandering pharaoh (Arnold Vosloo), who regenerates his body by sucking the life-juices out of an assortment of extras. *The Mummy* attempts to readdress the joyous nostalgia of *Raiders* to a younger audience, with over-obvious references to Harryhausen movies and 1970s–80s horror films like *Shivers*, *Dr. Phibes Rises Again*, *Evil Dead* and *Terminator*. Along with Fraser's faux-baritone growl, fethistic weapon fondling and tough guy posturing ("I only gamble with my life, never my money"), the movie's pulp-era milieu similarly lacks conviction. As strained and artificial as the secondary world of *Conan the Destroyer*, *The Mummy* shares the same knowing humor. Clichés like the ominous breeze that suddenly ripples the campfire are excused with lines like, "It does that a lot around here."

In striving to muster an infectious spirit for his clamorous sequel, *The Mummy Returns* (2001), Sommers winds up with the antithesis of everything *Raiders* got right. The movie's unintelligible plot somehow concerns an attempt by Vosloo's revived mummy to resurrect a long-dead Theban warlord known as the Scorpion King, taking control of his world-conquering army with a magic bracelet strapped to the wrist of the irksome young son of Fraser and Weisz. Suffering from a bad case of Harry-hausenitis, as well as torrential narrative diarrhea, the film dashes from set-piece to set-piece, held together with appalling contrivances and a vain hope the whole thing is moving too fast for anyone to realize nothing makes sense.

The movie argues that its narrative doesn't have to sum up to any kind of logic, that this is fantasy; therefore, anything goes, just as it did for Indiana Jones. The laws of reality are indeed marvellously supple in fantasy films, but only according to a given set of narrative rules (unless a film deals in surrealism, in which case anything really *does* go). The first two Indiana Jones movies crucially establish their narrative regulations early on and stick to them like barnacles. The *Mummy* films make up their rules on the fly. Their characters can stroll away from a pulverizing tidal wave one minute but be susceptible to a stab wound the next, while a hitherto unremarkable rod of *somethingorothor* inexplicably becomes a spear of *wotchmacallit*, which just happens to be the one weapon in all the world that can destroy the bad guy.

Indy's pulp-era legacy comes to a halt with the *Mummy* films, which themselves backtrack into the legendary past with their prequel *The Scorpion King* (2002). Modern neopulp adventuring looks more to the future, and the magic-obscuring encroachment of technology that comes with it. The adventurer heroine of Simon West's *Lara Croft: Tomb Raider* (2001) comes not from the pulps but from that most modern of art forms, the computer game. Yet she remains a conscious composite of pulp superheroes gone by. She has Batman's limitless wealth, techno hideaway, faithful butler and lost parents, James Bond's penchant for gadgets and love of the high life and Indiana Jones' redoubtable brawn and bookish intellect.

Although essayed with a compelling feral grace by Angelina Jolie, her character remains nothing but tits, lips, hips and guns, as superficial a feminist icon as the barbarian swordswoman of *Red Sonja*. A true child of the information age, Lara relies on her ability to manipulate nifty gadgets in her search for the two halves of a time-warping talisman. Forged by an extinct and unspecified culture from an alien metal that fell to earth inside a meteor, this artifact implies that Lara's time-slip meeting with her long-dead father (Jolie's real-life dad Jon Voight) is the result of cosmic rather than specifically magical forces. Otherwise the movie has a strong sense of the mysteries awaiting discovery in Lara's world, like its animated statues borrowed from *The Golden Voyage of Sinbad* and a spooky little girl who offers enigmatic observations throughout.

Jan De Bont's stilted sequel, *Lara Croft: Tomb Raider — The Cradle of Life* (2003), is as oddly inert as its predecessor, and displays more of an interest in technology than in the magic it is employed to retrieve. Lara's promotion of the scientific would appear to sow the seeds of her own repudiation. As in the first film, she must prevent capitalist forces exploiting an ancient source of magic, in this case a well of primordial slime from which all life derives and in which nestles Pandora's Box. This mystic site is located amid a Third World culture whose reverence for superstition has yet to be extinguished by the commercial onslaught of McDonald's and MTV (although the rot has apparently already set in, as Lara interrupts a family of Vietnamese boat people eating their dinner before an episode of *SpongeBob Square-Pants*).

Hello boys! Angelina Jolie sums up Lara Croft's contribution to feminist heroic fantasy in this publicity shot from Jan De Bont's *Lara Croft: Tomb Raider—The Cradle of Life* (Paramount/Mutual/BBC/Tele-München/Toho-Towa/Lawrence Gordon/Lloyd Levin/Edos, 2003).

Like Indy, Lara respects these native custodians, although her motives for trespassing in their hallowed enclave remain ambiguous. Indy does so for reasons other than himself—for his country, for an oppressed people, and for his family. He never benefits financially from his exploits, and his personal zeal for "fortune and glory" evaporates by the end, as he sheds his skepticism (repeatedly) and learns to believe and respect the forces of magic. Lara is more cavalier in her adventuring, which itself appears only a distraction from roughhousing with her training robot or toning her body with the narcissism of a peplum strongman. "She's in it for the glory," remarks her lover, although the artifacts she destroys and the invaluable tombs she helps demolish afford her a swish lifestyle that makes her little better than a villain. Despite a dinner guest obliquely accusing him of being just such a grave robber in *Temple of Doom*, the treasures Indy recovers all remain intact by the end, either rightfully restored or wisely rehidden. Mysticism gives little ground to science in Indy's world, while Lara, it seems, would be happy to see the last sanctuaries of earthbound magic destroyed, leaving successive neopulpsters with no more Atlantises or Shangri-Las to explore.

Sentimental Strongmen and New Age Barbarians: Heroic Fantasy Rides into the Sunset

Once exploitationeers like Ator and Deathstalker had bled the last drops of dignity from heroic fantasy, it was left to television to nurse the genre back to health. Since the mid–'90s, most American movies featuring strongmen, monster-battling mariners or barbarian swordsmen are characterized by the laid-back humanism of the successful heroic fantasy TV series *Hercules: The Legendary Journeys* (1995–99) and its superior spin-off *Xena: Warrior Princess* (1996–2001).

Heroic fantasy's inexhaustible superheroes and episodic storylines naturally lend the genre to television, but all attempts to launch such a series prior to *The Legendary Journeys* never made it further than a pilot. Heroic fantasy cinema's unlikely godfather Joseph E. Levine made the first attempt back in 1964, when he announced his intention to bring the peplum strongman to the small screen for the ABC network, but only got as far as *Hercules and the Princess of Troy* (1965), starring an unbecomingly bearded Gordon Scott coming to the rescue of a city under threat from a jerky mechanical sea-beast. Nicholas Corea fared no better with his dismal NBC pilot *The Archer: Fugitive from the Empire* (1981), while Terry Marcel failed to carry out his threat to produce a *Hawk the Slayer* spin-off series for Britain's Palladium Entertainment in 1989.

The literal-minded notion that secondary worlds must command expensive special effects proved prohibitive, and Hercules, Sinbad and Conan were barred from TV until they could grapple with the kinds of monsters they did on the movie screen. The curse of Harryhausen endured with the advent of CGI, which meant even the most impoverished TV studio could turn out passable centerpiece effects. Having got by in the past without any interference from fantasy, familiar TV superheroes now found themselves facing off against tentacled beasties in newly fantasized escapades like *Tarzan: The Epic Adventures* (1996) and *The New Adventures of Robin Hood* (1997–99).

Heroic fantasy TV's facelift extended to its adventurers' surroundings. *Hercules* and *Xena* discovered the verdant landscapes of New Zealand as an attractive alternative to the familiar dustbowl backdrops of Hollywood. This forced producers to look further than their Arizona backyard. The coastlines of South Africa provided the locations for *The Adventures of Sinbad*, rural Mexico for the embarrassing TV exploits of *Conan* and the forests of Lithuania for Sherwood in *The New Adventures of Robin Hood*. But scenic as these and their progenitors were, they retained that unique tackiness which had been a feature of American heroic fantasy since the days of *Beastmaster* and *Deathstalker*. They added strident modern lingo, *Melrose Place* melodramatics and a very '90s "can't we all just get along?" sensibility, to a world already populated by blow-dried hairdos, toy swords and well-scrubbed Californians. The legendary past here melds with the Californian present, creating a secondary world as anchored to the '90s as the peplum's was to the '60s, with Steve Reeves's brilliantined pompadour and Sylva Koscina's beehive hairdo looking just as conspicuous amid the Doric columns and Grecian statuary.

In *The Legendary Journeys*, Mills & Boon poster boy Kevin Sorbo embodies a strongman struggling with neuroses different from those that Steve Reeves and his chums keep in the closet throughout the peplum. In the five telefeatures that preceded the series in 1994, Hercules is established as the child of a broken home, caught between his absent father Zeus (a distinctly ungodly Anthony Quinn) and the hateful mother-figure of Hera, to whom Hercules is a living reminder of her husband's dalliance with a mortal woman. Consequently, Sorbo is strongly conservative, frowning on free love and anti-family values. He tells those he puts to rights to think for themselves for a change, and stop sacrificing their lunch (and each other) to a bunch of flawed gods who have even less of a clue than they do. Such altruism flies in the face of heroic fantasy's traditional egotism, but somehow works in its own peculiar way, lending these telefeatures an undeniably fresh perspective on the strongman archetype.

Bill L. Norton's *Hercules and the Amazon Women* is typical in its combination of overt sentimentality and engaging silliness. Sorbo's Hercules is captured by a band of militant feminist Amazons, who tear off his shirt and parade him around their village in time-honored fashion. They then make him realize the error of his sexist ways, ingrained in him by various chauvinist father figures. Although it purports to be a feminist yarn, the film cannot resist a peek as the girls prepare for battle, oiling each other up by firelight and strapping their curves into flattering war-gear. In a very funny scene, the timid men of a local village besieged by these ravenous women act on Hercules' progressive advise by attempting to placate their ravishers with dinner, flowers and serenades.

Directed by Harley Cokeliss (whom Milton Subotsky had lined up to direct his abortive *Thongor in the Valley of Demons* 15 years earlier), *Hercules and the Lost Kingdom* is a much livelier effort. Sorbo helps restore Renee O'Connor's petulant orphan to the throne of Troy, and in a colorful scene he crawls through the innards of a beady-eyed sea serpent and hugs its heart to bursting. Doug Lefler's risibly sentimental *Hercules and the Circle of Fire* has Sorbo impassively declare, "I love you too," when Zeus tearfully confesses he would rather see all humanity freeze to death under a new ice age, than have his son risk his life retrieving the magic flame that will thaw the world.

Bill L. Norton's *Hercules in the Underworld* has the strongman revisit Hades to rescue his dead wife, Deianeira (Tawny Kitaen). The underworld has not been redecorated since Reg Park's day, still featuring that dry-ice carpet, electric-blue mood lighting and those kitsch cobweb drapes. But a couple of amusing characters have since taken up residence. Bantering with Charon, ferryman of the dead, who speaks with the seen-it-all cynicism of a Brooklyn cabbie, Hercules also meets a platoon of dead soldiers sent to retrieve a runaway three-headed hound, and who grumpily reattach their dismembered limbs after every failed attempt. The final film, Josh Becker's *Hercules in the Maze of the Minotaur*, is padded with footage of previous labors, as Hercules learns that the wretched human-bull hybrid, which wraps its victims in slimy cocoons for some reason, is actually his half-brother.

While the peplum strives for the merely operatic, the *Legendary Journeys* movies attempt the soap operatic in mythological drag, although they stay truer to their borrowings from Greek myth than anything in the peplum. Yet the secondary world of Sorbo's Hercules is almost willfully unconvincing, and tries to compensate with its tongue-in-cheek sense of fun. Consequently, the films have little identity, with scenic New Zealand locations just another element disconnectedly shuffled into the deck. The same problem affects Sorbo's hero, apparently modelled on the Apple Pie decency of American sporting legend Joe Montana. Introduced by an opening voiceover as a Lone Ranger figure possessing "a strength surpassed only by the power of his heart," Sorbo appears driven purely by mindless nobility, betraying no underlying emotion to suggest he is any more human than the angelic strongman of the peplum.

As an icon, Hercules embodies the masculine values of a given culture. The ancient Greeks emphasize his commitment to duty, while the Italian pepla worship his physical splendor. *The Legendary Journeys* telefeatures present him as a kind of super-powered "New Man," while in Disney's animated *Hercules* (1997) he personifies the American hero-image of the jock, winningly lampooning previous embodiments like Sylvester Stallone's *Rocky*. Disney's Hercules (voiced by Tate Donovan) begins life as an infant god prophesized to aid Olympus in a coming war with the elemental Titans, but is rendered half-mortal by the power-hungry Hades (a piranha-toothed devil with an inflammatory hairdo, whose devious patter is voiced by James Woods). Raised like Superman by mortal rubes, Hercules learns of his divine heritage and becomes as Oedipally committed as Kevin Sorbo, struggling to live up to Zeus' expectations by proving himself a "true hero" and thus regaining his godhood. Ferried by Pegasus, his bird-brained steed, and coached by Danny DeVito's truculent Satyr, Hercules rids the land of monsters and becomes a merchandizing phenomenon, in an affectionate send-up of America's commercial love affair with sports superheroes like Michael Jordan. But Hercules learns the difference between celebrity and heroism when he sacrifices himself for the woman he loves.

Having previously only touched upon Greek myth in the pastoral sequence of

Fantasia (1940), Disney's feature-length retelling proves energetic but as unsuccessful as *Pocahontas* (1995) and *The Hunchback of Notre Dame* (1996) at appropriating
a morally complex text. *The Legendary Journeys* at least understands that the gods of
Greek myth embody life's contradictions. Disney presents a Manichean view, with
Hades, the personification of evil, neatly done away with at the end, leaving the question of who will now govern the dead left unanswered. The classically impartial Three
Fates become evil harridans sharing a single moist eyeball and delighting in cutting
the strings of mortal life. Despite this moral tidying (which extends to having Hercules born within immortal wedlock), Disney's *Hercules* does work as a heroic fantasy comedy. Saturating the world of its strongman with anachronistic gags about
sneakers and sports commentary, the movie accurately mocks the conventions of the
strongman epic from its very first scene. Defusing the traditional It-Was-a-Time-of-
Darkness monologue (voiced here by Charlton Heston), a Greek chorus of Muses
give an exasperated cry of "lighten up, dude."

A similarly modish view of the past was presented by the comic book adventures of *Asterix*, which appeared at the height of the peplum strongman's fame and
poked fun at his shortcomings as successfully as Disney. Created by French writer
Réné Goscinny and Italian artist Albert Uderzo, Asterix first appeared in the debut
issue of French comic *Pilote* in 1959, effectively turning the tables on the cultured
Greco-Roman strongman by placing his superhuman strength in the hands of the
coarse barbarians who oppose him.

Claude Zidi's crowded mega-franc adaptation, *Astérix & Obélix contre César*
(*Asterix & Obelix Take on Caesar*) (1999), retains the comics' basic premise, if little
else. In pre–Biblical Gaul, a tiny coastal village holds out against Caesar's all-
conquering Roman legions with the aid of their resident druid's magic potion, which
turns the drinker into an instant strongman. The film recreates the effects of this
potion amusingly enough, with face-contorting swigs all around and unfortunate
Roman soldiery orbited in every direction by the pugnacious Gauls. Diminutive
superhero Asterix and his rotund companion, Obelix (upon whom the potion's effects
are permanent, since he fell into a cauldron of the stuff as a baby), are pestered by
Roberto Benigni's excitable Centurion, while suffering boorish portrayals by a loud-
mouthed Christian Clavier and a blundering Gerard Depardieu. Alain Chabat's more
reserved sequel, *Astérix & Obélix: Mission Cléopâtre* (*Asterix & Obelix: Mission
Cleopatra*) (2002) recalls the more chivalrous charm of the strongmen of old, as the
duo (Clavier and Depardieu on better form this time) lend a superhumanly strong
hand in building a magnificent palace for Monica Belluci's imperious Cleopatra, just
so she can win a bet with Caesar.

While the strongman continues to adopt new and interesting guises, Sinbad
finds himself marooned in his post–Harryhausen years, with only a soggy TV series
and a couple of limp animated features to his name. If only future Sinbad movies
could be as enjoyable as Gore Verbinski's eighteenth century heroic fantasy *Pirates
of the Caribbean: The Curse of the Black Pearl* (2003). Sinbad must envy the movie's
reeling scalawag Captain Jack Sparrow, so agreeably sent up by Johnny Depp. Stepping ashore just as his rapidly sinking ship disappears beneath the waves (an outstanding visual gag), a destitute Jack agrees to help Orlando Bloom's winsome

blacksmith rescue Keira Knightley's equally winsome damsel, kidnapped by the gnarled sea dog Barbossa (Geoffrey Rush).

Along with the entire crew of iniquitous pirate vessel the *Black Pearl*, Barbossa suffers the blight of undeath until he returns every piece of loot from a cursed Aztec haul. In a neat gimmick, moonlight reveals these pirates as the mouldering corpses they truly are. An arrestingly creepy underwater shot sees their skeletal forms stealing across the moonlit sea bottom, while Sparrow (now similarly cursed) and Barbossa weave through columns of moonlight during a macabre duel, phasing between their fleshed and unfleshed selves. Unlike many a Sinbad movie, *Pirates of the Caribbean* moors its fantasy conceit securely to its narrative and attacks the story with a self-deprecating humor and swashbuckling brio that future Sinbad movies would do well to emulate.

The barbarian swordsman always has a tougher time on screen than the strong-man or Sinbad. His anti-heroic propensity for dismembering transgressors makes him unsuitable for hero status in family fluff like Disney's *Hercules* or *Pirates of the Caribbean*. His temperament makes him a more likely candidate for the role of the villain's strong-arm lieutenant in epic fantasies like *Willow* (1988) or *Dungeons and Dragons* (2000). The presence of characters packing razor-sharp steel realistically heralds bloodshed, and yet a barbarian swordsman movie without swords is rather like a Western without guns. Marc Singer's barbarian in the *Beastmaster* movies rarely draws steel in anger, preferring to rely on his Tarzan-like empathy with animals to get his point across. Yet he suffers as much as his fellows from the anti-violence, tongue-in-cheek constraints imposed by *The Legendary Journeys*.

Gabrielle Beaumont's risible telefeature *Beastmaster III: The Eye of Braxus* (1995) lacks even the wit to mock itself. David Warner's evil sorcerer requires periodic sacrifice to prevent him morphing into an old man. He needs the immortality-bestowing eye of the god Braxus so he can continue spouting ridiculously arch dialogue amid wobbly sets for all eternity. Casper Van Dien (wearing what has to be the most gloriously ridiculous wig of any heroic fantasy movie) plays good king Tal, who owns one half of the Eye, while Marc Singer's wrinkly Beastmaster owns the other. A throwback to the impoverished barbarian capers of the '80s, with a cut-rate climax lifted from *Conan the Destroyer*, *Beastmaster III* ended Dar's movie career, although the character limped on with Daniel Goddard in a similarly anodyne TV series, *Beastmaster: The Legend Continues* (1999–2002).

Those heroic fantasy TV series that follow the lead of *The Legendary Journeys* all abide by the rules for violent conduct laid down by kid's TV. The only beings allowed to be dismembered are bloodless robots, while flesh-and-blood bad guys may only be hurled across the screen in harmless *A-Team* fashion. But these rules did not seem to apply to Lucy Lawless's Xena, who made her first appearance as a *Legendary Journeys* antagonist. She was the kind of sword-waving maniac who would have led the first-act charge against every peaceable settlement burned to the ground since *Conan the Barbarian*. Based on Brigitte Lin's feminist ogre in Ronny Yu's fairy tale *Bai fa mo nu zhuan* (*The Bride with White Hair*) (1993), Xena proved so appealing that she landed her own series, through which she struggled to redeem herself, accompanied by the Jiminy Cricket figure of her sidekick Gabrielle (Renee O'Connor).

More deadly than the male! Lucy Lawless strikes a genuine blow for feminist heroic fantasy in the popular TV series *Xena: Warrior Princess* (MCA, 1996-2001).

Symptomatic of the barbarian swordsman's plight in the '90s, Xena is forced to rein in her urge to cut loose and bust heads, and has be nice to people for a change. The series' producers made much of their breaking with masculine tradition and added beheadings, ritual beatings, crucifixion and casual maiming, as well as a good deal of suggestive flirting between the superheroine and her cute female sidekick. Xena's male counterparts are allowed nothing like the same license. Notably Conan himself suffers the indignity of playing nice in his Saturday morning cartoon, *Conan the Adventurer* (1992), and a truly horrible one-season series, *Conan* (1997), starring gangling German body builder Ralf Moeller as a caring, sharing Cimmerian, flanked by representative sidekicks.

Featuring another misrepresented Howard hero, John Nicolella's farcical *Kull the Conqueror* (1997) typifies the kind of neutering the barbarian swordsman underwent throughout the '90s. Producer Raffaella De Laurentiis (Dino's daughter) originally developed the film in 1989 as a second *Conan* sequel, but switched characters when Arnold turned the movie down. *Kull* misguidedly casts *Legendary Journeys* nice-guy Kevin Sorbo as the brooding barbarian axe-man who thundered from the troubled id of Robert E. Howard. Reluctant to spill blood or cavort with his concubines, Sorbo's Kull is the sort of barbarian warlord you could take home to Mother. Crowned by the dying king, Sorbo sets about bringing justice to the oppressed people, while the dead monarch's relatives resurrect Tia Carrere's porno-wigged demonologist to depose him. Kull must retrieve the breath of an ice-god in order to destroy her, resulting in a ridiculous finale, which has him literally smooching a monster to death. Thoughtlessly grafting Sorbo's easygoing strongman persona onto its axe-wielding opposite, the movie also picks up the residuals of '80s secondary world fantasy, with all its mid-battle wisecracks, cheap sets, bad hair and tongue-in-cheekiness.

While drivel like *Beastmaster III* and *Kull* woo the child audience that enjoy *The Legendary Journeys*, Christophe Gans' *Le Pacte des Loups* (*Brotherhood of the Wolf*) (2001) unashamedly offers its far-fetched events to adults. French cinema is not known for its barnstorming action pictures, making this baroque cocktail of period melodrama, monster movie and kung fu flick all the more extraordinary. Based on French folk legend, the plot crossbreeds *Jaws* with *Sleepy Hollow*. In 1764, some elusive monster preys upon the peasantry of the Gévaudan province. King Louis XV sends his best men to investigate: stalwart gamekeeper Grégoire de Fronsac (Samuel Le Bihan playing a naturalist-adventurer somewhere between Ichabod Crane and John Rambo) and his Iroquois blood brother Mani (martial artist Mark Dacascos). As the superstitious nobility greet their scientific methods with skepticism, a wolf cull takes place, but fails to prevent further deaths. (A key scene is missing from overseas prints, in which the King orders Fronsac to construct an elaborate monster, paraded through Paris as official proof of the beast's death.)

Brotherhood moves to the beat of heroic fantasy throughout, with Le Bihan's indestructible superhero wreaking sword-slinging havoc against an apparently supernatural agency. He does so before a luxurious backdrop of autumnal forests, vine-draped ruins and torch-lit masonry. One extraordinary shot exemplifies the film's sensual texture, as the camera glides over Monica Belluci's nude torso and dissolves into a tracking shot of a snow-covered landscape. The main story forms the recollections of its hidden monarch (Jérémie Rénier's young Marquis), and the movie stays on to describe what happens to him after the superhero has departed and the new regent has healed the land. A prologue and epilogue set during the French Revolution see the Marquis (now an aging aristo) dragged before Madam Guillotine, symbolizing the fresh social upheaval that will summon further superheroes, and where dies the truth of the entire Gévaudan affair.

The beast of legend itself is the tool of a religious cabal spreading superstitious terror across France, in order to preserve the veneration of God in the Age of Reason. The film foreshadows its own rationalist resolution when Fronsac presents a furry trout to his astonished hosts, only to reveal, "My taxidermist is a clever man." With its conclusion that magic and religion are the same lie, the movie rules itself out as fantasy proper. Unlike a true fantasy film like Tim Burton's *Sleepy Hollow* (1999), in which rationality is conquered by the fantastic, *Brotherhood* concludes along the lines of Conan Doyle's *The Hound of the Baskervilles*. The prowling monster is finally revealed as an unspecified genus of African carnivore, trained and sheathed in a suit of bristling armor (the obvious implausibility of this scientific revelation locates the film somewhere in the region of science-fantasy). *Brotherhood of the Wolf* successfully harnesses sci-fi, surrealism, fairy tale and heroic fantasy, standing as a superior example of the creative freedom afforded by the genres of the fantastic, and which so often confounds the filmmakers working within them.

While the hot sex and bone-crunching violence of *Brotherhood* recall the piquant days of the early '80s, Chuck Russell's enjoyable sleeper hit *The Scorpion King* (2002) is bland, benign, coldly calibrated to please its pre-pubescent demographic, and the most likely model of any barbarian swordsman movie to follow. Conceived as backstory to the character who fleetingly appears in the prologue of *The Mummy Returns*, the movie plants itself in a mythic Middle East, a stone's throw from the Grecian Neverland of the peplum. Tyrannical general Memnon (Steven Brand) sweeps his armies across the land, conquering all with the help of a loyal seer who can predict the outcome of every battle. Dwayne Johnson (a.k.a. pro wrestling megastar The Rock) plays the mercenary assassin Mathayus, hired by the free peoples to kill Memnon's pet sorcerer. But on discovering this sorcerer is actually a captive sorceress (Kelly Hu), Mathayus is betrayed and his brother murdered, propelling him on a quest for revenge with the help of a standard-issue cowardly sidekick (Grant Heslov), a dotty inventor (Bernard Hill) and a grizzled Nubian warrior (Michael Clarke Duncan).

The Scorpion King retains ample good humor, yet unlike *The Legendary Journeys* and its acolytes the movie does not employ irony to guard against the audience sniggering at the sight of The Rock in ancient Egyptian drag. A pop-eyed hulk with a formidable smile, Johnson makes a thoroughly likable hero, displaying a very '90s understanding when he catches a rosy-cheeked urchin stealing his gold. Like the pirate hero of *Sinbad: Legend of the Seven Seas* (2003), one wonders how such a softie could ever cut it in the business of murdering people. The movie gets around the swordplay issue by capitalizing on its star's talent as a wrestler, although an incongruous rock'n'roll soundtrack blares from the ringside during fight scenes. Unlike most heroic and epic fantasies for children, which tend to emphasise colorful stuff

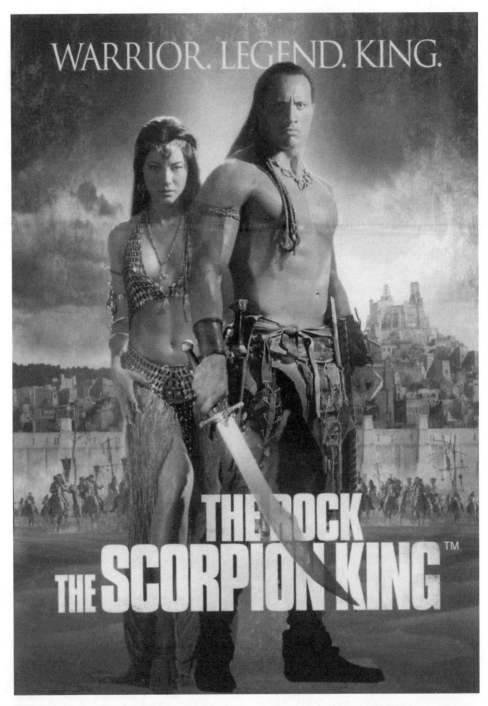

Dwayne Johnson (aka "The Rock") cooks up a storm as the mercenary Mathayus, posing along-side Kelly Hu, as rescued sorceress Cassandra, in this publicity still for Chuck Russell's agree-able barbarian picture *The Scorpion King* (Universal/WWF/Alpahaville/Stephen Sommers/Misher, 2002).

like lightning-hurling wizards, Russell's film is better for downplaying its single fantasy component (Kelly Hu's seeress), lending a quiet sense of the legend Mathayus will become. During a *Conan*-style resurrection scene, Hu remarks he is not destined to die at Memnon's hand and that the scorpion venom, lacing a near-fatal arrow, will forever taint his soul.

Given the calamities of the past, the barbarian swordsman's future does not look entirely bleak in the footsteps of *The Scorpion King*, and the archetype's breakthrough movie has yet to be made. Milius' *Conan* properly colors his world, while *The Scorpion King* gives him something to do. But for reasons of kismet, no film has yet merged these qualities.

Failing to realize they are at least three decades behind the comics they patronize, movies like Ang Lee's unbearably smug *The Hulk* (2003) and Pixar's (very funny) send-up *The Incredibles* (2004) continue to believe they have it all figured when it comes to the superhero genre. Struggling to keep up as its big brother makes headway with more progressive movies, like Bryan Singer's *X-Men 2* (2003), heroic fantasy (in its own small way) can presently be likened to the '30s Western, before the breakthrough success of Henry King's *Jesse James* (1939) elevated a genre previously typified by the Republic B Western and Gene Autry's singing cowboy. Although unlikely, heroic fantasy may one day achieve its *Stagecoach* (1939), the movie that achieves a poetry and resonance undreamed of in an apparently inconsequential genre.

6

Epic Fantasy

Exposing the Heart

Its influence trickling down into the rest of the genre, the full weight of myth itself rests on the shoulders of epic fantasy. Joseph Campbell was not exaggerating when he wrote of the magnitude of this burden in his 1949 study *The Hero with a Thousand Faces*, "It would not be too much to say that myth is the secret opening through which the inexhaustible energies of the cosmos pour into human cultural manifestation. Religions, philosophies, arts, the social forms of primitive and historic man, prime discoveries in science and technology, the very dreams that blister sleep, boil up from the basic, magic ring of myth." Along with those of Jung and Tolkien, Campbell's ideas are among the most influential in fantasy. Yet he was wrong to disregard myth's cousin, the fairy tale. "Fairy tales are for children," he told interviewer Bill Moyers. "As you grow older, you need a sturdier mythology." Campbell disregards the correspondence between the two forms, which actually brings the fantasy genre full circle.

As cultural manifestations of Story, myth and fairy tale share common traits, differing only in scope. Both prescribe models of conduct or reveal timeless human conditions, defining one's place in the world and our various courses through it. Both have no single identifiable author beyond their present relator, with countless personalities contributing to their existing form, like a mountain's distinguishing surface directing the course of a spring. Both are flavored by the accumulated persona of entire cultures, by whatever ideological assumptions prevail at the time of their telling. Yet the spiritual verities of fairy tale are more precise than those of myth, more gender- and community-specific. Fairy tale addresses the individual psyche, while myth addresses the world, embracing the most sweeping themes in the most audacious symbolic language.

Epic fantasy has its roots in literature just as much as fairy tale, the great national epics like Homer's *Odyssey* (c. 9th–8th centuries B.C.), Malory's *Le Morte d'Arthur* (1485) and Wagner's opera cycle *Der Ring des Nibelungen* (1869–76) provided early cinema with prime sources of inspiration. Like the ancient literary precursors of heroic fantasy (paeans to superheroic valor like *Gilgamesh* and *The Iliad*), the epics form part of the same free-floating repository of story as the folkloric wonder tale, until prose, rhyme or song freeze it into a snapshot. Whether straightforwardly adapting familiar legendary tales, and especially if attempting to create new ones, an epic fantasy movie must seek to connect with the grand rhythms of myth, through which it can relate the insight of the ages.

Just as heroic fantasy movies occupy the larger field of the superhero genre, so epic fantasy films naturally form part of the epic, a genre which embraces settings historical (*Spartacus*), modern (*Gone with the Wind*) or space age (*Star Wars*), their sweeping gestures emulating myth whatever the milieu.

Putting life into the grandest perspective, epic fantasy movies broadcast stories from the tower of myth itself. Yet this brazen genre attracts few *auteurs*. Great epic filmmakers like Kurosawa, Ford and Lean (whose influence sadly has hardly penetrated the genre) prefer to ground their films in the historical rather than the fantastical. Paradoxically, the personality of a director is often at its most invisible in epic fantasy, where invented worlds require a sense of verisimilitude that may not be conducive to the filmmaker's personal expression. Epic fantasies seeking to recreate mythic stories in this way cannot use irony to distance themselves from their own histrionics; to do so will short-circuit the absorptive experience. These movies demand total commitment to their premise, belonging to what critic Stephen Hunter calls in his *Washington Post* review of *The Return of the King* "a species of drop-dead melodramatic plotting." While fairy tale employs a candid host to address the audience where they stand, epic fantasy attempts to arrest them itself, and in so doing exposes its heart to be shot at.

Epic fantasy attempts then a kind of seduction, which romantic audiences need little encouragement in succumbing to. Uptight rationalists on the other hand remain more difficult to unbutton. Their resistance lies in the genre's perceived abandonment of intellectualism. Just as a religious experience requires faith, so epic fantasy demands an acceptance of the correlation between myth and reality, a willingness to open one's ears to what Campbell calls "the music of the spheres." The hard-line skeptic will dismiss all this as superstitious hogwash, and balk at the suggestion that myth or religion point to some discernable design behind man's existence. Ironically, this spiritual abstainer becomes as dogmatic in his thinking and as isolated in his own private domain as the misguided escapist who retreats into fantasy believing he has eluded the real world.

Epic fantasy should present a symbolic reflection of our world, the presentation and maintenance of which is a central concern. The genre reflects a world furthest from our own, free of perceptual clutter so that one may comprehend a more comprehensive view. For this reason, epic fantasy almost invariably takes place in archaic worlds, which have the least to distract us from the primacy of nature, of which (the genre asserts) we are ultimately a part. Faerie makes a display of its own artifice and allows transport to the earthbound world through its rabbit holes and wardrobes, while the ideal epic fantasy world is hermetically sealed and autonomous. It refers to the real world at its peril, since even the slightest twang of an inappropriate accent or a chance remark about "dwarf-tossing" can break the spell and yank the audience back to earth.

For the private world of epic fantasy to have any relevance to the public world, it must share the same process of life. For this reason, epic fantasy takes place out-side the prelapsarian bubble that encloses heroic fantasy and sets itself inside Camp-bell's "field of time," where all things are subject to the passage of life and its attendant woes. Here the narrative variables of magic must be tightly controlled. Epic fantasy demands the strictest marshalling, its worlds often more precisely detailed and fully realized than its inhabitants.

A defining characteristic of an epic fantasy world is ultimately its vulnerability. Like the lost worlds of earthbound fantasy, the entire world of epic fantasy (and hence the magic sustaining it) will be threatened with some kind of diminishment or a fall into entropy, which must be stemmed or prevented. Clute and Grant's *Ency-clopaedia of Fantasy* refers to this effect as "thinning," a process usually personified by (and the work of) some "Dark Lord." Ignoring the natural laws of the world in favor of their own, these villains are usually seen gliding about some gothic hide-away, leering at the outside world through a crystal ball and barking orders at incom-petent minions.

Occasionally the solipsist who brings about the collapse of an epic fantasy world may do so in complete innocence, like the Arthurian knight Balyn, whose pride comes before the so-called "dolorous stroke" that plunges King Arthur's realm into darkness. What the Dark Lord achieves through action, a character like Perceval achieves through inaction, failing to question the significance of the Grail procession in Arthurian myth. This brings about the thinning that (unless averted by heroic action) will ultimately conclude in the wasteland, the world abandoned by God like the medieval dystopia of *The Seventh Seal*, or else subdued by machinery like the nightmare technocracy of *Brazil*.

The task of lighting a candle against this curse of darkness falls to a reluctant champion. The epic fantasy hero does not possess the monster-taming muscle or firepower of the heroic fantasy superhero. He's the little guy selected to represent the multitude of his world, the fallible human (or humanoid) responsible for assuring the survival of the fantasy world after the superhero has defined its boundaries. Often the only significant weapon these heroes have to hand is the quotidian virtue of cour-age, specifically in facing up to their desperate, often suicidal missions.

The hero's journey is the engine that drives Joseph Campbell's theory of the "monomyth," the idea that all religio-mythic archetypes share a similar arrange-ment, the same underlying meaning and spring from universal human needs that transcend culture. An elaboration of Jung's nekyia, Campbell's monomyth finds perfect articulation in the typical narrative arc of the epic fantasy hero, who will abandon (or be forced to abandon) some comfortable domestic sphere and enter a perilous outdoor world of adventure. Here he will face guardians, win allies and over-come trials, before confronting some ultimate personal challenge even he had no idea he had the strength to overcome. He will then complete the circle by return-ing home, often finding his experiences have matured him to such an extent that he no longer has a place there.

Several early trick films miniaturize the hero's journey as it appears in chival-ric romance, focusing on the archetypal set-up of rescuing a distressed damsel. In W.R. Booth's *The Magic Sword; or, A Medieval Mystery* (1901), the damsel (representing the purity and fertility of the land) is abducted by her shadow-self, a Plutonian crone who spirits her away to a lair beneath the earth. A thrusting young knight comes to her rescue and, with supernatural assistance (in this case an angelic fairy who lends him her magic sword), he defeats several guardian ogres before confronting the witch. The villain gives him a final test of his worth before she is banished, and the knight is allowed to return to the outside world with the damsel in his arms. The Thomas Edison–produced *Fantasma* (1914) expands the formula by allowing a kindly clown and his pet goat to accompany the film's Prince Arthur on the same quest. Another Edison multi-reeler, *The Princess' Necklace* (1917) explicitly connects the plight of the hero to that of the land, as a magical choker that ensures the kingdom's prosperity is stolen by a jealous dwarf and must be retrieved.

Since the distinction between religion and mythology has become ever more acute since Homer's day, it is from the conceited view of the modern Westerner that Indian cinema can be regarded as the first to adapt a native mythology with any seriousness. The so-called "mythologicals," inspired by D.G. Phalke's breakthrough film *Raja Harischandra* (1912), concern the exploits of the Hindu gods, adapted from literary epics like the *Ramayana* and the *Mahabharata*. Its partner-genre, the "devotional" details the fraught lives of the gods' mortal followers, like the persecuted villager eventually carried to Heaven on the back of a giant bird in V.G. Damle and S. Fattelal's *Sant Tukaram* (1936).

It is important to emphasize that it is only the Westerner who regards the subject of these enduring genres as "myth." In India they have been known to resurrect the religious careers of small provincial gods and saints, as believers erect new shrines in the wake of successful movies. Showing off to the rest of world, the expensive grandeur of the mythologicals and the devotionals is also a salute to patriotism. Myth is unavoidably informed by national identity, yet movies harnessing this quality for nationalistic purposes may be concealing precarious political motives.

Legendary German director Fritz Lang gave sci-fi the gift of *Metropolis* (1926), while his equally brilliant contribution to fantasy became something of a poisoned chalice. Comprising two silent films (*Siegfried* and *Kriemhild's Revenge*), Lang's monumental *Die Nibelungen* (1924), a baroque masterpiece and one of the greatest films of its genre, adapts elements of Wagner's *Ring* cycle and the Teutonic saga upon which it is based. The first half of Lang's diptych escorts its innocent shock-haired hero (Paul Richter) to his death at the hands of a sinister man-at-arms, Hagen Tronje (Hans Adalbert Schlettow). In the second half, Siegfried's widow Kriemhild (Margarethe Schön) extracts her revenge with maniacal determination. Shot back to back and released months apart, the film achieved worldwide success and became a key film of Weimar cinema.

Hitler loved it. Possibly he recognized its potential as a tool of propaganda and thought he saw something of himself in the radiant *Übermensch* Siegfried, who pours gold into the hands of his impoverished countrymen. Perhaps the Nazi leader felt reassured by the absolving sense of fatalism driving Siegfried to exterminate the subhuman race of trolls known as the Nibelungs, depicted here as hook-nosed, treasure-grubbing monsters. Lang himself stated he was recalling the exuberance of myth in an attempt to dispel the cloud of pessimism hanging over his country after the First

World War. However, the interior motives of his wife, Thea von Harbou (the film's author), may be discerned by the fact that she later became a devoted Nazi.

Although *Die Nibelungen* makes its nationalist intentions clear with an opening dedication ("To the German People"), the fascists would actually have had a hard time persuading people with a film so relentlessly anti-authoritarian. *Kriemhild's Revenge* plays like Pythonesque tragedy. Kriemhild turns from shy violet to livid gargoyle, a malign totem pole at the foot of which hundreds sacrifice themselves for her greater good. The longer everyone stays devoted to the intractable principles of their superiors, the higher their corpses pile. Nevertheless, *Die Nibelungen* was promoted with an aggressively nationalistic advertising campaign. On release the movie was championed by the right and attacked by the left in equal measure. Its themes so ingeniously layered and its symbolism so carefully ambiguous, the film can be read from a dozen conflicting perspectives, successfully translating the relativism of myth, which presents a sort of blank screen upon which the beholder projects his or her own prejudices.

Flexing the considerable muscle of German expertise before an admiring world, inspiring filmmakers from Douglas Fairbanks to Sergei Eisenstein, *Die Nibelungen* cast its most significant influence over fantasy through the magisterial secondary world of *Siegfried*. The film's columnated woods, murky ravines, rainbow-crowned peaks and yawning caverns were built entirely on the Ufa backlot. No Western studio would lavish so much money on this kind of fantasy again until the '80s, when the studio-bound realms of several films (notably Germany's own *The Neverending Story*) would emulate the visual achievements of Lang.

Although spectacular, *Siegfried*'s primal world has a pleasing matter-of-factness, which few successive films have sought to replicate. Lang's direction seems almost blasé in this respect, never drawing attention to the obvious artifice of his set and encouraging the audience to take its wonders for granted. The film's star monster, the dinosaur-like dragon Fafnir (a life-size mechanical model), is revealed without preamble, as though it were just another bit of wildlife, and exactly what one might find on a ramble through these enchanted woods.

By bathing in the conquered dragon's blood, Siegfried renders himself impervious to mortal weapons (but for a single vulnerable spot where a leaf settles on his back). Thus baptized as a superhero, Siegfried becomes as unconquerable as Achilles, yet as symbiotically attached to the land as King Arthur. When Hagen Tronje impales Siegfried on a spear, the natural world dies in sympathy with its champion. In an eerie shot, the grieving Kriemhild recalls her husband reaching out to her by a blossoming tree, which now dissolves into a withered bush and then into a ghostly skull.

Its hero's fate determined by the Odin-figure of Hagen Tronje, *Siegfried* ends as its world expires, as magic passes and the world is left to mundane mankind. Picking up where movies like *The Lord of the Rings* leave off, *Kriemhild's Revenge* offers epic fantasy a chilling epilogue. As Kriemhild is forced to marry the misshapen King Attila of the Huns (the film reveals an undeniable racist streak here), the film slides down the slope of inevitability erected by the first film. The second now has only to let its characters destroy each other like over-wound clockwork soldiers, each conceding to their principles with absurd devotion, whatever the cost in blood. Without the guidance of myth, it seems, man is lost to his own natural urge to destroy himself.

Despite *Die Nibelungen*'s ultimate rejection of the fascist ideal, the movie's association with the Third Reich has remained an ideological stain on its genre, which critics have always been quick to point out. The modern-day Arthurian Romance *L'Eternal Retour* was long condemned by critics for the Aryan hue of its lovers, while Thomas Sutcliffe expresses a similar sentiment in his review of *The Fellowship of the Ring* for the British newspaper *The Independent*: "You cannot help feeling that Hitler would have adored this film, with its hideous Untermenschen, its homeland-loving Hobbits and its Aryan beauties." Yet the critic correctly exposes the genre's hazardous potential: "[Hitler] would have recognized that elemental myths don't dictate how their power is to be exploited."

During the Soviet "thaw" of the '50s, Russian cinema's honored fantasist, Aleksandr Ptushko, belonged to a dwindling generation of old-guard directors who continued to produce didactic films in the face of his country's artistic rallying cry, "Make room for youth!" Like Lang, Ptushko helped raise his country's spirits by recalling the mythic heroism of the past. His loose trilogy of epic fantasies, all based on national myths (*Sadko* [1952], *Ilya Muromets* [1956] and *Sampo* [1958]) were bought up for American distribution by AIP, eager to fill the market for colorful fantasy opened by Ray Harryhausen. Although subjected to appalling recuts that excised any obvious trace of their Communist origin, the original director's simplistic take on socialism remains just about discernable.

Ptushko's balancing act of agitprop and epic fantasy is at its most awkward in *Sadko* (retitled *The Magic Voyage of Sinbad*). Its Marxist hero (Edward Stolar) swears to retrieve a fabled bird of happiness in order to reconcile the unjust social divide in his native city. With its naïve special effects and hearty Fairbanksian gestures, the film feels like a throwback to the silents, even stopping off at a distinctly Méliès-esque undersea kingdom. A similar combination of pretension and ingenuousness affects *Sampo* (retitled *The Day the Earth Froze*). This Soviet-Finnish co-production adapts a story from the Finnish epic song-cycle, the *Kalevala*, or "land of heroes." The industrious folk of Kalevala have forged an enchanted "sampo," a mill capable of producing unlimited food and wealth, which the evil witch Louhi (Ingrid Elhardt), queen of the gloomy neighboring kingdom of Pohiela (Lapland), covets for herself.

Ilya Muromets (retitled *The Sword and the Dragon*), however, emerges from its transfer suggestive of something truly spectacular. Seemingly as visually impressive as anything in *Die Nibelungen*, the movie reflects the rugged character of its burly, bearded hero (Boris Andreyev) through the landscape he embodies, with its tiers of brittle forest, chilly mountain streams and devastated battlefields. The film is based on an epic song about a peasant cripple who became a strongman, and fought to defend his country from the invading Mongols. Furnished with evocative asides like the giant who gives Ilya his sword before calcifying into a mountain, and a magic tablecloth that nourishes Ilya in prison, Ptushko's secondary world feels pleasingly substantial.

Ilya defeats a succession of adversaries, including a wind demon with Dizzy

Gillespie cheeks, but really goes to town in the film's tremendous battle scene. Hordes of armed extras converge on the Steppes beneath charcoal skies. Dying soldiers are hoisted into the air on spears in Reinigerian silhouette. Ilya flings swathes of enemies aside with every sweep of his mace. A Mongol chief surveys the battlefield atop a mountain of living bodies. A Ghidorah-like dragon incinerates the Russian lines with streams of fire. There is a genuine sense of transport here, as the film shows absolute conviction in its mythic premise.

The Italian Alessandro Blasetti had a far more sophisticated handle on politicizing myth than Ptushko. His fantastical Mussolini-era costume epic *La corona di ferro* (*The Iron Crown*) (1941) carries a covert criticism of nationalism into the fantasy peplum, where the strongman symbolically wrestles with Italy's feelings of guilt over its fascist past. Yet Italian cinema has always been less interested in what myths might mean, and more in how they look on screen. The sheer narcissism of Italian fantasy films in the '50s and '60s had a significant influence on epic fantasy's development. Movies like *Hercules* take the bones of meaning out of myth and dress up the rest as shallow spectacle. Unfortunately, this preference for incident over insight obscured epic fantasy's underlying potency well into the '90s.

Although they achieved something rather special in transforming one of Greek mythology's less distinguished heroes into a genuine cinematic original, the Italians were rather less successful in their attempts to mount more sustained and thoughtful mythological narratives. First adapted by Francesco Bertolini in 1911 and later by Dino De Laurentiis for Italian TV in 1968 (recut and released abroad as a feature), the Italians' most significant retelling of Homer's *Odyssey* is Mario Camerini's *Ulysses* (1954), starring Kirk Douglas as the cocky wanderer. Like the pepla it precedes, this compressed account is geared towards a family audience, foregrounding anything that features fights and monsters, while relegating human episodes, like the suitor's romantic siege of Penelope (Silvana Mangano). Yet *Ulysses*' sense of spectacle is decidedly lacking, often playing like a Harryhausen film without the Harryhausen.

The peplum's inability to capture the reality of Homer's world (a frustration unexpectedly shared by Fritz Lang himself in Jean-Luc Godard's 1963 film *Le Mépris* [*Contempt*]), stems in part from their insistence on beating all myths into the same shape. For them, Greco-Roman myth is no different in character from the German *Nibelungenlied*, which Giacomo Gentilomo filmed as *Sigfrido* (*The Dragon's Blood*) (1963) and Emimmo Salvi as *Il tesoro della foresta pietrificata* (*The Treasure of the Petrified Forest*) (1965), starring Gordon Mitchell. Spectacle, however impoverished, takes precedent over anything the myths themselves might have to say, and the same fate befell the 1966 West German remake of *Die Nibelungen*. Lang sensibly turned down the offer to direct this, leaving Harold Reinl to create a hopelessly vacant spectacular, which was cut together for overseas audiences as *Whom the Gods Wish to Destroy*.

Although the fantasy pepla are heedlessly omnivorous, they do manage to make some distinction between epic and heroic fantasy, if only in realizing that certain myths do not lend themselves as readily as others to the superheroic presence of the strongman. Although the big guy's staple weedy companion sometimes lands a film of his own (like *Theseus Against the Minotaur* and *Medusa Against the Son of Hercules*), their adventures invariably follow the same arc as their brawny buddies, with peace restored after the death of a tyrant and no questions asked as to what happens next. There is no sense of the consequences of the hero's triumph, no sense of connection between the hero and the land he has liberated.

The protagonist of Schneer and Harryhausen's *Jason and the Argonauts* (1963) is a true epic fantasy hero in this sense, understanding there is more to healing an oppressed nation than regime change. "It will not be enough to fight," declares ousted prince Jason (Todd Armstrong) before he has even begun his quest to win back his father's crown from wicked King Pelias (Douglas Wilmer). "The people need more than a leader, they must believe the gods have not deserted them." The fantastical travelogue that follows takes on a greater significance, becoming a gesture of heroism that will inspire the people and bring about lasting amity long after their ruler has been deposed.

Fondly remembered by generations, *Jason and the Argonauts*, next to *The Golden Voyage of Sinbad*, is certainly one of the best fantasy films Schneer and Harryhausen ever produced. Benefiting from a pounding score by Bernard Herrmann and a strong screenplay (which borrows tics from *Sadko*, *Hercules* and *The Giants of Thessaly*), the movie also contains two of the most effective stop-motion sequences Harryhausen ever devised. In the first (and stronger) half of the film, Jason lands on a secret island where two of his Argonauts raid the vault of Talos the Titan, whose colossal bronze likeness creaks to life above them. "It must have been the wind," chuckles one, and in a shivery moment the statue's head swivels down and glares. Less impressive, but equally memorable are the rescue of the starving prophet Phineas (Patrick Troughton) from ravenous Harpies and the (non-stop-motion) sea-god Triton, who holds gnashing cliffs apart long enough for the Argo to slip through.

Once the Argonauts reach their destination, the movie seems to glance at its watch and make a sudden dash for a climax it never reaches anyway. It hurries through what should have been two major set-pieces: Jason's disappointingly easy dispatching of the Hydra and the resurrection of his mortally wounded girlfriend, Medea (Nancy Kovack).

But Harryhausen's final card is a real showstopper: With Jason and two of his men cornered on a cliff, the villain summons a platoon of malicious sword-wielding skeletons, who burst out of the earth and frantically attack the Argonauts. Possibly Harryhausen's finest hour, this technically astonishing sequence has deservedly become one of the most iconic scenes in the cinema of the *fantastique*. But it is also one of the few instances where Harryhausen's self-important special effects are allowed to transcend themselves, suggesting they operate as part of a larger world, where wonders continue to go about their business long after the cameras have moved on.

Jason himself is not so much bound to this magical world, as he is to the gods that pervade it. Subverting the fatalism of Greek myth into a reassuring irony, the script suggests that with courage a mortal's destiny is his own, while the omnipotent gods are just as clumsy as their worshippers. Jason is skeptical of the gods' existence until Hermes spirits him away to Olympus, a cloudy Club Med where the disinterested immortals idly play chess with mortal lives. Hera, Queen of the Gods (a splendidly feline Honor Blackman), warns Jason of the nigh-impossibility of

The gods themselves struggle: Zeus (Niall MacGinnis) and his wife Hera (Honor Blackman)
decide the fate of Jason in Don Chaffey's much-loved *Jason and the Argonauts* (Columbia, 1963).

retrieving the Fleece, but he initially refuses the offer of Olympian assistance, choosing instead to place his faith in human resourcefulness and courage. Demonstrating
a basic compassion for humanity generally lacking in Harryhausen movies, the
human characters actually have a sense of purpose beyond introducing the next stop-
motion monster. Nicely upstaging his animated co-stars, Nigel Green's memorably
vivacious Hercules steals the show every time he opens his mouth. ("If I meet a girl
with a firm leg, a full bosom and a warm heart, let no man try and stop me.")

Although its mythic source material has to be subsumed to the demands of
formula (Jason's apparent willingness to steal the object of another kingdom's
prosperity is necessarily ignored, while the classically homicidal Medea does little
here but fret from the sidelines), *Jason and the Argonauts* successfully redefined the
secondary world fantasy spectacular. But the cycle of historical epics to which it
belonged was already in decline. The youthful exuberance of the '60s had little time
for the mumblings of dusty antiquity, as filmmakers inspired by the French New
Wave expressed far more interest in today's goings-on. The kids who were
enthralled by *Jason* would not be paying homage in movies of their own until the
'70s, by which time memories of Talos and sword-fighting skeletons would be far
more immediate than the film's evocative secondary world. Through *Die Nibelungen* and *Jason and the Argonauts*, the voice of myth had spoken, but had yet to be
fully heard.

Between Dragons and Democrats

That *Monty Python and the Holy Grail* is the most significant contribution to Arthurian cinema from the legendary king's own kingdom just about sums up British cinema's doubtful attitude towards its own reservoir of myth. Not that England ever had much to do with Arthur. The French invented most of what we recognize as his chronicle (the code of chivalry, the Grail quest, courtly romance), all of which an Englishman, Sir Thomas Malory, definitively compiled in the fifteenth century in *Le Morte d'Arthur*, from which most Arthurian art has since derived.

During the Reformation, English literature regarded Malory's Arthur the way the punctiliously middle-class Dursleys treat Harry Potter, as a social carbuncle to be closeted in case the neighbors see it. Banished into literary limbo, Arthur made friends with the fairy tale, a fellow exile, and for a while they resided together in Faerie. Arthur became the heroic suitor in Edmund Spenser's *The Faerie Queene* (1599) and played host in several versions of *Tom Thumb*. By the eighteenth century, English literature had locked away all evidence of its pagan heritage, yet continued to express fantasy safely and more appropriately through stories of foreign extraction, like the "Grub-street" edition of the *Arabian Nights* (c. 1704) and William Beckford's best-selling Oriental pastiche *Vathek* (1786).

Previously patronized as the reserve of imbeciles and foreigners, Arthurian myth (also known as The Matter of Britain) was brought down from the cultural attic by those fairy-fancying Victorians. Lady Charlotte Guest's definitive 1849 edition of *The Mabinogion*, the medieval Welsh story cycle that kick-started the Arthur myth, and Alfred Lord Tennyson's 1859 sequence of swooning Malorian poetry, *The Idylls of the King*, helped restore Arthur's mythic crown. The Matter of Britain appealed to the Victorian sense of moral responsibility and fueled bourgeois nostalgia for the deference of feudalism. But this Christian romanticism buckled under the theories of Darwin, which led a cultural revolt at the close of the century.

With the country having suffered two World Wars, it is easy to sympathize with Britain's view in the '40s that the cute, seemingly evasive fantasies of Michael Powell were considered inappropriate, if not profoundly offensive. Yet it is the assumption that fantasy amounts to nothing but rambling conservative escapism that persists in Britain and earns the genre such critical contempt. Despite the fact that Britain has produced the majority of fantasy's most influential exponents, the nation continues to disregard the genre unless its works can be passed of as kid's fiction or appropriated as magic realism. British author Philip Pullman's brilliant Miltonian sequence *His Dark Materials* won several awards for children's fiction in Britain, but was otherwise ignored by the critical mainstream, until American publishers successfully marketed the first book, *Northern Lights* (1995), as an adult novel. In a remarkable volte-face, Britain immediately awarded the third volume, *The Amber Spyglass* (2000), Whitbread Book of the Year (and rightly so), but critics canonized it for use as a stick with which to beat purveyors of "fantasy" like Tolkien and (perhaps more deservedly) C.S. Lewis.

With a home reception as hostile and hypocritical as this, no wonder Arthur went abroad for his first film appearance. Based on Wagner, produced by Edison and shot by Edwin S. Porter, *Parsifal* (1904) was followed by *Lancelot and Elaine* (1910), Charles Kent's adaptation of Tennyson's *The Lady of Shalott*. Although Arthur and his knights are as classically British as any other epic fantasy hero— doubtful, cautious, steered by a sense of fair play and courageous under pressure (as opposed to the fast, sexy, all–American swashbuckling of the heroic fantasy superhero)— they nevertheless appeal to the American mindset through their unquenchable idealism, which the Brits (who actually know what living under a monarchy is like) never let themselves fall for. The first British film to engage in Arthuriana was a wartime comedy that laughs down its sleeve at kingly heroism. Marcel Varnel's *King Arthur Was a Gentleman* (1942) stars Arthur Askey as Arthur King, a fanciful squaddie posted to occupied France and inspired into performing acts of heroic lunacy after his mates present him with a rusty sword he fancies to be Excalibur.

Yet a British literary taste for the exploits of the Round Table never quite died with the Victorians, and by the early twentieth century Arthurian fiction had become a definite literary genre, trends in which carried over into film. Mark Twain's *A Connecticut Yankee at King Arthur's Court* influenced cinema, not only through the medieval fish-out-of-water comedy of its three film adaptations, but in movies like *L'Eternal Retour* and Terry Gilliam's *The Fisher King* (1991), which find Arthurian romance in modern-day settings.

Typified by the early stories of popular U.K. novelist Warwick Deeping, a superficially realistic strain of Arthurian literature strove for a degree of historical accuracy, leaving all that stuff about wizards and magic swords to children's storybooks and the Boy's Own papers. Nominally based on Malory, MGM's pompous historical epic *The Knights of the Round Table* (1953), directed by Richard Thorpe, did the same in its attempt to capture the seriousness and grandeur of medieval England. It was the studio's first CinemaScope feature, filmed in glowing Technicolor on the vivid green hills of Ireland, and the Matter of Britain according to MGM takes place in an age far from dark. Revealing an Anglo-American contrast as abnormal as that of Twain's *Connecticut Yankee*, *Knights of the Round Table* turns Malory into a modern Mardi Gras of color and heraldic design, jazzy with the anachronistic American accents of Robert Taylor's Lancelot, Ava Gardner's Guinevere and Mel Ferrer's Arthur.

Audiences responded better to Thorpe's earlier stab at medieval romance, which presents another variant melding of American modernism and British archaism. A pre–*Superman* George Reeves was the first to lend the Arthurian knight a Roy Rogers sense of galloping derring-do in the Columbia serial *The Adventures of Sir Galahad* (1949), but it was MGM's tremendously popular *Ivanhoe* (1952) that sparked a short cycle of boisterous historical epics, accurately termed the "Arthurian Western" by critic Jeffrey Richards.

Noisy, violent, childish and tremendous fun, with grown men running about like schoolboys thrashing each other with wooden swords, the antics of Robert Taylor's melodious Sir Wilfred are hardly authentic but immensely influential. Columbia followed suit and blacked-up Peter Cushing as a dastardly Saracen, opposed by

King Arthur's humble blacksmith (Alan Ladd) in the equally dotty *The Black Knight* (1954), directed by Tay Garnett (director of the Bing Crosby *Connecticut Yankee*). Cornel Wilde brought wife Jean Wallace to England to film his *Lancelot and Guinevere* (1962), while Columbia reconstituted much of *Black Knight*'s excitable battle footage for Nathan Juran's *Siege of the Saxons* (1963). These romps all owed far less to Malory than to Hal Foster's popular U.S. comic strip *Prince Valiant*, the story of a Viking noble who earns a place at the Round Table. Fox made Robert Wagner wear a very silly wig for Henry Hathaway's 1954 adaptation of the strip, a better film than Anthony Hickox's best-forgotten 1997 effort with Stephen Moyer in the lead and a panda-eyed Joanna Lumley embarrassing herself as Morgan le Fay.

Not wanting things to appear too childish, the Arthurian Westerns also feel it best to ban wizardry. This way they can get on with the easier business of clattering about in armor, saving damsels in pointy hats, and toppling off the battlements with an arrow in the chest. As if to justify their decision, Bert I. Gordon, the schlockmeister responsible for movies like *Attack of the Puppet People* (1958), had a go at Arthurian fantasy with *The Magic Sword* (*The Sorcerer's Curse*) (1962). Poor Basil Rathbone spits clichés as a turbaned sorcerer threatening to feed the hero's girlfriend to his two-headed pet dragon, while a spellbound company of multicultural knights ride to the rescue. "All you had to do was destroy that Frenchman," snarls Rathbone at one bungling lackey, before turning her into a tarantula.

Although he plays the villain in the *Connecticut Yankee* films and pops up as Arthur's doddery advisor in several Arthurian Westerns, Merlin the magician had to wait for Disney's scruffily animated *The Sword in the Stone* (1963) before his legendary magical nature could be revealed. Dramatizing Arthur's boyhood and his tutelage under Merlin, the film is adapted from the first book in T.H. White's milestone Arthur sequence *The Once and Future King* (collected in four parts in 1958). Echoing a constant of Arthurian cinema, White's book employs anachronisms, conceiving Merlin as a man "born at the wrong end of time," cleverly explaining his gift for prophecy by his already having lived through the future.

But in Disney's shallow adaptation, Merlin's forward thinking works itself into Anglo-American schizophrenia. Setting up magical assembly lines to deal with the washing-up and tinkering absent-mindedly with models of future machinery, Disney's Merlin (given a stuffy British accent by Karl Swenson) is as much an entrepreneurial capitalist as the Great American Oz. This fits in rather well with White's anachronistic conception, but otherwise fails to make much sense. Transforming the boy into a sequence of animals, Merlin teaches young Arthur the American way of standing up for one's self and refusing to give in to fate. Yet the wizard seems happy to let the boy draw Excalibur from the stone and become king by divine decree. Fans of White generally loathe the film, although there is fun to be had with a shape-shifting duel between Merlin and sorceress cheat Madam Mim ("Did I say 'no purple dragons'?").

Having waited for White's literary reputation to grow in the U.S. ever since they bought the rights to his first book in 1939, Disney hastened into production after hearing Warners were on their way to producing *Camelot* (1967). A mega-budget adaptation of Lerner and Loewe's Broadway musical, also based on White's books, Joshua Logan's epic can be credited, through little fault of its own, with delivering the Dolorous Stroke that crippled Arthurian cinema. Like the studios that burnt out the cycle of historical epics before it, Warners lavished so much money on the project that it lost a king's ransom despite box office popularity. But rather what killed the movie was the merciless savaging it received from the critics, who delighted in deflating such Hollywood pomposity.

Although certainly haphazard, often downright silly (witness Lancelot's soaringly camp *C'est moi*), *Camelot* is nowhere near the farrago the critics made out, and at least grants Arthur an actor worthy of his stature (how many unforgettable performances of the role can *you* think of?). Richard Harris finds easily cinema's most humane King Arthur, bewildered by a destiny he has no idea what to do with until he falls in love with Vanessa Redgrave's vixenish Guinevere. Sharing his wedded bliss with all of England, he founds the order of chivalry ("might *for* right") and its standard, the Round Table. His appeal inspires Franco Nero's impeccably virtuous Lancelot, who Arthur embraces as a brother, and Guinevere as a lover. Although carefully de-fantasized (Laurence Naismith's deciduous Merlin appears only as a memory, his shape-shifting schooling a metaphor), *Camelot* is probably the first film to treat the Arthurian cast as real people, human beings swimming against the tides of circumstance. While Lancelot and Guinevere give in and are dragged under, Arthur stands resolute ("The fates must not have the last word").

With Harris realizing he has achieved the immortality of legend, the movie ends on a triumphant survival of Arthurian idealism, while its present cultural downfall had already been prefaced. Produced by the ultra-conservative Disney, *The Sword in the Stone* presents its storybook prologue as a traditionalist metaphor, with a divided England awaiting reunification under the patriarchal rule of Arthur while liberalism runs amok. By the time of *Camelot*, the anti-establishment '60s were in full swing. How fitting then that one of the decade's icons, David Hemmings of *Blow-Up* (1966), should be cast as Mordred, Arthur's illegitimate son, who destroys the conservative utopia of Camelot by exposing its hypocrisy.

Opening with an empty-handed return from the Grail quest and closing on a scrap-yard battlefield, Robert Bresson's sensate *Lancelot du Lac* (1974) summarizes the state of post–*Camelot* Arthurian fantasy. But the genre's most enduring deconstruction begins when Graham Chapman's horseless King Arthur pretends to rein in a charger while his squire clatters two empty halves of coconut in Terry Jones and Terry Gilliam's *Monty Python and the Holy Grail* (1974). Britain's satiric salvo on its own Arthuriana has done more damage to epic fantasy than a dozen *Krull*s.

Held together by an irrelevant quest for the Holy Grail, this inspired parody relentlessly and comprehensively debunks the conventions that most serious epic fantasies must hold sacred. Arthur's heroic dignity is first scuppered by a ranting socialist serf ("Strange women lying in ponds distributing swords is no basis for a system of government"), and then by a gang of rude French knights who pelt him with livestock from the battlements. Arthur's famous knights hardly prove themselves the "goodliest fellowship" of Tennyson. The chaste Sir Galahad (Michael Palin) is reluctantly rescued from a bevy of sex-starved damsels, while Lancelot (John Cleese) answers what he thinks is a cry of distress and accidentally massacres a wedding party ("I just got a bit carried away"). Such pathological heroism finds its ultimate expression in the indefatigable Black Knight, who insists on fighting even after all his limbs have been hacked off ("'Tis but a scratch"), while the archetype of the guardian dragon is mockingly embodied by a cuddly white rabbit with the temperament of a startled Velociraptor.

It all works brilliantly, while the film's authentically filthy and violent medieval milieu slings mud in the eye of Hollywood polish. With a budget that only just managed to accommodate cut-out castles, knitted woollen chain-mail, a smoke machine and lots of mud, the world of *Monty Python and the Holy Grail* is at times more credible than that of any mega-budget Arthurian epic you care to mention, dispelling the myth that convincing secondary world fantasy requires a budget the size of a national debt. Unfortunately, the movie's setting works so well every serious medievalist epic since (*Lord of the Rings* included) has to work hard to avoid evoking the memory of their slapstick predecessor.

Terry Gilliam returned to his own Dark Age milieu in his first solo feature *Jabberwocky* (1977), a jumbled medieval comedy based on the nonsense rhyme by Lewis Carroll. Michael Palin plays the village cretin who inadvertently saves a stagnant kingdom from a terrifying peasant-chewing monster somewhere between Tenniel and Hieronymus Bosch. With budget and plot only fractionally less negligible than those of *Holy Grail*, *Jabberwocky* crams its revolting historical world with peasant squalor, religious clamor, careless violence and brutal humor. Impressed by the vividness of this Brueghelian world, John Boorman apparently screened the movie several times during the making of *Excalibur*, although Gilliam's film gives Arthurian manners yet another pasting. Hulking inhuman knights clump around like automatons, their tournaments so bloodthirsty that spectators get more of a soaking than the front row at Seaworld. Like that of the Python film, Gilliam's comedy attacks fundamentalist interpretations of the Arthur myth, and here Palin's reluctant hero must ride away into the sunset with a hopelessly romantic princess whether he likes it or not.

After the damage wrought by the Pythons, it was now impossible to approach Malory with a straight face. Films seeking to capture his elevated spirit had to look elsewhere within The Matter of Britain. While the '50s and '60s favor the story of Lancelot and Guinevere to see to the downfall of Arthurian chivalry, independent movies of the '70s and early '80s see to its restoration, adapting the missionary tales of Grail seekers like Gawain and Perceval. British director Stephen Weeks takes a fair stab at the great medieval poem, albeit for children, in *Gawain and the Green Knight* (1973), which for some reason he rehashed as the atrocious *Sword of the Valiant* (1983), starring *Ator*'s Miles O'Keeffe in Prince Valiant bangs and Sean Connery as a Christmas tree. Eric Rohmer looks to another of Malory's antecedents, twelfth century French writer Chrétien de Troyes, whose *Le Conte del Graal* is faithfully adapted in Rohmer's extraordinary, theatrical *Perceval le gallois* (1978). Hans-Jürgen Syberberg turns to Wagner for his febrile psychological epic *Parsifal* (1982). Plunging deepest into Arthurian pre-history, British director Barney Platts-Mills bases his Gaelic-language *Hero* (1982) on the Celtic folktale of Diamuid Ua Duibhne, a sort of Irish Lancelot who runs away with the wife of warrior king Finn MacCool.

But for this small creative fringe, determinately poetic Arthur movies had been beaten into dormancy by the early '80s, while epic fantasy as a whole stood on the brink of stardom. The movie brats had become the "New Hollywood" and brought about an box-office Indian summer that lasted from *The Godfather* (1972) to *Star Wars* (1977). Their success encouraged a re-evaluation of the popular *fantastique* long disregarded by "old school" Hollywood. Epic fantasy finally had a chance to prove itself, but at a time when, in terms of cinema, the genre still groped in the dark.

As traditionalist critics struggled with this apparently jejune outburst, it was as though Mordred had taken over the court of Hollywood. For epic fantasy, however, it was a time when Arthurian conservatism had come to an end, its death knell sounded not by *Excalibur*, that heroic rallying cry to reclaim Arthur's majesty, but by Desmond Davis' *Clash of the Titans* (1981), Charles Schneer and Ray Harryhausen's last-gasp attempt to relive their past successes in classical fantasy.

Returning to Greek myth with a $16 million budget that surpassed those of all their previous films combined, Schneer and Harrryhausen's *Clash of the Titans* relies on futile nostalgia, adopting the paternalism that died with *Camelot*. Its hero, Perseus (Harry Hamlin), is a vacuous pretty-boy, privileged by his godly father, Zeus (Laurence Olivier). His Mordred-like alter ego is Calibos (played by Neil McCarthy and a stop-motion stand-in), whom Zeus turns into a Satyr for crimes never dramatized, leaving us feeling rather more sympathy for the movie's misshapen villain than for its spoiled, pouting hero. Ever since *Star Wars*, weird beasties were no longer the default bad guys. Friendly aliens like Yoda and E.T. embodied a new spirit of imaginative tolerance, which *Clash of the Titans* ignores. Calibos' immediate rejection by his sweetheart, the lovely princess Andromeda (Judy Bowker), further shows up the shallowness of the forces of good.

The film is also broken-backed and only in its more entertaining second half does anything in *Clash of the Titans* work as epic fantasy. In the first half, Perseus frees the city of Joppa from Calibos' reign of terror. Meanwhile the film saddles its distinguished performers with unspeakable lines ("She sits alone, away from these accursed, hell-sent swarms of blood-gutted marsh-flies") and the RSC-types assembled to play the watchful immortals stand around like novelty chess-pieces. The film's epic scope needs some elemental humanity, but grasps only fairy tale sentiment. Its second half is more dynamic, as Perseus gallops off to save his marriage after catty sea goddess Thetis (Maggie Smith), Calibos' mother, demands Andromeda's life in compensation for her son's injury. At this point, the film almost captures the sense of monumental human endeavor the story needs, as Perseus and his crew struggle up a mountain to ask a coven of cackling, eyeless witches for directions. But the stakes never seem high enough. There is no sense of mortal outrage at the unfairness of the gods, since the demands of Thetis seem as justified as those of Zeus.

Harryhausen's stop-motion monsters feel more perfunctory than ever. Encounters include an annoying clockwork owl (which the animator insists he thought up

Opposite: Medusa loses her head, thanks to Harry Hamlin's Perseus, in the best scene from Desmond Davis' drowsy spectacular *Clash of the Titans* (MGM, 1981).

before Lucas's Artoo-Detoo), a two-headed guard dog, a clutch of giant scorpions and the Kraken, a gurgling Kong-like sea monster that pauses just long enough in its damsel-munching duty for Perseus to show up and kill it. The film only manages a substantial secondary world encounter when it gets to Medusa, whose tense scene proves a fine epitaph for her animator. Her shadow writhing and her tail rattling in anticipation, Harryhausen's serpentine archer slithers among the columns and braziers of her infernal lair, picking off her prey from in between the statues of fallen heroes. Otherwise, *Clash of the Titans* proves the animator's number was up. The movie was not well-received; still reeling from its scathing reviews, Harryhausen announced his retirement.

By contrast, John Boorman's *Excalibur* (1981) is that most rare of things, an intellectual epic fantasy for adults, a concept which seemed somehow offensive to critics, who thought the film even funnier than *Camelot* and *Monty Python* combined. Although released much too soon after *Python* and at a time when its ambitions appeared outrageously pretentious next to juvenilia like *Clash of the Titans*, the film actually works very well indeed. The script is perfectly in synch with the mythic rhythms of the Malory stories it adapts, while the movie's visuals echo their splendor. The lakes and hills of Ireland look like the Amazon, while nature's metal totem, the sword Excalibur, weirdly radiates the same shimmering green. The violence of men by contrast is realistically clumsy, with battered armor, crashing blades and spurting blood.

Like *Camelot* (Warners' other Arthurian epic), *Excalibur* recalls the tragedian structure of *Die Nibelungen*, dramatizing the death of a supernatural age and examining its spiritual legacy. (It even opens to the boom of *Siegfried's Funeral March*.) The tragedy to come is foreshadowed by the death of Arthur's father (Gabriel Byrne), whose pact with the Duke of Cornwall (Corin Redgrave) is broken by his lust for the other man's wife (critics cracked up at the scene in which Byrne rudely mounts her without pausing to remove his armor). Nicol Williamson's Merlin spirits away the fruit of their union, who as a young man (Nigel Terry) draws Excalibur from the stone and unites England under its divine banner.

What threw everyone was the film's mystical rather than literal reading of Malory. As Merlin tutors Arthur in the ways of kingship, he speaks of "the dragon," referring not to the fire-breathing variety that rampages through Hollywood movies like *Dragonslayer*, but metaphorically to the energy of life itself. Arthur must become an avatar of this force, and synchronize himself with its flow, so its otherwise ineffable blessings can be bestowed upon others. (George Lucas, Joseph Campbell and Lao Tzu have all been here before.) In *Excalibur*, the clearest expression of this force is nature, through which man comes closest to experiencing life's vitality. Echoed by the disappearance of Merlin himself, man's rapport with nature inexorably fades as he takes the Fall into religion and science. Boorman's complex film is practically a treatise on myth itself.

There is much debate over the film's seriousness, however, particularly Nicol Williamson's decidedly odd performance as Merlin. His voice churning and wafting through lines like "For it is the doom of men that they forget," it's difficult to tell whether or not he is having us on. But Merlin's jester slyness and peculiar inhumanity are perfectly appropriate, aside from a few bits of conventional slapstick. A visitor from beyond akin to the angelic wizards of *Lord of the Rings*, Merlin's presence binds the film, and it feels his loss when he disappears. Ironically, Boorman himself occasionally loses his grip on the reins, cutting from story to story without so much as a dissolve. Often the only indication that years have passed is the length of everyone's beard. Also, some of the early scenes have trouble making the barefaced dialogue work. Yet it all seems more believable as the stakes mount.

The apocalypse comes with Arthur's discovery of the love affair between Nicholas Clay's peerless Lancelot and Cherie Lunghi's Guinevere, Wagner's *Prelude to Tristan und Isolde* clumsily chiming in whenever the lovers exchange a thwarted glance. As Merlin evaporates, the armored knights gleam like the burnished droids at the climax of *Star Wars*, while the castle of Camelot and the Round Table itself resemble the squared metallic corridors of the Death Star. As in Lucas' film, a self-righteous civilization is destroyed by a primal seed, in this case Lancelot and Guinevere's irresistible animal passion. When Helen Mirren's serpentine Morgana goads Gawain (Liam Neeson) into accusing his Queen of infidelity, Arthur and his court, like the damned players of *Kriemhild's Revenge*, must abide by their own laws, doomed by their own fundamentalist decree.

Depicting the quest of Perceval (Paul Geoffrey) to heal the land and its dying king, *Excalibur*'s final half is more obtuse, but yields some memorable imagery. Symbolically mocking his father's fate, Mordred (Robert Addie) sports both the armor of a sinister Michelangelo cherub and the mask of a Greek tragedian. Trees spring into blossom as a revived Arthur rides into war against his son to the crash of *Carmina Burana*. In a bitter filial embrace, Arthur heaves himself along the spear that impales him and plunges Excalibur into son's chest (Boorman clearly knows his Freud).

Mainstream audiences who easily saw through *Clash of the Titans* were unprepared for *Excalibur*'s dense erudition. While movies like the *Spider-Man* films have to dumb themselves down for the benefit of a wider audience unfamiliar with the sophistication of modern comics, many big-budget fantasies of the '80s borrowed directly from literary sources long matured and refined, but which were foreign to most cinemagoers.

Owing a great deal to Tolkien, Disney's *Dragonslayer* (1981), possibly the most unconventional and unsentimental family film the studio has ever produced, was another commercial failure, but emerges next to *Excalibur* as the most accomplished epic fantasy of its time. In the Celtic kingdom of Urland, villagers placate a crotchety dragon known as Vermithrax Pejorative with an annual virgin sacrifice. Wizard's apprentice Galen Bradwarden (Peter MacNicol) agrees to help the cowering peasants following the death of his mentor, Ulrich (a nicely judged turn by Ralph Richardson). It would have been easy for director Matthew Robbins to turn out the slapstick kid's movie everyone expected, but the film (which he co-wrote) proves bravely dramatic. Unlike Elliott, the blubbery star of *Pete's Dragon*, the film makes sure we know this fire-breather means business, as an early shot from a rearing dragon's-eye view sees the pitiless beast incinerate a screaming victim.

The wonderful thing about *Dragonslayer* is that everyone (even the dragon) acts

True Brit: Nigel Terry holds court as King Arthur in John Boorman's much-maligned but really very good *Excalibur* (Orion/Warners, 1981).

out of motive rather than convention. The king's daughter is appalled to discover she was excluded from the lottery that selects an eligible virgin, and bravely puts herself up for sacrifice. She refuses to play along when Galen rescues her, and runs into the dragon's lair seeking a heroic demise that the movie surprisingly lets her find. If anything, the actions of Galen, its morally obliged hero, are the most questionable, since it is his attempts to slay the dragon that bring about the greatest disaster.

Like the irate Xenomorph queen in *Aliens* (1986), Vermithrax (a vicious bat-like creature deftly rendered in computer-assisted stop-motion) is enraged by the death of her hatchling brood, which Galen grimly dispatches with a razor-sharp harpoon. Their knightly duel is everything it should be, man and beast, technology and nature driven to mortal combat by private outrage.

By the '80s, fantasy films appealed to audiences through the technology of special effects just as much as sci-fi, for which the box office returns of *E.T. The Extra-Terrestrial* (1982) and *Return of the Jedi* (1983), next to those of *Dragonslayer* and *Krull*, expressed a clear audience preference. No wonder thoughtful epic fantasies felt the nebulous world of magic was in decline. In *Dragonslayer*, Ulrich (resurrected in the glowing white robes of Gandalf) confronts the dragon on a mountaintop (in an iconic scene clearly modelled on Tolkien's Balrog encounter). The only way Vermithrax can be killed is by banishing all magic from the world. With his master carried away in the dragon's claws, Galen smashes the wizard's amulet, destroying Ulrich, Vermithrax and the world of magic itself.

After the dragon's charred remains plunge Smaug-like into a quenching lake, the film's cowardly Arthurian king, flanked by his clerics, ceremonially thrusts his sword into the beast's lifeless carcass. As Merlin prophesizes in *Excalibur*, "The one god comes to drive out the many gods." Pagan magic becomes Christian miracle, as mankind erects religion to (as Jung puts it) defend himself against the experience of God. Joseph Campbell calls this "the reduction of mythology to theology," when the democracy of everyday spiritual experience becomes the reserve of the few, when infinite mystery becomes a definite code, which the fundamentalist cleaves to at the expense of his own humanity.

For all their swish technology and darting lasers, sci-fi movies like *E.T.* and *Jedi* seek the same spiritual rapture as medieval fantasies like *Dragonslayer*. These sci-fi films make a mystic appeal to their own technocratic characters, while epic fantasy asks the same, but of its audience. For characters inhabiting an epic fantasy, the task of faith is made redundant by the palpable miracles that surround them; even the Olympian gods are so obvious as to be irrelevant. As far as its audience is concerned, epic fantasy must strike a delicate balance in its reading of myth, creating a world that is literal, but not too literal, symbolically ambiguous, yet definite enough for the audience to sense that the hero's story in some way mirrors their own.

This was the genius of the original *Star Wars*. Out to repeat Lucas's trick, epic fantasies set in similarly invented realms, like *The Dark Crystal* and *Krull*, overtook those derived from earthbound classics. Arthurian Europe disperses into medieval movies like Giacomo Battiato's cheap and nasty *Excalibur* ripoff *Hearts and Armour* (1983), the limp *Ladyhawke* and Paul Verhoeven's rampant *Flesh and Blood* (both 1985), whose depiction of the Dark Ages is so wilfully repulsive as to make Terry Gilliam's look like Disneyland. Other movies again grasp at sources outside the traditional Greek and Arthurian canon. *Holy Grail* co-director Terry Jones adapts his own mock Norse saga in the intermittently amusing *Erik the Viking* (1989), which confirms the suspicions of *Bruce Almighty* when Tim Robbins' baby-faced Viking discovers the gods of Asgard are just a bunch of vicious little kids. Disney's dreadful animated feature *The Black Cauldron* (1985) attempts to make a scaled-down *Lord of the Rings* out of the first two books in Lloyd Alexander's *The Chronicles of Prydain* sequence. This was itself based on *The Mabinogion*, which got a straightforward retelling in Derek Hayes' gory Welsh animated feature *Otherworld* (2002).

A low-budget Canadian epic fantasy based on North American Inuit legend, *Atanarjuat: The Fast Runner* (2000) occupies a unique place in fantasy cinema, skipping from oral folklore to modern-day filmmaking without centuries of literature in between. Evoking the spontaneity of oral storytelling by shooting on handheld digicam, director Zac Kunuk (among the first generation of Inuit to take up filmmaking) achieves the cultural equivalent of Homer picking up a camera and shooting *The Odyssey*. Filmed in the Arctic, the alien world of *Atanarjuat* seems at times like some negative outer space, a blinding blue-white tundra ridged with ice-blue shadow, where the Inuit camp of Igloolik hangs like a precarious satellite.

Having murdered the previous chief and installed a cruel successor, the lingering spirit of a malignant shaman poisons the fortunes of the rightful heir, the nimble Atanarjuat (Natar Ungalaaq). His brother murdered by the chief's vicious son and his home life ruined by the advances of the chief's idle daughter, the hero is chased naked across a sea of tilting ice floes (in a scene made all the more startling by the fact it was filmed for real). Guided to safety by the spirit of the murdered chief, Atanarjuat makes a violent Odyssean return with magical assistance from a friendly shaman. The hero becomes chief and prelapsarian perfection is restored as his antagonists are banished from the camp like Adam and Eve.

Like *Excalibur*, the movie is about living in synch with nature, but also about maintaining the unified community needed to survive in a hostile wilderness. Similarly this often-impenetrable film does not welcome outsiders, making no concession to anyone used to slick Hollywood storytelling. Like several other epic fantasies, *Atanarjuat* is a product of nationalism, and strives to preserve a storytelling culture that has suffered since the arrival of Christian missionaries. "How can you teach the Burning Bush to a culture that has never seen trees?" said the director in an interview. Winning the Camera d'Or at Cannes 2001 for Best First Feature, *Atanarjuat: The Fast Runner* defies the Western hegemony on mythic film threatened by a global (read Hollywood) film culture. The movie affirms that the value of myth is relative to the diversity of its language.

While mythic cinema continues to flourish abroad, it remains suppressed in Britain, whose film culture, rather like its literary culture in the eighteenth century, seems happy to patronize any product of the *fantastique* but its own. By the '90s, Arthuriana had fallen back into the incapable hands of Hollywood. Kevin Costner revived the spirit of the Arthurian Western, goading Saracen jailors with his "English curge" in Kevin Reynolds' rather likeable *Robin Hood: Prince of Thieves* (1991); while Jerry Zucker's distinctly drab *First Knight* (1994) retells the story of Lancelot and Guinevere for the Mills and Boon set. These were the first intimations that the historical epic was about to undergo a CGI–age revival, which began in earnest with Mel Gibson's schoolboy epic *Braveheart* (1995). Again Arthurian magic was left to nursery movies like Frederick Du Chau's *The Magic Sword: Quest for Camelot* (1998). Although probably the first film after *Hearts and Armour* to make its chivalric hero a girl, Du Chau's antiseptic animated feature undoes a good idea by leaving her helpless in the face of peril.

Another one of those sentimental airbrushed fantasies in which the '90s specialized, Rob Cohen's *Dragonheart* (1996) finds itself somewhere between historical epic and children's fable, emerging as an Arthur story by way of *Hercules: The Legendary Journeys*. Set in Arthurian Britain, this anemic tale stars a growling Dennis Quaid as Sir Bowen, a disillusioned knight who turns freelance dragonslayer after a mortally wounded prince (to whom a dragon donates half of its heart) grows up to become a tyrant (David Thewlis). Sean Connery voices the puppy-faced fire-breather Draco (a vivid but weightless CGI creation), with whom Bowen strikes up a friendship. The heart-sharing device is a twee fairy tale touch that doesn't work in the context of an epic fantasy, serving only to contrive a tragic ending as Bowen is forced to kill his friend in order to do away with the villain.

The only big-budget secondary world fantasy Hollywood produced in the '90s, *Dragonheart* reads the mythic trope of dragonslaying with the credulity of a child. *Jabberwocky* and *Dragonslayer* understand that the monster symbolizes some negative mental barrier on the part of the hero, which must be overcome, just as Dorothy evolves into a woman with the dowsing of the Wicked Witch. *Dragonheart* is appalled by the idea that people are going around killing dragons and adopts the euphemistic sweetness of conservationist kiddie pictures like *Pete's Dragon* and *Dragonworld* (1994).

Since *Dragonheart*, the burden of magic, shunned by most serious epics, has been comfortably shouldered by *Lord of the Rings*, whose emphasis on pitched battles and medieval adventure prompted otherwise classical epic fantasies to shrug off wizardry entirely and find human meaning behind the magic. This would be a fruitful angle if the movies presented anything approaching reality. The de-fantasized versions of *Beowulf* in John McTiernan's *The 13th Warrior* (1999), *The Iliad* in Wolfgang Petersen's *Troy* (2004) and The Matter of Britain in Antoine Fuqua's *King Arthur* (2004) are reality by way of the Arthurian Western.

Nevertheless, de-fantasizing classical myth has an interesting effect on the story, leaving what was once the responsibility of the gods in the hands of humanity. *Troy*'s secular account of the Trojan war defies the fatalism of the ancient Greeks (while avoiding comparison to the lounging gods of the Harryhausen epics), but gives no equivalent sense of human beings as their own ruling deitys. Brad Pitt's petulant star quarterback of an Achilles takes the modernist view that belief in the gods is absurd. We agree with him because the film does nothing to suggest why the ancients may have feared the gods and been driven to commit legendary deeds in their name. Without divine motivation, the actions of *Troy*'s all-human cast seem positively psychopathic, and the entire Trojan war an expression of the same lunatic fundamentalism that propels *Kriemhild's Revenge*. The movie translates Homer's warrior paean into something revealing the spiralling madness of war. Indeed, Achilles' contemptuous desecration of his dead enemy, Hector (Eric Bana), felt horribly pertinent the week it was released in the U.S. (just after the first Abu Ghraib pictures hit the American media).

Epic fantasy (whether de-fantasized or not) must leave room for the collective imagination to have its say. It must avoid the extremes of literalism, whether the credulous fundamentalism of *Dragonheart* or the utilitarian banality of *Troy* and

King Arthur (whose deadpan Clive Owen is hardly the man about whom legends are told). Unlike *Troy*, with its clear, god-free skies, the ideal epic fantasy leaves room for interpretation, for a sense of divine mystery. How could that have happened? What does it all mean? What movies like *King Arthur* fail to understand is that the reality behind the mythic hero, whether King Arthur or Jesus Christ, is unimportant next to the legend he inspires. Even when fantasy makes the mysteries of the imagination concrete, the conversion must stop halfway. Like the punchline to a joke or the suspense in a horror film, the viewer's imagination must be allowed to complete the circuit. Movies like *Dragonheart* and *Troy* do all the work for them. Of course, this leaves room for fanatics or fascists to translate scripture for their own allegorical ends, but such is the democracy of myth.

A Fine and Public Place

Once upon a time this author worked as a cinema projectionist. As a trainee I was taught the code of presentation (as it existed before the just-sling-it-on-the-screen approach of the multiplex). Every join in the reel, every change in the sound, every twitch in the focus, every switch from one reel to the next must be invisible. Nothing must distract the audience from being absorbed by the separate reality of the movie. "They come here to see the film," I was told, "not to see you doing your job." J.R.R. Tolkien engendered the same policy in fantasy through his concept of the autonomous secondary world.

Before Tolkien, most of fantasy's secondary worlds, among them Wonderland, Narnia and Oz, were tethered to the real world by portals allowing free passage between the two. William Morris' masterpiece *The Well at the World's End* (1896), E.R. Eddison's humanist fantasy *The Worm Ouroboros* (1922) and Mervyn Peake's rococo *Gormenghast* trilogy (1946–59) had already explored the idea of a universe operating without reference to our own, but it was Tolkien who drew the map. Expressed through fairy tale in *The Hobbit* (1937), explained in his 1939 lecture *On Fairy-Stories*, and exemplified by his *The Lord of the Rings* (1954–55), Tolkien's definitions opened up a new sphere of operation for fantasy.

"Neoclassicism" may appear a lofty term to apply to this kind of fantasy, but it shares with Dryden and Pope a desire to recall the style and structure of the classics, namely classical myth. The term may thus apply to any epic fantasy text whose mythic substance is entirely original, the imaginative product of a single person (or occasionally a group), rather than an entire culture. Neoclassic epic fantasy creates new myths from the old, seeking to sidestep the confines of modernity, which might otherwise get in the way of the story's imaginative sweep. However, its venues are not restricted to the autonomous secondary world prescribed by Tolkien, or the medieval variant he employed himself. A neoclassic epic fantasy may take place in the real world, albeit from an alternative perspective, as in *Watership Down* or *The Navigator: A Medieval Odyssey*. Yet few realize the genre offers such freedom and choose to mimic the second-hand example of Tolkien.

It is through *Lord of the Rings*, or more accurately through the many derivative books and role-playing games that disseminated its ideas in the '70s, that a popular conception of the entire fantasy genre derives. As John Clute points out, Tolkien's influence has in this way had something of a "thinning" effect on fantasy culture itself. To the skeptical, to the uninitiated and to writers of limited imagination, fantasy comprises a sort of kitsch toybox, offering fairy tale kingdoms, Prince Valiant–type heroes and fluttering fairies, all of which bear about as much resemblance to *Lord of the Rings* as Disney's *Sleeping Beauty* bears to the Grimms' fairy tale.

Most books and films that lift ideas from Tolkien favor the debilitating credo of "anything goes," retreating into escapism and losing contact with the real world. Such an approach owes more to the romanticism of fairy tale than the meticulous neoclassicism of Tolkien. Yet *Lord of the Rings* remains indirectly responsible for all those indeterminate volumes of medieval epic fantasy wasting shelf space at your local bookstore. In attacking the mindless formalism of this spin-off genre, too many critics (from both inside and outside the field) make the mistake of blaming Tolkien for the laziness of his imitators.

Not that the author is in any way immune to criticism, as many of his acolytes would like to believe. In Britain, *Lord of the Rings* has topped just about every poll for the nation's favorite read, but could just as easily take the prize for the most hated. British critics especially seem to regard the book with the kind of detestation the Ayatollah Khomeini reserved for *The Satanic Verses*. They routinely cite Tolkien's reactionary coda, his insistence on unambiguous morality, his absence of emotional range, his disregard for feminism, his seemingly autistic devotion to his own invented world, his arch prose ("For the main wall of the City was of great height and marvellous thickness, built ere the power and craft of Númenor waned in exile"), and even more away-with-the-fairies dialogue ("Hey! Come merry dol! Derry dol! My hearties!").

But such arguments all too often miss the point, lacking a proper understanding of how this kind of fantasy must work. Although a product of the twentieth century, *Lord of the Rings* is not a post–Joyce, post–Woolf mimetic novel. (According to Humphrey Carpenter's excellent biography, Tolkien had little interest in anything published after Chaucer.) So attempts to measure the book by the standards of modern literature are surely a case of square pegs and round holes. Accusations of inherent racism and xenophobia are also deflated by the fact that the book has been hijacked over the years by both the left and the right; such is the ambiguity of myth.

The book is genuinely *sui generis*. Out of the Cauldron of Story, Tolkien ladles the roots of classic myth, among them Beowulf and Gawain, in order to, in his own words, "make a body of more or less connected legend." A saga so immense it had to be published as three separate volumes, *The Fellowship of the Ring* and *The Two Towers* (both 1954) and *The Return of the King* (1955), *Lord of the Rings* concerns Frodo, a Hobbit (of a rustic, diminutive race distinguished by their large hairy feet). His mission is to destroy a malignant magical ring that will otherwise destroy the secondary world of Middle-earth. The influence of this story on modern fantasy film and literature is difficult to overestimate, although its legacy has been corrupted.

To borrow a Buddhist metaphor, *Lord of the Rings* is like a finger pointing to the Moon, with too many in awe of the finger and too few following its direction. Like Jung's take on religion, the veneration of Tolkien is a defense against the experience of myth. The formula his fiction has become makes a commodity of the archetypal stories that connect us with a shared humanity, reducing them to a formula that can be repeated and repackaged *ad infinitum.*

The only film to really understand what Tolkien was getting at was the science-fantasy *Star Wars* (the 1977 version that may now qualify as a "lost" film, following several debilitating CGI makeovers). Returning to the Cauldron of Story, rather than scavenging from Tolkien's plate, Lucas' deceased classic recognized that myth need not be medieval, or even take the form of fantasy. However, most neoclassic epics have regrettably taken the fundamentalist route, persisting in abortive efforts to recreate on screen what Tolkien achieves on the page, and doing much to diminish the identity of the genre in the process. Peter Jackson's conclusive adaptation of fantasy's reluctant ur-text may only serve to ghettoize the genre further, cementing neoclassic epic fantasy in medieval form. Widely recognized as the first "fantasy" film to win a Best Picture Oscar (if you disregard *American Beauty*, which was narrated by a dead guy), the success of Jackson's epics may limit conceptions of the genre even further, unless a wider comprehension of fantasy's expansive remit can be achieved.

Lord of the Rings may have become part of popular culture through an Anglicized New Zealander, but it first gained momentum on the American fringe. The youth culture of the '60s embraced the book like a Bible, and it quickly became a campus cult, a testament to the anti-war cry, "Power to the Imagination." As enthusiasm for the doings of Hobbits spread, American fantasy activist Lin Carter outlined the development of pre–Tolkien fantasy in his *Tolkien: A Look Behind the Lord of the Rings* (1969). He illustrated his point by reprinting the author's neglected antecedents in the "Ballantine Adult Fantasy" series. But a regrettably long tailback of Tolkien imitators followed, mostly comprising Americans born in the '40s and young enough to have underwent the *Lord of the Rings* experience at college. All this fuss and attention baffled Tolkien, quiet Oxford gent that he was.

The year of Tolkien's death, 1973, also saw the appearance of the role-playing game *Dungeons and Dragons*, created by American entrepreneurs Gary Gygax and Donald Kaye. The game's storytelling mechanics borrow elements from disparate, often-incompatible sources, throwing Tolkien's adventurers in with Robert E. Howard's barbarians, and a bestiary taken from *Famous Monsters of Filmland*. With its anything-goes approach to fantasy, early *Dungeons and Dragons* has unfortunately had the most profound influence on epic fantasy cinema after Tolkien himself.

The first crack at filming *Lord of the Rings* took place long before the book became a cult. In 1957, Tolkien rejected a treatment from *Famous Monsters* editor Forrest J Ackerman, who proposed the Fellowship be ferried about Middle-earth on the backs of giant eagles. Years later, The Beatles, instead of seeing out their contract with *Let It Be* (1970), almost starred in *The Hobbits*. With Michelangelo Antonioni reportedly signed to direct, this was to star Paul as Frodo, Ringo as Sam, George as Gandalf and John as Gollum. (One wonders if Yoko may have guest-starred as

Sauron.) While Disney were rumored to be mounting a Tolkien project of their own, following the success of *The Sword in the Stone*, John Boorman spent six months in 1970 developing a condensed script for United Artists, set for filming in Ireland.

By the end of the '60s, most of Hollywood's revenue was coming from small, daring movies like *Bonnie and Clyde* (1967) and *Midnight Cowboy* (1969). Appealing to the literate campus crowds who raved over Tolkien, these movies encouraged Hollywood to produce more "youthpics." While making possible the fantasy boom of the '80s, this trend also culminated in cinema's first Tolkienian fantasy, which combined the psychedelic counterculture movie, typified by Brian De Palma's *Hi, Mom!* (1969), with the activist questing of the road movie, born of Dennis Hopper's *Easy Rider* and Coppola's *The Rain People* (both 1969).

Written and directed by pugnacious underground animator Ralph Bakshi, *Wizards* (1977) is in many ways the flower generation's response to Tolkien, romantic about his themes, but lacking his artistic rigor. Like *Star Wars* (which opened in the U.S. two weeks after this), Bakshi's film predicts our downfall through technocracy and our salvation through mysticism, as swarms of swattable fairy-folk awake from dormancy after terrorists blow up the world. Bony-elbowed necromancer Blackwolf (voiced by Steve Gravers) excites a desire for war with Nazi propaganda discovered in the ruins of civilization. His weary, Hobbit-footed brother, Avatar (Bob Holt), journeys across the groovy post-apocalyptic fairyland of Montagar in order to stop him, accompanied by a buxom apprentice fairy, a bat-eared elf and "Peace," a robot assassin in a baggy red boiler suit.

Caught somewhere between fable and epic fantasy, all this erratic tale can do is gibber like a groupie full of LSD. The supposed conflict between technology and magic is blurred, both sides as technocratic and warlike as each other. Good guy Avatar even cold-bloodedly guns down his brother with a Luger. Not that this is any conscious irony on Bakshi's part; his ideas just swirl into one big chaotic collage, like the psychedelic chiaroscuro he uses to animate Blackwolf's armies, culling footage from *Alexander Nevsky* and *Zulu*. But the movie occasionally picks out an image whose slouched funkiness is rather appealing, like the rifle-toting Peace cantering across the prairies on an alien steed like some Martian cowpoke.

A surprise hit, *Wizards* proved to the studios that this fantasy stuff could actually work at the box office, even though only the kids understood it. Perhaps then it was John Boorman's artistic maturity that helped put UA off producing his expensive live-action *Lord of the Rings*. Given the density of *Excalibur*, Boorman (well into his thirties by now) would almost certainly have developed the deeper themes propelling Tolkien's story, of less interest to his younger more superficial peers. Whatever the reason for UA's cold feet, the studio passed the property onto Ralph Bakshi.

In the light of Peter Jackson's dexterity, it is easy to see how the difficulty in nailing Tolkien's sonorous, often abstract prose completely overwhelms Bakshi's animated *The Lord of the Rings* (1978), whose insistence on a fundamentalist reading of the book attempts to satisfy Tolkien's fans. Like Jackson, Bakshi regards Tolkien's words as holy writ, but only Bakshi seems overawed, hardly daring restructure. Although marched along nicely by Leonard Rosenman's grand score, the story is not so much dramatized as narrated, truncating exactly half the entire book into a two-hour film that only really comes to life when Bakshi or screenwriter Peter S. Beagle (a notable fantasy author himself) have the confidence to think for themselves. This only happens occasionally, as in a menacing scene (which Jackson borrows) where one of the cowled Ringwraiths sniffs out the Ringbearer as he cowers amid the roots of a tree.

Bakshi's film never connects with Tolkien the way Jackson's do. The effusive rotoscoped figures act out of concert with their imaginative but static backgrounds, forever disconnected from the world they are fighting to save. Jackson's cast is so smothered in the dirt and grime of Middle-earth that they become part of it. Nor does Bakshi empathize with the unenviable predicaments of his rather precious Frodo (voiced by Christopher Guard) or his obsequious Gollum (Peter Woodthorpe), the cuddly Hobbit tragically reduced to a ravening goblin by his hunger for the ring. Aragorn (John Hurt), Frodo's protector and Middle-earth's dormant monarch, remains stony. The movie's simpering bumpkin Sam (Michael Scholes), Frodo's stalwart retainer, and its grumpy Boromir (Michael Graham-Cox), the pragmatic human soldier who covets the ring himself, are vivid enough, but somehow the irascible Gandalf (William Squire) emerges as the most appealing character in the film.

With all his Zen conceitedness and suspicious fondness for "pipe-weed," Gandalf flew the flag for '60s mysticism which, by the '70s, had revived interest in Joseph Campbell. George Lucas kept a copy of *The Hero with a Thousand Faces* next to *Lord of the Rings* while writing *Star Wars* (which Campbell himself applauded before his death in 1987). But Campbell's book had already been fruitfully employed in fiction. One of the more unusual neoclassic fantasies to emerge in the wake of Tolkien, Richard Adams' 1972 bestseller, adapted by Martin Rosen's British animated feature *Watership Down* (1978), sees the world through the eyes of a rabbit. Promoting to the stature of myth what could essentially be told as an animal fable, Adams drew from Campbell in creating an entire mythology according to "rabbitkind," transforming the familiar human world into an alien secondary world through the eyes of his long-eared protagonists.

Set somewhere in the English countryside, this naturalistic adult fantasy turns the Golden Afternoon of Carroll and Tolkien into the charnel house dawn of Conan's Hyboria. A terrified rabbit named Fiver (voiced by Richard Briers) foresees the destruction of his burrow in a nightmare vision straight out of *The Shining*. He convinces his cunning brother (John Hurt) and several others to hop across the perilous wilds in search of a new home. Spookily heralded by the bounding shadow of rabbitkind's own Grim Reaper, death is everywhere in *Watership Down*, as this rapidly dwindling fellowship suffer the depravations of swooping hawks, choking snares and graveyard rats. The movie presents the world of nature as red in tooth and claw not only to offset its occasionally over-arch soulfulness (like the mournful montage for Art Garfunkel's *Bright Eyes*), but also to command respect for a premise many adults find risible. The first live-action neoclassic epic written for the screen approached a more forgiving child audience.

Yet another gallant failure of early '80s, Muppet creator Jim Henson's fearlessly ambitious *The Dark Crystal* (1982) succeeds only in creating a ravishing secondary world, inspired by the chitinous artwork of Brian Froud (who designed both this

Elf service: Prince Legolas (center, voiced by Anthony Daniels) consoles Sam (left), while helping an ailing Frodo (top) along with Aragorn (right) in Ralph Bakshi's animated *The Lord of the
Rings* (Fantasy Films/United Artists, 1978).

and *Labyrinth*). Embraced by Trevor Jones' faraway score, the movie is a landmark
in special effects (the entire cast consists of animatronic puppets) and its fixtures are
certainly beguiling. Lanky, wingless bats lope across the horizon like giraffes across
the Serengeti. Potato-faced gnomes jig away like Leprechauns in secret villages. Hulking crablike storm troopers patrol the landscape like Tolkien's Ringwraiths.

But having taken so much time over the creation of this alien playground, Henson makes the schoolboy error of making sure we appreciate it. The movie gives a
play-by-play of some unfathomable stone-smashing contest, gazes in awe at a huge
revolving model of the solar system, and documents what happens in a forest while
no one is around. All of this has little to do with the business of driving the story,
but also leaves little room for the viewer's imagination. What entices readers of
Tolkien is the wealth of undisclosed material of which *Lord of the Rings* forms just
a part. Eager to give away all its secrets, *The Dark Crystal* doesn't realize that it is
what the audience do not see in a secondary world that reels them in.

The film's titular crystal is a floating monolith that once radiated goodness over
the land until it somehow cracked. This metaphorical Fall splits the world's benevolent ruling race in two, creating the contemplative Mystics (a race of equine
hippies) and the degenerate Skeksis (capitalist pterodactyls who dress like Miss Hav-
isham and have wonderfully gross table manners). Gamine Gelflings, Jen and Kira,
replace the crystal's missing shard and restore their world to prelapsarian bliss.

Unfortunately, a voiceover relating another one of those blasted prophesies tells us this within the first five minutes. Jen has to play catch-up for the rest of the film, his quest lacking that vital sense of urgency in a world conceived too preciously for the brutalities of drama to penetrate.

In contrast to Henson's dedicated fantasy, Peter Yates' equally unsuccessful *Krull* (1983), the last big-budget fantasy of the early '80s (squished at the box office by *Return of the Jedi*), suffers from its own opportunism. Hoping to cash in on the vogue for medieval fantasy, the movie hurriedly dropped its original title (*The Dragons of Krull*) following the box office demise of *Dragonslayer*, while launching its medieval secondary world into the more commercial setting of outer space. An evil alien known as The Beast flies through the galaxy in his Black Fortress (one of those strongholds of evil that crumbles to bits the moment its owner gets his comeuppance). Stopping off to vandalize planets with his faceless Giger-esque army (whose squealing brains scurry out of their heads like face-huggers when they get shot), The Beast lands on the medieval planet of Krull and kidnaps Princess Lyssa (Lysette Anthony), the bride of boyish Errol Flynn wannabe Prince Colwyn (Ken Marshall). Having retrieved an ancient magical weapon (a sort of lethal designer Frisbee), Colwyn enlists a motley crew of cutthroats, a glum Cyclops and an aggravating pantomime magician, before setting off to locate The Beast's teleporting castle.

Krull's *Dungeons and Dragons*–style eclecticism never gels, yet it all moves at such an agreeable clip, with adventurers clambering through mountains and swamps, or dashing about dodging laser bolts in the bad guy's lair, that despite the hand-me-down feel you cannot help getting carried along and, well, rather enjoying it. The movie's problem is that it assumes all kinds of fantasy are alike and attempts to cover the bases of fairy tale, heroic and epic fantasy (not to mention sci-fi) in the hope that since it all comes under the heading of fantasy it should all somehow work. The one scene that does click does so in isolation.

The team's wise man, Ynir (Freddie Jones), is forced to consult his former lover, the Widow of the Web (Francesca Annis). This desiccated old woman was imprisoned inside the snare of a monstrous crystal spider for their murder of her and Ynir's son. In a scene that clearly borrows from Tolkien's subterranean detour into the Mines of Moria, as well as from Korda's *Thief of Baghdad*, the old man heroically traverses jangling cords of silk suspended over a bottomless chasm. Meanwhile, the sands of the Widow's hourglass run out and the crystal spider slavers in anticipation. The scene approaches genuine fairy tale poignancy as Ynir reminisces with his lover, who redeems herself by giving up her own life so that Ynir might escape and help save the world. It also lends the traditionally obtuse archetype of the wise old mentor something that feels like humanity.

The mediocre box office of epic fantasies like *Dark Crystal* and *Krull* failed to justify their colossal budgets; both cost over double the average for a feature film and put paid to live-action stabs at the genre for many years. The cheaper avenues of animation, television and video allowed the genre to tap its niche market while avoiding those monumental budgets. Arthur Rankin, Jr., and Jules Bass snatched up the TV rights to Tolkien's work back in the '60s and cheekily bookended Bakshi's *Lord of the Rings* with their animated greetings-card adaptations, *The Hobbit* (1977)

I got no strings: Gelflings, Kira (left) and Jen (right), with mantrap-mouthed furball Fizig, wander off in search of the titular monolith in Jim Henson and Frank Oz's. ***The Dark Crystal*** (Universal/ITC, 1982).

and *The Return of the King* (1980). Their best animated fantasy is probably *The Last Unicorn* (1982), adapted by Peter S. Beagle from his own 1968 book. With music by '60s *Wunderkind* Jimmy Webb, this telefeature falls somewhere between groovy eco-concern and *My Little Pony*, as its eponymous mythical beast (voiced by Mia Farrow) goes in search of her lost kin. Yet Beagle's masterful grasp of fantasy shines through the frilly animation.

Based on the book by Peter Dickinson and Wayne Anderson, the Rankin Bass' *The Flight of Dragons* (1982) is less cohesive, but more representative of '80s fantasy, particularly in its giving the mainstream so much to sneer at it. After having to listen to Don McLean croon the wistful title song, we learn the advance of science threatens a pastoral Wonderland full of friendly talking dragons. The malicious warlock Ommadon (voiced by James Earl Jones) hopes to coax this new technocracy into atomic extinction, while his wizard brethren summon a daydreaming nerd from the future (source-book author Dickinson) to stop him. After the beautiful princess he has created wilts into his scrawny arms, Dickinson has great fun as a result of being accidentally turned into a dragon. As its hero happily scuds about the sky like a fire-breathing zeppelin, the movie revels in the role-playing mindset at its most escapist.

Dungeons and Dragons also gives the film its push-button plot and oddball crew

A spider's touch: This stop-motion arachnid features in the best scene from Peter Yates' scattershot epic *Krull* (Columbia, 1983). It is also one of the many monstrous spiders scuttling through fantasy cinema, from the stuffed monster that grapples with Douglas Fairbanks in *The Thief of Baghdad* (1924) to the loathsome Shelob in *The Lord of the Rings: The Return of the King* (2003).

of player-characters. A tea-obsessed English knight, a talking wolf, a flame-haired archeress and a potato-nosed pixie neatly dispel every threat with an appropriate magical artifact. With its entreaties about the inspirational power of fantasy, *Flight of Dragons* preaches to the converted, but at least has the gumption to commit to its own rules. Restored to human form, Peter defeats Ommadon by denouncing the existence of magic, forbidding him to return to the very world he has denied.

Along with unspeakably wretched straight-to-video dreck like Hector Olivera's *Wizards of the Lost Kingdom* movies (1984 and 1988), role playing game–influenced programming continued to embarrass epic fantasy well into the '80s on CBS. Pitched by veteran producer Don Reo as "Butch and Sundance in Camelot," *Wizards and Warriors* (1983) was a jokey caper set in a future where technology is the sole reserve of wizards. Every week, drag queen–wigged hero Eric Greystone (Jeff Conaway) and his smart-mouthed sidekick Marko (Walter Olkewicz) attempted to save the world from a camp villain named Dirk Blackpool (Duncan Regehr). And they wondered why it only lasted four episodes. Far more promising was *Dungeons and Dragons* (1983–87), a Saturday morning cartoon about six teenagers thrown into the role-playing world by a theme park ride. Co-produced by game co-creator Gary

Gygax, the series benefited from several memorable episodes scripted by Michael Reaves and ran for two seasons.

Based on producer Rona Jaffe's book, the CBS telefeature *Mazes and Monsters* (1982), like *Return to Oz*, questions the stability of the imaginative mind, as Tom Hanks' unbalanced role-player takes the monster-slaying game a little too seriously. The appeal of role playing games derives from their encouraging a player's creativity, as they assume the role of a Tolkien-like storyteller or a Conan-like character, creating secondary worlds to their own liking. *Mazes and Monsters* sees this as a form of ritualized neurosis (although Balzac said a similar thing about fiction), as gamers create heroic characters to compensate for earthbound feelings of inadequacy and rejection.

The question of whether or not the author or role-player is of sound mind depends here on the degree by which the creator is fooled by his creation. Tolkien's fiction instigated this question by severing umbilical ties to the real world. Previously, authors kept their own fantasies safely at arm's length, never having to worry about Alice's sanity (and by extension their own) since she never visits Wonderland in her waking hours. (She does so in *Dreamchild* when her mind is crumbling with senility.) Yet the question only exists in the mind of those who see the imaginative process as a flight from reality, which is, of course, an impossibility, whether the fantasist likes it or not.

Like life, fantasy is an inescapable confrontation. Exclamations to the contrary are the reserve of snake-oil merchants like Germany's big-budget *Die unendliche Geschichte* (*The Neverending Story*) (1984), directed by Wolfgang Petersen, and badly adapted from the soporific bestseller by Michael Ende (who hated the film so much, he had his name removed from the credits). Bullied youngster Bastian (Barret Oliver) childishly ignores his father's advice to grow and face his problems. Instead, the boy loses himself in a woolly escapist world that sweeps away life's difficulties *gratis*. Having borrowed the titular book from one of those curious old shops that might as well form a chain (perhaps "Artifacts-R-Us"), Bastian reads about Fantasia. Composed of human whimsy, this world is presently decaying under a billowing fog known as the Nothing (an apocalyptic variant of the fairy-killing denial in *Peter Pan*). Bastian's heroic surrogate in this world is the curiously androgynous child-warrior Atreyu (Noah Hathaway), who must find a cure for Fantasia's consumptive avatar, the Childlike Empress (Tami Stronach).

As Bastian reads on, he learns that he is to become Fantasia's savior, and restores the world by wishing on its last remaining grain of sand. The story is well-intentioned, but so insular that the consequence of Fantasia's survival is meaningless. The film's spurious optimism is epitomized in the scene where Bastian somehow rides his Labrador-faced dragon into the real world, elatedly chasing away the bullies who beat him up in the first reel. This moment speaks only hollow comfort to any bullied kids in the audience.

Along with *The Dark Crystal*, *The Neverending Story* tailors epic fantasy for kids, but blunts its meaningfully sharp edges in doing so. Any drama, even kid's drama, thrives on conflict, yet the closest *Neverending Story* can bring itself to tears is by drowning Atreyu's horse. Fantasia itself is as boringly capricious as it is in the book.

Eyes to wonder: Scrawny boy warrior Atreyu (Noah Hathaway) touches down at the Ivory Tower astride Falcor the Luck Dragon (voiced by Alan Oppenheimer of *Masters of the Universe* fame) in Wolfgang Petersen's *The Neverending Story* (Warner/Producers Sales/Bavaria, 1984), at the time the most expensive movie ever produced in Germany.

Survival here relies on nothing so exciting as the state of one's mood. Atreyu's cheerfulness buoys him in quicksand, while his confidence deflects the eye-lasers of a pair of stone sphinxes. Had the movie a tighter grip on its material, the results could have been significant. Instead it offers few pleasures beyond endearing turns from the child leads, some pleasingly tactile (if all too obviously fake) monsters, some diverting scenery and a likeably bad Europop anthem. The sequels are even worse. George Miller's *The Neverending Story II: The Next Chapter* (1989) suffers from narrative bowels even more volatile than those of *The Mummy Returns*; the less said about Peter McDonald's utterly rancid *Neverending Story III* (1994), the better.

By the mid-'80s, it was as though the Nothing had devoured epic fantasy itself. All attempts to puncture the mainstream had by now failed, whether neoclassic originals, adaptations of *Lord of the Rings* or the fantasy novels it inspired. (Michael Powell planned an adaptation of Ursula Le Guin's popular *Earthsea* sequence in 1981, while working as a studio consultant at Coppola's American Zoetrope, but failed to find backing.) The genre had become the spiritual wasteland prophesized by *Excalibur* and *Dragonslayer*. But through the eyes of the time-travelling peasants in Vincent Ward's *The Navigator: A Medieval Odyssey* (1988), this mechanistic dystopia blossoms into a world as strange and magical as any Middle-earth. A busy motorway becomes as impassable as a mountain range. Cars flash past like stampeding beasts. A breaching submarine becomes a sea monster, and the claws of scrap-yard cranes dangle like monstrous spiders.

The Navigator suggests that the opposing forces of the wasteland and the Eden, which clash for supremacy over the epic fantasy world, are really only a matter of perception (one man's Eden is another man's wasteland, and vice versa). The movie also implies that these conditions are cyclic, each containing the seed of its own downfall, like the complementary principles of Yin and Yang. The one coherent idea *Wizards* comes up with proposes the human urge to destroy lays dormant beneath the Eden, just as the human urge to heal lays dormant beneath the wasteland, the latter's quiescence signified by the sinking of the sword at the end of *Excalibur*. And so the dramatic cycle rolls on, every "happily ever after," prefacing the next "once upon a time." "There are no happy endings," says the diffident magician of *The Last Unicorn*. "Because nothing ever ends."

With the emergence of Don Simpson and Jerry Bruckheimer's vision of "high concept" Hollywood, preceded by the return of pop storytelling under Lucas and Spielberg, the narrative studies of Joseph Campbell became as much a commodity as Tolkien had become in the '70s. Since Campbell's *Hero with a Thousand Faces* can be construed as outlining a mythic formula, whose box office benefit the *Star Wars* movies had proved three times over, Hollywood turned Campbell's book into a screenwriting manual. Now any family film with lavish special effects was laid down according to the "dictates" of Campbell, while the heroes of these neoclassic legends came free with a packet of cereal, thanks to *Star Wars* having also successfully exploited the ancillary market of merchandising. In Ron Howard's competent yet profoundly bland epic fantasy *Willow* (1988), executive producer George Lucas seems strangely intent on confessing the marketing sins he instigated.

The movie approaches Campbell like a recipe book, stitching together a patch-work of archetypes lifted undisguised from Homer, the Old Testament, Shakespeare, Tolkien, and even *Star Wars*. Not that *Willow*'s narrative works better for it. With its familiar subtitles ("It is a time of dread" and so on), the film blows its own ending with another prophecy. We learn a baby will be born who will end the evil reign of Queen Bavmorda (Jean Marsh). The chosen tot escapes her Herod-like cull on Moses' bed of reeds and is taken in by a tribe of diminutive "Nelwyn" (basically Hobbits with shoes). Accompanied by a pair of irksome French Brownies (with "out-raaaaaaageous" Monty Python accents) and a grinning mercenary named Madmartigan (Val Kilmer, the liveliest thing in the film), magician's apprentice Willow Ufgood (Warwick Davis) must protect the child from Bavmorda's soldierly daughter (Joanne Whalley) and her Darth Vader–impersonating henchman.

Designed with contributions from fantasy artists Chris Achilleos and Jean "Moebius" Giraud, *Willow*'s secondary world looks passably functional, but to little purpose. The movie's fairy tale sense of enclosure reveals nothing of the world apparently under threat from Bavmorda. One of those villains kept shuttered up in her castle, the Queen has little to do but rant about the incompetence of her cronies. As the baby is passed from player to player in a game of narrative football, the bad guys almost score a touchdown as they carry her off to Bavmorda's castle. But this is one of those movies where the baddies hold out just long enough for the goodies to get their act together. The film climaxes with two soggy old women punching the snot out of each other (reminiscent of a similarly goofy wizard's duel in *The Fellowship of the Ring*). Clearly if George Lucas, the godfather of modern secondary world fantasy, could not invigorate the genre, then it was surely dead to the mainstream.

Then along came the movie that confirmed everyone's suspicions. Gamer and novice filmmaker Courtney Solomon daringly bought the film rights to Gary Gygax's role playing game with his own money, perhaps qualifying *Dungeons and Dragons* (2000) as a heroic effort, but still the most comprehensively ghastly fantasy film ever made. *Ator: the Fighting Eagle* is a model of judgment by comparison. The movie summarizes just about everything that can go wrong with epic fantasy. Set in a gaudy freakshow world somewhere between *Xena* and *Star Trek*, it deftly illustrates the pitfalls of applying contemporary dialogue, pantomime acting and Hanna-Barbera slapstick, and borrowing ideas from *The Phantom Menace*.

Elitist wizards boss around the muggle peasants of the CGI city of Izmir, while Thora Birch's anesthetized Empress petitions for social reform and Jeremy Irons' guffawing warlock plots to gain the throne. In search of the dragon-summoning scepter that will thwart him are the usual gang of idiots, a pair of bungling thieves (Justin Whalin and an unbearably shrill Marlon Wayans), a bewildered sorcerer's apprentice (Zoe McLellan), a dwarf who talks to camera in a Brooklyn accent, and an intense elf tracker even sillier than the one in *Hawk the Slayer*. On their trail is Bruce Payne's ludicrous villain, trying hard to look sinister with blue lipstick and tentacles exuding from his ears.

When it was rumored in 1996 that Peter Jackson, the relatively untried talent behind several outrageous splatter flicks and the feverish true-life drama *Heavenly Creatures* (1994), was set to attempt a live-action adaptation of *Lord of the Rings*, audiences would have been justified in fearing the worst. Given that, at the time, Hollywood's idea of Tolkienesque fantasy was *Dragonheart*, one could already picture the casting. (How about Warwick Davis as Frodo, Sean Connery as Gandalf, Dennis Quaid as Aragorn, Marlon Wayans as Legolas and maybe Dennis Hopper as Gandalf's wizardly rival Saruman?) But when Miramax balked at the idea of producing anything other than a single two-hour feature, "art-house indie" New Line Cinema made the unprecedented move of backing Jackson's proposal to adapt Tolkien's three books as three films, all shot back to back. Based on a book that had been a bestseller for generations, the project offered unique "synergy" (merchandising opportunities) and the potential to create a global franchise that could rival Warners' *Harry Potter* series. No other literary fantasy property (with the possible exception of Howard's Conan) has quite the same potential to become the global fantasy film that could follow Jackson's.

With *Lord of the Rings* driven into the geek niche by *Dungeons and Dragons*, Jackson faced the Herculean task of adapting a cherished and unwieldy book into a film that had to appeal to both cultists and newcomers. The production was shrewd in its approach. Taking pains to convince the aficionado market of their movie's proposed fidelity to the book, producers welcomed Internet correspondence from Tolkien fans, whose responses to casting proposals reportedly swayed final decisions. Shooting entirely in Jackson's native New Zealand proved another canny choice, offering exactly the kind of varied terrain Tolkien's vast world required. Illustrators Alan Lee and John Howe were hired to help design the film, their previous work on a multitude of Tolkien publications amounting to a collective vision that fans would recognize when they saw it on screen.

Although New Line's gamble paid off both artistically and commercially, it's difficult to see Jackson's *The Lord of the Rings* (2001–03) having the impact it did without the digital-age revival of both the historical epic under Ridley Scott's *Gladiator* (2000) and of bespectacled nerd culture in general under the *Harry Potter* phenomenon. Although inextricably a product of the digital age, with extended (and superior) versions of the films available only on DVD, Jackson's films avoid the trap of becoming a CGI free-for-all. Relying on Méliès-like sleights-of-hand (like the false perspectives needed to shrink actors to the size of Hobbits) just as much as grandstanding computer technology, Jackson seemed to recognize the rut epic fantasy was in. Echoing the words of John Milius years before on *Conan the Barbarian*, Jackson said he approached the movies as though they were historical epics rather than "fantasy films." By creating a pseudo-historical world comparable to those of blockbusters like *Gladiator* and *Crouching Tiger, Hidden Dragon* (2000), Jackson cleverly aligns himself with the mainstream and avoids association with the inanity epic fantasy becomes through movies like *Willow* and *Dungeons and Dragons*.

The movies work as well as they do through this correspondence between reality and fantasy, a virtue made most of in the first installment, *The Fellowship of the Ring* (2001), the most intimate, substantial and immediately likable of the three films. The lost ring into which the faceless dark lord Sauron long ago embodied his evil powers is uncovered in the bucolic Eden of Hobbiton. Ian McKellen's Gandalf convinces its present owner Bilbo Baggins (Ian Holm) to pass the malevolent bauble on to his credulous nephew Frodo (Elijah Wood). As Frodo and his pal Sam (Sean Astin) flee their home with cousins Merry and Pippin (Dominic Monaghan and Billy Boyd), the film is propelled by a dramatic terror most epic fantasy leaves out for the sake of the kids. As Sauron's shrieking Ringwraith servants pursue the helpless Hobbits, the film is not afraid to get ugly or scary, as when the wraiths gather around their sleeping quarry like something out of an infant's nightmare.

The transporting grandeur of *Fellowship* really kicks in once Viggo Mortensen shows up. Bringing wiry gypsy vigor to the role of Aragorn, he delivers the Hobbits from the wild and forms part of the fellowship that sets off on the seemingly hopeless quest to dissolve the otherwise indestructible ring in the fire that forged it. As the heroes start trekking across awesome natural landscapes, and get on with credibly mundane stuff like camping out and bickering about directions, the movie evokes Tolkien's Middle-earth every bit as tangibly as the author himself. Taking for granted lines like, "They have a Cave Troll," everyone knuckles down to the gritty business of sweating, fighting and smoking, rather than tipping winks to the audience about what fools the movie might be making of them. Only the occasional crack about pipe-weed (for all those crusties left over from the '60s) and a few irksome jokes at the expense of dwarf warrior Gimli (John Rhys-Davies)—which unfortunately escalate in the second and third films—break an otherwise immaculate spell.

Picking up after Sean Bean's hawkish Boromir has broken the fellowship by making a play for the ring himself, *The Two Towers* (2002) is based on the most awkward of the three books to adapt, sensibly choosing to cut back and forth between timelines Tolkien lays end to end. Now the faltering Frodo and the resolute Sam pick their way among the crags to the fires of Mordor, guided by the wheedling Gollum (an often eerily lifelike creation, part–CGI, part-performed by actor Andy Serkis), whose schizophrenic personalities quarrel from reverse angles in one inspired scene. Carried away by hulking Orc soldiers, Merry and Pippin escape into a brooding forest where they meet Treebeard, a lovable walking oak who gets all the best lines. The booming tree-man also signifies the thematic conflict between nature's Eden and the mechanistic wasteland threatened by the inventions of Gandalf's adversary, Saruman (Christopher Lee).

A veteran of the Somme, Tolkien always maintained his experience of war had little bearing on his fiction, although watching *The Two Towers* makes this difficult to believe. Nazi imagery is a constant throughout Tolkien-derived fantasy, from the Nuremberg addresses in Bakshi's *Wizards* and *Lord of the Rings*, to the Auschwitz nightmares and *Führer* villain of *Watership Down*. Even the fascist Skeksis of *The Dark Crystal* include a Mengelean scientist in their ranks. With humanity bunkered against Saruman's tramping Orc legions, it's easy to imagine the siege of Helm's Deep was for Tolkien an unconscious working-through of the inevitable trauma he suffered during the war. Jackson's film does all it can to make sure this exhausting sequence seems like the desperate last stand it is. As the crows gather, the storm breaks, and men and boys hurl themselves against the weapons of their reckless enemy, Jackson lends human ballast to the crashing spectacle, as terrified children cower in the caves below and their proud king (Bernard Hill) wonders how it all came to this.

Gone fishing: Gollum (Andy Serkis) breaks for lunch in Peter Jackson's *The Two Towers* (New Line/Wingnut/Lord Zweite/Deutschland, 2002), the second and most thoughtful of New Line Cinema's groundbreaking *The Lord of the Rings* trilogy.

Released after the bombing of Afghanistan, *The Two Towers* was read by many critics as a commentary on George W. Bush's "War on Terror" (there was even debate as to whether the movie should retain its title after 9/11). But the significance of Sauron's distinctly Eastern allies and that of some hard-line dialogue ("Open war is upon you, whether you would risk it or not") can be countered by the suggestion that the film sides with terrorists. In defiance of neo-imperialist Hollywood epics like *Troy* and Oliver Stone's *Alexander* (2004), Frodo weaves undetected through a hostile empire hoping to cause the detonation that will bring freedom for his people. But as if to deflect all such contemporary readings, the extended DVD gives Boromir's surviving brother, Faramir (David Wenham), the last word: "What lies or threats lead him on this long march from home," he wonders, pausing to consider the dead body of his foreign enemy. "War will make corpses of us all."

By *The Return of the King* (2003), the sheer volume of Jackson's triptych starts to work against it. By now the characters have already been saved from the brink of death once too often, while the Churchwellian rhetoric and desperate last stands feel too comfortably familiar. Even the lunatic swashbuckling of elf prince Legolas (Orlando Bloom) seem more like he is having us on (he takes down a war elephant single-handed and surfs down its trunk for an encore). As the innumerable hosts of

Mordor lay siege to the panicking city of Minas Tirith, the battle often takes on the arid quality of a CGI cartoon like *Attack of the Clones*.

But Jackson still manages to involve his audience by tethering the fantastic clamor to quiet human pauses. Merry and Pippin fearfully part company and ride to uncertain ends. Cloistered shield-maiden Eowyn (Miranda Otto) seethes for the chance to prove herself in battle. Best of all, Faramir leads a suicidal charge in an attempt to win favor with his bedevilled father (John Noble), who picks absently at his food and forces Pippin to sing Faramir's eulogy. Everyone is prepared to forfeit his or her life in order to distract Sauron's all-seeing eye just long enough to let Frodo get the drop on him.

Yet it is the stalwart Sam (a character even lower down Middle-earth's pecking order than Frodo) who emerges as the ultimate hero of *Lord of the Rings*. With Frodo almost completely consumed by the ring's influence, Sam wrestles with the machinations of a relapsed Gollum, who tricks Frodo into the lair of the bloated spider, Shelob. Making several protective stands that range from cheer-worthy (fending off Shelob like Sigourney Weaver) to tear-worthy ("I can't carry it for you, but I can carry you!"), the stalwart Sam brings the adventure to a close in a moving and justifiably prolonged epilogue. It is this warmth of character (arguably lacking in Tolkien) that gives *Lord of the Rings* consequence, although its humanism may appear one-sided. The movies never consider the forces of evil in the same way as the forces of good, because evil here stands for the faceless adversity of life itself, against which one's defiant faith in humanity, friendship, courage, love or one's own resourcefulness will be rewarded.

In *The Two Towers*, Sam has a tearful speech about the inspirational power of Story, expressing in words the showboating delight all three films take in the act of storytelling. In the first film, Bilbo enthralls Hobbit children with tales of his adventures from *The Hobbit*, while a worm is hooked in much the same way as the audience for the opening image of the third film. Jackson's vertiginous camera penetrates all like the eye of an omniscient narrator. What Sam calls "the stories that meant something" are those myths that spur Frodo and himself on to epic deeds, which will themselves become one of "the great stories," and be recalled with inspiration. But this continuation relies on reinvention and reinterpretation, something that precious little epic fantasy has realized beyond its medieval incarnation in Tolkien.

In *On Fairy-Stories*, Tolkien asserts that fantasy serves three functions: recovery, escape and consolation. His use of plain nouns has unfortunately lent them to misinterpretation. For Tolkien, "escape" means simply ignoring the superficial furnishings of modernity, in order to recognize (or "recover") the Jungian roots they obscure. Fantasy must then look beyond the mask to the face behind it, by looking at the familiar from an unfamiliar perspective. Not to be mistaken for the idea of comfort in the face of disappointment, Tolkien's "consolation" comprises two aspects: the superficial—"the imaginative satisfaction of ancient desires"—and the profound—the realization that all is not lost and can never be lost.

Fantasy is the eternal optimist. The genre knows the cycle of life will endure, and forms the Yang to the horror genre's Yin. Fantasy's insistence on always seeing the sun behind the clouds is something that Tolkien terms the "eucatastrophe," the reversal of the existential despair evoked by tragedy (and, ideally, horror). In *Return of the King*, Gandalf reassures Pippin, as the forces of Mordor close in, that death is an inevitability to be embraced, not feared, and recalls the world beyond, which he as an angelic being has already been privy to. But then Tolkien was an assured Catholic, whose questions about death had all been answered. His "eucatastrophe" is the "design in everything" promised by Christian fantasy like *Here Comes Mr. Jordan*. Yet, such rapture is not the reserve of the devout (whatever they may say) and concerns life just as much as death. This state of mind, the crowning theme of fairy tale and fantasies earthbound, heroic and epic, is open to all, and it also has a secular name: Hope.

Bibliography

The American Film Institute. *Catalog of Motion Pictures Produced in the United States.* Berkeley: University of California Press, 1993.

Barbour, Alan G. *Cliffhangers: A Pictorial History of the Motion Picture Serial.* A & W Publishers, 1977.

Bettelheim, Bruno. *The Uses of Enchantment: The Meaning and Importance of Fairy Tales.* New York: Penguin, 1976.

Broecker, Randy. *Fantasy of the 20th Century: An Illustrated History.* Portland, OR: Collector's Press, 2001.

Campbell, Joseph. *The Hero with a Thousand Faces.* London: Fontana, 1949.

_____ with Bill Moyers. *The Power of Myth.* New York: Anchor Books, 1988.

Carpenter, Humphrey. *J.R.R. Tolkien: A Biography.* New York: HarperCollins, 1977.

Clute, John, and John Grant. *The Encyclopaedia of Fantasy.* London: Orbit, 1997.

Clute, John, and Peter Nicholls. *The Encyclopaedia of Science-Fiction.* London: Orbit, 1999.

Cohan, Steve. *Masked Men, Masculinity and the Movies in the Fifties.* Bloomington: Indiana University Press, 1997.

Cotterell, Arthur. *The Illustrated Encyclopaedia of Myths and Legends.* London: Guild, 1989.

Cross, Robin. *The Big Book of B Movies, or How Low Was My Budget.* London: Frederick Muller Ltd., 1981.

Dyer, Richard. *White Man's Muscles* From *Race and the Subject of Masculinities*, edited by Harry Stecopoulos and Michael Uebel. Durham: Duke University Press, 1997.

Falsetto, Mario. *Personal Visions: Conversations with Independent Film-makers.* London: Constable, 1999.

Frazer, John. *Artificially Arranged Scenes: The Films of Georges Méliès.* Boston: G.K. Hall and Co., 1979.

Frazetta, Frank. *Icon: A Retrospective of the Grand Master of Fantastic Art.* Vancouver: Evergreen, 1998.

Freud, Sigmund. *The Interpretation of Dreams.* James Strachey, trans. London: Hogarth Press, 1971.

Giannetti, Louis. *Understanding Movies.* Eighth Edition. Englewood Cliffs, N.J.: Prentice Hall, 1999.

Grant, John. *Masters of Animation.* London: Batsford, 2001.

Hammond, Paul. *Marvellous Méliès.* London: Gordon Frazer, 1974.

Hammond, Stefan, and Mike Wilkins. *Sex and Zen and a Bullet in the Head.* New York: Fireside, 1996.

Hardy, Phil, ed. *The Aurum Film Encyclopaedia: Horror.* London: Aurum, 1993.

_____. *The Aurum Film Encyclopaedia: Science Fiction.* London: Aurum, 1984.

_____. *The Aurum Film Encyclopaedia: The Western.* London: Aurum, 1995.

Harryhausen, Ray. *An Animated Life.* London: Aurum, 2003.

Hollis, Richard, and Brian Sibley. *The Disney Studio Story.* London: Octopus, 1988.

Hughes, David. *Tales from Development Hell.* London: Titan Books, 2003.

Jung, C.G. *Alchemical Studies.* First Edition. R.F.C. Hull, trans. London: Routledge & Kegan Paul, 1967.

_____. *The Practice of Psychotherapy.* Second Edition. R.F.C. Hull, trans. London: Routledge & Kegan Paul, 1966.

Kaminsky, Stuart M. *American Film Genres.* Second Edition. Chicago: Nelson-Hall Publishers, 1985.

Karney, Robyn, ed. *Cinema, Year by Year, 1894–2000.* New York: Dorling Kindersley, 2000.

Katz, Ephraim. *The Film Encyclopaedia.* Revised by Fred Klein and Ronald Dean Nolen. New York: HarperPerennial, 1998.

Klepper, Robert K. *Silent Films, 1877–1996. A Critical Guide to 646 Movies.* Jefferson, N.C.: McFarland, 1999.

Lacy, Norris J., ed. *The Arthurian Encyclopaedia.* Woodbridge, Suffolk: Boydell Press, 1986.

Larkin, Colin. *The Encyclopaedia of Stage and Film Musicals.* London: Virgin, 1999.

Lucanio, Patrick. *With Fire and Sword: Italian Spectacles on American Screens; 1958–1968.* Metuchen, N.J.: Scarecrow Press, 1994.

Mast, Gerald, and Bruce F. Kawin. *A Short History of the Movies.* Seventh Edition. Boston: Allyn & Bacon, 2000.

Mathews, Tom Dewe. *Censored: What They Didn't Allow You to See, and Why: The Story of Film Censorship in Britain.* London: Chatto & Windus, 1994.

Meyers, Richard. *Great Martial Arts Movies, from Bruce Lee to Jackie Chan and More.* New York: Citadel Press, 2001.

Moorcock, Michael. *Wizardry and Wild Romance.* London: Victor Gollancz, 1987.

Neale, Steve. *Genre and Hollywood.* London: Routledge, 2000.

Nicholls, Peter. *Fantastic Cinema, An Illustrated Survey.* London: Ebury Press, 1984.

Nowell-Smith, Geoffrey, with James Hay and Gianni Volpi. *The Companion to Italian Cinema.* London: Cassell, 1996.

Palmerini, Luca M. *Spaghetti Nightmares: Italian Fantasy-Horror.* Key West: Fantasma Books, 1996.

Pringle, David, ed. *The Definitive Illustrated Guide to Fantasy.* London: Carlton, 2003.

Pringle, David. *Imaginary People, A Who's Who of Modern Fictional Characters.* London: Paladin, 1989.

Richards, Jeffrey. *Swordsmen of the Screen: From Douglas Fairbanks to Michael York.* London: Routledge and Kegan Paul, 1977.

Rickitt, Richard. *Special Effects: The History and Technique.* London: Virgin Books, 2000.

Robinson, David. *Georges Méliès: Father of Film Fantasy.* London: BFI, 1993.

Sadoul, Georges. *Georges Méliès.* Paris: Editions Seghers, 1961.

Salisbury, Mark. *Burton on Burton.* London: Faber and Faber, 1995.

Sibley, Brian. *The Lord of the Rings: Official Movie Guide.* New York: HarperCollins, 2001.

Swartz, Mark Evan. *Oz Before the Rainbow: L. Frank Baum's* The Wonderful Wizard of Oz *on Stage and Screen to 1930.* Baltimore: Johns Hopkins University Press, 2000.

Tasker, Yvonne. *Spectacular Bodies: Gender, Genre and the Action Cinema.* New York: Routledge, 1993.

Thompson, David. *The New Biographical Dictionary of Film.* Fourth Edition. Boston: Little, Brown Books, 2002.

Thompson, Kristin, and David Bordwell. *Film History, An Introduction.* Second Edition. Boston: McGraw-Hill Higher Education, 2003.

Todorov, Tzvetan. *The Fantastic: A Structural Approach to a Literary Genre.* Translated from the French by Richard Howard. Ithaca, N.Y.: Cornell Paperbacks, 1993.

Tolkien, J.R.R. "On Fairy-Stories." From *The Monsters and the Critics and Other Essays*, edited by Christopher Tolkien. New York: HarperCollins, 1997.

Warner, Marina. *From the Beast to the Blonde.* New York: Vintage, 1994.

Weisbrot, Robert. *Hercules: The Legendary Journeys, The Official Companion.* New York: Doubleday, 1998.

_____. *The Official Guide to the Xenaverse.* New York: Bantam, 1998.

Wright, Nicky. *The Classic Era of American Comics.* London: Prion, 2000.

Zipes, Jack, ed. *The Oxford Companion to Fairy Tales.* Oxford: Oxford University, 2000.

Index

Numbers in **bold italic** indicate illustrations.

Aaron, Paul 110
Abbott and Costello 124, 169
ABC 222
Aberson, Helen 39
Abraham, F. Murray 100
Absurdism 11, 23, 35, 52, 83, 108, 122
Academy Awards 1, 39, 40, 45, 56, 58, 73, 256
Ace Ventura, Pet Detective (1993) 75
Achilleos, Chris 266
The Acid House (1998) 96
Ackerman, Forrest J 256
Adams, Richard 258
Addie, Robert 249
Adolescence 63, 66–7, 68, 72, 74, 144, 153, 160, 163
Adolfi, John G. 28
Adventure of Sinbad (Shindbad no bôken, 1962) 188
The Adventures of Baron Munchausen (1988) 55, 71–2
Adventures of Captain Marvel (1941) 166, **167**, 168
The Adventures of Pinocchio (1996) 78
The Adventures of Prince Achmed (Die Abenteuer des prinzen achmed, 1926) 43–4
The Adventures of Robin Hood (1938) 165
The Adventures of Rocky and Bull-winkle (2000) 118
"The Adventures of Sinbad" (TV series) 189, 223
The Adventures of Sinbad the Sailor (Dobrodruzství Námorníka Sindibáda, 1971) 188
"The Adventures of Sinbad the Sailor" (TV series/aka "Sinbad Jr.") 188
The Adventures of Sir Galahad (1949) 242
Aeschylus 97

Aesop 20, 39, 54, 81
Affleck, Ben 90, 91
After Life (1998) 136
Afterlife 12, 87, 98, 106, 122, 124, 136–9
Agar, John 101, 182
L'Âge d'or (The Golden Age, 1930) 13, 14, 46
Agnosticism 3, 214
AIP 183, 237
Ajax (1921) 169
Aladdin (1992) 73, 80, 114
Aladdin and the Marvellous Lamp (Aladdin et la lampe mer-veilleuse, 1906) 28
Aladdin and the Wonderful Lamp (1917) 29
Aladdin's Other Lamp (1917) 101, 114
Albers, Hans 46
Albertini, Luciano 169
Alexander (2004) 269
Alexander, Lloyd 252
Alexander Nevsky (1938) 257
Alf's Button (1920) 101, 114
Alf's Button (1930) 101
Alf's Button Afloat (1938) 101
Alf's Carpet (1929) 101
Algol (1920) 43
Ali, Muhammad 4
Ali Baba and the Forty Thieves (Ali Baba et les quarante voleurs, 1902) 28
Ali Baba and the Forty Thieves (1918) 29
Ali Baba and the 40 Thieves (1944) 180
Alias Nick Beal (1949) 93
Alice (1969) 61
Alice (1981) 63
Alice (Něco z Alenky, 1988) 71, 72, 102, 103
Alice in Acidland (1969) 61
Alice in Cartoonland 31
Alice in Wonderland (1903) 30–1
Alice in Wonderland (1915) 31

Alice in Wonderland (1931) 31
Alice in Wonderland (1933) 31–**32**
Alice in Wonderland (1935) 32
Alice in Wonderland (1951) 46, 49, 50
Alice in Wonderland (Disney, 1951) 2, 9, 50, 52, 61
Alice in Wonderland (1966) 59, **60**, 76
Alice in Wonderland (1976) 61
Alice's Adventures in Wonderland (1910) 31
Alice's Adventures in Wonderland (1972) 59
Aliens (1986) 209, 251
All of Me (1984) 110–1
All That Money Can Buy (1941) 93
Allan Quatermain and the Lost City of Gold (1986) 216
Allegory 10, 14, 38, 95, 254
Allen, Corey 61
Allen, Joan 135
Allen, Karen 214
Allen, Tim 106, 110
Allen, Woody 81, 98, 100, 110, 134
Allende, Isabel 7, 84
Almost an Angel (1990) 90, 95
Alonso, Chelo 175
Altain, Laura 176
Altman, Robert 80, 110, 150
Alves, Joe 189
Always (1989) 127
Ama (1991) 151–2
Amadio, Silvio 174
The Amazing Mr. Blunden (1972) 126, 128
"Amazing Stories" (TV series) 213
Amazons (1986) 205, 209
Ameche, Don 93, 123
Amélie (2001) 9, 145
Amenábar, Alejandro 120
America 18, 23, 27, 31, 35, 36, 59, 66, 74, 78, 90, 102, 122–4, 137, 141, 149, 166, 169, 173, 213, 224, 241, 242, 243, 253, 256–7
American Beauty (1999) 256

275

American cinema 30, 33, 41–2, 52, 59, 63, 67, 78, 102, 105, 106, 115, 118, 120, 122–4, 128–9, 130, 156, 168, 169, 182, 195, 197, 199, 200, 205, 211, 222, 223, 237
Amos, John 199
Andersen, Hans Christian 28, 34, 36, 39, 48, 51, 61, 68, 72, 80, 115, 158
Anderson, Eddie 95
Anderson, Michael 218
Anderson, Paul 131
Anderson, Wayne 261
Andersson, Bibi 110
Andre the Giant 70
Andress, Ursula 131, *132*
Andrews, Julie 58, 89
Andreyev, Boris 237
Angel, Heather 140
An Angel Comes to Brooklyn (1945) 87
The Angel Levine (1970) 89
Angel on Earth (1966) 89
Angel on My Shoulder (1946) 93, 106–7
The Angel Who Pawned Her Harp (1954) 89
Angels 13, 15, 16, 22, 47, 84, 86–92, 94, 95, 97, 98, 99, 120, 121, 123, 127, 128, 137, 139, 150, 151, 224, 235, 249, 271
Angels in the Outfield (1951) 89
Angels in the Outfield (1995) 89
Animal fables 38, 39, 54, 73–4, 76, 81, 258
Animals 39, 40, 58, 73, 76, 80, 101, 102, 108–9, 116–8, 146, 186, 199, 212, 226, 243
Animation and animated films 3, 13, 31, 33, 36–41, 43–4, 50–1, 54, 56, 57, 58, 66, 71, 72–3, 74–5, 76, 78, 80–2, 102–3, 106, 108, 111, 134, 135, 180, 182, 187–90, 194, 200, *201*, 209–10, 224, 225, 228, 243, 246–8, 251, 252, 257–8, *259*, 260–3, 270
Aniston, Jennifer 149
Annakin, Ken 115, 117
Annaud, Jean-Jacques 3
Annis, Francesca 260
Anstey, F. 112, 114
Anthony, Lysette 260
Anthony, Tony 216
Anti-heroes 100, 226
Anton, Amerigo 176
Antonini, Gabriele 173
Antonioni, Michelangelo 256
Antz (1998) 81
Apollonius of Rhodes 168
Apuleius, Lucius 25
Arabian Adventure (1979) 63
Arabian fantasy and the Arabian Nights 21, 28–30, 32, 43, 44–5, 48, 54, 55, 63, 73, 101, 179–90, 191, 200, 241

Arabian Nights (1942) 180
Arabian Nights (Il fiore delle mille e una notte, 1974) 56, 63
Arabian Nights: The Adventures of Sinbad (Arabian Naito: Shin-dobaddo no bôken, 1975) 188
Arau, Alfonso 160
The Archer and the Sorceress (1981) *see* "The Archer: Fugitive from the Empire"
"The Archer: Fugitive from the Empire" (The Archer and the Sorceress, 1981— TV series) 195, 222
Archetypes 15, 16, 21, 26, 73, 134, 181, 191, 212, 223, 231, 234, 256, 266
Arddino, Emile 107
The Ark of the Sun God (I sopravvlssutl della cittá morta, 1986) 216
Armendariz, Pedro 183
Arminus the Terrible see Massacre in the Black Forest
Armor of God (Long Xiang Hu Di, 1986) 216
Armstrong, Todd 239
Army of Darkness (1992) 143
Arrival of a Train at Ciotat Station (1895) 17
Arthurian fantasy 5, 15, 68, 87, 102, 120, 129, 132, 141, 193, 198, 216, 234, 236, 237, 241–6, 248–9, 254
Artifacts 42, 59, 84, 100–6, 114, 163, 214, 216, 219, 220, 262, 263
Ashman and Menken 72
Askey, Arthur 242
Asner, Ed 126
Asterix & Obelix: Mission Cleopatra (Astérix & Obélix: Mission Cléopâtre, 2002) 225
Asterix & Obelix Take on Caesar (Astérix & Obélix contre César, 1999) 225
Astin, Sean 268
The Astronomer's Dream, or the Man in the Moon (La Lune à un metre, 1898) 20
At the Earth's Core (1976) 192, 214
Atanarjuat: The Fast Runner (2000) 252
Atheism 3, 145
L'Atlantide (1921) 130
Atlas Against the Cyclops (Maciste nella terra dei cyclopi, 1961/aka: Monster from the Unknown World) 175, 177
The Ator Fighting Eagle (Ator l'invincibile, 1982) 201–2, 266
Attack of the Clones (2002) 270
Attack of the Puppet People (1958) 243

Auberjonois, Rene 108
Autant-Lara, Claude 93
Autry, Gene 231
"The Avengers" (TV series) 184
Aylmer, Felix 125

Babe (1995) 81
Babe: Pig in the City (1998) 81
Babes in Bagdad (1952) 182
The Babes in the Wood (1917) 27
Babes in Toyland (1934) 32–3, 36
Babes in Toyland (1961) 57
Baby: Secret of the Lost Legend (1985) 114
The Bacchantes (1961) 96
Bacharach, Burt 131
Baker, Kenny *143*
Baker, Rick 26, 190
Baker, Roy Ward 141, 192
Baker, Tom 184
Bakshi, Ralph 200, 201, 257–8, 259, 260, 268
Baky, Josef von 46, 55, 72
Balderston, John L. 140
Baldi, Ferdinando 201, 216
Baldi, Marcello 96
Baldwin, Alec 109, 126, 150, 219
Balk, Fairuza 64, 65, 154, *155*
Ball, Lucille 101
Ball of Fire (1941) 45
Ballet 21, 42, 48, 51, 188
Balzac, Honoré de 263
Bambi (1942) 36, 39, 40, 73
Bana, Eric 253
Banks, Lynne Reid 105
Baran, Jack 96
Barbarian Queen (1985) 205, 209
Barbarian Queen II: The Empress Strikes Back (1988) 209
Barbarian swordsmen 171, 180, 191–2, 193, 194, 198, 199, 200, 201, 204, 205, 206, 209, 210, 212, 213, 222, 226–8, 229, 231
The Barbarians (1987) 211
Barber, Frances 120
Barberini, Urbano 133, 211
Barkin, Ellen 109
Baron Munchausen 24, 46, 160, 181
Baron Münchausen's Dream (Les Hallucinations du Baron de Münchausen, 1911) 23
Barrera, Alessandro 201
Barrie, J. M. 2, 28, 30, 50, 79, 134
Barron, Steve 78, 108
Barrymore, Drew 52, 77
Barrymore, Lionel 87, 98, 123
Barton, Mischa 77
Basile, Giambattista 25
Baskett, James 39
Bass, Jules 260–1
Bates, Alan 150
Batman (1989) 11, 164, 218, 219

Batman Returns (1992) 74
Battiato, Giacomo 251
Bauer, Belinda 195
Baum, L. Frank 23, 27, 28, 30, 34, 36, 52, 64, 66, 68, 78, 158
Bava, Mario 177–8
Bazhov, Pavel 54
B.B.C. 4, 44, 54, 59, 156
Beacham, Stephanie 119
Beagle, Peter S. 258, 261
Bean, Sean 268
The Beastmaster (1981) 63, 191, 199–200, 205, 223, 226
Beastmaster 2: Through the Portal of Time (1991) 212
Beastmaster III: The Eye of Braxus (1995) 203, 228
"Beastmaster: The Legend Continues" (TV series) 226
The Beatles 256
Beatty, Warren 93, 107, 138, 218
Beaumont, Gabrielle 203, 226
Beaumont, Kathryn 50
Beautiful Vasilisa (Vasilisa prekrasnaya, 1939) 53
Beauty and the Beast 25, 26
Beauty and the Beast (1991) 72–3, 77, 82
Beauty and the Devil (La Beauté du diable, 1950) 93
Becker, Josh 224
Beckford, William 241
Bedazzled (1967) 93, 94–5
Bedazzled (2000) 92, 93, **94**
Bedknobs and Broomsticks (1971) 153
Beetlejuice (1988) 74, 125, 126–7, 133, 137
Being John Malkovich (1999) 35, 111
Belafonte, Harry 126
Belasco, David 121
Belief 10, 18, 41, 47, 63, 72, 85, 97, 99, 100, 106, 215
Bell, Book and Candle (1958) 147, 153
La Belle et la bête (1908) 26
La Belle et la bête (1946) 47–8, 57
Beller, Kathleen 199
Belluci, Monica 225, 228
Belushi, James 144
Ben-Hur (1959) 169
Benigni, Roberto 225
Bennet, David 67
Bennett, Compton 213
Bennett, Constance 122
Benny, Jack 87, 169
Benoît, Pierre 130, 131
Benson, Jodi 72
Benson, Robby 72
Benton, Barbi 205, 211
Berenger, Lisa 209
Berger, Ludwig 44
Bergese, Micha 63, **65**
Bergman, Ingmar 55, 98, 110, 125, 136

Bergman, Sandahl 197, 203, 207, 209
Berkeley, Busby 215
Berkeley Square (1933) 140, 141
Berlin, Irving 31
Berova, Olinka 131
Bertolini, Francesco 238
Besser, Joe 181
Besson, Luc 79
La Bête (The Beast, 1975) 61
Bettelheim, Bruno 37, 62
Between Two Worlds (1944) 136
"Bewitched" (TV series) 147, 153
The Bewitched Inn (L'Auberge ensorcelée, 1897) 20
Beyond Tomorrow (1940) 122
The Bible 20, 37, 38, 39, 56, 85, 86, 90, 91, 94, 95, 121, 177, 218, 266
Big (1988) 70, 112–**113**, 114
The Big Boss (Tangshan Daxiong, 1971) 179
Big Fish (2003) 160–1
"The Big Read" (TV series) 4
Big Top Pee-wee (1986) 67
Big Trouble in Little China (1986) 133
Bigfoot (1969) 114
Biggles (1986) 218
Bill and Ted's Bogus Journey (1991) 98, 138
Bill and Ted's Excellent Adventure (1988) 11
Birch, Thora 266
The Bishop's Wife (1947) 87, 89, 122
Bison Pictures 23
Blaché, Herbert 140
The Black Cauldron (1985) 66, 251–2
The Black Hole (1979) 66
Black Knight (2001) 143
The Black Knight (1954) 242–3
Blackbeard's Ghost (1967) 125
Blackman, Honor 239, **240**
Blackmore, Peter 115
The Blade Master (Ator l'invincibile 2, 1983) 202
Blair, George 124
The Blair Witch Project (1998) 12
Blasetti, Alessandro 238
Blasphemy 3, 85, 95
Blatt, Edward A. 136
Blithe Spirit (1945) 12, 121, 124, 128
Blondell, Joan 122
The Blood of Jesus (1941) 86, 95
Bloom, Orlando 225, 269
Blow-Up (1966) 244
The Blue Bird (1940) 37
The Blue Bird (1976) 62
Bluebeard (Barbe-Bleue, 1901) 20
The Bluebird (1918) 28
Blyth, Ann 115

Blyth, Betty 130
Boccaccio, Giovanni 25
Bodin, Ljuba 176
Bodyswaps 18, 35, 83, 84, 106–14
Boehm, Karl 57
Boem, Jeffrey 218
Bogart, Humphrey 100
Bogart, Paul 95
Boles, John 182
The Bolex Brothers 78
Bolger, Ray 33, **34**, 57
Bonnie and Clyde (1967) 257
The Book of Life (1998) 95
Boorman, John 245, 248–9, 250, 257
Booth, W.R. 234
Borgnetto, Ramono Luigi 169
Borowczyk, Walerian 61
The Borrowers (1997) 133
Borzage, Frank 106
The Bottle Imp (1917) 101
The Bouwmeestero 119
Bower, Dallas 46, 49
Bowie, David 68
Bowker, Judy 246
The Boy Who Could Fly (1986) 151
The Boy with Green Hair (1948) 151
Boyd, Billy 268
Boyer, Charles 106
Boyle, Danny 90
Brackett, Leigh 203
Bradbury, Ray 7
Bradley, Marion Zimmer 203
Bradley, Tom 108
Bragaglia, Carlo Ludovico 175
Branagh, Kenneth 157
Brand, Steven 229
Brandis, Madeline 28
Brandon, Henry 33
The Brass Bottle (1964) 114
Braveheart (1995) 252
Brazil (1985) 79, 234
Brenon, Herbert 28, 115
Brescia, Alfonso 211
Breslin, Spencer 145
Breslow, Lou 108
Bresslaw, Bernard 193
Bresson, Robert 244
Brest, Martin 99
Brewster McCloud (1970) 108, 151
Brick Bradford (1947) 165
The Bride with White Hair (Bai fa mo nu zhuan, 1993) 226
Bridget Jones's Diary (2001) 40
Briers, Richard 258
Brigadoon (1954) 131, 135
Bright, Matthew 76, 78
Brighton Rock (1947) 49
Brill, Steven 94
Britain 33, 41, 42, 44, 49, 51, 56, 61, 63, 67, 78, 84, 137, 141, 156, 176, 188, 193, 194, 216, 237, 242, 252, 255

British cinema 18, 48, 59, 63, 64, 78, 90, 101, 105, 110, 114, 115, 117, 120, 121, 128, 130, 133, 137, 142, 148, 162, 192, 193, 210, 222, 241, 245, 258
Broca, Philippe de 189
Broderick, John C. 206
Broderick, Matthew 70
Bromley, Alan 89
Bronski, Jacek 63
Bronson, Betty 28
Brooker, Richard 205–6
Brooks, Albert 136
Brother Bear (2003) 108
Brotherhood of the Wolf (Le Pacte des loups, 2001) 228–9
The Brothers Quay 78
Brown, Clarence 89
Brown, Pamela 49
Brown, Reb 204
Brown, Ritza 201
Browne, Coral 70
Browning, Robert 26
Bruce Almighty (2003) 13, 95, 144, 149, 150, 160, 251
Bruckheimer, Jerry 265
Bruhl, Heidi 183
Brundage, Margaret 190
Bruno, John 194
Bucquet, Harold S. 98
Buechler, John Carl 119
A Bug's Life (1998) 81
Bull, Peter 58, 59
Bullock, Sandra 154
Bunin, Lou 46, 49, 50
Buñuel, Luis 13, 14, 46
Bürger, Berthold *see* Kästner, Erich
Burns, George 95
Burns, Robert 119
Burr, Raymond 101
Burroughs, Edgar Rice 130, 192, 200, 213, 214
Burton, Richard (actor) 93
Burton, Richard (author) 28
Burton, Tim 12, 66–7, 74–5, 77, 78, 79, 80, 126–7, 137, 160, 218, 229
Bush, George W. 149, 269
But My Love Does Not Die! (Ma l'amour mio non muore, 1913) 169
The Butcher's Wife (1991) 152
Butler, David 141
Buzzell, Edward 119
Bye Bye Red Riding Hood (Piroska e farkas, 1988) 64
Byrd, Ralph 165
Byrne, Gabriel 248

Cabin in the Sky (1943) 89
The Cabinet of Dr. Caligari (1919) 33, 37, 43
Cabiria (1914) 169
Cabot, Sebastian 182
Cage, Nicolas 89, 144
Caine, Michael 144

Camelot (1967) 243–4, 246, 248
The Cameraman's Revenge (1912) 54
Camerini, Mario 174, 238
Camp, Joe 108
Campbell, Bruce 143
Campbell, Joseph 164, 232, 233, 234, 248, 251, 258, 265–6
Campbell, Neve **155**
Campogalliani, Carlo 175
Campos, Victor 195
Canale, Gianna Maria 171
Cannon Films 204, 216
The Canterbury Tales (I raconti di Canterbury, 1971) 56
The Canterville Ghost (1944) 124
Capitalism 54, 94, 259
Capra, Frank 16, 83, 87, 88, 130
Capshaw, Kate 215
Captain America (1944) 165
Captain Blood (1935) 181
Captain Sindbad (1963) 183
Cardona, René 99, 216
Cardos, John 211
Carew, James 101
Carlei, Carlo 108
Carne, Marcel 47
Carnera, Primo 170
Caro, Marc 79, 80
Caron, Leslie 52
Carousel (1956) 106
Carpenter, Humphrey 255
Carpenter, John 133
Carradine, David 179, 206
Carrere, Tia 228
Carrey, Jim 75, 80, 102, 110, 149
Carroll, Jonathan 7
Carroll, Lewis 2, 15, 30, 32, 41, 49, 50, 52, 59, 61, 68, 71, 78, 245, 258
Carroll, Pat 72
Carter, Angela 7, 40, 63, 64, 84, 115, 153
Carter, Helena Bonham 160
Carter, Lin 184, 191, 192, 210, 256
Cartwright, Veronica 153
Casarès, Maria 137
Cascorelli, Don 199
Caserini, Mario 169
Casper (1995) 128
Castellari, Enzo G. 189
Castle, Nick 151
Castle, William 150
The Cat in the Hat (2003) 52, 80
Cates, Phoebe 100
Cats and Dogs (2001) 117
Cattrall, Kim 103, 104
Caudell, Lane 195
Cavazos, Lumi 160
The Cave of the Demons (La Caverne maudite, 1898) 20
Caviness, Cathryn 86
CBS 57, 262, 263
Celano, Guido 175

Celedonio, Maria 78
Censorship 7, 35, 37, 44, 53, 61, 109, 177, 194, 198, 203, 207, 216
Čepek, Petr 94
CGI *see* Special effects
Chabat, Alain 225
Chadwick Pictures 28
Chaffey, Don 240
Chamberlain, Richard 4, 216
Chamberlain, Wilt "The Stilt" 207
Chamisso, Adelbert von 42, 43
Chan, Jackie 101, 216
Chances Are (1989) 107
Chaney, Lon, Jr. 182
Channing, Stockard 154
Chaperones 32, 46, 55, 58, 74
Chapman, Edward 149
Chapman, Graham 244
Charleson, Ray 193
Charley and the Angel (1973) 89
Chase, Chevy 108
Chaucer, Geoffrey 25, 255
Cheadle, Don 144
Chechik, Jeremiah 96
Cheh, Chang 175
Cher 153, **154**
Chicken Run (2000) 76, 78, 81, 133
Un Chien andalou (An Andalusian Dog, 1929) 13, 46
Childhood 7, 8, 26, 37, 39, 55, 100, 113, 134, 159, 187, 213
Children 14, 27, 28, 29, 33, 41, 59, 62, 64, 66, 67, 71, 74, 77–9, 81, 102, 105, 112–4, 119, 133, 134, 153, 156, 159–60, 215, 232, 251, 265, 268
Children's fantasy 10, 27, 28, 78, 119, 153, 156–60, 167–8, 192, 197, 205, 216, 229, 241, 242, 245, 249, 253, 263
Chill Wills 116
The Chimes (1914) 140, 145
A Chinese Ghost Story (1987) 126
The Chips Are Down (Les Jeux sont faits, 1947) 136
Chitty Chitty Bang Bang (1968) 2, 58–9, 62, 71, 78
Christianity 3, 38, 85, 86–7, 89, 95, 96, 106, 107, 127, 133, 146, 214, 241, 251, 252, 271
A Christmas Carol (1938) 121
A Christmas Carol (1984) 126
The Christmas Dream (Le Rêve de Noël, 1900) 21
Cimino, Michael 192
Cinderella 28, 40, 43, 52, 73, 77
Cinderella (Cendrillon, 1899) 20
Cinderella (1914) 28
Cinderella (Der verlorene Schuh, 1923) 43
Cinderella (1947) 54

Cinderella (1949) 40–1, 50
Cinderella and the Fairy God-mother (1898) 26
Cinderella, or the Glass Slipper (Cendrillon ou la pantoufle mystérieuse, 1912) 23
Cinema 16, 17, 18, 20, 21, 22, 24, 25, 27, 28, 30, 42, 43, 46, 48, 83, 92, 100, 135, 142, 165, 192, 232, 235, 246
Circle of Iron see The Silent Flute
City of Angels (1998) 89
The City of Lost Children (La Cité des enfant perdus, 1995) 79, **80**, 82, 142
Civilization 83, 131, 164, 171, 192, 198, 257
Clair, René 24, 93, 121–2, 123, 140, 146, 147, 148
Clark, Marguerite 28, 119
Clark, Spencer Treat 152
Clarkson, Lana 206
Clary, Robert 182
Clash of the Titans (1981) 63, 96, 187, 191, 246–**247**, 248, 249
Clavier, Christian 143, 225
Clay, Nicholas 249
Cleese, John 142, **143**, 244
Clemans, Brian 184
Clery, Corine 204
Close, Glenn 110
Close Encounters of the Third Kind (1977) 63
Clouzot, Henri-Georges 8
Clouzot, Vera 8
Clute, John 3, 12, 234, 255
Cobb, Ron 197
Cochran, Robert 149
The Cockeyed Miracle (aka: Mr. Griggs Returns, 1946) 124
Cocteau, Jean 47–8, 59, 63, 67, 73, 133, 137, 142
Coghlan, Frank, Jr. 166
Cohan, Steve 172
Cohen, Howard R. 212
Cohen, Rob 253
Cohn, Harry 52
Cohn, Michael 64
Cokeliss, Harley 223
Colicos, John 213
College Holiday (1936) 169
Collette, Toni 129
Collins, Ray 204
Collodi, Carlo 37, 78
Colman, Ronald 13, 131
Coltrane, Robbie 156
Columbia Pictures 31, 52, 101, 131, 166, 181, 182, 242, 243
Columbus, Chris 156, 157, 158
Comic-books and strips 9, 11, 152, 164, 165, 169, 178, 190, 195, 197, 199, 200, 204, 207, 218, 225, 231, 243
Communism 54, 151, 160, 237
The Company of Wolves (1984)

8, 61, 63–4, **65**, 66, 67, 68, 70, 71, 72
"Conan" (TV series) 223, 228
Conan Doyle, Arthur 114, 120, 229
"Conan the Adventurer" (TV series) 228
Conan the Barbarian (1981) 3, 10, 14, 63, 166, 189, 191, 193, 194, 195–**196**, 198, 199, 200, 201, 202, 203, 206, 207, 212, 226, 231, 267
Conan the Destroyer (1984) 192, 196, 206–7, **208**, 209, 219, 226
Conaway, Jeff 262
A Connecticut Yankee (1931) 141, 142
A Connecticut Yankee in King Arthur's Court (1920) 141, 142
A Connecticut Yankee in King Arthur's Court (1949) 141, 142, 243
Connelly, Jennifer 68
Connelly, Marc 95
Connery, Sean 13, 91, 142, 164, 218, 245, 253, 267
Connor, Kevin 63, 214
Conquest (1983) 194, 203
Conrad, Joseph 198
Conried, Hans 52
Conservatism 35, 51, 241, 244, 246
Conspirators of Pleasure (Spiklenci slasti, 1996) 102–3
Constantine, Storm 203
Conway, Gerry 200, 207
Cook, Peter 59, 70, 93, 94–5
Cool World (1992) 118
The Cooler (2002) 150
Cooper, Gary 32, 45, 134
Cooper, Jeff 179
Cooper, Merian C. 130
The Coppelia Animated Doll (Copélia ou la poupée animée, 1900) 21, 26
Coppola, Francis Ford 119, 144, 183, 257, 265
Cordeliers' Square in Lyon (1895) 17
Corea, Nicholas 195, 222
Corman, Roger 66, 195, 205, 206
Cornell, John 89–90
Corona, Alfonso 212
Cort, Bud 151
Cosby, Bill 93
Costello, Maurice 23
Costner, Kevin 87, 128, **129**, 139, 252
Cottafavi, Vittorio 175, 176
Cotton, Joseph 125
The Countryman and the Cinematograph (1901) 18
Coward, Noël 121, 124
Cozzi, Luigi 194, 204
Crabbe, Larry "Buster" 165, 166
The Craft (1996) 153–4, **155**, 156

Craven, Wes 12
Cregar, Laird 93
Crosbie, Annette 193
Crosby, Bing 141, 243
Cross, Beverley 186
Crouching Tiger, Hidden Dragon (2000) 267
The Crow (1994) 98–9, 102
Crudup, Billy 160
Cruise, Tom 67
Crystal, Billy 70, 95, 134
Cuarón, Alfonso 157
Cukor, George 62
Cummings, Constance 124
Cummings, Robert 87
Curry, Tim 67
Curtis, Jamie Lee 112
Curtis, Tony 109
Cusack, Joan 75, 106
Cusack, John 111
Cushing, Peter **132**, 192, 242

D'Abo, Olivia 207
Dacascos, Mark 228
Dahl, Roald 2, 59, 61–2, 77, 78, 153, 158
Daisy's Adventures in the Land of the Chrysanthemums (1904) 134
Daitozoku (aka: The Lost World of Sinbad/Samurai Pirate, 1964) 183
Damiano, Gerard 118
Damle, V.G. 235
Damn Yankees (1958) 93
Damon, Matt 90
Dana, Viola 101
Dance, Charles 133, 136
Dance of Death (Totentanz, 1919) 97
Danforth, Jim 57
Daniels, Anthony 259
Daniels, Bebe 27
Daniels, Jeff 135
Daniels, Rod 112
Danning, Sybil 205, 209
Dante, Joe 101
Danziger, Edward J. 182
Darabont, Frank 152
Darby O'Gill and the Little People (1968) 13, 119
The Dark Crystal (1982) 8, 63, 191, 251, 258–60, **261**, 263, 268
Darlington, W.A. 101
Darwin, Charles 3, 16, 130, 241
Dassin, Jules 124
Date with an Angel (1987) 89
A Daughter of the Gods (1916) 28
Davidtz, Embeth 77, 143
Davis, Desmond 246
Davis, Geena 80, 126
Davis, Warwick 119, 266, 267
Dawley, J. Searle 28, 119
The Dawn of Freedom (1916) 141
Dawn of the Dead (1979) 201
Day, Josette 47

Day, Robert 132
The Day the Earth Froze see *Sampo*
Déa, Marie 137
The Dead Can't Lie see *Gotham*
Dead of Night (1945) 124
Dear, William 89
Deardon, Basil 110
Death 12, 16, 17, 38, 39, 42, 43, 55, 57, 90, 97–9, 107, 108, 111, 120–1, 122, 123, 124, 128, 130, 134, 136, 137, 138, 140, 160, 258, 271
Death Becomes Her (1992) 111
Death Takes a Holiday (1934) 98, 99
Deathstalker (1983) 194, 195, 205–6, 209, 211, 212, 223
Deathstalker II: Duel of the Titans (1987) 205, 212
Deathstalker III: The Warriors from Hell (1988) 212
Deathstalker IV: Match of the Titans (1990) 212
De Bont, Jan 220, 221
The Decameron (1970) 56
De Camp, L. Sprague 162, 191
De Carlo, Yvonne 181
Deeping, Warwick 242
DEFA (Deutsche Film Aktien Gesellschaft) 54
Defending Your Life (1991) 136
Delannoy, Jean 47, 136
De Laurentiis, Dino 197, 206, 207, 238
De Laurentiis, Raffaella 228
Delman, Jeffrey 64
Delusions 10, 71
De Martino, Alberto 171, 174
Demy, Jacques 61
Deneuve, Catherine 61
Denizot, Vincenzo 169
Dent, Lester 218
Denton, Donna 211
Deodato, Ruggero 201, 211
De Palma, Brian 257
Depardieu, Gerard 225
Depp, Johnny 12, 74, **75**, 225
The Desert Hawk (1950) 181
Desert Romance 101, 114, 180, 181–2, 189
De Sica, Vittorio 169
Destiny Turns on a Radio (1995) 96
The Devil 19, 20, 22, 42, 47, 64, 67, 84, 91–95, 97, 99, 107, 109, 153, 154
The Devil and Max Devlin (1981) 93
The Devil in a Convent (Le Diable au Couvent, 1899) 22
The Devil with Hitler (1942) 93
The Devil's Money-bags (Les Trésors de Satan, 1901) 22
The Devil's Widow see *Tam-Lin*
DeVito, Danny 77, 156, 160, 224
"Devotionals" 235

Les Diaboliques (The Fiends, 1954) 8–9
Diaz, Cameron 81, 90, 111
Dick Tracy (1937) 165
Dick Tracy (1990) 218
Dickens, Charles 2, 121, 140, 158
Dickinson, Peter 261
Die Hard (1988) 200
Dieterle, William 33, 44, 93, 125
Disney (studio) 14, 33, 36–41, 44, 45, 47, 48, 49–51, 52, 54, 61, 64, 65, 66, 72, 74, 77, 78, 80, 81–2, 89, 93, 103, 108, 112, 114, 118, 119, 125, 127, 145, 150, 153, 224, 225, 243, 244, 249, 251, 255, 257
Disney, Walt 31, 33, 36, 51, 66, 226
A Diva's Christmas Carol (2000) 126
Divine Intervention (2002) 84
Divoff, Andrew 114
Dixie National Pictures 121
Dixon, Malcolm **143**
Doc Savage: The Man of Bronze (1975) 218
Doctor Dolittle (1967) 58, 116
Doctor Dolittle (1998) 117, 152
Doctor Dolittle 2 (2001) 117, 152
Doctor Faustus (1967) 93
Dr. Phibes Rises Again (1972) 219
Dr. Seuss 52, 53, 66, 74, 78, 80
"Doctor Who" (TV series) 184, 186
Dodgson, Charles Lutwidge see Carroll, Lewis
Dogma (1999) 13, 90–1, 96
The Dollmaker's Daughter (1906) 26
The Doll's Revenge (1907) 105
Dominici, Arturo 170
Dommartin, Solveig 89
Dona Flor and Her Two Husbands (1977) 124
Donat, Robert 121, **123**
Donen, Stanley 93
Donlevy, Brian 87, 123
Donne, John 61
Donner, Clive 63, 126
Donner, Richard 68, 126, 217
D'Onofrio, Vincent 191
Donovan, Martin 95
Donovan, Tate 224
Doody, Alison 218
Dorothy and the Scarecrow in Oz (1910) 27
The Double Life of Véronique (1991) 110
Douglas, Kirk 238
Douglas, Sarah 207
Dowd, Kay 87
Down to Earth (1947) 96
Down to Earth (2001) 107, 138
Downey, Robert, Jr. 107
Doyle, Richard 120

Dragon Gate Inn (Long menke zhen, 1967) 175
Dragonheart (1996) 253, 254, 267
Dragons 10, 15, 30, 51, 57, 157, 212, 236, 238, 245, 249–51, 253, 260, 263, **264**, 266
The Dragon's Blood (Sigfrido, 1963) 238
Dragonslayer (1981) 63, 66, 191, 249–51, 253, 260, 265
Dragonworld (1994) 253
Dream a Little Dream (1989) 112
The Dream Doll (1917) 105
Dreamchild (1985) 66, 70–1, 263
Dreams and dreaming 4, 7, 8, 9, 10, 13, 16, 17, 25, 30, 31, 39, 41, 47, 51, 52, 55, 56, 57, 60, 61, 63, 65, 68, 71, 79, 80, 87, 101, 108, 134, 139, 140, 151, 232
DreamWorks SKG 81, 190
Drew, Sidney 109
Driscoll, Bobby 39
Drop Dead Fred (1991) 100
Drums of Fu Manchu (1940) 215
Dryden, John 254
Du Chau, Frederick 252
Duigan, John 77
Dumas, Alexandre 181
Dumbo (1941) 38–9, 40
Duncan, Michael Clarke 152, 229
Dungeons and Dragons 45, 189, 198, 256, 260, 261–2; *see also* Role-playing games
"Dungeons and Dragons" (TV series) 203, 262–3
Dungeons and Dragons (2000) 193, 226, 266, 267
Dunne, Griffin 153
Dunne, Irene 124
Dunsany, Lord 7
Duprez, June 44
Durante, Jimmy 169
Durgnat, Raymond 176
Duvall, Shelley 110, 151
Duvivier, Julien 98
DVD 67, 267, 269
Dyer, Richard 170
"Dynamation" *see* Special effects

"Early Edition" (TV series) 140
Earth vs. the Flying Saucers (1956) 182
Earthbound (1920) 121
Earthbound (1940) 121
Earthbound fantasy 13, 14, 15, 16, 83–161, 163, 213, 234
Eastwood, Clint 178, 205
Easy Rider (1969) 257
Echoes of Wizardry see *Iron Warrior*
Eddison, E.R. 254
Eden 39, 62, 164, 265, 268
Eden, Barbara 114
Edison, Thomas 18, 19, 26, 235, 242

Education for Death (1943) 41
Educational Pictures 42
Edward Scissorhands (1990) 14, 67, 74, **75**, 79, 80, 82, 160
Edwards, Blake 109
Edwards, Cliff 38
Edwards, Henry 121
Edwards, Mike **143**
18 Again! 112
Eisenstein, Sergei 236
Ekerot, Bengt 55
Ekmann, Gösta 92
Elf (2003) 134
Elhardt, Ingrid 237
Elliott, Denholm 218
Elwes, Cary 70
Emilfork, Daniel 79, **80**
The Empire Strikes Back (1980) 192, 202
Emshwiller, Ed 191
The Enchanted Cottage (1945) 9
The End of Koshchei the Deathless (Kashchey Bessmertny, 1943) 53
Ende, Michael 156, 157, 263
Endfield, Cyril 98
English, John 167
Ephron, Nora 90
Epic fantasy 3, 12, 14, 15, 16, 26, 63, 65, 67, 85, 96, 97, 101, 114, 133, 139, 142, 159, 163–4, 167, 168, 171, 174, 183, 184, 187, 191, 193, 205, 226, 229, 232–271
Eraserhead (1976) 78
Erhard, Bernard 205
Erik the Viking (1989) 251
Erikson, Leif 180
Ernest Saves Christmas (1988) 99
The Erotic Adventures of Pinocchio (1971) 61
Escapism 4, 8, 40, 41, 44, 47, 48, 57, 58, 59, 68, 77, 79, 82, 134, 151, 233, 241, 255, 263
E.T.: The Extra Terrestrial (1982) 1, 116, 251
L'Eternal Retour (The Eternal Return, 1943) 47, 237, 242
Europe 18, 23, 27, 28, 30, 34, 36, 41, 78, 97, 122, 123, 146, 200, 251
Ever After (1998) 52, 70, 77
The Evil Dead (1982) 12, 143, 219
Excalibur (1981) 3, 11, 63, 101, 191, 193, 206, 216, 245, 246, 248–9, **250**, 251, 252, 257, 265
The Execution of Mary, Queen of Scots (1895) 19
Expressionism 13, 21, 41, 44, 55, 76
Eyer, Richard 183
Eyes of Youth (1919) 140

Faerie 25, 26, 30, 31, 33, 34, 37, 38, 44, 46, 48, 49, 50, 52, 54, 55, 59, 62, 63, 70, 72, 74, 77, 79, 82, 83, 84, 99, 102, 118, 133–4, 163, 233, 241

Fairbanks, Douglas **29**–30, 31, 32, 42, 44, 180, 181, 182, 236, 237, 262
Fairbanks, Douglas, Jr. 181, 182
Fairies 10, 22, 25, 27, 38, 50, 51, 67, 68, 69, 118–120, 132, 235, 257
Fairy Godmothers 40, 41, 52, 77, 119, 207
The Fairy of the Black Rocks (La Fée des roches noires, 1904) 119
Fairy Tale: A True Story (1997) 120
Fairy tale films 3, 12, 14, 15, 16, 20, 25–82, 83, 84, 85, 97, 101, 114, 115, 116, 117, 119, 133, 139, 158, 163, 186, 188, 195, 198, 226, 229, 232, 233, 241, 253, 254, 260, 266, 271
Fairy tales (literary) 20, 23, 25, 26, 27, 28, 36, 42, 47, 52, 80, 146, 156, 182, 255
Fairyland, or The Kingdom of the Fairies (Le Royaume des fées, 1903) 21–2
Faith 15, 38, 79, 85, 89, 138, 233, 251
Falk, Peter 70, 89
The Fall of Troy (Il caduta de Troia, 1910) 169
Family Man (2000) 144, 145
Famous Players 23
Fanaka, Jamaa 110
Fanny and Alexander (1982) 55, 125
Fantasia (1940) 36, 38, 61, 225
Fantasma (1914) 235
Fantasizing 7, 15, 55, 160–1, 263
"The Fantastic" 8–9
The Fantastic Night (La Nuit fantastique, 1942) 47
Fantasy: adult audiences and 8, 10, 27, 41, 46, 47, 50, 113; adult fantasy 10, 27, 46, 73, 168, 192, 211, 228, 248, 258; ambiguity in 9, 52, 56, 76, 99, 100, 120, 137, 151; audiences and 10, 14, 15, 19, 30, 33, 34, 44–5, 49, 55, 56, 66, 67, 68, 71, 73, 84, 85, 107, 124, 139, 161, 163, 169, 210, 233, 249, 251, 254, 259, 270; child audiences and 8, 27, 36, 37, 39, 41, 49–50, 52, 54, 73, 77, 78–9, 81, 113, 182, 207, 215, 219, 226, 228, 229, 268; critical regard for 1, 3–4, 8, 9, 10, 16, 33, 35, 36, 38, 46, 48, 49, 50, 52, 73, 116, 169, 176, 177, 194, 195, 198, 206, 237, 241, 244, 248, 255; cultural impact of 4, 7, 15, 53–4, 169, 198, 232; cultural regard for 7, 16, 27, 36, 39, 169, 179, 190, 192, 206, 241, 255, 256; defining 3, 4, 5, 7–10, 12, 15, 35, 254; Eastern and western

attitudes to 16, 20, 101–2, 125, 131, 132, 133, 164, 179, 180, 235, 236, 252, 269; euphemisms for 4, 5, 7, 84; functions of 4, 15; identifying 4, 8, 12, 13; literature of 7, 8, 20, 21, 23, 27, 31, 39, 84, 125, 162–3, 181, 190–1, 192, 194, 197, 203, 210–1, 212, 213–4, 232–3, 235, 254–6, 265, 267; misconceptions of 4, 5, 7, 15, 134, 151, 157, 220; postmodern 66, 68, 73, 157; returning from 4, 151; social class and 93, 107, 134, 138, 149, 181; structure of 7; wish-fulfilment in 7, 134, 164
Fantoni, Sergio 173
Faraway, So Close! (In weiter Ferne, so nah!, 1993) 89, 94
Farrow, John 93
Farrow, Mia 135, 261
Fascism 40, 73, 170–1, 198, 210, 237, 238, 254, 268
Fattelal, S. 235
Faust 16, 22, 42, 43, 72, 79, 87, 92, 93, 95, 102
Faust (1926) 43, 92
Faust (Lekce Faust, 1994) 94, 102
Faust and Marguerite (1897) 22
Favreau, Jon 134
Feast, Michael 97
Feldman, Corey 112
Fellini, Federico 125
Felton, Tom 156
Feminism 40, 51, 72, 77, 103, 109, 115, 153–6, 203, 209, 221, 223, 226, 227, 255
Ferrara, Abel 207
Ferrati, Rebecca 211
Ferrer, Mel 242
Ferrigno, Lou 189, 194, 204–5
Ferris, Pam 77
Ferroni, Giorgio 96
Fiddler's Three (1944) 142
Field of Dreams (1989) 12, 87, 128–**129**, 139
Fields, W.C. 32
Fight Club (1999) 100
Filmation 188
Fincher, David 100
Finding Nemo (2003) 81
Finger, Bill 218
Finian's Rainbow (1968) 119
Finley, Joe 209
Finney, Albert 126, 160
Fire and Ice (1982) 200, **201**, 207, 209
Fire Monsters Against the Son of Hercules (Maciste contro i mostri, 1962/aka: Colossus of the Stone Age) 178
First Knight (1994) 70, 252
Fisher, Jason 153
The Fisher King (1991) 242
Fist of Fury (Jingwu Men, 1972) 179

A Fistful of Dollars (Per un
    pugno di dollari, 1964) 178
Fitzhamon, Lewin 26
The 5,000 Fingers of Dr. T (1953)
    3, 8, 52, *53*, 55
Flaherty, Paul 112
Flash Gordon (1936) 165
*Flash Gordon Conquers the Uni-
    verse* (1940) 165
Flash Gordon's Trip to Mars
    (1938) 165
Fleischer, Charles 118
Fleischer, Richard 58, 206, 207,
    208
The Fleischer Brothers 180
Fleming, Andrew 153, 155
Fleming, Ian 59
Fleming, Victor 33, 34, 123
Flesh and Blood (1985) 251
Flight 28, 103, 151
Flight of Dragons (1982) 68, 108,
    261–2
The Flintstones (1994) 80, 111
A Florida Enchantment (1914)
    109
Fluke (1995) 108
The Fly (1986) 108
Flying carpets *29*, 45, 101
Flynn, Emmet J. 141
Flynn, Errol 165, 180, 181, 199
Folklore and folktale 15, 16, 20,
    21, 38, 42, 57, 84, 114, 118, 120,
    130, 147, 173, 183, 228, 232,
    245, 252
Fonda, Bridget 160
Fonuielle, Lloyd 127
For a Few Dollars More (Per
    qualche dollari in più, 1965)
    178
For Heaven's Sake (1950) 89
Forbes, Bryan 62
Ford, Harrison 187, 213, *214*,
    217, 219
Ford, John 233
Ford, Mick 151
Forest, Mark 173, 175, 176
Forever Darling (1956) 89, 122
Foster, Hal 243
Foster, Jodie 112
Fox *see* 20th Century–Fox
Fox, Gardner F. 191
Fox, Michael J. 80
France 20, 25, 28, 33, 42, 44,
    46–7, 54, 61, 98, 130, 169, 176,
    225, 228, 241, 242, 245
Francis (1950) 116
Francis Covers Big Town (1953)
    116
Francis Goes to the Races (1951)
    116
Francis Goes to West Point (1952)
    116
Francis in the Haunted House
    (1956) 116
Francis Joins the Navy (1955)
    116
Francis Joins the Wacs (1954) 116

Francisci, Pietro 168, 172, 173,
    174, 179, 183
Frankenstein (1931) 43
Frankenweenie (1984) 66
Franklin, Chester and Sidney
    27, 28–9, 122
Fraser, Brendan 76, 93, 94, 101,
    189, 219, 220
Frazetta, Frank 191, 197, 200, 207
Freaky Fairy Tales (1986) 64
Freaky Friday (1976) 83, 111, 112
Freaky Friday (2003) 83, 111, 112
Freas, Frank Kelly 191
Freda, Riccardo 178
Frederick, Lynne 126
"Freedom Force" (TV series) 188
Freeman, Morgan 95, 149
Freeway (1996) 76
*Freeway II: Confessions of a
    Trickbaby* (1999) 78
Freud, Sigmund 7, 37, 62, 130,
    153, 173, 249
Friday the 13th (1980) 194
Friedman, Ed 210
Froud, Brian 68, 258
Fulci, Lucio 194, 201, 203
Fullerton, Fiona 59
Fundamentalism 3, 4, 85, 87,
    91, 145, 214, 245, 249, 251,
    253, 256, 257
Fuqua, Antoine 253
Furst, Anton 63
Fury, Ed 175

Gabriel and Me (2001) 90
The Gabriel Grub Surly Sexton
    (1904) 119
Gabrielle, Monique 211, 212
Gahagan, Helen 130
Gaiman, Neil 7, 158
Galeen, Heinrich 42
Galland, Antoine 28
Gallo, Vincent 78
Gambino, Domenico 169
Gambon, Michael 75, 144, 157
A Game with Stones (Spiel mit
    Steinen, 1965) 102
Gans, Christophe 228
Ganz, Bruno 89
Gardner, Ava 96, 103, 119, 125,
    242
Gardner, Joan 149
Garfunkel, Art 258
Garland, Judy 4, 33, *34*, 50, 153
Garnett, Tay 141, 243
Garrani, Ivo 168
Gaskill, Charles L. 28
Gassman, Vittorio 189
Gaudreault, André 23
Gaumont 134
Gawain and the Green Knight
    (1973) 245
The Geiselodore *see* Dr. Seuss
Gellar, Sarah Michelle 102
Gender 15, 37, 38, 40, 50, 51,
    64, 73, 84, 90, 109–11, 114,
    140, 146–7, 150, 169, 173, 198,

203–4, 209–10, 211, 223, 224,
    232
Genies 27, 44, 45, 73, 80, 101,
    106, 114, 183, 184, 189
Gentilomo, Giacomo 175, 238
Geoffrey, Paul 249
German Expressionism 37, 43,
    46, 97
Germany 27, 33, 39, 41, 42–4,
    46, 54, 89, 235–6, 238, 263,
    264
Gesner, Zen 189
Ghost (1990) 127–8, 129, 152
Ghost and Mrs. Muir (1947)
    125, 140
Ghost Chase (1987) 126
Ghost Dad (1990) 126
The Ghost Goes West (1935)
    121–2, *123*
The Ghost Goes Wild (1947) 124
Ghostbusters (1984) 11, 126
Ghosts 19, 20, 38, 55, 66, 83,
    84, 85, 98, 100, 109, 110,
    120–30, 139, 140, 162, 214
The Ghost's Holiday (1907) 127
The Ghosts of Berkeley Square
    (1947) 124–5, 126
Gianetti, Louis 13, 83
The Giants of Thessaly (I giganti
    della Tessaglia, 1961) 239
Gibson, Mel 3, 78, 252
Gibson, Walter B. 166
Gilbert, Brian 112
Gilliam, Terry 24, 55, 56, 63,
    71, 72, 96, 142, 143, 145, 242,
    244, 245, 251
Ginger Snaps (2000) 108
Giraud, Jean "Moebius" 266
Gladiator (2000) 267
The Glass Slipper (1954) 51
Gleason, Jackie 181
Gliese, Rochus 43
The Gnome-Mobile (1967) 119
God 16, 85, 87, 89, 92, 94–6, 99,
    106, 120, 125, 138, 142, 145,
    149, 150, 164, 171, 214, 229,
    234, 251
Godard, Jean-Luc 238
Goddard, Daniel 226
Goddard, Gary 210
Goddard, Paulette 182
The Godfather (1972) 246
Gods 55, 96–7, 101, 103, 108,
    133, 148, 160, 171, 190, 192,
    205, 213, 223, 224, 225, 226,
    228, 235, 239–*40*, 246, 251,
    253
Godzilla movies 169, 183
Goebbels, Josef 44, 46
Goethe, Johann Wolfgang von
    16, 27, 42, 92, 93, 102
Golan and Globus 189, 204
Goldberg, Whoopi 74, 127,
    152
The Golden Arrow (La Freccia
    d'oro, 1962) 182
The Golden Blade (1953) 182

The Golden Child (1986) 101, 133
The Golden Key (Solotoi kluchik, 1938) 54
The Golden Voyage of Sinbad (1973) 8, 45, 184–**185**, 186, 220, 239
Goldman, William 70
Goldwyn, Tony 127
Der Golem (1914) 42, 103
Der Golem (1920) 43, 103
Goliath Against the Giants (Golia contro i giganti, 1960) 174
Goliath and the Dragon (La vendetta di Ercole, 1960/aka: The Vengeance of Hercules) 175, 177
Goliath and the Vampires (Maciste contro il vampiro, 1961) 175–6
Golino, Valeria 67
Good and evil 36, 38, 67, 92, 95, 96, 136, 142, 159, 164, 171, 198, 225, 246, 260, 270
A Good Little Devil (1914) 119
Goodbye Charlie (1964) 109
Gooding, Cuba, Jr. 136
Goodman, John 80, 134
Goodwin, Leslie 87
The Goonies (1985) 217
Gone with the Wind (1939) 233
Gor (1987) 133, 211
Gordon, Bert I. 243
Göring, Hermann 41
Goring, Marius 48, 137
Goscinny, Réné 225
Gotham (aka: The Dead Can't Lie, 1988) 127
Goto, Island of Love (Goto, l'île d'amour, 1968) 131
Gottlieb, Michael 103, 104
Gould, Chester 218
Gould, Will 64
Gounod, Charles 92
Graham-Cox, Michael 258
Grahame, Kenneth 76
Granger, Marc 126
Granger, Stewart 213
Grant, Cary 32, 85, 87, 90, 112, 122
Grant, John 3, 118, 234
Grant, Kathryn 182
Grant, Richard E. 110
Grapewin, Charley 121
The Grasshopper and the Ant (La Cigale et la fourmi, 1897) 20
The Grasshopper and the Ant (1912) 54
Gravers, Steve 257
Gravey, Fernand 47
Gray, Helen 61
Great Expectations (1946) 48
The Great Muppet Caper (1981) 118
Green, Nigel 240
The Green Mile (1999) 152

The Green Pastures (1936) 95
Greene, Richard 181
Greer, Germaine 3
Gregorio, Eduardo de 125
Grieco, Richard 189
Grieco, Sergio 200
Griffith, D.W. 21, 23, 92
Griffiths, Richard 156
Grimm, Brothers 26, 27, 28, 34, 36, 42, 43, 54, 56, 59, 61, 63, 68, 77, 158, 255
Grimm's Fairy Tales for Adults (1970) 61
The Grinch (2000) 52, 80
Grint, Rupert 156
Groundhog Day (1993) 145–6
Gruza, Jerzy 63
Guard, Christopher 258
Guazzoni, Enrico 169
Guerrini, Mino 216
Guest, Lady Charlotte 241
Guest, Christopher 70
Gulliver's Travels (Le Voyage de Gulliver, 1902) 21
Gura, Sascha 97
A Guy Named Joe (1943) 123–4, 127
Gwenn, Edmund 99
Gygax, Gary 256, 262–3, 266

Hackett, Buddy 57 103
Haggard, H. Rider 121, 130, 131, 178, 213
Haggard's "She": The Pillar of Fire (La Colonne du feu, 1899) 21, 130
Hagman, Larry 114
Hale, Jennifer 189
Hale, Sonnie 142
Haley, Jack 33, **34**
Hall, Alexander 85, 86, 89, 96
Hall, Jon 180
Hallucinations 9, 34, 39, 71, 137
Hamilton, Margaret 33, 34
Hamlin, Harry 246, **247**
Hammond, Kay 124
Hampshire, Susan 96
Hanks, Tom 106, 112–3, 116, 263
Hanna-Barbera 80, 188, 266
Hannah, Daryl 116
Hannah, John 145
Hannon, Sean 200
Hans Christian Andersen (1952) 51
Hansel and Gretal 78
Hansel and Gretal (1909) 26
"Happily ever after" 70, 265
Happy Land (1943) 123
The Harboua von 236
Harding, Ann 134
Hardwicke, Cedric 98, 141, 213
Hardwicke, Edward 120
Hargitay, Mickey 175
Harlequin (1980) 150
Harring, Laura Elena 110

Harris, Barbara 112
Harris, Brad 174
Harris, James B. 62
Harris, Joel Chandler 40
Harris, Leigh 204
Harris, Lynette 204
Harris, Richard 157, 244
Harrison, Dan 183
Harrison, M. John 7
Harrison, Rex 58, 124, 125, 152
Harrison, Tony 97
Harry Potter 85, 156, 241
Harry Potter and the Chamber of Secrets (2002) 157, **158**, 159
Harry Potter and the Philospher's Stone (aka: Harry Potter and the Sorcerer's Stone, 2001) 156–7, 159
Harry Potter and the Prisoner of Azkaban (2004) 144, 157
Harry Potter movies 10, 13, 15, 49, 84, 132, 133, 144, 156–60, 267
Harryhausen, Ray 26, 45, 54, 57, 131, 157, 174, 180, 182–3, 184–7, 188, 189, 190, 192, 202, 219, 220, 222, 225, 237, 238, 239–40, 246–8, 253
Hartley, Hal 95
Hartman, Don 100
Harvey (1950) 100, 119
Harvey, Laurence 56–7
Harvey, P.J. 95
Has, Wojciech 55
Haskin, Byron 183
Hatch, Richard 133
Hathaway, Henry 134, 243
Hathaway, Noah 263, **264**
Hauer, Rutger 70
Haughton, David Cain 202
The Haunted Curiosity Shop (1901) 102
The Haunted Mansion (2003) 127
Hauser, Wings 212
Hawk the Slayer (1980) 133, 191, 193, 194, 195, 211, 222, 266
Hawks, Howard 45, 112
Hawn, Goldie 111
Hayek, Salma 96
Hayes, Derek 252
Hayes, Helen 103
Hayes, Robert 209
Hayward, Louis 140
Hayworth, Rita 96
He-Man and She-Ra: The Secret of the Sword (1985) 210
"He-Man and the Masters of the Universe" (TV series) 209–10, 264
Heard, John 113
Hearts and Armour (1983) 251, 252
Heaven and hell 22, 85, 87, 90, 92, 93, 107, 121, 122, 127, 136–9
Heaven Can Wait (1943) 93

Heaven Can Wait (1978) 107, 138–9
Heaven Only Knows (aka: Montana Mike, 1947) 87
Heavenly Creatures (1994) 266
The Heavenly Kid (1985) 89
Heaven's Gate (1980) 192
Heavy Metal (1981) 194, 204
Hecht, Ben 121
Heisler, Stuart 122
Helm, Brigitte 130
Helpmann, Robert 49, 59
Hemmings, David 244
Henreid, Paul 182
Henry, Buck 107
Henry, Charlotte 32, 33
Henson, Brian 69
Henson, Jim 68, 69, 118, 258 60, 261
Henson, Leslie 101
Hepburn, Audrey 40
Hepworth, Cecil 105
Herbert, James 108
Herbert, Victor 32
Herbie Goes Bananas (1980) 103
Herbie Goes to Monte Carlo (1979) 103
Herbie Rides Again (1974) 103, 106
Hercules: 14, 179, 189, 209, 213, 215, 222, 224, 240
Hercules (Le fatiche di Ercole, 1958) 56, 166, 168, 169, 170–1, *172*, 174, 178, 238, 239
Hercules (1983) 194, 204–5
Hercules (1997) 224–5, 226
Hercules and the Amazon Women (1994) 223
Hercules and the Captive Women (Ercole alla conquista di Atlantide, 1961/aka: Hercules Conquers Atlantis) 176
Hercules and the Circle of Fire (1994) 223
Hercules and the Lost Kingdom (1994) 223
Hercules and the Princess of Troy (1965) 222
Hercules in New York (1969) 96
Hercules in the Haunted World (Ercole al centro della terra, 1962) 177–8
Hercules in the Maze of the Minotaur (1994) 224
Hercules in the Underworld (1994) 224
Hercules, Prisoner of Evil (Ursus, il terrore dei Kirghisi, 1965) 178
"Hercules: The Legendary Journeys" (TV series) 189, 212, 222–4, 225, 226, 228, 229, 253
Hercules II (Avventure dell' incredibile Ercole, 1984) 205
Hercules Unchained (Ercole e la regina di Lidia, 1959) 170, 173, *174*

Here Comes Mr. Jordan (1941) 85–8*6*, 87, 90, 93, 96, 98, 107, 122, 123, 127, 137, 141, 271
Hero (1982) 245
Heroes and heroines 11, 12, 14, 15, 19, 38, 40, 50, 51, 59, 63, 64, 71, 84, 101, 102, 159, 163–4, 167, 171, 184, 193, 198, 224, 234–5, 236, 239, 242, 251, 253, 254, 265
Heroic fantasy 12, 14, 15, 16, 35, 56, 63, 83, 85, 97, 114, 133, 139, 162–231, 232, 233, 234, 238, 242, 260, 271; *see also* Anti-heroes; Superheroes
"Hero's journey" 234–5
Die Herrin von Atlantis (1932) 130
Herrmann, Bernard 183, 239
Herzfeld, John 95
Heslov, Grant 229
Hesser, Edwin Bower 96
Hessler, Gordon 184, 185
Heston, Charlton 95, 225
Hewitt, Peter 98, 133
Hi, Mom! (1969) 257
Hickox, Anthony 243
Hicks, Seymour 121
High Spirits (1988) 127
Highlander (1986) 11, 90, 91
Highlander II: The Quickening (1990) 11
Hilde Warren und der Tod (1917) 97
Hill, Bernard 229, 268
Hill, Jack 204
Hill, Richard 194, 205
Hilton, James 131
His Majesty Scarecrow of Oz (1914) 27
Historia Naturae (1967) 102
Hitchcock, Alfred 81
Hitler, Adolf 41, 44, 46, 93, 94, 164, 170, 235, 237
The Hobbit (1977) 260
Hocus Pocus (1993) 153
Hoffman, Dustin 134
Hoffmann, E.T.A. 26, 42, 74
Hoffmanns Erzählungen (1915) 42
Hogan, Paul 90
Hogan, P.J. 79, 116
Holden, William 123
Holloway, Sterling 169
Hollywood 1, 23, 28, 30, 31, 33, 35, 36, 37, 39, 41, 42, 43, 44, 45, 48, 51, 52, 56, 57, 63, 78, 82, 87, 89, 92, 98, 110, 111, 124, 127, 136, 143, 156, 169, 191, 193, 200, 205, 211, 223, 244, 245, 246, 252, 257, 265, 267, 269
Holm, Christopher 202
Holm, Ian 70, 142, 267
Holt, Bob 257
Homer 232, 235, 238, 252, 253, 266

Homosexuality 61, 64, 93, 147, 172–3, 209, 210
Hong Kong 126, 203, 216
Hook (1991) 134
Hopper, Dennis 257, 267
Horn, Camilla 92
The Horn Blows at Midnight (1945) 87
Horror 3, 4, 8, 11, 12, 14, 43, 64, 66, 92, 108, 114, 119, 120–1, 124, 153, 177–8, 219, 270, 271
Horsley, Lee 194, 199
Horton, Edward Everett 86
Hoskins, Bob 118
The Hot Chick (2002) 108
Hough, John 218
Hour of the Wolf (Vargtimmen, 1967) 55
House! (1999) 150
The House in the Square (aka: I'll Never Forget You, 1951) 141–2
Houston, Robert 195
How to Get Ahead in Advertising (1989) 110
Howard, John 131
Howard, Leslie 122, 140
Howard, Robert E. 7, 162–3, 165, 166, 168, 171, 181, 190–1, 192, 193, 195–8, 199, 203, 207, 210, 211, 212, 213, 228, 256, 267
Howard, Ron 80, 116, 265
Howard, Shemp 180
Howard, Trevor 151
Howdy Doody 50
Howe, John 267
Howitt, Peter 144
Hu, Kelly 229, *230*, 231
Hu, King 175
Huddleston, David 100
Hudson, Rock 182
Hughes, Ken 58
Hughes, Terry 152
The Hulk (2003) 231
Human Feelings (1978) 95, 96
Humberstone, H. Bruce 124
The Hunchback of Notre Dame (1996) 225
Hundra (1983) 204, 216
Hunter, Holly 90
Hunter, Kim 137, *138*
Hunter, Stephen 233
Hunter, T. Hayes 121
Hunter, Tab 182
Hunters of the Golden Cobra (I cacciatori del cobra d'oro, 1984) 216
Hurley, Elizabeth 93, *94*
Hurst, Brian Desmond 121
Hurt, John 150, 159, 258
Hussein, Muhammad 131
Hussein, Saddam 93
Huston, Angelica 77, 153
Huston, Walter 93
Huxley, Aldous 50
Hyams, Peter 11, 93

"I Dream of Jeannie" (TV series) 114
I Dream of Jeannie: 15 Years Later (1985) 114
I Married a Witch (1942) 146–147, **148**
I Still Dream of Jeannie (1991) 114
Iaccino, James F. 16
Idealism 36
I'll Never Forget You see *The House in the Square*
Illusions 18, 19, 21, 25, 49
Ilya Muromets (aka: The Sword and the Dragon/The Epic Hero and the Beast, 1956) 237–8
Imaginary Friends 100
Imagination 4, 7, 8, 15, 16, 20, 25, 31, 34, 36, 44, 45, 48, 49, 58, 64, 66, 68, 72, 74, 81, 106, 119, 139, 142, 159–60, 253, 254, 256, 263
Immortals and Immortality 11, 16, 67, 84, 89, 90, 96, 109, 111, 134, 160, 164, 166, 192, 226, 239, 244
In the Bogie Man's Cave (La Cuisine de l'ogre, 1908) 21
The Incredibles (2004) 231
India 131, 235
The Indian in the Cupboard (1995) **105**–106
Indiana Jones and the Last Crusade (1989) 218
Indiana Jones and the Temple of Doom (1984) 59, 215–6, **217**, 218, 222
The Infernal Cakewalk (Le Cake-walk infernal, 1903) 22
The Infernal Palace (Le Manoir du Diable, 1890) 19
Ingram, Rex 44, 95
Institute Benjamenta, or This Dream People Call Human Life (1995) 78
Interview with the Vampire (1994) 147
Into the West (1992) 119
Invincible Barbarian (Gunan il guerriero, 1983) 194, 202, 203
Invitation to the Dance (aka: The Magic Lamp, 1954) 188
Ireland, Dan 191
The Iron Crown (La corona di ferro, 1941) 238
Irons, Jeremy 73, 266
Iron Warrior (aka: Echoes of Wizardry, 1987) 211
Isaac, Frank K. 205
Isaacs, Jason 79
It Came from Beneath the Sea (1955) 182
It Grows on Trees (1952) 102
It Had to Be You (1947) 100
Italy 20, 21, 25, 38, 56, 61, 96, 131, 162, 168–71, 176–7, 178, 182, 183, 189, 191, 194, 197,

200–3, 204, 205, 206, 208, 211, 216, 224, 225, 238–9
It's a Wonderful Life (1946) 1, 3, 14, 16, 84, 85, 87, **88**, 98, 121, 123, 128–9, 139, 140
Ivanhoe (1952) 242
Ives, Tony 114
Iwerks, Ub 180

Jabberwocky (1977) 245, 253
Jack and the Beanstalk (1902) 26
Jack and the Beanstalk (1917) 27
Jack Frost (1998) 107
Jack the Giant Killer (1961) 57, 183
Jackman, Hugh 142
Jackson, Mick 103
Jackson, Peter 1, 3, 14, 118, 256, 257–8, 266–7, 269
Jackson, Samuel L. 152
Jacob, Irene 110
Jacobs, Alan 189
Jacobs, W.W. 108
Jaffe, Rona 263
Jaffe, Sam 131
Jakes, John 191
James, Henry 8, 140
James and the Giant Peach (1996) 78
Jane and the Lost City (1987) 218
Jannings, Emil 43, 92
Jarman, Derek 14, 141
Jarrott, Charles 131
Jason and the Argonauts (1963) 57, 97, 239–**40**
Jaws (1975) 228
Jaws: The Revenge (1987) 72
Jayston, Michael 59
Jeanmaire 51
Jefferson Airplane 59
Jeffries, Lionel 59, 126
Jesse James (1939) 231
Jesus Christ 87, 91, 95, 95, 254
La Jetée (The Pier, 1962) 145
Jeunet, Jean-Pierre 9, 24, 79, 80
The Jewel of the Nile (1985) 217
Joe's Apartment (1996) 117
Joffe, Mark 99
John Dough and the Cherub (1910) 27
Johns, Glynis 58, 115, **117**
Johns, W.E. 218
Johnson, Dwayne "The Rock" 229, **230**
Johnson, Julanne **29**, 30
Johnson, Laura 61
Johnson, Van 124
Johnston, Joe 102, 218
Jolie, Angelina 101, 164, 220, **221**
Jones, Dean 103
Jones, Dickie 38
Jones, Freddie 260
Jones, Grace 207, 209
Jones, Griffith 115
Jones, James Earl 12, 73, 128, 189, 197, 261
Jones, Jeffrey 93

Jones, Jennifer 125
Jones, Terry 68, 76, 78, 244, 251
Jones, Trevor 259
Jong, Ate De 100
Jonze, Spike 111
Jordan, Michael 224
Jordan, Neil 63, 64, 65, 127, 147
Jory, Victor 166
Jubilee (1978) 14, 141
Judd, Ashley 76
Jugnot, Gérard 189
Juliet of the Spirits (Giulietta degli spiriti, 1965) 125
Jumanji (1995) 83, 102, 106, 216
Jung, Carl 15–6, 38, 232, 234, 251, 256, 270
Junger, Gil 143
Jupiter's Thunderbolts, or the Home of the Muses (Le Tonnerre de Jupiter, 1903) 21
Juran, Nathan 57, 182, 243
Just Visiting (2001) 143
Justin, John 44

Kachivas, Lou 210
Kadár, Ján 89
Kaminsky, Stuart M. 8, 16
Kamiyama, Sojin 30
Kane, Bob 218
Karloff, Boris 43
Karma 106–7, 154
Kästner, Erich 46
Kate and Leopold (2001) 142
Kaufman, Charlie 111
Kaye, Danny 51, 124
Kaye, Donald 256
Keaton, Michael 107, 126
Keener, Catherine 111
Keighley, William 95
Keitel, Harvey 94
Kellaway, Cecil 147
Keller, Harry 114
Kellerman, Sally 151
Kelly, Gene 188
Kemp, Julian 150
Kemper, Charles 87
Kennedy, George 195
Kent, Charles 242
Kerr, Deborah 213
Kershner, Irvin 192
Keyes, Evelyn 45, **86**
The Kid (2000) 145
Kidman, Nicole 120, 154
Kiersch, Fritz 211
Kierska, Marga 97
Kieślowski, Krzysztof 110
Kilmer, Val 100, 266
Kinetoscope 19
King, Henry 106, 231
King, Stephen 152
King, Martin Luthor 39
King Arthur (2004) 253, 254
King Arthur Was a Gentleman (1942) 242
King Features Syndicate 165
King Kong (1933) 1, 11, 33, 42, 114, 130, 183

King of the Mounties (1942) 213
King of the Rocket Men (1949) 218
King of the Royal Mounted (1940) 165
King Solomon's Mines (1937) 213
King Solomon's Mines (1950) 213
King Solomon's Mines (1985) 216
King Solomon's Treasures (1978) 213
King-Smith, Dick 81
Kirkwood, James 28
A Kiss for Cinderella (1925) 28
Kiss Me Goodbye (1982) 124
Kitaen, Tawny 224
Kleiser, Randal 67
Knight, Felix 33
Knight of the Snows (Le Chevalier des neiges, 1912) 23
Knightley, Keira 226
The Knights of the Round Table (1953) 242
Knox, Teddy 101
Korda, Alexander 44, 45, 46, 47, 48, 73, 121, 260
Koreeda, Hirokazu 136
Korkarlen (aka: Thy Soul Shall Bear Witness!, 1920) 97–8
Koscina, Sylva 168, 173, 223
Kosheverova, Nadezhda 54
Koster, Henry 87, 100, 119
Koteas, Elias 91
Kovack, Nancy 239
Kramer, Eric Allen 211
Kramer, Stanley 52
Kramer, Wayne 150
Kristofferson, Kris 67
Kruek, Kristen 75
Krull (1983) 63, 67, 175, 191, 244, 251, 260, *262*
Kubrick, Stanley 11
Kuleshov, Lev 21
Kull the Conqueror (1997) 192, 228
Kumel, Harry 96
"Kung Fu" (TV series) 179
Kung-fu avengers 179, 180, 197, 216
Kunuk, Zac 252
Kurosawa, Akira 206, 233
Kuttner, Henry 191
Kwan, Teddy Robin 216
Kyo, Machiko 125
L.A. Story (1991) 103
The Laboratory of Mephistopheles (Le Cabinet de Mephistophélès, 1897) 22
Labyrinth (1986) 3, 66, 68, *69*, 70, 71, 72, 174, 259
Ladd, Alan 243
Ladyhawke (1985) 68, 70, 71, 251
LaGallienne, Eva 31
Lahr, Bert 33
Lake, Veronica 146, *148*, 156
Lamb, John 116
Lambert, Christopher 90, *91*

Lamont, Charles 122
La Motte Fouque, Friedrich de 28
Lancaster, Bruce 128
Lancelot and Elaine (1910) 242
Lancelot and Guinevere (1962) 243
Lancelot du Lac (aka: Le Graal, 1974) 244
Lanchester, Elsa 147
The Land of Oz (1910) 27
The Land That Time Forgot (1974) 11, 214
Landon, Laurene 204, 209, 216
Landor, Rosalyn 126
Lane, Allan 165
Lang, Fritz 42, 43, 97, 106, 235–6, 238
Lang, Walter 169
Langella, Frank 210
Lansbury, Angela 64, 153
Lanyon, Anabelle 67
Lao Tzu 248
Lara Croft: Tomb Raider (2001) 220
Lara Croft: Tomb Raider — The Cradle of Life (2003) 101, 220, *221*
La Rocque, Rod 166
La Rue, Eva 212
The Last Action Hero (1993) 98, 118, 134–6
The Last Adventure of Galaor (Ultime avventure di Galaor, 1921) 169
The Last Days of Pompeii (Gli ultimi giorni di Pompei, 1908) 169
The Last Unicorn (1982) 261, 265
The Last Wave (1977) 4, 133, 152
Last Year at Marienbad (L'Année dernière à Marienbad, 1961) 12, 145
Laurel and Hardy 28, 32–3, 34, 57, 169
Laurie, Hugh 80
Law, John Philip 184, *185*
Lawless, Lucy 209, 226, *227*
Lawn Dogs (1997) 77, 79
Lawrence, D.H. 36
Lawrence, Florence 23
Lawrence, Martin 143
Lawson, Priscilla 165
La Zar, John 212
Lazenby, George 165
Leake, Cynthia 200
Lean, David 48, 124, 233
Le Bihan, Samuel 228
Lee, Alan 267
Lee, Ang 231
Lee, Brandon 98, 99, 102
Lee, Bruce 126, 179
Lee, Christopher 142, 177, 178, 179, 268
Lee, Gypsy Rose 182

Lee, Tanith 40
Lefler, Doug 223
Legend (1985) 57, 67, 68
Legend of Bagger Vance (2001) 89
Legend of the Golden Pearl (Wai Si-Lei Chuen Kei, 1985) 216
Leggatt, Alison 59
Le Guin, Ursula 7, 265
Leiber, Fritz 162, 191
Leisen, Mitchell 98
Leni, Paul 43
Leon (aka: The Professional, 1994) 79
Leone, Sergio 178, 193
Leoni, Téa 144
Leonviola, Antonio 173, 175, 176, 200
Leprechaun (1993) 119
Leprechauns 13, 119
Leprince de Beaumont, Madame Jeanne-Marie 26, 47
Lerner and Loewe 243
Leslie, Joan 140
Let It Be (1970) 256
Let My Puppets Come (1977) 118
Levant, Brian 80
Levine, Joseph E. 168, 169, 177, 222
Levinson, Barry 75
Levy, Eugene 116
Lewin, Albert 125
Lewis, C.S. 2, 158, 241
Lewis, Geoffrey 114
Lewis, Reg 178
L'Herbier, Marcel 47
Liar Liar (1996) 110
Liddell, Alice 49
Life 4, 12, 15, 26, 39, 57, 70, 97, 98, 105, 106, 107, 108, 122, 131, 136, 138, 139, 146, 234, 263, 270, 271
A Life Less Ordinary (1997) 90
Light Years Away (Les Années lumière, 1981) 151
Like Father and Son (1987) 112
Like Mike (2002) 102
Like Water for Chocolate (Como agua para chocolate, 1991) 160
Lilith und Ly (1919) 97
Lilliom (1930) 106, 121
Lilliom (1935) 106, 121, 136, 137
Limbo 86, 136
Lin, Brigitte 226
Lindo, Delroy 90
The Lion King (1994) 39, 73–4, 81
Liotta, Ray 128
Litefoot 105
Little Giant (1946) 169
The Little Humpback Horse (Koniok Gorbunok, 1942) 53
Little Lady Eileen (1916) 119
The Little Mermaid (1989) 41, 72
Little Monsters (1989) 133

Little Mook (Die Geschicte vom kleinen Muck, 1953) 54
Little Nicky (2000) 94
Little Red Riding Hood 33, 55, 63–4, 65, 76
Little Red Riding Hood (Le Petit Chaperon rouge, 1901) 20
Little Red Riding Hood (1918) 28
Little Tom Thumb (Le Petit Poucet, 1903) 26
Livesey, Roger 112, 137
Lloyd, Christopher 118
Lloyd, Frank 140
Loch Ness (1994) 114
Lofting, Hugh 58
Logan, Joshua 244
Loggia, Robert 113
Logic 15, 32, 46, 68, 71, 81, 83, 142, 153, 178, 220
Lohan, Lindsay 112
Lommel, Uli 216
Lone, John 219
The Lone Ranger (1938) 165
Looney Tunes: Back in Action (2003) 101, 118
Lopez, Gerry 197
Lopez, Sylvia 173
Lord, Peter 76
The Lord of the Rings (1978) 200, 257–8, **259**, 260, 268
The Lord of the Rings (2001–3) 1, 3, 4, 11, 14, 15, 37, 43, 101, 134, 142, 159, 163, 193, 197, 206, 219, 236, 245, 249, 253, 266–71
The Lord of the Rings: The Fellowship of the Ring (2001) 237, 266, 267–8
The Lord of the Rings: The Return of the King (2003) 1, 233, 262, 269–70, 271
The Lord of the Rings: The Two Towers (2002) 268–**269**, 270
Losey, Joseph 151
Lost Horizon (1937) 13, 130–1, 135, 136
Lost Horizon (1973) 131
Lost films 19, 27, 256
The Lost Kingdom (Antinea, l'amante della città sepolta, 1961) 131
The Lost Shadow (Der verlorene Schatten, 1921) 43
The Lost World (1925) 114
The Lost World of Sinbad see *Daitozoku*
Lost worlds 13, 84, 130–9, 163, 187, 213, 234
Love and Death (1975) 98
The Love Bug (1968) 103
The Loves of Hercules (Gli amori di Ercole, 1960/aka: Hercules vs. The Hydra) 175
Lubin, Arthur 56, 102, 116
Lubin, Sigmund 26
Lubitsch, Ernst 93
Lucas, George 11, 63, 82, 192,
203, 213, 214, 218, 248, 256, 258, 265–6
Lucifer *see* The Devil
Luck of the Irish (1948) 119
Lucky Ghost (1942) 121
Luhrmann, Baz 9
Lugosi, Bela 165
Lumet, Sidney 62
Lumière Brothers 17, 18, 24
Lumley, Joanna 243
Lundgren, Dolph 210
Lunghi, Cherie 249
Lynch, David 110
Lynch, Richard 199, 211
Lyonne, Natasha 78

MacArthur, Charles 121
MacCorkindale, Simon 199
MacDonald, J. Farrell 27
MacGinnis, Niall **240**
Maciste (1915) 169
Maciste on Holiday (Maciste in vacanza, 1921) 169
Maciste the Athlete (Maciste atleta, 1918) 169
MacNicol, Peter 249
Macy, William H. 135, 150
Mad About Men (1954) 115
Madden, Harry 109
Maddin, Guy 78
Maddona 218
Made in Heaven (1987) 138
Madigan, Amy **129**
Madison, Guy 200
Maeterlinck, Maurice 28
Maggi, Luigi 169
Magic 10, 11, 12, 13, 19, 20, 36, 43, 47, 48, 52, 58, 61, 72, 75, 83, 84, 85, 97, 100, 102, 103, 106, 116, 130, 132, 134, 146, 147, 149, 154, 156, 159, 160, 163, 164, 174, 175, 179, 214, 232, 234, 236, 251, 253, 257, 262
The Magic Carpet (1951) 101, 182
The Magic Cloak of Oz (1914) 27
The Magic Lamp see *Invitation to the Dance*
Magic realism 5, 8, 84, 145, 151, 160, 241
The Magic Sword (aka: The Sorcerer's Curse, 1962) 243
The Magic Sword: or, A Medieval Mystery (1901) 234
The Magic Sword: Quest for Camelot (1998) 252
The Magic Voyage of Sinbad see *Sadko*
Magritte, René 75
Maguire, Tobey 135
Maharis, George 199
Majors, Lee 126
Mako 207
Malatesta, Guido 174, 178
Malcolm, Robert 179, 184
Malika Salomi (1953) 131
Malkovich, John 111
Malleson, Miles 44
Mallick, Anne-Marie 59, **60**
Maloney, Michael 128
Malory, Sir Thomas 232, 241, 242, 243, 245, 248
Malpertuis (1971) 96
The Man in the Iron Mask (1939) 180
The Man in the Mirror (1936) 110
Man or Mouse (1948) 169
The Man Who Could Work Miracles (1936) 144, 148–9
The Man Who Haunted Himself (1970) 110
The Man Who Sued God (2001) 99
The Man with the Rubber Head (L'Homme à la tête de caoutchouc, 1902) 19, 22
Mancori, Alvaro 178
Mangano, Silvana 238
Mangold, James 142
Manhattan (1979) 81
Manhunt of Mystery Island (1945) 215
Mankiewicz, Joseph L. 32, 125
Mann, Stanley 207
Mannequin (1987) 103, **104**
Mannequin on the Move (1991) 103
Manners, David 169
Mansfield, Jayne 175
Marais, Jean **47**, 61, 137
Marcel, Terry 133, 192, 193, 218, 222
March, Fredric 98, 122, 147, 148
Margheriti, Antonio 178, 182, 204, 216
Marguerite de la nuit (1955) 93
Marin, Cheech 74
Marin, Edwin L. 121
The Mark of Zorro (1940) 165
Marker, Chris 145
Marlowe, Christopher 92, 93, 102
Marquez, Gabriel Garcia 7, 84
Marquis (1989) 118
Mars Attacks! (1996) 11
Marsh, Carol 49
Marsh, Jean 64, 65, 266
Marshall, Ken 260
Marshall, Penny 89, 112, 113
Martin, Steve 103, 110
Marton, Andrew 213
"The Marvellous" 9, 10
Marvin, Michael 114
Marxism 77
Mary Poppins (1964) 1, 57–8, 78, 89
Masina, Giulietta 125
The Mask (1994) 102, 111
Mask of the Demon (La maschera del demonio, 1960) 177

Mason, James 107, 125
Massaccesi, Aristide 201, 202, 211
Massacre in the Black Forest (Il massacro della foresta nera, 1967/aka: Arminus the Terrible) 201
Massey, Raymond 137
Masters of the Universe (1987) 206, 210
Mate, Rudolph 125
Matheson, Tim 188
Mathews, Kerwin 57, 131, 182, 184, 186
Matilda (1996) 77–8, 79, 156
Mattei, Bruno 205
A Matter of Life and Death (aka: Stairway to Heaven, 1947) 48, 136–7, *138*
Matthews, Paul 112
Mattsen, Arne 98
Maxie (1985) 110
Mazes and Monsters (1982) 263
Mayall, Rick 100, 143
Mayo, Archie 93
McAdams, Rachel 108
McCallum, John 115
McCarthy, Andrew *104*
McCarthy, Neil 246
McCloud, Norman Z. 31, 122
McClure, Doug 192, 214
McDonald, Kelly 150
McDonald, Peter 265
McDonough, Glen 32
McDowall, Roddy 119
McDowell, Andie 146
McGregor, Ewan 90, 160
McGrory, Matthew 160
McGuigan, Paul 95–6
McKellen, Ian 98, 136, 267
McKenzie-Litten, Peter 128
McLean, Don 261
McLellan, Zoe 266
McLoughlin, Tom 89
McShane, Ian 119
McTiernan, John 134, 135, 253
The Medallion (2003) 101
Medoway, Gary 89
Medusa Against the Son of Hercules (Perseo l'invincibile, 1963) 174, 238
Meet Joe Black (1998) 99
Meet the Feebles (1989) 118
Mehrez, Alan 189
Meins, Gus 32
Méliès, Georges 1, 18–24, 25, 26, 27, 28, 30, 31, 32, 35, 41, 43, 57, 92, 130, 142, 237, 267
The Melomaniac (Le Mélomane, 1903) 19
Memory 17, 45, 55, 100
Mendes, Lothar 148
Menjou, Adolphe 92
Menzies, William Cameron 30, 32, 44
Mephistopheles *see* The Devil
Le Mépris (Contempt, 1963) 238

Mercer, Jack 180
Meredith, Judi 57
Merlin 15, 99, 146, 189, 202, 243, 244, 248–9, 251
Merlin: The Return (2000) 142–3
The Mermaids of Tiburon (1962) 116
Merpeople 21, 28, 30, 42, 50, 72, 84, 115–6, *117*
The Merry Frolics of Satan (Les 400 Farces du diable, 1906) 22
Mészaro, Márta 64
Metropolis (1926) 43, 235
Meurisse, Paul 8
Meyrink, Gustav 42
Mezzanotte, Luigi 202, 203
MGM 33, 34, 37, 183, 242
Michael (1996) 90
The Middle East 28, 73, 89, 114, 180, 184, 190, 193, 197, 229
Middleton, Charles 165
Middleton, Jonas 61
Midler, Bette 153
Midnight Cowboy (1969) 257
A Midsummer Night's Dream (1935) 33, 44
Miéville, China 7
Mifune, Toshiro 171, 183
Mighty Aphrodite (1995) 100
The Milagro Beanfield War (1987) 89
Milius, John 191, 194, 196, 197–8, 199, 203, 206, 207, 231, 267
Milland, Ray 93
Miller, Garry 126
Miller, Gavin 70
Miller, George 81, 93, 154
Miller, George, II 265
Miller, Jonathan 59, 60, 76
Miller, Penelope Ann 67, 219
Miller, Troy 107
Milne, A.A. 78, 105
Milton, Ernest 49
Milton, Robert 136
The Mines of Kilimanjaro (1985) 216
Minghella, Anthony 128
Minkoff, Rob 80
Minnelli, Vincente 89, 109, 131
Mioni, Fabrizio 168, 178
Miracle in Milan (1951) 89
Miracle in the Rain (1956) 125
The Miracle of Life (1915) 121
Miracle on 34th Street (1947) 99, 100
Miracle on 34th Street (1994) 99
Miracles and the miraculous 10, 11, 15, 19, 26, 85, 251
Miramax 66, 267
Miranda (1948) 115, 116, *117*
Mirren, Helen 249
Mischievous Puck (1911) 119
Mr. Destiny (1990) 144
"Mister Ed" (TV series) 117

Mr. Griggs Returns see *The Cockeyed Miracle*
Mr. Peabody and the Mermaid (1948) 115, 116
Misumi, Kenji 195
Mitchell, Gordon 173, 175, 238
Mittet, Judith 79
Mizoguchi, Kenji 125
Modine, Matthew 108
Moeller, Ralf 228
The Mole Men Against the Son of Hercules (Maciste, l'uomo più forte del mondo, 1961/aka: Maciste, Strongest Man in the World) 173, 176
Molnár, Ferenc 106
Monaghan, Dominic 268
Monkey Business (1952) 112
Monogram 166
"Monomyth" 234
The Monster Club (1980) 192
Monsters, Inc. (2001) 81, 134
Montana, Joe 224
Montana Mike see *Heaven Only Knows*
Montand, Yves 93
Monte, Marlo 110
Montez, Maria 131, 180
Montgomery, Elizabeth 147
Montgomery, George 213
Montgomery, Robert 85, *86*, 107, 123
Monty Python 218, 236, 245, 266
Monty Python and the Holy Grail (1974) 241, 244–5, 248, 251
Monty Python's The Meaning of Life (1983) 98
Moon, Elizabeth 203
Moorcock, Michael 7, 162, 191, 194
Moore, Catherine L. 191, 203
Moore, Demi 127, 152
Moore, Dudley 93, 95
Moore, Richard 179
Moore, Roger 110
Morality 27, 36, 38, 63, 81, 93, 106, 121, 159, 165, 171, 198, 210, 225, 241, 255
Moreau, Jeanne 77
Morgan, Frank 34, 124
Mori, Masayuki 125
Morley, Robert 125
Morricone, Ennio 193
Morris, Kirk 176, 178
Morris, Mary *45*
Morris, William 254
Morrisette, Alanis 96
Mortal Kombat (1995) 132
Mortensen, Viggo 76, 92, 159, 268
Moscow, David *113*
Mother Goose 32, 46, 55
Moulin Rouge (2001) 9, 145
Mowbray, Alan 93
Moyer, Stephen 243
Moyers, Bill 232

Ms. 45 (1980) 207
Der müde Tod (The Weary
  Death, 1921) 42, 43, 46, 97
Mulcahy, Russell 90, 91, 218
Mulholland Drive (2001) 110
Muller, Harrison 203
The Mummy (1999) 218, 219,
  220
The Mummy Returns (2001)
  187, 219–20, 229, 265
Münchhausen (1943) 46, 55, 72
Muni, Paul 106
Munro, Caroline 184
The Muppet Christmas Carol
  (1992) 126
The Muppet Movie (1979) 118
The Muppets Take Manhattan
  (1984) 118
Murnau, F.W. 43, 92
Murphy, Eddie 81, 133, 152
Murray, Bill 126, 145
Murray, Stephen 49
Musicals 2, 27, 32, 33, **34**, 37,
  40, 49, 50, 51, 52, 56, 57–9,
  61, 62–3, 72–3, 74–5, 86, 87,
  106, 117, 126, 131, 141, 180, 243
Mussolini, Benito 170, 171, 238
My Fair Lady (1964) 1, 40, 103
Myers, Mike 80, 81
The Mysterious Island (Ulysse et
  le géant Polyphème, 1905) 21
Myth 1, 15, 16, 21, 67, 76, 84, 97,
  99, 101, 103, 164, 174, 175, 178,
  182, 183, 204, 206, 224, 225,
  232–3, 234, 235, 236, 237,
  238, 239, 240, 241, 245, 246,
  248, 251, 253, 254, 255, 256,
  265, 270
"Mythologicals" 235
"Mythopoeic Imagination" 15, 16

Naismith, Laurence 126, 244
Nammour, Edouard 134
Narrative 12, 15, 20, 21, 23, 26,
  31, 36, 43, 46, 56, 63, 64, 71,
  77, 83, 135, 139, 151, 156, 157,
  170, 184, 198, 199, 206, 220,
  226, 234, 265, 266
Nationalism 52, 63, 235–6, 238,
  252
Nature 9, 10, 171, 233, 252, 258,
  268
*The Navigator: A Medieval
  Odyssey* (1988) 142, 254, 265
Nazis 23, 41, 44, 46, 214, 215,
  235–6, 257, 268
NBC 222
Neale, Steve 8, 10
Neame, Ronald 126
Neeson, Liam 249
Neilan, Marshall 101
"The Nekyia" (aka: "The Night-
  Sea Journey") 15–6, 38, 234
Nelson, Bob 204
Nelson, Gary 216
Neoclassic fantasy 254, 255,
  256, 258, 265

"Neomythologism" 176, 178
Neopulp adventurers 212–22
Neptune's Daughter (1914) 115
Nero, Franco 244
Nervo, Jimmy 101
Nesher, Avi 209
Neumann, Kurt 213
The Neverending Story (Die
  unendliche Geschichte, 1984)
  133, 236, 263–**264**, 265
*The Neverending Story II: The
  Next Chapter* (1989) 265
Neverending Story III (1994) 265
Neville, John 71
"The New Adventures of Robin
  Hood" (TV series) 222, 223
The New Gulliver (Novyi Gul-
  liver, 1935) 54
New Horizons 205
New Line Cinema 267
New World 195
Newell, Mike 119
Newley, Anthony 112
Newton-John, Olivia 95
The Next Voice You Hear ...
  (1950) 95
Die Nibelungen (1924) 12, 42,
  43, 165, 235–7, 238, 240, 248;
  Kriemhild's revenge 236–7,
  249, 253; Siegfried 236
Nichetti, Maurizio 111
Nicholls, George, Jr. 121
Nicholls, Peter 3, 10, 187
Nicholson, Jack 93, 94, 153, **154**
Nicolella, John 228
Nielsen, Brigitte 207
Nietzsche, Friedrich 198
The Night Life of the Gods (1935)
  96
Night of the Living Dead (1968)
  12
"The Night-Sea Journey" *see*
  "The Nekyia"
The Nightmare Before Christmas
  see *Tim Burton's The Night-
  mare Before Christmas*
A Nightmare on Elm Street
  (1985) 12
Nimoy, Leonard 189
9/11 149, 269
Niven, David 87, 137, **138**
Nixon, Richard M. 130
No Retreat, No Surrender (1985)
  126
Noble, John 270
Nonguet, Lucien 26
Noonan, Chris 81
Norman, John 210–1
North (1994) 79
Norton, Andre 199, 211
Norton, Bill L. 223, 224
Norton, Edward 100
Norton, Mary 133
Norton, Randy 200, 201
Nosferatu (1922) 43
Novak, Kim 147
Novalis 27

Oakie, Jack 123
O'Brien, Austin 135
Occhipinti, Andrea 203
O'Connell, Jerry 117
O'Connor, Donald 116
O'Connor, Renee 223, 226
Odd Man Out (1947) 48
O'Farrell, Peter 193
O'Ferrall, George 32
Offenbach, Jacques 42, 49
Offending Angels (2000) 90
Oh, God! (1977) 95
Oh, God! Book Two (1980) 95
Oh, God! You Devil (1984) 95
Oh, Heavenly Dog (1980) 108
O'Hara, Maureen 181
O'Hara, Paige 72
O'Hara's Wife (1982) 126
O'Keeffe, Miles 201, 202, 211,
  245
Oldman, Gary 157
Oliver, Barret 263
Olivera, Hector 205, 209, 262
Oliveros, Ramiro 204
Olivier, Laurence 246
Olkewicz, Walter 262
The Omen (1976) 92
On Borrowed Time (1939) 98
On Her Majesty's Secret Service
  (1969) 165
"Once Upon a Time" 31, 139,
  265
The One-Armed Swordsman
  (Dubei dao, 1966) 175
One Magic Christmas (1985) 99
The One-Man Band (L'Homme
  Orchestre, 1900) 19
One Million Years B.C. (1966)
  11, 202
One Touch of Venus (1948) 96,
  103, 216
Opera 18, 21, 32, 42, 49, 92, 232
Oppenheimer, Alan 264
Orfei, Moira 176, 209
Orlando (1992) 84, 90, 109
Orphée (1950) 47, 137
Orr, James 144
Osment, Haley Joel 120, 156
Ostrum, Peter 62
Oswald, Richard 42
The Others (2001) 120–1
Otherworld (2002) 252
Ottaviano, Matteo 204, 216
Otto, Henry 28
Otto, Miranda 270
Outland (1981) 11
Outlaw of Gor (1987) 211
Outward Bound (1930) 136
Owen, Clive 254
Owen, Reginald 121
Owusu, Kwesi 151
Oz, Frank 105, 261
Oz Film Manufacturing Com-
  pany 27

Pabst, G.W. 130
Pagano, Bartolomeo 169

The Pagemaster (1994) 134
Pal, George 54, 56, 78, 150
The Palace of the Arabian Nights (Le Palais des mille et une nuits, 1905) 21
Palance, Jack 193, 211
Palin, Michael 76, 244, 245
Palmara, Mimmo 173
Palminteri, Chazz 138
Paltrow, Gwyneth 144
Pandora and the Flying Dutchman (1950) 125
Paramount Pictures 28, 30, 31
Park, Nick 76
Park, Reg 173, 176, 177, 178, 224
Parker, Albert 140
Parker, Jean *123*
Parker, Trey 99
Parsifal (1904) 242
Parsifal (1982) 245
Pasolini, Pier Paolo 56, 61, 63
Pasquin, John 110
The Passion of Darkly Noon (1995) 76, 79
The Passion of the Christ (2004) 3
Pastrone, Giovanni 169
The Patchwork Girl of Oz (1914) 27
Pathé, Charles 23
Pathé Frères 23
Patinkin, Mandy 70
Patterson, Sarah 63
Paul, David 211
Paul, Peter 211
Paul, Robert W. 18, 102
Payne, Bruce 266
Peacocke, Captain Leslie T. 115
Peake, Mervyn 7, 41, 254
Pearl, Harold 39
Peau d'âne (The Magic Donkey, 1970) 61
Pee-wee's Big Adventure (1985) 66–7
Peggy Sue Got Married (1986) 144, 145
The People That Time Forgot (1977) 214
Peploe, Clare 160
Peplum 169–79, 182, 183, 191, 194, 200, 204, 205, 206, 208, 209, 210, 211, 213, 222, 223, 224, 225, 229, 238
Perception 1, 3, 8–9, 48, 49, 55, 72, 76, 99, 120, 139, 152, 161, 233, 265
Perceptual fantasy 9, 49, 120, 145
Perceval le gallois (1978) 245
Perils of Nyoka (1942) 215
Perkins, Elizabeth 113
Perlman, Rhea 77
Perlman, Ron 79
Perrault, Charles 20, 26, 28, 36, 40, 51, 52, 61, 63–4, 80
Persona (1966) 110
Die Pest in Florenz (The Plague in Florence, 1919) 97

Peter Ibbetson (1935) 134
Peter Pan 66, 134, 164, 175, 263
Peter Pan (1924) 28
Peter Pan (1953) 50–1
Peter Pan (2003) 79, 116
Petersen, Wolfgang 253, 263, 264
Pete's Dragon (1977) 118, 249, 253
Pett, Norman 218
Pfeiffer, Michelle 70, 94, 153, *154*, 190
Phalke, D.G. 235
Phantasm (1978) 199
The Phantom (1996) 218, 219
The Phantom Creeps (1939) 165
The Phantom Menace (1999) 11, 266
The Phantom of Liberty (Le Fantôme de la liberté, 1974) 14
Phillips, Augustus 101
Phoenix, River 218
Phoenix the Warrior (1988) 209
Photographing Fairies (1997) 120
Pichel, Irving 115, 121, 123
Pickford, Mary 23, 28, 31, 119
Picnic at Hanging Rock (1975) 132–3
The Pied Piper (1907) 26
The Pied Piper (1971) 61
The Pied Piper of Hamlyn (Der Rottenfänger von Hameln, 1918) 43
Pigozzi, Luciano 204
Pinocchio (1940) 37–8, 40, 41, 44, 51, 55, 58
Pintoff, Ernest 95
Pirandello, Luigi 135
Pirates of the Caribbean: The Curse of the Black Pearl (2003) 225–6
Pitt, Brad 99, 100, 190, 253
Pixar 81, 82, 106, 134, 231
Platts-Mills, Barney 245
Play It Again, Sam (1972) 100
Pleasantville (1998) 135
Pocahontas (1995) 225
Podesta, Rossana 200
Poe, Edgar Allan 42, 97, 137, 189
Poire, Jean-Marie 143
Polanski, Roman 9, 12
Poledouris, Basil 197, 207
Pollard, "Bud" 31
Pollard, Harry 121
Pope, Alexander 254
Popeye (1980) 80
Popeye the Sailor Meets Sindbad the Sailor (1936) 180
Pornography 7, 23, 61, 118, 209
Porter, Cole 215
Porter, Edwin S. 26, 31, 119, 130, 242
Portman, Natalie 79
Portrait of Jennie (1948) 125
Postlethwaite, Pete 108

Poston, Tom 150
Potente, Franka 145
Potocki, Jan 55
Potter, Sally 90
Potterton, Gerald 194
Powell, Dick 108, 140
Powell, Michael 44, 48–9, 50, 136, 137, 138, 180, 187, 189, 241, 265
Powell, William 115
Power, Taryn 186, *188*
Power, Tyrone 141, 165
Practical Magic (1998) 153, 154–6
Prasad, Udayan 90
Pratchett, Terry 158
The Preacher's Wife (1996) 89
Predator (1987) 200
Prelude to a Kiss (1992) 109
Presley, Elvis 100
Pressburger, Emeric 48–9, 138, 180, 187, 189
Pressman, Edward R. 197
Pretty in Pink (1986) 77
Pretty Woman (1990) 40, 77
Price, Vincent 74, *75*, 181
Prince Valiant (1954) 243
Prince Valiant (1997) 243
The Princess Bride (1987) 70, 71, 72, 77
The Princess' Necklace (1917) 235
A Princess of Baghdad (1913) 28
Principal, Victoria 110
Pringle, David 3
The Prisoner of Zenda (1937) 180
Prisoners of the Lost Universe (1983) 133
Prometheus (1998) 96–7
Propaganda 41, 44, 46, 54, 93, 114, 137, 146, 235, 257
The Prophecy (1995) 91
Prosperi, Franco 194, 200, 201, 202, 203
Proyas, Alex 98
Pryce, Jonathan 71, 79, 150
Psychosis 9, 12, 66, 76, 78, 100, 263
Ptushko, Aleksandr 54, 112, 183, 237–8
Pudovkin, V.I. 15, 21
Pullman, Bill 128
Pullman, Philip 4, 7, 241
Punch and Judy (Rakvičká, 1966) 102
Purdom, Edmund 202
The Purple Rose of Cairo (1985) 134–6
Purvis, Jack *143*
Pyun, Albert 199

Quaid, Dennis 253, 267
Qualen, John 180
Quan, Ke Huy 215
Queen of the Sea (1918) 28, 115

Questel, Mae 180
Quest for Fire (La Guerre du feu, 1981) 3, 202, 203
Quest for the Mighty Sword (aka: Ator III: The Hobgoblin/The Lord of Akili, 1989) 211
Quests 15, 16, 35, 65, 87, 101, 164, 165, 175, 239
Quine, Richard 147
Quinn, Anthony 223
Quo Vadis? (1913) 169
Quo Vadis (1951) 169

Race and racism 39–40, 73, 86, 95, 107, 121, 127, 143, 152, 236, 255
Radar Men from the Moon (1952) 218
Radcliffe, Daniel 156, *158*, 159
Radvanyi, Geza von 89
Raiders of the Lost Ark (1981) 202, 213, *214*–5, 218, 219
Raimi, Sam 143
The Rain People (1969) 257
Rains, Claude 85, 90, 93, 107
Raja Harischandra (1912) 235
Rajan, Andrew 90
Rakoff, Alvin 213
Rambo: First Blood, Part II (1985) 200
Ramis, Harold 93, 94, 145
Randall, Tony 114, 150
Rankin, Arthur, Jr. 260–1
Rappaport, David *143*
Rat (2000) 108
Rathbone, Basil 164, 243
Rationalisation 9, 10, 11, 12, 63, 66, 84, 134
Rationality 4, 10, 11, 12, 13, 14, 31, 35, 68, 77, 87, 100, 118, 163, 166, 229
Ratoff, Gregory 114
Ratner, Brett 144
Raymond, Alex 165
Realism 8, 13, 14, 23, 30, 43, 48, 52, 70, 71, 77, 83, 84, 101, 119, 151, 163
Reality 3, 4, 8, 9, 10, 11, 13, 15, 19, 32, 35, 41, 43, 46, 48, 49, 57, 63, 65, 71, 72, 76, 82, 83, 85, 89, 118, 120, 128, 132, 146, 161, 163, 175, 213, 233, 238, 253, 254, 263
Reason 4, 9, 11, 46, 71, 77, 79, 229
Reaves, Michael 263
The Red Shoes (1948) 48–9, 51, 52, 55
Red Sonja (1985) 192, 206, 207, 209, 211, 220
Redford, Robert 89
Redgrave, Corin 125, 148
Redgrave, Michael 59
Redgrave, Vanessa 244
Reed, Barbara 166
Reed, Carol 48
Reed, Oliver 211

Reeves, George 242
Reeves, Keanu 98
Reeves, Steve 168, *172*, 173, *174*, 179, 190, 200, 223
Regehr, Duncan 262
Regnoli, Piero 178
Reincarnation 85, 90, 106–7, 108, 109, 125, 130, 145
Reiner, Carl 110
Reiner, Rob 70, 79
Reinhardt, Max 33, 42, 44
Reiniger, Lotte 43, 44, 238
Reinl, Harold 238
Reis, Irving 136
Religion 4, 26, 38, 84, 85, 90, 99, 145, 146, 229, 232, 233, 234, 235, 248, 251, 256
Religious adaptations 3, 23, 95, 235
The Remarkable Andrew (1942) 122–3
René, Norman 109
Rénier, Jérémie 228
Reno, Jean 79, 143
Reo, Don 262
Repeat Performance (1947) 140, 144
Republic 166, 218, 231
Repulsion (1965) 9
Resnais, Alain 145
Restivo, Mario 169
Rettig, Tommy 52, *53*
The Return of Peter Grimm (1926) 121
The Return of Peter Grimm (1935) 121
Return of the Jedi (1983) 251, 260
Return of the King (1980) 261
Return to Oz (1985) 64–6, 67, 71, 72, 154, 263
Reubens, Paul 66
Revenge of the Stolen Stars (1985) 216
Reyes, Ernie, Jr. 209
Reynolds, Debbie 109
Reynolds, Kevin 252
Rhys-Davies, John 189, 218, 268
Ricci, Christina 128
Ricci, Teodoro 201, 202
Richards, Jeffrey 181, 242
Richardson, John *132*
Richardson, Miranda 75
Richardson, Ralph 96, 149, 249
Richey, Ruth 42
Richman, Charles 141
Richmond, Kane 166
Richter, Hans 24
Richter, Paul 235
Rickman, Alan 128, 157
Ricks, Evan 189
Ridley, Philip 76
Rip's Dream (La Légende de Rip van Winkle, 1905) 21
Ritchie, Michael 133
Rites of passage 35, 40, 64, 74, 106, 113, 197

Rivero, Jorge 203
RKO 93, 130, 180
Roach, Hal 93, 109, 122
Robbins, Matthew 249
Robbins, Tim 251
Roberts, Julia 40
Roberts, Tanya 199
Robertson, Dale 181
Robertson, Harry 193
Robin Hood: Prince of Thieves (1991) 252
Robinson, Bruce 110
Robinson, David 18
Robinson, Phil Alden 128, 129
Robison, Arthur 42
Robson, Flora 59
Rock, Chris 91, 107, 152
The Rocketeer (1991) 218
Rockwell, Sam 77
Rocky (1976) 224
Roeg, Nicolas 153
Roëves, Maurice 96
Rogell, Albert S. 87
Rogers, Charles 32
Rogers, Ginger 100, 112
Rogers, Jean 165
Rogers, Roy 242
Rogers, Will 141
Rohmer, Eric 245
Role-playing games 198, 255, 256, 262–3, 266; *see also* Dungeons and Dragons
Romancing the Stone (1984) 217
Romano, Maria 203
Romero, George A. 12, 201
Rosemary's Baby (1968) 12, 92
Rosen, Martin 258
Rosenman, Leonard 257
Ross, Diana 63
Ross, Gary 134
Ross, Tiny *143*
Rossellini, Roberto 169
Rou, Aleksandr 52
Rough Magic (1995) 160
Rounseville, Robert 49
Rowland, Roy 52, 53
Rowling, J.K. 156
Rudolph, Alan 138
Ruehl, Mercedes 112
Ruffo, Leonora 177
Rule, Janice 147
Runacre, Jenny 141
Rush, Geoffrey 226
Rushdie, Salman 8, 84
Rushton, Jared 112
Russell, Chuck 102, 229, 230, 231
Russell, Kurt 133
Russia 15, 52–4, 183, 237–8
Rutherford, Margaret 124
Ryan, Meg 89, 109, 142
Ryan, Thomas Jay 95
Ryder, Winona 74
Rye, Stellen 42

Sabatini, Rafael 181
Sabu 44, 45, 180

Sadko (aka: The Magic Voyage of Sinbad, 1952) 183, 237, 239
Sadler, William 98
Sadoul, Georges 23
Saetta Against Sherlock Holmes (Saetta più forte di Sherlock Holmes, 1922) 169
Salten, Felix 39
Salvi, Emimmo 96, 238
Sampo (aka: The Day the Earth Froze, 1958) 237
Samson (Sansone, 1917) 169
Samson in King Solomon's Mines (Maciste nelle miniere de re Salomone, 1964) 178, 211
Sander, Otto 89, 94
Sandford, "Tiny" 169
Sandler, Adam 94
Sandor, Steve 200
Sant Tukaram (1936) 235
Santa and the Ice Cream Bunny (1972) 99
Santa Claus 74, 99–100, 110, 126, 134
Santa Claus (1959) 99
Santa Claus Conquers the Martians (1964) 99
Santa Claus: The Movie (1985) 78, 99–100, 113
The Santa Clause (1994) 110
The Santa Clause 2 (2002) 119
Santa vs. Jesus (1995) 99
Santa Visits the Land of Mother Goose (1967) 99
Sara, Mia 67
The Saragossa Manuscript (Rekopis znaleziony w Saragossie, 1964) 55, 63
Sarandon, Chris 70, 74
Sarandon, Susan 153, *154*
Sergeant, Dick 147
Satan *see* The Devil
Satan in Prison (Satan en prison, 1907) 22
Saunders, Norman 191
Savage, Fred 70
Sawalha, Julia 78
Sayles, John 132
Scardino, Hal *105*
Scarfiotti, Ferdinando 75
Schertzinger, Victor 121
Schiller, Johann Christoph Friedrich von 15
Schlettow, Hans Adalbert 235
Schneer, Charles H. 45, 182, 184, 185, 186, 187, 239, 246
Schneider, Rob 108
Scholes, Michael 258
Schön, Margarethe 235
School Spirit (1985) 126
Schultz, John 102
Schwartz, Yevgeni 54
Schwarzenegger, Arnold 96, 135, 136, 163, 194, *196*, 197, 200, 206, 207, *208*, 209, 228
Science 10, 11, 14, 16, 17, 26, 79, 111, 130, 133, 134, 135, 143, 163, 166, 220, 222, 232, 248
Science-fantasy 11, 14, 75, 79, 117, 126, 175, 194, 204–5, 206, 210, 229
Science-fiction 3, 8, 11, 12, 21, 23, 43, 66, 79, 112, 114, 139, 140, 163, 165, 182, 194, 204–5, 218, 229, 235, 251, 260
Scither, George 162
Scooby-Doo in Arabian Nights (1994) 189
The Scorpion King (2002) 220, 229–*230*, 231
Scott, Dougray 77
Scott, George C. 126
Scott, Gordon 173, 175–6, 222
Scott, Ridley 67, 267
Scott, Tony 100
Scotti, Raimondo 169
The Scoundrel (1935) 121
Scrooge (1935) 121
Scrooge (1951) 121
Scrooge (1970) 126
Scrooged (1988) 126, 145
The Sea Hawk (1940) 180
The Sea's Shadow (Der Schatten des Meeres, 1912) 42, 97
Seaton, George 89, 99
Secondary worlds 13, 14, 16, 19, 20, 22, 30, 34, 49, 55, 83, 84, 85, 101, 114, 132, 133, 134, 135, 146, 156, 159, 160, 163, 174, 175, 177, 184, 187, 190, 191, 193, 197, 198, 199, 200, 206, 211, 212, 213, 219, 222, 223, 224, 228, 236, 237, 240, 245, 248, 253, 254, 258, 259, 260, 263, 266
The Secret Adventures of Tom Thumb (1993) 78, 79
The Secret of Roan Inish (1993) 132
Seidelman, Arthur A. 96
Seiter, William A. 103
Selick, Henry 75, 78
Selig Polyscope Company 27
Sellers, Peter 56
Semon, Larry 28
Sendak, Maurice 68, 174
Sérail (1976) 125
Serials 165–8, 213, 215, 218, 242
Serkis, Andy 268, *269*
Sernas, Jacques 175
Sessa, Alex 205
The Seven Castles of the Devil (Les Sept Chateâux du diable, 1901) 92
The Seven Dwarfs to the Rescue (I sette nani alla riscossa, 1952) 56
7 Faces of Dr Lao (1964) 150
The Seven Magnificent Gladiators (1983) 205
The Seven Samurai (1954) 81
The Seven Swans (1917) 28
The Seventh Seal (Det Sjunde Inseglet, 1956) 10, 55, 98, 234
The 7th Voyage of Sinbad (1958) 57, 174, 180, 181, 182–3, 186, 187
Sewell, Vernon 124
Sex 7, 36, 37, 48, 50, 51, 61, 63, 74, 76, 93, 103, 109, 110–1, 113, 115, 135, 147, 156, 164, 192, 203, 206, 210–1, 212, 213, 229, 244
The Sex Pistols 141
Sexuality 67, 109, 171–3
Seymour, Jane 108, 186, *188*
The Shadow (1939) 166
The Shadow (1994) 218–9
The Shadow Returns (1946) 166
The Shadow Strikes (1937) 166
Shadyac, Tom 110, 149
The Shaggy D.A. (1976) 108
The Shaggy Dog (1959) 108
Shakespeare, William 55, 115, 127, 141, 266
Shankar, Ravi 59
Shapiro, Mikhail 54
Sharpe, Albert 119
Shaw, Fiona 156
Shawn, Dick 114
Shawn, Wallace 70
She (1916) 130
She (1917) 130
She (1925) 130
She (1935) 130
She (1965) 13, 131, *132*, 136
She (1983) 209
She-Creature (2001) 116
"She-Ra: Princess of Power" (TV series) 209–10
Shearer, Moira 48
Shearer, Norma 122
Sheffer, Craig 143
Shepherd, Cybill 107
Sher, Jack 131
Sherman, George 114
Sherman, Lowell 96
The Shining (1980) 130, 258
Shivers (aka: The Parasite Murders/They Came from Within, 1974) 219
Shogun Assassin (1980) 195
The Shout (1978) 150
Shrek (2001) 36, 38, 68, 81–2, 134
Shrek 2 (2004) 82
Shyamalan, M. Night 120, 152
Siani, Sabrina 202, 203
Sica, Vittorio de 89
Siege of the Saxons (1963) 243
Siegfried see *Die Nibelungen*
Signoret, Simone 8
Silberling, Brad 89, 128
Silence Is Golden (Silence est d'or, 1947) 24
The Silent Flute (aka: Circle of Iron, 1978) 179, 207
Silenti, Vira 175
Silly Symphony cartoons 31, 50
Silvers, Phil 45
Sim, Alistair 121

Simon, S. Sylvan 124
A Simple Wish (1997) 119
Simply Irresistible (1999) 102
Simpson, Don 265
Sinbad 14, 103, 179–90, 198, 200, 209, 213, 215, 222, 225, 229
Sinbad and the Caliph of Baghdad (Simbad e il califfo di Bagdad, 1973) 179, 183
Sinbad and the Eye of the Tiger (1977) 186–7, **188**, 190
Sinbad: Beyond the Veil of Mists (1997) 189–90
"Sinbad Jr." (TV series) *see* "The Adventures of Sinbad the Sailor"
Sinbad: Legend of the Seven Seas (2003) 190, 229
Sinbad of the Seven Seas (Simbad il marinaio, 1989) 189
Sinbad: The Battle of the Dark Knights (1998) 189
Sinbad the Sailor (1935) 180
Sinbad the Sailor (1947) 180–1
Sinbad versus the Seven Saracens (Simbad contro i sette saraceni, 1964) 183
Singer, Bryan 231
Singer, Marc 199, 212, 226
The Singing Ringing Tree (Das singende klingende Bäumchen, 1957) 54
Siren of Atlantis (1949) 131
The Sixth Sense (1999) 83, 120–1, 129
Sjöström, Victor 55, 97
Skolimowski, Jerzy 150
Slater, Christian 100
Slave of Rome (La schiava di roma, 1960/aka: Slave Warrior) 200
Sleeping Beauty 41, 62
Sleeping Beauty (1959) 12, 40, 41, 51, 72, 255
Sleepy Hollow (1999) 12, 127, 228, 229
Sliding Doors (1997) 144–5
The Slipper and the Rose (1976) 62
Small, Edward 57, 183
Smilin' Through (1932) 122
Smith, Clark Ashton 186, 191, 200
Smith, Dick 199
Smith, G.A. 26
Smith, Kevin 90–1
Smith, Maggie 246
Smith, Mel 70
Smith, Thorne 109, 122, 146
Snow, Marguerite 130
Snow White 36, 39, 45, 55, 56, 68
Snow White (1916) 28
Snow White (Schneewitchen, 1916) 42
Snow White (2001) 75, 76

Snow White and the Seven Dwarfs (1937) 1, 33, 36–7, 40, 44, 46, 50, 64, 81
Snow White: A Tale of Terror (1996) 64
Socialism 52, 97, 119, 237
Solomon, Courtney 193, 266
Some Call It Loving (1973) 62
Somerville, Jimmy 90
Something Wicked This Way Comes (1983) 150
Sommers, Stephen 218, 219
The Son of Hercules in the Land of Darkness (Ercole l'invincibile, 1964) 178
Song of the South (1946) 39–40, 46, 71
Sorbo, Kevin 223–4, 228
The Sorcerer's Curse see *The Magic Sword*
Sorceress (1983) 204
The Sorrows of Satan (1926) 92–3
Soul Vengeance see *Welcome Home, Brother Charles*
"South Park" (TV series) 99
South Park: Bigger, Longer and Uncut (2000) 93
Spacek, Sissy 110
Spain, Fay 176
Sparks, Ned **32**
Sparrow, Walter 97
Spartacus (1960) 233
Special effects 20, 21, 23, 26, 28, 30, 35, 41, 54, 56, 58, 63, 65, 67, 68, 70, 71, 79, 112, 128, 157, 184, 186–7, 199, 202, 214, 222, 237, 239, 251, 259, 265; animatronics 39, 259
CGI 39, 79–81, 106, 107, 111, 117, 120, 127, 134, 189, 222, 252, 253, 256, 266, 267, 268, 270; "Dynamation" 57, 182, 187; stop-action 18–9, 21, 27; stop-motion animation 33, 49, 54, 57, 74, 76, 182–3, 184, 186–7, 190, 202, 239, 246–8, 251
Spenser, Edmund 241
Spider-Man (2002) 11, 164, 249
Spielberg, Steven 63, 83, 127, 134, 213, 214, 215, 216, 217, 218, 265
Spinrad, Norman 170
The Spirit of the Conqueror (1914) 107
Splash (1984) 116
Splash, Too (1988) 116
"SpongeBob SquarePants" (TV series) 220
Squire, William 258
Stagecoach (1939) 231
Stairway to Heaven see *A Matter of Life and Death*
Stalin, Joseph 54
Stallone, Sylvester 224
Stamp, Terence 64
Stanton, Harry Dean 99
Stanwyck, Barbara 45
The Star Prince (1918) 28

Star Wars (1977) 1, 11, 15, 63, 79, 82, 156, 187, 192, 195, 197, 200, 233, 246, 249, 251, 256, 257, 258, 265, 266
Starewicz, Wladyslaw 54
Stark, Curt A. 42
Staudte, Wolfgang 54
Staunton, Imelda 108
Stay Tuned (1992) 93, 135
Steele, Tommy 119
Stefani, Francesco 54
Steig, William 81
Steiner, John 189, 204
Stephens, Toby 120
Sterling, William 59
Stevenson, Juliet 128
Stevenson, Robert 213
Stevenson, Robert Louis 101
Stewart, James 16, 84, 87, 100, 119, 139, 147, 149
Stockwell, Dean 151
Stokes, Jack 194
Stolar, Edward 237
Stone, Matt 99
Stone, Oliver 197, 269
Stone, Sharon 81
The Stone Flower (Kamenni Tsvetok, 1946) 54
The Stone Forest (Il tesoro della foresta pietrificata, 1965) 238
Stop-motion animation *see* Special effects
Stork Bites Man (1947) 98
Stormquest (1988) 205
Story 4, 13, 20, 23, 56, 84, 232, 255, 256, 270
Storybooks 31, 32, 36, 38, 46, 48, 50, 51, 81, 244
Storytellers and storytelling 2, 10, 13, 15, 20, 25, 28, 33, 36, 40, 41, 46, 49, 50, 51, 55, 56, 65, 71–2, 74, 83, 139, 160–1, 181, 198, 252, 256, 263, 265, 270
Stow, Percy 26, 30, 31, 32
Straparola, Giovan Francesco 25
Streep, Meryl 111
Stronach, Tami 263
Strongmen 70, 79, 169–79, 180, 182, 190, 191, 194, 198, 200, 204, 209, 213, 218, 222, 223, 224, 225, 226, 237, 238
Stuart Little (1999) 80–1
Stuart Little 2 (2002) 80
Stuart, Mel 61, 62
The Student of Prague (Der Student von Prag, 1913) 42, 43, 49
Student Tour (1934) 169
Sturridge, Charles 120
Subotsky, Milton 192, 193, 223
Sumpter, Jeremy 79
Superheroes and superheroines 11, 14, 15, 152, 163–8, 171, 177, 178, 184, 189, 197, 199, 200, 204, 207, 210, 213, 215, 218,

219, 220, 222, 225, 228, 229, 231, 232, 233, 234, 236, 238, 242
Superman (1978) 164, 205
Superman II (1980) 11, 202
Suratt, Valeska 130
Surrealism and Surrealists 13, 14, 15, 24, 26, 35, 46, 52, 57, 62, 71, 76, 102, 131, 178, 195, 220, 229
Suspension of disbelief 10, 99
Sutcliffe, Thomas 237
Sutherland, A. Edward 122
Sutherland, Kiefer 76
Sutton, John 182
Svankmajer, Jan 24, 71, 94, 102
Swartz, Mark Evan 27
Swashbucklers 30, 180, 181, 198
Swayze, Patrick 127
Swenson, Karl 243
Swinton, Tilda 90, 109
Switch (1991) 109
The Sword and the Dragon see *Ilya Muromets*
The Sword and the Sorcerer (1981) 12, 63, 191, 194, 195, 199, 211, 212
The Sword in the Stone (1963) 243, 244, 257
Sword of the Barbarians (Sangraal, la spada di fuoco, 1983/aka: Barbarian Master) 202–3
Sword of the Valiant (1983) 245
Syberberg, Hans-Jürgen 245
Sydow, Max von 55
Szwarc, Jeannot 99

Tabet, Sylvio 212
Tailspin Tommy (1934) 213
A Tale of Lost Time (1964) 112
The Tale of the Fox (Le Roman de Renard, 1928) 54
The Tales of Hoffmann (1951) 49, 55
Tales of 1001 Nights (Pohádky Tisíce a Jedné Noci, 1974) 188
Tall Tale (1994) 96
Tallas, Gregg 131
Tam-Lin (aka: The Devil's Widow, 1971) 119
Tamblyn, Russ 56
Tamburella, Paolo William 56
Taniguchi, Senkichi 183
Tanner, Alain 151
Tarantino, Quentin 96
Tarlov, Mark 102
The Tarzan Ape Man (1932) 165
"Tarzan: The Epic Adventures" (TV series) 222
Tasker, Yvonne 206
The Taur King of Brute Force (Taur, il re della forza bruta, 1962/aka: Tor, Mighty Warrior) 200
Taylor, Robert 242

Tchaikovsky, Pyotr Ilyich 42, 51
Teague, Lewis 217
Technology and the technological 11, 52, 65, 70, 74, 79, 82, 103, 118, 134, 140, 141–3, 166, 173, 213, 216, 220, 232, 251, 257, 261, 262
Television 33, 57, 62, 87, 112, 114, 117, 140, 147, 168, 177, 179, 188–9, 203, 209, 212, 213, 218, 222–4, 225, 226–8, 238, 260, 262–3
The Ten Commandments (1956) 3
Tennant, Andy 77
Tennyson, Alfred Lord 241, 242, 244
Terlesky, John 212
The Terminator (1984) 209, 219
Terry, John 193, 194
Terry, Nigel 248, **250**
Thanhouser Company 130
Thatcher, Torin 57, 182
That's the Spirit (1945) 122–3
Thayer, Otis 28
Theater 20–1, 22, 23, 27, 28, 31, 42, 49, 97, 115, 121, 136, 140
Theseus Against the Minotaur (Teseo contro il Minotauro, 1960) 174, 238
Thesiger, Ernest 149
Thewlis, David 253
The Thief of Baghdad (1924) **29**–30, 31, 42, 181, 182, 262
The Thief of Baghdad (1940) 8, 44–**45**, 46, 47, 48, 165, 180, 187, 189, 260
The Thief of Baghdad (Il Ladro di Bagdad, 1960) 56
The Thief of Baghdad (1978) 63
Thief of Damascus (1952) 182
Thiele, Rolf 61
The 13th Warrior (1999) 253
Thomas, Damian 186, **188**
Thomas, Elton see Fairbanks, Douglas
Thomas, Ralph 115
Thomas, Roy 197, 200, 207
Thomas, Terry 56, 57
Thomas and the Magic Railroad (2000) 134
Thompson, Caroline 74, 75, 76
Thompson, J. Lee 216
Thomson, David 36
Thongor in the Valley of Demons 192, 193, 223
Thor the Conqueror (Thor il conquistatore, 1982) 202, 203
Thorburn, June 56
Thorpe, Richard 242
A Thousand and One Nights (1945) 45
A Thousand and One Nights (Les Mille et une nuits, 1990) 189
Three Husbands (1950) 136
The Three Musketeers (1921) 181
Three Wise Fools (1946) 119
Three Women (1977) 110

The 3 Worlds of Gulliver (1960) 131
The Throne of Fire (Il trono di fuoco, 1983) 202, 203
Through the Looking Glass (1976) 61
Thy Soul Shall Bear Witness! see *Korkarlen*
Tieck, Ludwig 27, 42
Tierney, Gene 125
Tim Burton's The Nightmare Before Christmas (aka: The Nightmare Before Christmas, 1993) 74–5, 160
Time and time-slips 17, 20, 26, 84, 102, 114, 118, 126, 136, 139–146, 164, 189, 210, 212, 213, 218, 220, 234, 265
Time Bandits (1981) 65, 79, 96, 142, **143**, 145
The Time of Their Lives (1946) 124
The Tin Drum (Die Blechtrommel, 1979) 84
"Tinkerbell's Law" 47
To Die For (1994) 128
Todorov, Tzvetan 8–9, 10
Tolkien, J.R.R. 2, 7, 36, 78, 84, 102, 158, 192, 193, 198, 232, 241, 249, 251, 254–9, 260, 263, 265, 266, 267, 268, 270–1; *The Lord of the Rings* 4, 7, 156, 191, 251–2, 254–6, 258, 259, 265, 266, 267; "On Fairy Stories" essay 13, 15, 25, 254, 270
Tolstoy, Alexei 54
Tom Thumb (1958) 56, 57
Tomlin, Lili 110
Tomlinson, David 58, 115
"Toons" 118, 119, 128
Tooth (2003) 134
Top Gun (1986) 67
Topper (1937) 85, 121, 122, 124, 125, 148
Topper Returns (1941) 122
Topper Takes a Trip (1938) 122
The Tor, Mighty Warrior see *Taur King of Brute Force*
Torn, Rip 199
Torrisi, Pietro 202, 203
A Touch of Zen (Xia Nü, 1970) 175
Touchstone 66
Tourneur, Maurice 28
Townsend, Bud 61
Toy Story (1995) 81, 106, 133
Toy Story 2 (1999) 106
Toys (1992) 75, 78, 113
Tracy, Spencer 123, 127, 137
Transformations 12, 19, 20, 26, 64, 101, 109, 159, 164
Travers, Henry 87
Travers, P.L. 2, 58
Travolta, John 90, 95
Treasure of the Amazons (1985) 216

Treasure of the Four Crowns (1982) 216
Trick films 19, 23, 27, 30, 99, 102, 105, 127, 234
Trinder, Tommy 142
A Trip to Paradise (1921) 106
A Trip to the Moon (Le Voyage dans la lune, 1902) 21, 22
The Triumph of Hercules (Il triomfo di Ercole, 1964/aka: Hercules vs. the Giant Warriors/Hercules and the Ten Avengers) 171
Triumph of the Son of Hercules (Il trionfo di Maciste, 1961) 176
The Triumph of Venus (1918) 96
Troll (1986) 119, 133
Tron (1982) 66
Troughton, Patrick 186, **188**, 239
Troy (2004) 253, 254, 269
Troyes, Chrétien de 245
True, Rachel **155**
True Romance (1993) 100
Truly, Madly, Deeply (1990) 128, 129
Tunney, Robin 153, **155**
Turnabout (1940) 109
Turner, Kathleen 144
Turner, Otis 27
Twain, Mark 141, 143, 144, 242
12 Monkeys (1995) 145
20th Century–Fox 27, 28, 37, 130, 243
20 Million Miles to Earth (1957) 182
The Twilight of the Ice Nymphs (1997) 78
2001: A Space Odyssey (1968) 11
Two of a Kind (1983) 95
Tykwer, Tom 145
Tyler, Tom 166, **167**

Uderzo, Albert 225
Ufa 46, 236
Ugetsu Monogatari (1953) 125, 128, 129
Ullmann, Liv 110
Ulmer, Edgar G. 131
Ulysses (Ulisse, 1955) 174, 238
Unbreakable (2000) 152–3, 160
"The Uncanny" 9, 10, 145
The Unconscious 7, 8, 15, 16, 35, 46, 55, 65
Underwood, Jay 151
Undine (1916) 28, 115
Ungalaaq, Natar 252
The Unholy Three (1925) 169
The Unholy Three (1930) 169
The Uninvited (1944) 124
United Artists 192, 257
Universal 165, 180, 181, 182, 210, 219
Updike, John 153
Ursus (aka: Mighty Ursus, 1961) 175

Ustinov, Peter 112, 125
The Usual Suspects (1995) 65

Vadis, Dan 171, 178, 205
Vallejo, Boris 205
Vance, Jack 191
Van Damme, Jean-Claude 126
Van Dien, Casper 226
Van Doren Stern, Philip 88
Van Dyke, Dick 58, 59
Vane, Sutton 136
The Vanishing Lady (Escamotage d'une dame chez Robert-Houdin, 1896) 18–9
Vari, Giuseppe 183
Varnel, Marcel 242
Varney, Jim 99
Veidt, Conrad 44, **45**
Vengeance of She (1967) 131
Venus Meets the Son of Hercules (Marte, dio della guerra, 1963) 96
Verbinski, Gore 225
Verhoeven, Paul 251
Verne, Jules 21
Vice Versa (1948) 108, 112
Vice Versa (1988) 112
Victor, Henry 130
Video 72, 200–1, 202, 205, 207, 209, 260, 262
Vidor, Charles 51
Vigo, Jean 46
Vincent (1982) 66
Vincent, Chuck 209
Violence 36, 61, 78, 192, 194–5, 197, 203, 206, 212, 213, 226, 229
The Virgin Spring (Jungfrukällan, 1959) 55
Les Visiteurs (1993) 143
"Visitors from beyond" 85–100, 121, 122, 136, 144, 146, 249
Visitors of the Evening (Les Visiteurs du soir, 1942) 47
Voight, Jon 220
Volere, Volare (1991) 111, 118
Voltaire 61
Vosloo, Arnold 219
Votocek, Otakar 136
Vulcan, Son of Jupiter (Vulcano, figlio di Giove, 1962) 96

Wagner, Karl Edward 191
Wagner, Richard 232, 235, 242, 245, 249
Wagner, Robert 243
Wakayama, Tomisaburo 195
Walbrook, Anton 48
Walken, Christopher 91
Walker, Nancy 96
Walker, Robert 103
Wallace, Jean 243
Walsh, Raoul 29–30, 87
Walston, Ray 93
Walter, Tracey 207
Walters, Charles 51
Wanamaker, Sam 186, 188

War of the Zombies (Roma contro Roma, 1963) 183
Warbeck, David 216
Ward, Vincent 139, 142, 265
Warner, David 142, 226
Warner, Marina 25, 36, 73
Warner Brothers 33, 44, 156, 243, 244, 248, 267
Warnock, Craig 142
The Warrior and the Sorceress (aka: Kain of Dark Planet, 1984) 205, 206
Warrior Queen (1987) 209
The Warrior's Husband (1933) 169
Warriors of Virtue (1996) 133
Watergate 61, 107, 108
Watership Down (1978) 142, 254, 258, 268
Watson, Emma 156
Watson, John 205
Watt, Harry 142
Watts, Naomi 110
Watusi (1958) 213
Waxworks (Der Wachsfigurenkabinett, 1924) 43
Wayans, Marlon 266, 267
Wayne, Patrick 186
Weaver, Sigourney 64
Webb, Jimmy 261
Webber, Diane 116
Weeks, Stephen 245
Wegener, Paul 43
Weir, Peter 4, 132, 133, 152
Weiser, Shari 69
Weissmuller, Johnny 165, 166
Weisz, Rachel 219, 220
The Weitz Brothers 107
Welch, Bo 80
Welcome Home, Brother Charles (aka: Soul Vengeance, 1975) 110
Welles, Orson 96
Wellman, William 95
Wells, H.G. 21, 148
Wenders, Wim 89
Wenham, David 269
Werckmeister, Hans 43
The Werewolf of Washington (1973) 108
Werker, Alfred 140
West, Simon 220
Westerns 2, 23, 165, 178, 179, 192, 193, 194, 198, 226, 231
Westfahl, Gary 12
Whale, James 43
Whalin, Justin 266
Whalley, Joanne 266
What Dreams May Come (1998) 136, 139
Whelan, Tim 44
Where Do We Go from Here? (1945) 114
Whipp, Joseph 209
White, E.B. 80
White, Richard 73
White, T.H. 243

Whiting, Margaret 186
Who Framed Roger Rabbit?
  (1988) 84, 118, 128, 134
The Whole Wide World (1996)
  191
Whom the Gods Wish to Destroy
  (Die Nibelungen, 1966) 238
Wickie, Gus 180
Widen, Gregory 91
Wiene, Robert 43
Wiest, Dianne 74, 154
Wild Strawberries (Smultronstäl-
  let, 1957) 55
Wilde, Cornel 243
Wilder, Gene **62**
Wilding, Michael 52
Williams, Guy 183
Williams, Robin 71, 73, 75, 134,
  136, 139
Williams, Spencer 86
Williams, Treat 219
Williamson, James 119
Williamson, Nicol 64, 65, 248
Willing, Nick 120
Willis, Bruce 111, 129, 145, 152
Willow (1988) 226, 265–6, 267
*Willy Wonka and the Chocolate
  Factory* (1971) 1, 61–**62**, 78
Wilmer, Douglas 184, 239
Wilmot, David 108
Wilson, Mara 77
Wincer, Simon 150, 218
The Wind in the Willows (1996)
  76, 78, 80, 118
Wings of Desire (Der Himmel
  über Berlin, 1987) 13, 89, 90,
  128
Wings of Fame (1990) 136
Winter, Alex 98
Winwood, Estelle 52
Wishman (1991) 114
Wishmaster (1997) 114
The Witches (1990) 153
Witches, crones and hags 19,
  21–2, 33, 34, 35, 37, 49, 51, 54,
  57, 64, 72, 78, 146–7, 150,
  153–6, 193, 199, 200, 237
The Witches of Eastwick (1987)
  92, 93–4, 153, **154**
The Witch's Curse (Maciste
  all'inferno, 1961) 178

Withers, Googie 115
Witherspoon, Reese 76, 135
Witney, William 167
The Wiz (1978) 62–3
Wizard of Baghdad (1960) 114
The Wizard of Oz (1939) 1, 3, 8,
  9, 33–**34**, 35, 37, 42, 46, 48,
  49, 57, 58, 62, 64, 65, 128, 165,
  243
Wizards (1977) 257, 265, 268
"Wizards and Warriors" (TV
  series) 262
Wizards of the Lost Kingdom
  (1984) 205, 262
Wizards of the Lost Kingdom II
  (1988) 205
Wizards, psychics, magicians
  and sorcerers 10, 13, 15, 16,
  26, 35, 50, 84, 100, 102, 116,
  127, 129, 132, 133, 142, 143,
  146, 149–153, 162, 163, 181,
  183, 189, 193, 199, 200, 202,
  204, 205–6, 209, 210, 213,
  226, 231, 242, 249, 261, 262,
  266
Wolfen (1981) 133
The Wolves of Kromer (1998) 64
Wonder Man (1945) 124
Wonder tales 25, 26, 27, 40, 42,
  232
The Wonderful Wizard of Oz
  (1910) 27
The Wonderful Wizard of Oz
  (1924) 28
*The Wonderful World of the
  Brothers Grimm* (1962) 56–7
Wong, Chen 202
Wood, Elijah 79, 268
Wood, Wally 191
Woods, James 224
Woodthorpe, Peter 258
World War I 23, 43, 46, 101,
  235–6, 268
World War II 23, 47, 48, 122–5,
  136–7, 140, 213
Wright, Robin 70
Wright, Samuel E. 72
Wuhrer, Kari 212
Wynn, Keenan 103
Wynorski, Jim 212
Wynter, Paul 176

X-Men (2000) 11
X-Men 2 (2003) 231
"Xena: Warrior Princess" (TV
  series) 189, 204, 209, 212,
  222, 223, 226–**227**, 228, 266
Xhonneux, Henri 118

Yabushita, Taiji 188
Yasbeck, Amy 116
Yates, Peter 260, 262
*Yellow Hair and the Fortress of
  Gold* (1984) 216
Yojimbo (1961) 206
Yolan, Jane 7, 40
Yolanda and the Thief (1945) 89
Yor: The Hunter from the Future
  (Il mondo di Yor, 1982)
  204
York, Dick 147
York, Susannah 130
You Never Can Tell (1951) 108
Young, Alan 56
Young, Clara Kimball 140
Young, Loretta 87
Young, Roland 122, 148
Young, W.W. 31
"The Young Indiana Jones
  Chronicles" (TV series) 218
Yu, Ronny 133, 226

Zabriskie, Grace 76
Zane, Billy 219
Zanotto, Juan 204
Zecca, Ferdinand 23, 28, 92, 119
Zelazny, Roger 7
Zelig (1983) 110
Zellweger, Renée 40, 191
Zeman, Karel 188
Zemeckis, Robert 111, 118, 217
Zero de Conduite (1933) 46–7
Zeta-Jones, Catherine 189, 190
Zeuxis 17
Zidi, Claude 25
Ziemer, Gregor 41
Zipes, Jack 26
Zorro's Fighting Legion (1939)
  215
Zotz! (1962) 150
Zucker, Jerry 127, 252
Zulu (1963) 257